RESURRECTING DAVID'S FALLEN TENT

TO USHER IN THE END-TIME HARVEST

ISBN: 978-0-6454918-0-7

Follow me on social media at "GIFT OF THE GAB" @JLF538 👆

👉 **gab.com/JLF538**

👉 **https://t.me/JLF538**

👉 **gettr.com/user/JLF538**

👉 **facebook.com/JLF538**

For free video teachings, please subscribe to my YOUTUBE CHANNEL 👆

👉 **youtube.com/giftgab** ▶️

SIGN UP FOR THE MAILING LIST

TO RECEIVE SPECIAL PDF BONUS OFFERS, BLOGS ALERTS FROM THE AUTHOR & INFO ON NEW RELEASES, subscribe at:

www.justinfarrugia.org

ACKNOWLEDGMENTS

To my gorgeous wife Bronwyn, loving mother to our two kids and co-editor. We got through it! And what a monumental task it was. Hopefully it will produce plenty of fruit for the kingdom of God.

To Diane Spicer: for kick-starting me along the step-by-step process towards publication. It was a massive help and I couldn't have completed this without your expertise. Thank-you for all your love and support as a spiritual mother to Bronwyn and I over the years.

To my Lord and Saviour Jesus Christ: You came into my life 18 years ago and set me free when I was on the brink of ending it all. Without Your divine intervention and immeasurable love I probably would not even be here, let alone an author. You thoroughly saved me from all the plans the enemy had to destroy me, and for that I am eternally grateful. Thank-you for dying on the cross for all my sins and granting me everlasting life through Your precious blood. This book is dedicated to You!

Last but not least: 'You all', my avid readers. Thank-you for taking precious time out of your busy lives to be inspired, entertained and educated by my writing. Without every one of you, this dream of mine ceases to exist. You are all wonderful people who are destined to experience the greatness of God in your lives!

SECTION I: EMERGENCY! CALL A COUNCIL

Attack of the Judaizers 9

A Prophetic Mandate for the times 17

Correct grafting into the Jewish root 26

Simplicity of Pure Devotion.. 34

The Final Verdict of the Council 40

'True' Circumcision.. 47

SECTION II: TABERNACLE OF MOSES

The Outer Court 61

An 'earthly' sanctuary 67

Altar of Incense 766

Table of Showbread 85

Golden Lampstand 96

SECTION III: THE ARK OF HIS GLORY

Ark of the Covenant 107

Beholding the Form of the Lord 114

Moses in the Tabernacle of David? 122

Moses' Defining Moment... 129

Glory in the Wilderness Wanderings 135

Post Tabernacle Glory 141

Synonyms for the Glory of Yahweh............................... 152

SECTION IV: THE ARK AWAY FROM HOME

Cast your mind back to Shiloh....................................... 163

Abiathar and Zadok 173

CONTENTS

The Lord abandons Shiloh 180

The Ark in Philistia 188

SECTION V: THE MAKING OF A KING

David's Loyal Endurance 199

David's Solemn Vow 208

Entrance Open 217

Where would my resting place be? 227

Your personal Zion 238

Making us feel right at home 245

A flourishing crown of revival 254

SECTION VI: ZION BOUND

A tragic false start 267

Servant of the Gentiles 276

Bearing proper weight 281

I desire mercy, not sacrifice 287

Spiritual sacrifices pleasing to God 296

Sacrifices 'once and for all' 307

Sacrifices brought to an end 314

Whose house do you live in? 323

Worship lives on 331

SECTION VII: END-TIME HARVEST

The Harvest: an 'ever-expanding' remnant 339

One things hot on the heels of another 349

The restoration of all things 358

LIST OF ABBREVIATIONS

- **TOD** = Tabernacle of David
- **TOM** = Tabernacle of Moses
- **LOM** = Law of Moses

SECTION I:

EMERGENCY! CALL A COUNCIL!

ATTACK OF THE JUDAIZERS

In the early days of the church, there were two primary congregations. The first of these was located in Jerusalem. This body of believers was birthed on the Day of Pentecost in Acts chapter 2, when the Holy Spirit was poured out upon all those present in the upper room. It was comprised exclusively by people of Jewish descent, and the presiding apostles were Peter (the stone), James (the Lord's brother), and John (the beloved).

The second congregation was located in Antioch, north of Israel, in Syria. In Acts chapter 7, Stephen was stoned to death for his bold testimony of Jesus Christ. On the back of his murder a tsunami wave of persecution broke out against the church at Jerusalem. All the believers except for the apostles were dispersed abroad, initially throughout Judea and Samaria, and then as far as Phoenicia, Azotus and Antioch. (Acts 8:1, 11:19a)

The scattered believers started preaching the gospel first to the Jews, and after experiencing limited success, they eventually turned their attention toward the Greeks. As they did, vast numbers of Gentile men and women came to the Lord and became Christians, and so the multicultural church in Antioch was born. (Acts 11:19-21)

News about this influx of Gentile converts travelled quickly down the grapevine and reached the ears of the apostles in Jerusalem. Upon hearing it, they immediately sent Barnabas with the precious task of encouraging the newly saved to stay true to the Lord (Acts 11:22-24). Barnabas quickly realised that the task was far too great for one man, so he went to Tarsus to look for Saul (later to become the Apostle Paul), and when he found him, he brought him to Antioch to lend a helping hand. Saul had been tucked away in seclusion for many years getting to know Jesus inside and out, and he was waiting patiently for his 'call-up' into the ministry God had promised him (Gal. 1:11-17, Acts 9:15-16). Little did he know that the surprise appearance of Barnabas at his door-step was the day when it would all begin. (Acts 11:25-26)

Pretty soon it became clear that Barnabas and Saul were going to remain permanently in Antioch as prophets and teachers. They were installed into the eldership of this vibrant, cosmopolitan body of believers, forming the Jewish contingent in the leadership group. The full list of leaders is found in Acts 13:1.

Antioch quickly became renowned as the first Gentile church; a diverse, multicultural church. Its composition was primarily Gentile converts to the faith, but there were some Jewish believers thrown into the mix as well.

◊◊◊◊◊

As the dust settled following the upheaval of the dispersion, trouble was brewing back in the church at Jerusalem. Within their own ranks, a sect emerged called 'Judaizers'. These believers were extremely fond of their Old Testament Judaism. They had accepted Christ, but still held the Mosaic Covenant dear to their hearts. Even after accepting Jesus as their Messiah, their overriding passion still involved following the rules Moses laid down for the children of Israel, rather than seeking a closer relationship with God through faith in Jesus Christ.

Peter, James, John, (and the Jewish church as a whole) also continued to adhere to the legalistic demands of Judaism alongside saving faith, but they maintained Judaism for cultural purposes only (Acts 21:20-25). At that time it was too difficult to uproot and still function in Jewish society, for these religious requirements are an integral part of the laws of the land. The difference was they were no longer adhering to these laws for the purpose of worship or salvation.

For example, if someone renounced Judaism, they would no longer be permitted into the Temple Complex (Acts 21:28b). We know from the book of Acts the early Christians held many meetings in and around the Temple, especially in a place called Solomon's Colonnade on the eastern side of the Temple's outer court (Acts 3:1, 11, 5:12). It would not have been advantageous for the church to be absent from these places.

To relinquish Judaism would also mean you were no longer welcome in most synagogues. We know that the Apostle Paul actually circumcised Timothy, (whose mother was a Jew, but father was a Greek), so that he could help them preach the gospel to the Jews inside the synagogue (Acts 16:3). Even in his introduction to the Jews in Rome, Paul began by stating; "I have done nothing against our people or *against the customs of our ancestors.*" (Acts 28:17)

If you broke free from these customs, you would also have problems finding shops to buy food and other necessities, because Jewish outlets would deny entry to anyone not eating kosher or remaining ceremonially clean. To top it off, there would also be unnecessary persecution to endure on a daily basis.

◊◊◊◊◊

It is abundantly clear throughout the New Testament writings that the apostles did not teach or believe that obedience to the laws of Moses 'added to' or was required for their salvation. They clearly recognised that it was the grace of God through faith in Jesus alone.

For this reason they did not advocate placing such a heavy burden upon the shoulders of the Gentile believers. These men had never been circumcised as children and they had no grid of reference for all of these laws, which, if enforced, would only be a major encumbrance. Hence their overall stance toward the Gentiles was for them to continue in their unique cultural heritage as long as they implemented Christian morality while denouncing any practices that were carnal or demonic.

Even Peter admitted in Acts 15:10 that the law was a weight that neither they nor their ancestors had ever been able to bear. In this verse he also emphasises that forcing Gentiles to attach 'Mosaic' policies to the Christian life 'tempts God' in a similar fashion to Ananias and Sapphira, who "tempted the Spirit of the Lord" when they lied to Him, costing them their lives (Acts 5:1-10). These two statements alone prove the chief apostle's belief concerning this issue.

The Judaizers were not going to have a bar of that. They render every single law given by Moses 'absolutely essential'. So without the apostles' authorisation they travelled north to Antioch and began to teach the Gentile believers;

> *"Unless you are circumcised, according to the custom taught by Moses, you cannot be saved."* (Acts 15:1)

In essence, what they were saying was;

> *"You have all received the initial salvation that comes by grace through faith. You have life in the Spirit. BUT... you're not 'fully saved' yet. You haven't completed all the steps necessary to guarantee eternal life. In order to progress into the full Christian experience, you must advance to*

the 'stage of maturity'. You must be physically circumcised and then start obeying all the laws of Moses."

This was adding human effort in the form of 'works of the flesh' and 'works of the law' to grace, faith and life in the Spirit: A mixture of faith and works. (Eph. 2:8-9, Gal. 3:3 NLT)

Paul and Barnabas disagree vehemently. They believe that the New Testament believer is sealed by the Holy Spirit with a spiritual circumcision of the heart, not a physical circumcision of the foreskin. Any attempt to adhere to a law as a means of earning salvation is a denial of the all-sufficiency of Jesus' blood atonement, an insult to the finished work of the cross, and treating the death of Christ as if it had been done in vain;

> *²Mark my words! I, Paul, tell you that if you let yourselves be circumcised, <u>Christ will be of no value to you at all.</u> ³Again I declare to every man who lets himself be circumcised that he is <u>required to obey the whole law.</u> ⁴You who are trying to be justified by the law have been <u>alienated from Christ;</u> you have <u>fallen away from grace.</u>* (Gal. 5:2-4)

In other words; *"If Jesus' sacrifice was the ultimate fulfilment of all these laws as the eternally, universally and continually effective substitute, why are you still enforcing them?"*

Now we know this legalism was also happening elsewhere because the entire book of Galatians was written by Paul to warn the church against these Judaizers! Evidently, this event in Antioch was not an isolated incident. Everywhere Paul and Barnabas travelled, these Judaizers were popping up and attempting to draw away disciples to themselves (Gal. 6:12-13). Paul was so incensed by this group of troublemakers that he retorted;

> *"As for those agitators* (who want to circumcise everyone), *I wish they would go the whole way and emasculate themselves!"* (Gal. 5:12)

Strong language! *"Hey guys, don't stop with merely the foreskin. Go the whole way and turn yourselves into eunuchs while you're at it."* Paul did not hold back in showing his disdain towards these characters that were undermining all his good work and causing the Gentiles to question the legitimacy of their salvation. He was not fond of them in the slightest! It is one thing to have unbelieving Jews or outright pagans attempting to strike you down, but these were Christians who believed that Jesus was their Messiah coming up against the Lord's work.

Paul and Barnabas eventually got fed up with being followed around. Desiring to establish an official, 'church-wide' ruling on this issue, they implore the Judaizers;

> *"Right you blokes, go back to Jerusalem where you came from. We'll go with you and set up a meeting with the pillars of the church (Peter, James and John). Get all the elders to come along and we'll gather to settle this matter once and for all!"*

This meeting became known as the Jerusalem Council documented in Acts 15.

◊◊◊◊◊

In Acts 15:5a we come to find out these *'agitators'* still had a greater affiliation with the Pharisees than the body of Christ. In part b of this verse, we find that they are the first to air their emphatic opinion; *"The Gentiles must be circumcised and required to keep the Law of Moses"*. And so the meeting begins…

The Bible says that all those present embarked on a long discussion (Acts 15:6-7a). No doubt it was one opinion after the other. Such and such aired his opinion. The next person aired that. Backwards and forwards it continued: One viewpoint after the next. They were clearly at loggerheads with little to no progress made. Belatedly, Peter thinks within himself;

> *"I'm supposedly the leader of this church. I better take control of this mess!"*

Rising to his feet, he proclaims;

> *"Listen everyone! I little while back I was on the rooftop at Simon the Tanner's house, and just before lunch I went into a trance. I saw a sheet coming down from heaven with various types of unclean animals in it. God said to me; 'Get up Peter! Kill and eat.' And I said 'surely not Lord, nothing impure or unclean has ever entered my mouth'. But God aptly replied; 'What I have made clean, do not call unclean'. God showed me that the blood of His Son shed on the cross has made all men clean. These Gentiles (the ones I was about to be sent to) had already been*

declared ceremonially clean and they weren't even saved yet, let alone circumcised!" (Acts 10:9-15)

In the Old Covenant the Jews viewed themselves as clean, and everybody else was unclean. First, they had the sign of circumcision, which meant they were sanctified unto God, set apart as holy, clean vessels unto the Lord. Second, they had a long list of dietary and hygienic laws to follow. If you 'touched this' you were unclean. If you 'ate that' you were defiled. If you came into contact with a dead body, you were contaminated. And if you fell short in any of these categories, there was an extensive process you had to go through to get yourself back to a 'clean state' once more. So while examining the Gentiles who followed none of these rules, the Jews naturally concluded; *"By touching items which cause defilement and eating all this unclean food, they're dirty!"*

Because of this, no Jew would ever associate with a Gentile. Not even give them an acknowledgment of "hello" down the street. If you remember in John chapter 4 when Jesus was talking to the Samaritan woman (whose lineage is a mixture of Gentile and Jew) at the well, His disciples questioned Him saying; *"Why are You talking with her?"* (John 4:27)

They wouldn't associate with Gentiles by any act of their own volition, let alone enter their house. That was a big no-no (Acts 10:28). Worse still would be to sit down with them and eat a meal *in their house*, because the Jews viewed a fellowship meal to be equal with coming into covenant. Interestingly enough, God ordered Peter to do these very things! (Acts 11:2-3) *"Go eat with them, they're clean"*, was the basic interpretation of the vision.

God revealed to Peter that Jesus' sacrifice had effectively done away with all these ceremonial, dietary and hygienic laws. From an external / outward / ceremonial point of view, all of humanity had been purified in God's sight, whether they followed the Law of Moses or not. Now all they required to be fully clean was an inward spiritual cleansing through the born again experience.

Peter continues... *"In response to the vision, I went with the servants to Cornelius' house and ate with them. When I preached the gospel, I wasn't even halfway through my message when the Holy Spirit came and filled them. They were divinely and sovereignly saved; they spoke in other tongues and declared the greatness of God* (Acts 10:44-46). *The whole time I was there I made no mention of circumcision. In fact, they are still uncircumcised to this very day, and God has not rejected them."*

Many in the meeting were in awe of Peter's story. *"That's amazing Peter. You have a vision, and you even have a testimony to back up the vision! Now if you can just give us a scripture to confirm all this, we can all be out of here a-sap."*

Now, I'm all for receiving visions from God and hearing testimonies about people's experiences with God. I love all that stuff, but how many of you know it has to be backed up with Scripture to be credible? So everyone present in the meeting is waiting with bated breath as Peter is about to bring forth his bible verse.

'A twiddle of the thumbs, a brush of his sweat-laden forehead';

Peter: *"Ummmmm, I don't have one."*

The council: *"Sit down. Next..! Anyone else wish to testify?"*

Next Paul and Barnabas stand up;

"We've just completed our first missionary journey. The Holy Spirit said; "Set apart for me Barnabas and Saul for the work I have called them to do" (Acts 13:2b) and we've been going out among all the Gentiles. There's been such power unleashed and the presence of God has been evident in every place we set our feet. In fact, there was such authority on our ministry that I had a name change from Saul to Paul and became an apostle along the way! (Acts 13:9) Everything that Peter said is true. In every Gentile town we are seeing salvations in great numbers. Gentiles are getting delivered. They're getting baptised in the Holy Spirit and speaking in heavenly languages. They've received a complete and entire experience of the New Covenant. All the blessings and privileges Barnabas and I have as Jewish Christians they have received as Gentile Christians. God is holding nothing back. They have the full package!"

In response the judging panel exclaim;

"Wow, more testimonies! This definitely adds more weight to the argument. The scales seem to be tipping in only one direction. Now if

you could just give us the scripture to back it up we will all be on our way."

Paul turns to Barnabas; *"Oh sorry Barnabas. I've been hogging the mic, you can say the scripture."*

Barnabas responds; *"Nah Paul, you're on a roll, man. Stay in the flow..."*

Paul: *"I insist; you can share some of the limelight".*

Barnabas: *"No, I insist!"*

Paul: *"Come on Barnabas! Do I have to do everything around here? Pull your weight and add some correspondence!"*

Barnabas: *"I, I, I... forgot my scrolls."*

Paul: *"Got anything off the top of your head?"*

Barnabas: *"No..."*

After much deliberation, Paul and Barnabas sigh and belatedly admit: *"Sorry, we don't have one..."*

"Oh, this is getting us nowhere", those in the meeting groaned. *"We're going to be stuck here forever!"*

But just when all hope seems lost; enter James, Jesus' half-brother and author of the book of James. Stepping up to the plate, he begins a rivetingly pivotal discourse...

Chapter 1

A PROPHETIC MANDATE FOR THE TIMES

James: *"Hi everyone. Let me state emphatically, I don't have a vision; I don't even have a testimony. In fact, to be perfectly honest, I've never associated meaningfully with a Gentile in my life! I am the stay at home pastor here in Jerusalem. I don't even travel outside the city; I'm securely entrenched here at home base (Gal. 2:12). Yes, I admit I haven't received a vision. I concede that there is no testimony I can share. But what I do have, I will share with all of you. Here is the scripture!"*

Isn't it amazing the way God works: He reveals the key bible passage to the person who has the least experience with Gentiles, the man *we* would deem least likely to receive insight on such a matter. Jesus loves using foolish things to confound the wise.

For your own reference, the scripture James is about to cite is found in Amos 9:11-12. However, it is more beneficial for us to examine it directly from Acts 15 in the exact form he quoted it. We will begin at verse 13;

¹³When they finished, (that is, Peter, Paul and Barnabas) *James spoke up: 'Brothers, listen to me* (because I have the key scripture). *¹⁴Peter has shown us how God first intervened by <u>taking from the Gentiles a people for himself</u>* (the story of Peter at Cornelius' house). *¹⁵The words of the prophets are in agreement with this* (Amos 9:11-12), *as it is written;*

¹⁶"After this I will return and <u>resurrect David's fallen tent</u> (Or, 'the tabernacle of David which has fallen'). *<u>Its ruins I will rebuild and I will restore it,</u> ¹⁷that the rest of mankind may seek the Lord, even all the Gentiles who bear my name, says the Lord, who does these things."* (Acts 15:13-17)

This achieves an immediate consensus;

> *"Right, that settles it then. No circumcision required. Let's go home. We're done here."*

What a startling turn of events!

While it certainly was a positive outcome to see such an emphatic resolution being achieved in the end, my question to you, the reader, is; how in the world does this Scripture resolve the dispute? Doesn't James' scripture seem completely out of context? There is no mention of circumcision, not even a mention *of the Law of Moses!*

Sure, the last portion does have a brief reference concerning the Gentiles being included in Covenant with God, and James himself admitted even before quoting Amos that the words of the prophets were in agreement with Peter's testimony about the Lord taking from the Gentiles a people for Himself. But this merely gives us the *timing* for when this prophecy in Amos was to begin its fulfilment. *It doesn't resolve the circumcision issue!* Everyone in attendance had already come to the revelation that the Gentiles were included within the blood atonement of Christ. They acknowledged that their Jewish Messiah was *also* Saviour of the world! This was not what they were disputing about, for there were many other Old Testament scriptures that pointed to a time when the Gentiles would share in the nourishing sap of the olive root (Rom 11:17). A comprehensive list is compiled by Paul in Romans 15:9-12.

The point of contention was whether these Gentiles (who had been converted) *had to be circumcised and obey the Law of Moses*, and on face value Amos 9:11-12 doesn't seem to address this topic at all.

Believe it or not, the answer is actually found in the first portion, *"After this I will return and rebuild the tabernacle of David which has fallen. Its ruins I will rebuild and I will restore it."* (Acts 15:16)

So then, the million dollar question remains: ***What is the tabernacle of David?***

You may recall the story in the Old Testament where David was dancing before the Lord while the people of Israel witnessed the Ark being brought into Jerusalem for the first time. This was when this tent came into existence. (2 Sam 6:12-17, 1 Chr. 15-16:1)

Why was David so jubilant? Why so exuberant in praise? Most people think it was merely the fact that David was bringing the Ark back as the centrepiece of Jewish society after so many years in obscurity. That was definitely part of it, but there was more to it than that.

God had showed David *'a new and living way through the curtain'* (Heb. 10:20). When David was tending the sheep as a young boy he would worship the Lord on his harp. As he partook of this revolutionary new form of connecting with Yahweh, he was shown the heavenly tabernacle (Heb. 8:2).

There was a High Priest ministering inside who was also a King. It was the Messiah! What's more, the curtain into the Most Holy Place was torn from top to bottom. Everyone had unrestricted access into the presence of God and could approach this High Priest (inside the Holy of Holies) whenever they pleased. Through these experiences, God showed David that He wanted to give him and all the people a foretaste of this coming reality.

David had just conquered the city of Jerusalem, known as the stronghold of Zion. This supposedly impenetrable fortress occupied by the Jebusites was miraculously taken over by David and his mighty men (Josh 15:63, Jud. 1:21). This was to become the capital city of Israel, and David called Zion; 'The City of David' (2 Samuel 5:6-7, 9). The City of David was an 11 acre plot of ground on top of Mount Zion, and it served as David's governmental and spiritual headquarters. The city of Jerusalem grew much larger, spreading primarily north and west across the nearby hills and valleys. Zion then, was the ruling city inside the greater city of Jerusalem. (Ps. 48:1-2)

Prior to this, David had already been reigning over Judah from a place called Hebron for 7.5 years. Just before this victory, King Saul's son Ish-Bosheth (king of the remainder of Israel), was viciously stabbed to death while he slept in his bed. In response to this sad tragedy, the people anointed David as king over the entire land of Israel (2 Samuel 4 & 5:1-5). Therefore, we find that the takeover of Mount Zion was David's first major achievement as the fully fledged king of Israel, and in light of God's prophetic mandate upon his life, he immediately implemented plans to shift his throne to Mount Zion, constructing a new palace that would stand alongside the tabernacle which was soon to be installed. (2 Sam 5:9-10, 7:1-2, 1 Chr. 15:1)

In order to institute this new reality, we can assume God instructed David along these lines:

[God instructed David] "Pitch a simple, single-room tent on top of Mount Zion representing what I have shown you in heaven. Place the Ark inside and you can preside as priest. Fold back the entry so that all who revere and honour My name may enter with bold confidence."

This is what would be known throughout Israel as 'the Tabernacle of David.'

The Lord set David up to rule as king from His throne and simultaneously operate as a priest inside this tabernacle. He was a king-priest foreshadowing Christ, who is now King of kings and eternal High Priest in the same likeness as Melchizedek. (Ps. 110:4, Heb. 7:15)

Unrestricted Access

Throughout his life, David was permitted to do things only the priests were allowed to do under Mosaic Law. Partaking of these 'priestly exemptions' proved his positioning by God as priest of Zion's tabernacle. At a time of desperate need he and his companions ate the consecrated bread from the Holy Place (Mark 2:25-26). At another crisis point he consulted God by wearing the High Priest's ephod (1 Sam 30:7-8). Continually on Mount Zion he would proceed through the veil into the Holy of Holies alongside the Ark and there he would gain divine inspiration in the form of prophetic songs and declarations, many of which we find recorded for us in the book of Psalms.

During this time period, the Tabernacle of Moses (the first tabernacle God revealed to Moses on Mount Sinai) was still in operation at Mt Gibeon (1 Chr. 21:29). The Ark had not been back in the Holy of Holies since the days of Eli the Priest. So wouldn't you think that David would have placed the Ark back into the Tabernacle of Moses, where it belonged?

I can hear the people saying; *"The Ark hasn't been inside Moses' Tabernacle for 80 years! The High Priest hasn't been in there to pour the blood on the mercy seat all that time! The Day of Atonement has been compromised for so long! Let's just get back on track, restore the status quo, business as usual, c'mon David!"*

But David's response is; *"No way. God has something far better in store. Just you wait and see!"*

At the Tabernacle of Moses (TOM), the Ark being placed inside formed a *barrier of separation*. It kept unregenerate humanity away from the presence of a holy God. But the tent David pitched on Mount Zion was a tent of UNRESTRICTED ACCESS.

Tradition states that at certain times all four sides would be folded up, and some historians also believe the roof could be taken off. The glory of the Lord would then emanate out to passers-by in the surrounding area. If this was so, we could logically conclude that the tent structure was only really there to protect the Ark from the elements, such as wind and rain. Anytime the weather permitted, the Ark would be placed on full display for everyone to enjoy. We cannot be dogmatic about whether the Tabernacle of David (TOD) was ever dismantled in this fashion, but one thing is undeniable, there was always an open entryway into the tent for anyone who would desire to worship the Lord and draw close to Him with a pure and sincere heart. That is all that matters!

The Shadow of His Wings

Within Jewish folklore lies a fascinating anecdote suggesting that on certain days (when there were clear blue skies) the roof would be entirely removed. The angle of the sun would cast a shadow from the Ark. This 'Ark of the Covenant' (which was a coffin-shaped rectangle box of acacia wood overlaid inside and out with gold), had two winged angelic beings called 'cherubim' seated on top. The wings of these golden angels covered the mercy seat or 'atonement cover' from either side (Ex. 25:10-21, Heb. 9:5a). The mercy seat was placed as a lid on the top of the rectangle box, the location where the High Priest would sprinkle the blood of an animal once a year for his own sins and the sins the people of Israel had committed in ignorance. (Heb. 9:7)

In 1 Chronicles 13:6, David went to Kiriath-jearim to retrieve the Ark and bring it into Jerusalem, stating that the Ark *"bears the name of the Lord who is enthroned between the cherubim"*. At that time, God's earthly throne was located between these two cherubim; technically on top of this mercy seat. The tangible reality of this still existed in heaven, but He resided in Spirit upon this earthly location as well. Therefore, you could say that the wings of the cherubim are 'the wings of the throne of God'; in shortened form, '*God's wings*'.

As the story goes, when the roof was removed, the sun would cast the 'shadow of God's wings' onto the limestone courtyard. People would enter the shade and find refuge and safety in the shadow of His wings. This imagery originated from Psalm 91 verses 1 and 4, where we are promised protection when we abide in the shadow of the Almighty. (Refer also to Davidic Psalms 17:8 & 36:7)

The glory of God was so strong in this shadow that people would find deliverance from strongholds in the shadow of His wings. They would find an anointing for provision in the shadow of His wings. They would be physically healed and receive prophetic guidance for their lives as their spirits were rejuvenated and refreshed. In fact, it is presumed that David even wrote some of the Psalms as he abided in the 'shadow of God's glorious presence'.

With this story in mind we can examine the Messianic prophecy of Malachi 4:2 in a new light; *'to you who fear My name, the Sun* (s 'U' n) *of Righteousness shall arise with <u>healing in its wings</u>'*. The Messiah is the sun that casts the shadow! The healing power of God is now experienced by abiding underneath the shadow of Jesus' wings (His presence), for the Ark was built to represent Him in the first place!

A New Testament confirmation of this is when Peter's shadow was healing everyone who came into contact with it (Acts 5:15). Jesus wants to dwell so mightily within us that as the 'Son shines' upon us, even our shadow brings healing and deliverance to the people who are within our vicinity.

All this alludes to the fact that God's wings and those of the Messiah's are one and the same, confirming that Jesus is the Lord Most High and it also emphasises nicely who He wants to be *through us*, His worshiping warriors.

Worshiping in Song

David's tabernacle is the birthplace of 'song-based' worship unto the Lord. The very same worship we enjoy as sons and daughters of God in the New Covenant was birthed here at this tent on Zion. The first official worship song that was sung on inauguration day is found in 1 Chronicles 16:7-36. It was eventually divided and incorporated into Psalm 96:1-13 and 106:1, 47-48. We would do well to study these verses thoroughly as they lay out the foundational blueprint for true Holy Spirit inspired worship.

It might be hard to believe, but before this time there was no such thing as song-based worship. When Moses went up Mount Sinai to receive the pattern for the first tabernacle, God did not mention a single word concerning this type of worship; nothing about music, nothing about singing. On the whole, the only way to show your appreciation to God through the Mosaic Covenant was through obedience to rules, rituals and regulations.

Prior to the law being given, Moses and Miriam did lead the Israelites in celebratory songs of deliverance after the Egyptians were drowned in the Red Sea. It was a break-away moment of utter jubilation in response to the glorious display of God's miraculous power! In this celebration, there was only one type of instrument at Israel's disposal; tambourines, which Miriam and some other women played. The slaves had been set free from their captivity; they just couldn't help but rejoice! (Ex. 15:1-21)

But when David combined his relentless pursuit of Yahweh with his passion for playing the harp, he began to tap into a new sound as he entered into an *ongoing lifestyle* of spontaneous worship. Without even knowing it, David was releasing this revolutionary worship from heaven into the earth realm!

As he progressed deeper, God increased his awareness of the heavenly reality. With his spiritual eyes opened, he saw the 24 elders, the four living creatures and the myriads of angels worshiping around the throne singing; *"Holy, Holy, Holy, is the Lord God Almighty who was, and is, and is to come"* (Rev. 4:8b). Suddenly it dawned on him that the songs he was playing to the sheep were breaking open the heavens in a similar fashion to the torn veil he had seen in the heavenly Holy of Holies. (Heb. 8:2)

When it came time to institute this order of worship in a corporate setting David set up a grand symphony comprising *'all kinds of musical instruments'* (2 Sam 6:5 NLT, 1 Chr. 15:16-24), accompanying the Ark in a grand procession as it travelled 10 miles from Abinadab's house in Kiriath-jearim into Jerusalem. Never had such an array of musical instrumentation been implemented into the worship of Yahweh. A new 'slice of heaven' was coming to earth!

Once the Ark was set firmly in place, David then selected 24 groups of Levites (gifted musicians and singers) and placed them inside the tabernacle (the Holy of Holies). The 24 groups were on continuous shifts day and night, all year round representing the 24 elders around God's throne in heaven (1 Chr. 16:1-6, 37, 25:9-31). Under the Law of Moses (LOM), it was illegal and punishable by death for Levites to be inside the Holy of Holies, or even look upon any of the furniture in the Holy Place (Lev. 16:2, Num. 4:17-20). By ministering before the Ark, they were breaking the law and should have dropped dead, but they didn't.

If that wasn't enough, the entrance of the tent being folded back meant *anyone* in Israel could enter the Most Holy Place and approach the Ark. Those who drew near were deeply impacted by the Spirit's transforming influence, being permitted to experience the glory of God and join in with the worship alongside the Levites (1 Chr. 16:28-30). Even those within close proximity could sense the power of God emanating from the Ark.

Rebuilding the Ruins through Worship

When Amos stated that God would *'raise up the Tabernacle of David's ruins and rebuild it as in the days of old'*, he was not referring to a literal material tent being placed back on physical Mount Zion. He was speaking of a restoration of the true worship David established at the pinnacle of Israel's response to the Lord.

In essence, David proclaimed to all Israel; *"I don't want to go back to the Tabernacle of Moses. I don't desire works, I desire worship. God doesn't desire sacrifices of bulls and goats. He desires sacrifices of praise and thanksgiving."*

Why did God allow this?

David had been shown a prophetic blueprint of the future. He had seen the High Priest after the order of Melchizedek. He replicated Hebrews 8:1-2 where Jesus *'sat down at the right hand of <u>the throne of the Majesty in Heaven</u>, ministering in the heavenly hagion (sanctuary/holy of Holies), the true tabernacle set up by the Lord and not by man.'*

What is *'the throne of the Majesty'*?

Psalm 110:1 and Acts 2:33 clarify that Jesus is seated at the right hand of the Father; therefore 'the throne of the Majesty' is actually referring to God *the Father's* heavenly throne.

There, at the Father's right hand, Jesus (from a seated position) ministers as High Priest in the heavenly Holy of Holies, which is the *true* tabernacle, set up by the Lord. The Greek text in this last portion of Hebrews 8:2 can be literally translated; 'the true tent **pitched** by the Lord, not by man', as we find it in the two most widely accepted word-for-word translations, NASB and KJV.

If we look in 1 Chronicles 15:1, we find that *'David pitched a tent'* on top of Mount Zion where the Ark was to be placed. He was pitching this tent in natural Jerusalem to imitate the genuine article pitched by the Lord in the heavenly Jerusalem, the true tabernacle mentioned here in Hebrews 8:2.

Intimacy caused David's spiritual eyes to be opened, and it was God's pleasure to transform David into an Old Testament type/pattern/foreshadowing of Christ, the eternal King-Priest. God showed David; *"You're a King from the tribe of Judah, and I'm also going to anoint you as a priest. You will show future generations what it looks like to function as a Royal Priesthood."*

This is in accordance with Hebrews 6:5, where it says that believers can *'taste the powers of the coming age'*. This means that if you see something prophetically in the Word of God, and believe it is promised in a future dispensation, you can experience it *now*: You can bring it 'into the now'.

David saw the New Covenant/the gospel age/the dispensation of grace which was the 'coming age' for him. Therefore, God allowed him to experience a *foretaste* in his day. (Bear in mind that a foretaste is merely a glimpse and not the full reality. For example, in David's time there was only this one *physical* location on the earth where people could come and experience the gospel age. Now in its fullness, we can worship the Lord in any location because we carry the Holy Spirit inside us)

In the same way, we can also experience a foretasting of the powers of our coming age, the *Kingdom* Age; the millennial reign of Christ. That's why in the New Testament it says that the kingdom is *coming* (Luke 19:11), whilst at the same time it has already *drawn near* (Matt 3:2, 4:17, 12:28, Mark 9:1). The latter is the 'good news of the kingdom', the *demonstrated gospel* of the King's superior rule over all things in every nation! (Matt 4:23, 9:35, 28:18)

~ Chapter 2 ~

CORRECT GRAFTING INTO THE JEWISH ROOT

Having come to a higher level of understanding, we can now re-examine what was said at the Jerusalem council in even greater detail;

> *After this I will return and rebuild David's fallen tent. Its ruins I will rebuild, and I will restore it,* [17]***that the rest of mankind may seek the Lord, even all the Gentiles who bear my name,*** *says the Lord, who does these things.* (Acts 15:16-17)

According to the Book of Acts; the inclusion of Gentiles in the Covenant with God (the gospel age) directly corresponds with the rebuilding of the Tabernacle *of David*.

God is rebuilding David's fallen tent so that *the rest of humanity* can seek the Lord alongside Israel, and these are *Gentiles who bear His name*. Notice that they are not 'former Gentiles' who must become proselyte Jews.

David's tabernacle is the only worship construct that would enable Gentiles *to remain true to their own national heritage* whilst still being permitted to enter into a relationship with God. It is the only framework that would allow covenantal access without forcing conversion into Judaism, because it is based on Jesus' 'once for all' sacrifice *that was not Mosaic*. This preserves differing cultural interpretations of worship and encourages unique demonstrations of adoration toward our Creator.

Interestingly, when God speaks about David's tabernacle in Scripture, there are no details given about the materials used or any references to measurements at all. Everything in the construction of the Tabernacle of Moses was stringent and precise, right down to minutest detail. On the other hand, it seems that God gave no specific guidelines to David about how He wanted the TOD to look. He was given creative license, allowing his own interpretation and individual expression of what connecting with God looked like for him.

This is what God desires for us in the New Covenant. We are encouraged to bring our own unique flavour into our relationship with God, derived from our own upbringing, culture and even personal taste. God wants us to be true to how He created us and where He placed us, rather than being forced into a religious formula that produces cookie-cutter copies.

The council in Jerusalem was organised to map out the way believers in *the Gentile churches (including all others that would follow)* ought to pursue Christian devotion. The final verdict was that by rebuilding David's tabernacle, each individual ecclesia should be free to embrace their own unique cultural style. That way, their worship would be truly genuine and free from facade. God wants us to be ourselves as we glorify and praise His name. Please understand; there is no obligation to embrace anything from Jewish culture in order to enter into 'Zion worship'. Every culture, regardless of nationality, colour or creed, has been liberated to discover and then develop their own organic expression of the Tabernacle of David. This is God's heart.

Roots we never had to begin with

Today, a large segment of the Body of Christ is consumed with getting back to 'Jewish roots'. But the Jewish root Paul mentions in Romans 11:17-18 is not an appeal for Gentiles to partake in Jewish culture. Rather, the Lord is making it clear to us that He has not utterly rejected His Old Testament people; the Jews according to the flesh. God has always kept their root intact through a faithful remnant from the physical descendants of Abraham, Isaac and Jacob, who, by believing that Christ was their promised Messiah, maintained covenant with Him. (Rom. 11:1-5)

The Jewish olive root is God's *'true Israel'*, labelled by Paul as *'the Israel of God'* in Galatians 6:15-16. This root has no cultural connotations; it simply refers to *'those currently connected in covenant with God'*. Therefore, whoever has been attached to this root at any given time in history has been one of God's holy people. At the time of Christ's resurrection, this root transformed from natural Israel into *'spiritual Israel'* or *'Israel after the Spirit'*. In order to stay vitally connected, those in the Mosaic Covenant had to transfer across. If they did not embrace Jesus as Messiah, they were broken off (Rom. 11:17-20).

> [28]*For a person is not a Jew who is one outwardly, and true circumcision is not something visible in the flesh.* [29]*On the contrary, a person is a Jew who is one inwardly, and circumcision is of the heart—by the Spirit, not the letter.* (Rom. 2:28-29 CSB)

The adjoining branches, the faithful remnant of Israel *along with* engrafted Gentiles, have become *spiritual Jews;* God's New Covenant people circumcised in their heart by the Holy Spirit.

*14For he himself is our peace, who has <u>made us both **one**</u> and has broken down in his flesh the dividing wall of hostility 15by <u>abolishing the law of commandments</u> expressed in ordinances, that he might create in himself <u>**one new man** in place of the two</u>, so making peace, 16and might reconcile us <u>both to God in **one body**</u> through the cross, thereby killing the hostility.* (Eph. 2:15-16 ESV)

We are all, 'One New Man'

Jesus has created one new man out of the two groups, and He did this by 'abolishing in His flesh the dividing wall of hostility' which came from *the Law of Moses and all its commands and regulations.* This is why the early church was known as 'the third race', even among outsiders. Those attached to this olive root, (whether natural or grafted in) are the 'elect' mentioned by Jesus and His apostles throughout the New Testament. [Matt 24:22-31, Luke 18:7, Rom 8:33, Col. 3:12, Tit. 1:1, 1 Pet. 1:2, Rev 17:14. (Greek word *eklektos*, only used of Jesus, Christians and angels)] According to 1 Peter 2:9, as a royal priesthood and holy nation we are God's 'chosen' or 'elect' race. This means that we, as the 'newly-formed third race', are God's elect.

11Therefore remember that at one time you Gentiles in the flesh, called "the uncircumcision" by what is called the circumcision, which is made in the flesh by hands— 12remember that you were at that time separated from Christ, <u>alienated from the commonwealth of Israel and strangers to the covenants of promise</u>, having no hope and without God in the world. 13But now in Christ Jesus you who once were far off have been brought near by the blood of Christ...19So then you are no longer strangers and aliens, but you are <u>fellow citizens</u> with the saints and members of the household of God, (Eph. 2:11-13, 19 ESV)

This is not about God discarding the physical descendants of Israel. Please don't get the wrong impression: It is an invitation for Gentiles to be included *within* the Commonwealth of Israel, becoming partakers *with them* in the Covenants of Promise (Noah, Abraham & David) *aside from the Covenant of*

Law. The hostility and segregation that resulted between Jew and Gentile *because of the law* has been discarded forever by the body of Jesus hung on the cross (Eph. 2:11-16, Rom. 4:14). To integrate Mosaic Law into the New Covenant actually re-establishes the enmity Jesus died to abolish. If this wall of separation has been detonated by Christ, why then should we rebuild it? Because of Jesus, the Jews were required to turn away from pursuing the law as a way of righteousness and place their hope in a righteousness that is by faith from first to last (Rom. 1:17). They had to transition away from obeying God through 'works of the flesh' and transfer across to 'Spirit-led obedience'.

> *30What then shall we say? That the Gentiles, who did not pursue righteousness, have obtained it, <u>a righteousness that is by faith</u>; 31but the people of Israel, <u>who pursued the law as the way of righteousness</u>, have not attained their goal. 32Why not? <u>Because they pursued it not by faith but as if it were by works</u>. They stumbled over the stumbling stone.*
> (Rom 9:30-32)

Jew and Gentile together in the Promise

*Through the Gospel the Gentiles are <u>heirs **together** with Israel</u>, <u>members **together** of one body</u>, and <u>sharers **together** in the promise</u> in Christ Jesus.* (Eph. 3:6)

You can clearly see (from the words in bold above) that with regard to Covenant there is *no separation* of Jew and Gentile any longer. All the covenants of promise pointed to Jesus, and *all* humanity (including Jews) must now enter them through Him. Jesus came first as a servant of the Jews, confirming the *promises made to them by the Patriarchs* **so that the Gentiles** might glorify God for His mercy (Rom. 15:8-9). Therefore, the Gentiles are connected with God through the covenant promises given to the Patriarchs (Abraham, Isaac & Jacob; all inheritors of the Abrahamic Covenant), not the law given through Moses. Jesus came *to serve the Jews* so that they could transition back into these covenants by placing their faith in Him, and by serving them He opened the way for Gentiles too.

> *He did not say this on his own, but as high priest that year he prophesied <u>that Jesus would die for the Jewish nation</u>, 5and <u>not only for that nation</u> but also for the scattered children of God, to bring them **together** and <u>make them **one**</u>.* (John 11:51-52)

*²⁶So in Christ Jesus **you are all** children of God through faith, ²⁷for **all of you** who were baptized into Christ have clothed yourselves with Christ. ²⁸There is neither Jew nor Gentile, neither slave nor free, nor is there male and female, for you are **all one** in Christ Jesus. ²⁹**If you belong to Christ, then you are Abraham's seed**, and heirs according to the promise.* (Gal. 3:26-29)

Whilst the Jews are still included in the plan of God, the cross unites all of us *as one body* by placing us into 'the Elect' as children of Abraham (Rom. 11:15-16). This entrance via citizenship into the Commonwealth of God's chosen people connects the Gentile with God through the Promise of Covenant relationship; the same experience Abraham had before Israel was even formed as a nation out of him. It does not demand that the new citizen discard their own national identity and embrace the culture of the Jewish people. (That culture stems primarily from Israel's compliance to the Laws given by Moses. For out of their deliverance from slavery in Egypt the nation's cultural heritage was derived). The sole focus here is son-placement into the family of God; the Father of every kindred, tongue, tribe and nation. Abraham experienced this imputed righteousness *before* he was ever physically circumcised, and well before the LOM came into existence. (Rom. 4:6-12)

*¹⁷If some of the branches have been broken off, and you, though a **wild olive shoot**, have been grafted in among the others and now share in the nourishing sap from the olive root, ¹⁸do not consider yourself to be superior to those other branches. If you do, consider this: you do not support the root, but the root supports you...²⁴After all, if you were cut out of an olive tree that is wild by nature, and contrary to nature were grafted into a cultivated olive tree, how much more readily will these, **the natural branches**, be grafted back into **their own olive tree**!* (Rom. 11:17-18, 24)

We must never forget that the Gentiles are being grafted into *the Jewish* olive root. It never changed and became the 'Gentile olive root'. Some of the branches may have changed, but the roots have not, for as Jesus told the Samaritan woman; *"salvation is of the Jews"* (John 4:22). For this reason, the Lord tells us through Paul that we should not 'show off' about being grafted in at the expense of Jews who have been cut off. Rather, we should be grateful toward the Jewish people and reach out to them people with the gospel; for if it weren't for them, there would be no root connecting humanity with God to begin with.

> [19]*You will say then, "Branches were broken off so that I could be grafted in." *[20]*Granted. But they were broken off because of unbelief, and you stand by faith. Do not be arrogant, but tremble.* [21]*For if God did not spare **the natural branches**, he will not spare you either.* [22]*Consider therefore the kindness and sternness of God: sternness to those who fell, but kindness to you, provided that you continue in his kindness. Otherwise, you also will be cut off.* [23]*And if they do not persist in unbelief, they will be grafted in, for God is able to graft them in again.* (Rom 11:19-23)

The people of Israel, as Abraham's chosen descendants according to the flesh, are the originators. This means they will always be regarded as 'natural branches', while the Gentiles remain 'wild olive shoots'. Therefore, we should not conclude that God has completely done away with Jewish people just because the majority of them rejected their Messiah. The 'Jewish root' and the 'religion of Judaism' are not the same thing. The former has been preserved *through belief in the Messiah* (being founded upon the everlasting Covenants of Promise), while the latter has been abolished *through the death of Jesus* (being based upon the Covenant of Law).

The people of Israel still have irrevocable promises in God's end-time plan, which were given to their forefathers long ago (Rom. 11:25-29). These promises will start being fulfilled when they, the original branches, are grafted back into *their own* olive root en masse. This will take place at a future time when many in Israel will acknowledge that Jesus was their Messiah (Rom. 9:27-28, 11:11-12). In Romans 11:12 Paul said; *"if their denial of Jesus meant riches for the world, and their severing from the cultivated olive tree riches for the Gentiles, how much greater riches will be brought forth by their full re-instatement!"* We are commissioned to help prepare the hearts of the Jewish people enabling God to bring this to pass. However, we must be careful which way we go about it. We are not required to become Jewish nor donate money to their ungodly, antichrist government (a false Zionism that despises Jesus). But we can do the following...

1) **Witness to their hearts by**: a) loving them with the *agape* of God
   b) Preaching the gospel of salvation.

2) **Provoke them to Jealousy through**: a) intimate fellowship with Jesus b) Carrying His glory c) Operating in the gifts of the Spirit with supernatural demonstration.

3) **Pray for the peace of Jerusalem (Psalm 122:6-9):** a) by following the framework found in Isaiah 62 b) that the Jewish people will acknowledge Jesus as their promised Messiah c) intercede against the antichrist agenda associated with the implementation of a one-world government in conjunction with the rebuilding of a third Temple.

Consensus Achieved

In the end, the Jerusalem Council was not in favour of the Gentile church embracing the culture of the Jerusalem church. Amos 9:11 liberated this vibrant multicultural church, breaking them free from any ritualistic practices subtly added to their simple faith in Christ and normal way of life. As James concluded;

> *It is my judgment, therefore, that we should not make it difficult for the Gentiles who are turning to God.* (Acts 15:19)

Any attempt to turn Gentile Christians toward Jewish customs makes it more difficult for them to embrace God authentically. Even the Jews, (who are meant to be provoked to envy by engrafted Gentiles living in the freedom of the Spirit), can only be jealous of something they don't have (Rom. 11:11). If we try to imitate them by joining in with the empty religion they are destined to be liberated from, what is there for them to envy about us?

There was no Law of Moses in operation at the tabernacle of David. There were no daily rituals and regulations in the Holy Place and therefore no Mosaic priestly function (there was only one room, the Holy of Holies), no daily animal sacrifices on an altar of burnt offering: *Not even an obligation to attend feast days!* THE INSTITUTION OF CIRCUMCISION FORMED NO PART OF THE WORSHIP OFFERED TO GOD ON MOUNT ZION. That's why when James quoted Amos 9:11-12 it was clear to everyone present that the Gentiles did not have to be circumcised or obey the LOM.

If Amos 9:11 had said; "The days are coming when I will rebuild the Tabernacle *of MOSES*", then the Gentiles would come under the Law Covenant. James would have concluded;

> *"Ok, we have to get the Gentile believers circumcised and teach them Levitical law. We will show them correct protocol for entering the temple complex, and all the specific offerings and sacrifices that must be observed. They must mark all the festivals down on their calendars, and we will show them how to celebrate each one, etc."*

But the Lord did not say that! God has *no* plans to rebuild the tabernacle of Moses. As glorious as it was, it is now a relic of the past, contained within an inferior and outdated covenant which was destined to vanish from the very get-go (Heb. 8:13). For from the moment Moses received the law, the glory upon his countenance began to fade, even as he descended the mountain. (2 Cor. 3:7)

It is evident then, that whatever pertains to the tabernacle of Moses and his law *passes away at the cross,* being nailed to it. Their spiritual reality is fulfilled through Jesus' death, burial and resurrection.

But the things that pertain to the Tabernacle of David *pass through the cross* and are retained in the New Covenant. The TOD, therefore, is the blueprint for the New Testament believer and God's heartbeat for the church of Jesus Christ. God desires to replicate everything that happened there in us and through us; His body, only on a much broader, world-wide scale.

~ Chapter 3 ~

SIMPLICITY OF PURE DEVOTION

The Tabernacle of Moses and its accompanying law is extremely complex. There are 613 laws that must be stringently obeyed. But the Tabernacle of David is so simple: 'The freedom to worship, uninhibited exposure to God's presence and full access into His goodness and grace.'

When we place our undivided attention on the Saviour in this way, it generates an earnest expectation for our own personal encounter with God. **David's tabernacle has a singular focus to it, and everything else God requires of us flows from this <u>simplistic devotion</u>.**

The serpent's plan to lead us astray

Paul taught the Corinthian church;

> *[2]I am jealous for you with a godly jealousy; for I betrothed you to one husband, so that to Christ I might present you as a pure virgin. [3]**But I am afraid that, as the serpent deceived Eve by his craftiness, your minds will be led astray <u>from the simplicity and purity of devotion to Christ</u>**.* (2 Cor. 11:2b-3 NASB)

The simplicity of pure devotion to Christ is the tabernacle of David lifestyle; a simplified life of devotion to worship and intimacy through relationship with our Creator. If there is one thing Satan wants to beguile or trick us out of, it is this sincere and pure devotion to our Lord. This is what he stole from Adam and Eve in the Garden of Eden. We need to ensure that we simplify our lives by unclogging our busy schedules so that we free up the necessary time to enter into this supernaturally favoured way of life. If we abide in Him, we will produce much fruit. (John 15:5)

In Daniel 7:25, God reveals one of the primary end-time strategies of the antichrist spirit. If the devil can't lure a believer into sin and debauchery, he has a Plan B up his sleeve;

> *He shall speak great words against the Most High, and shall <u>wear out the saints</u> of the Most High.* (KJV)

We may be unwavering in our dedication *to serve* Jesus, but if we are over-committed to outward works the 'spirit at the end of this age' will stop curtailing us from 'doing'. Instead, it will get behind and propel us forward into an ultra-busy state. The enemy knows that if we bombard our schedule with *'worldly commitments'* and get engaged in too many *'good works'*, we will eventually burn out and lose all connection with the Head. We need to get the balance right.

Adam and Eve had simple, unhindered fellowship with God. They walked with Him in the cool of the day (Gen. 3:8). As long as they maintained this, they were able to experience the fullness of the blessings of God as they tended and expanded the garden (Gen. 2:15). BUT THE SERPENT LURED EVE AWAY FROM THIS BY USING A TACTIC THAT SEEMED FAIR AND REASONABLE.

This is also his plan for us. In the same way that Eve lost sight of what really mattered and abandoned her first love, the devil's plan is to get us distracted in all kinds of religious obligations and ceremonial tradition. This is a modern day equivalent of becoming circumcised and obeying the LOM. If we're not careful, we'll start rebuilding the Tabernacle of Moses instead of the Tabernacle of David, and in Galatians 2:18 it says that when we rebuild the lifestyle of law we previously destroyed (works of religion/human striving), we make ourselves into a transgressor. This is serious stuff!

Godly Jealousy

*²**I am jealous for you with a godly jealousy**; for I betrothed you to one husband, so that to Christ I might present you as a pure virgin. ³But I am afraid that, as the serpent deceived Eve by his craftiness, your minds will be led astray from the simplicity and purity of devotion to Christ.* (2 Cor. 11:2-3 NASB)

The first statement in this section of scripture is somewhat unusual. Paul says that he is jealous for the Corinthians with a jealousy that comes *from God*. In doing so, he is exhibiting holy jealousy in a righteous form. God told Moses in Exodus 34:14;

Do not worship any other god, for the Lord, whose name is Jealous (NIV), *is a God who is jealous about his relationship with you.* (NLT) (For further context, read verses 15-16)

God is not jealous *of* us, He is jealous *for* us. He wants to be number one in our lives. In fact, James told us in his epistle that the Spirit God caused to dwell in us wants our attention so desperately He envies intensely for it. (Jam. 4:5)

Without Stain or Blemish

*²I am jealous for you with a godly jealousy; **for I betrothed you to one husband, so that to Christ I might present you as a pure virgin**. ³But I am afraid that, as the serpent deceived Eve by his craftiness, your minds will be led astray from the simplicity and purity of devotion to Christ.* (2 Cor. 11:2b-3 NASB)

During this lifetime, we are engaged to Jesus and are waiting for Him to return for the marriage supper of the Lamb. But this is no ordinary engagement like the ones in the western world today. In a formal Jewish betrothal you obtain marriage status immediately. Upon engagement, the bride is considered a married woman and the groom is considered a married man, but they are not yet physically a married *couple*. That is why the scriptures call us 'the Bride of Christ' *right now*.

Paul's overriding passion was to present God's betrothed to Him as a *pure virgin*. We are to remain faithful to Jesus during our engagement period (our time on this earth). Therefore, we must rid ourselves of idolatry, which is spiritual adultery against Christ. This is why James 4:4-5 links idolatry (v4) with the Spirit in us envying intensely for our attention (v5):

*⁴"**Adulteresses!** Don't you know that <u>friendship with the world</u> (idols, both religious and carnal) is hostility toward God? So whoever wants to be the world's friend becomes God's enemy. ⁵Or do you think it's without reason the Scripture says that <u>the Spirit who lives in us yearns jealously</u>?"* (Jam. 4:4-5 HCSB)

According to Ephesians 5:27, Jesus is coming back to present us to himself as a radiant church: a holy and blameless bride without stain, wrinkle or any other blemish. That's a pure virgin! 'Without stain' refers to her 'purity'. 'Without wrinkle' refers to her 'perpetual youthfulness'. **This 'Tabernacle of David**

lifestyle' is how we renew our youth, clean ourselves up and make ourselves ready. It unleashes the Harvest, ushering in the second coming of Christ.

Revelation 19:7 says; "For the wedding of the Lamb has come, and His bride has _made_ herself ready." In the Greek, to be 'made ready' means to make the necessary preparations and get everything in order. Making ourselves ready _is a choice on our part._ All we need to do is _decide to pursue the Lord with full commitment_ and let God's grace do the rest as we submit daily to the Holy Spirit's leading. (Jam. 4:6)

Some of you might be thinking, _"Well, it's too late for me, I've already _made_ myself dirty!"_ If this is the case, Revelation 7:14b is for you;

> _They have washed their robes_ (the wedding garment) _and made them white in the blood of the Lamb_ (NASB)

Why don't you start right now? Repent of your past compromise and wash your wedding garment white in the blood of the Lamb. Jesus the Bridegroom offers a fresh start to everyone reading this today. Dedicate your life from this moment on to the Tabernacle of David pattern of worship in Spirit and truth.

True Worshipers

In John 4:20 the woman at the well questions Jesus concerning one of the fiery disputes between Samaritans and Jews. She said; _"Our ancestors worship right here on Mount Gerizim, but you Jewish people claim that the place where we must worship is in Jerusalem"._ (John 4:20)

Jesus demolishes her previous paradigm. To her amazement, He imitates the Captain of the Lord's Army, who, when questioned by Joshua regarding whose side He was on, answered; "neither" (Josh 5:13-14).

> _"Woman,"_ Jesus replied, _"believe me, a time is coming when you will worship the Father _neither_ on this mountain nor in Jerusalem."_ (John 4:21)

Jesus doesn't side with His own people - the Jews, but neither does He side with the Samaritans. Instead, He introduces this woman to the New Covenant soon to be unleashed upon humanity. Once officially ratified, there will no longer be certain geographical locations where God must be worshiped, or any particular people group God favours over another.

Through the blood of Christ, all of us can now connect with God in our own unique style, any place, any time. In private, this is known as the secret place (Matt 6:6). In corporate settings of two or more, there He is in the midst (Matt 18:20). John 1:14 states that *'Jesus became flesh and tabernacled among us'*. Therefore, Jesus' earth suit was a tabernacle. In 2 Corinthians 5:1, Paul referred to our bodies as "earthly tents". We are not only *the temple* of the Living God (2 Cor. 6:16). We are *portable tabernacles* transporting Him wherever we go.

Unlike the City of David in days of old, the Father is no longer seeking a particular location to sustain an ongoing manifestation of His glory. He is searching for an end-time GENERATION clothed in the Spirit of Elijah, CARRYING the manifest glory in an unprecedented, ongoing display in every nation on the planet. This is the great fulfilment of "the raising up of the ruins of David's fallen tent" in the *very* last days.

After answering the Samaritan woman's question, Jesus carries on teaching;

> *But the time is now here when the true worshipers will worship the Father in Spirit and in truth. These are the worshipers THE FATHER SEEKS.* (John 4:23)

In the same way that Jesus told us to "seek first the kingdom of God," so *the Father* seeks out those who are true worshipers. The Greek word for *'true'* here is the same word used in Hebrews 8:2 describing the heavenly Holy of Holies as the *'true'* tabernacle pitched by the Lord. *True* worshipers will be found worshiping the Lord Jesus inside the *true* tabernacle! It is the "true place of worship". (Translated as such in ERV, NCV, NLT, NLV and ICB)

From this location the Father will seek us out because He is seated on the throne of the Majesty right next door! (Heb. 8:1) Forgive me for poor humour, but the point I am making is that the true worshiper will be sought by God. When you seek after the Father in truth (and not religion) it places you on a collision course with your Creator. You won't need to search for God any longer. *He is going to jump out from behind the bushes and surprise you!*

> *For the eyes of the Lord move to and fro throughout the earth that He may strongly support those whose heart is completely His.* (2 Chr. 16:9a NASB)

The eyes of the Lord 'darting back and forth' implies that God is seeking. His eyes are constantly searching for a certain type of person to lavish His abundant love and favour upon. The ones whom he marks and identifies are the true worshiper's; those who have yielded their entire heart over to Him. In selecting such, the Lord quenches His passionate desire to form a deep, personal bond with His children. This heart-quality is the Father's focal point. Once you allow God to find you in this way, He will STRONGLY SUPPORT you; so long as your heart *continues* to remain COMPLETELY HIS. This is no seasonal fad: It is a lifelong devotion.

As you cultivate an environment to grow in your dedication to worship and intimacy with your Heavenly Father, this purity of sincere devotion will be the facilitator of personal encounters with God. This creates for you a platform, granting you a spiritual authority to take the impartations you received in these personal encounters and release them to a dying world.

As each individual personally establishes their tabernacle of David, we will be prepared as a corporate body to usher in 'God's thorough work of speed and finality' (Rom. 9:28); the Great End-time Harvest, also prophesied in Amos 9, where *"the plowman shall overtake the reaper and the treader of grapes Him who sows seed."* (Amos 9:13 KJV)

~ Chapter 4 ~

THE FINAL VERDICT OF THE COUNCIL

In the Book of Galatians, the Judaizers had turned the saints away from Paul's gospel to a fake gospel. It was one that made them slaves through the integration of Judaism to their Christian walk. Paul described it as *"a way that pretends to be the Good News, but is not the Good News at all."* (Gal. 1:6-7 NLT)

Paul was so alarmed at their conduct that he made a desperate plea, saying;

> *⁸Formerly, when you did not know God, you were slaves to those who by nature are not gods. ⁹But now that you know God – or rather are known by God – how is it that you are <u>turning back to those weak and miserable principles</u>? Do you wish to be enslaved by them all over again? <u>¹⁰You are observing special days and months and seasons and years!</u> <u>¹¹I fear for you</u>, that somehow I have wasted my efforts on you.* (Gal. 4:8-11)

Originally, many of the Galatian Christians had been rooted in paganism. Now the Judaizers came along and took advantage of their previous 'works-based' religion. They did this by teaching them that they should depart from these demonic paganistic practices and convert over to the 'God-kind' of practices, which of course for the Judaizers, was Moses' Law. But Paul actually classifies paganism *and the Law of Moses* in the same category of 'weak and miserable principles' that don't bring anyone closer to God! For a person of strong Pharisaical background, such a comment shows the totally revolutionised state of Paul's mind.

A Mixed Crowd

In Acts 13, Paul and Barnabas launched their first missionary journey. All the testimonies they shared at the Jerusalem Council in Acts 15 came from this expedition. After beginning on the Island of Cyprus, they entered the mainland into the region of Pamphylia and headed north-bound to Pisidian Antioch, where they would birth the first church in the region of Galatia. (Pisidian Antioch is not to be confused with Antioch of Syria, Paul and Barnabas' home base.)

In Acts 13:14-43 we find there were three groups of people attending the Synagogue.

Verses 16, 26 and 43 reveal that 'Jews by birth' were present; those born into the covenant of Moses, circumcised on the eighth day.

In verse 43, we find 'proselytes' or 'converts to Judaism'. These were Gentiles who fully and devoutly converted to Judaism. Being circumcised, immersed in a 'mikvah' style bath, and committed to the 613 commandments (which encompassed the entire Mosaic Law) enabled them to be considered full members of the Jewish people in every way and called *"righteous Proselytes"*.

The third group of people (verses 16 and 26) are 'God-fearing Gentiles'. These 'God-fearers' were not full converts to Judaism, but sympathised with the religion and reverentially worshiped the God of Israel. For this reason they were still regarded as 'resident aliens,' but were allowed a few privileges outright pagans were denied. They did not agree to circumcision or comply with the whole of the Torah, but they did commit in stern obedience to what is known as the seven laws of Noah. Because of this, they were granted entry to worship in the Synagogue and had access to the Old Testament Scripture. They were known as *'righteous Gentiles'*, 'gate proselytes', 'limited proselytes, or 'half Proselytes'. These God-fearing Gentiles ('strangers in the land') were accepted in society (Exodus 20:10, Deut. 14:28-29) but still came under the category of unclean with regard to their homes, fellowship meals etc. As their name suggests, they were 'at the gate of the Jewish religion' peering in, but did not have full covenant standing with the Jewish race. Cornelius, the Roman Centurion from Caesarea, was most likely one of these 'God fearers'. (Acts 10:1-2)

The seven laws of Noah were agreed upon by the Rabbi's through critical analysis of God's dealing with Noah after the flood. They are: 'do not worship idols', 'do not curse God', 'establish courts of justice', 'do not murder', 'do not commit any form of sexual immorality', 'do not steal', and 'do not eat the flesh torn from a living animal'. As long as these were kept and maintained, a Gentile became a God-fearer in the sight of Jews. (Be aware that in recent times the United Nations has been using these laws for nefarious, anti-Christian purposes referred to as the 'Noahide Code'. For example: Under this code worshiping Jesus is seen as idol worship punishable by death)

Therefore, in the *churches of Galatia* you would find Christians who came from these four backgrounds 1) Jews from birth 2) Converts to Judaism 3) God-fearers and 4) those who were *outright pagans* before accepting Christ.

Into Christ, then back to Moses?

Judaizers found it relatively easy to convert 'ex-pagan believers' to the Law of Moses. Some may have objected, but as stated earlier, it would be simply swapping 'pagan practices' for the *so called* 'God-kind of practices', and that would have seemed reasonable to their 'works orientated' minds.

Most of the Jews and converts to Judaism would not have disapproved either: The LOM had always been, and was still, their natural way of life. For cultural reasons, they continued to follow Jewish law alongside saving faith anyway, so it *outwardly* wouldn't affect them. However, what had become cultural preference was now being re-established as a binding law of works-based salvation.

Then we have the Christians from the third group, who previous to salvation had been in the 'God fearer' category. These people would have taken offence to what the Judaizer's were proposing. For when Judaism became their number one religious persuasion, they were not forced to be circumcised. Most did not like the thought of circumcision, regarding it as unappealing and extremely unpleasant. Many did not want to be seen in the Roman gymnasiums and public baths deprived of their foreskins.

Under Judaism, they had been accepted as 'righteous Gentiles' who would be assured a place in the world to come. Now under Christianity, adherence to the seven laws of Noah was not enough? Did accepting Jesus as Messiah result in bondage to 613 extra laws; regulations that they were not required to follow even under the watchful eye of the Rabbi's in the synagogue?

This is where the decision made by James and the apostles at the Jerusalem Council becomes very important. After James quoted from Amos 9, (concerning God's desire to rebuild the Tabernacle of David in the last days), it was instantly concluded that subjection to the Law of Moses was *not* required for salvation or eternal life. However, there were a few small stipulations given to the Gentile believers by James, which seemed good to the Holy Spirit and to everyone present at the meeting. (Acts 15:28)

[19]It is my judgment, therefore, that we should not make it difficult for the Gentiles who are turning to God. [20]Instead we should write to them, telling them to <u>abstain from food polluted by idols, from sexual immorality, from the meat of strangled animals and from blood</u>. [21]For

the law of Moses has been preached in every city from the earliest times and is read in the synagogues on every Sabbath. (Acts 15:19-21)

If Scripture declares Gentiles free from Mosaic Law, why add these four rules into the mix? The reason James gives for the institution of these four laws is this; 'the law of Moses had been preached *in every city* from the earliest times and was still being read in the synagogues every Sabbath'.

This was a season where Jews and Gentiles were now mixing in full fellowship as the Ecclesia, while the Jewish contingent were still operating in Judaism, and this was occurring in every city where new churches were being formed. What James effectively states is a revised version of the seven laws of Noah. Abstaining from *'the meat of strangled animals and from blood',* is obeying the law that prohibits the consumption of flesh torn from a living animal, because the blood is not drained and is still present.

The other two (sexual immorality and idolatry) are identical to what is stated in the laws given to Noah. James considers it wise that wherever there is strong emphasis on the Synagogue and Judaism, all Gentile Christians should live in the lifestyle of the 'God-fearer' or 'limited Proselyte'. That way they would continue to be accepted in everyday Jewish society, the synagogues, and in church fellowship without causing major rifts and upheavals.

Promoting Peace and Unity

All Christians *of that era* would either be full adherents to Judaism, (because of their previous way of life) or they would follow these four rulings and be accepted in society as God-fearers. They would *not have to be circumcised or obey the Law of Moses.* This is what seemed good to the Holy Spirit, because it kept everyone unified and at peace. It was a godly compromise *for that time period* in that region of the world.

The reason we can determine that this letter was only temporary and localised in nature is because there are scriptures which show us that *later on* Christians were no longer required to obey three out of the four. Let's start with food sacrificed to idols. Paul said;

[25]*Eat anything sold in the meat market without raising questions of conscience,* [26]*for, 'The earth is the Lord's, and everything in it.* (1 Cor. 10:25-26)

⁴So then, about eating food sacrificed to idols: we know that 'An idol is nothing at all in the world' and that 'There is no God but one.' (1 Cor. 8:4)

The basic principle of what Paul is trying to show us is that we can eat any food, even food which *had previously* been sacrificed to an idol. According to 1 Corinthians 8:10, you can even eat food *in an idol's Temple* and it does you no harm. What Paul strictly prohibits is involvement in *the ritual* when the food is *being sacrificed* to the idol. That's why he says;

¹⁹Do I mean then that food sacrificed to an idol is anything, or that an idol is anything? ²⁰No, but the sacrifices of pagans are offered to demons, not to God, and I do not want you to be participants with demons. ²¹You cannot drink the cup of the Lord and the cup of demons too; you cannot have a part in both the Lord's table and the table of demons. (1 Cor. 10:19)

The food sacrificed is nothing; the idol is nothing, *but these sacrificial acts* of pagans are offered to demon spirits, who are powerfully active during these rituals. It is clear that Paul is emphasising pagan ceremony because of his statement '*the table* of demons'. He is deliberately contrasting it with the ceremony of the 'communion *table*'. They were not merely buying food of an animal previously sacrificed to an idol. They were *drinking the cup of demons* by partaking in the pagan ritual.

Therefore, we are permitted to eat anything we like without needing to check if the food was used as a part of a demonically engineered sacrifice or idolatrous ritual. The only other time Paul says we should consider what we eat is regarding another's conscience, so that a weak believer will not be emboldened to commit sin by doing something *they believe* is wrong. This wounds their weak conscience (1 Cor. 8:7-12, 10:27-29).

In Mark 7:17-19 we find that 'Jesus declared all foods clean' giving us permission to eat absolutely anything. However, indulging our flesh by feeding an addiction to any sort of food is clearly sinful behaviour (Num. 11:31-34, Prov. 23:20-21). The Apostle Paul made a similar statement to Jesus when stated in Romans 14:14 that he was fully convinced in the Lord Jesus that no food was unclean in and of itself. He then summed up this passage by explaining that the kingdom of God was not about what we eat or drink, but of righteousness, peace and joy *in the Holy Spirit.* (Rom 14:17)

The second law: abstaining from sexual immorality; is the only rule of the four that is clearly still in effect under the moral law. Under Christ's law, we are to obey Jesus' commandments, and in this we show our love for God (1 Cor. 9:21, John 14:15, 1 John 5:3). Immediately after Jesus calls all foods clean in Mark 7, He then states many of His commandments which are still in effect today.

> [20]*He went on: 'What comes <u>out of a person</u> is what defiles them. [21]For it is from within, out of a person's heart, that evil thoughts come – <u>sexual immorality</u>, theft, murder, [22]adultery, greed, malice, deceit, lewdness, envy, slander, arrogance and folly. [23]All these evils <u>come from inside and defile a person</u>.'* (Mark 7:20-23)

Under the New Covenant, there is a new way to become unclean. It is not by what we touch, or the foods we eat. Rather, it is by all these things stated by Jesus in verse 21-22. They come from the *inside, not the outside.* Look what the first one is; 'sexual immorality'. It is the head of the bunch!

Refraining from eating meat of strangled animals and consuming blood are tied to the Law given to Noah in Genesis 9:4: *"You must not eat meat that still has its life-blood in it."* Following this law helped people live within the Jewish society of kosher. Keeping this simple dietary requirement also enabled them to enter the synagogue. Those who became Christians at this time would follow this, but it was clearly not a permanent rule for the body of Christ moving forward. Jesus declared all foods clean, and Paul elaborated on this further;

> *They forbid people to marry and order them to abstain from certain foods, which God created to be received with thanksgiving by those who believe and who know the truth. [4]<u>For everything God created is good, and nothing is to be rejected</u> if it is received with thanksgiving, [5]because it is consecrated by the word of God and prayer.* (1 Tim 4:3-5)

It is also important to understand that under the Old Covenant the blood of animals was required to make atonement for the people's sin upon the altar. The expiation of their sins in the sight of God was brought about through animal blood.

> [10]*"I will set my face against any Israelite or any foreigner residing among them who eats blood, and I will cut them off from the people. [11]For the life of a creature is in the blood, and I have given it to you to make atonement for yourselves on the altar; <u>it is the blood that makes atonement for one's</u>*

life. *¹²Therefore I say to the Israelites, 'None of you may eat blood, nor may any foreigner residing among you eat blood.'* (Lev. 17:10-12)

The great news for us living in the New Covenant is that the blood of Jesus Christ, the true human sacrifice to which all these animal sacrifices pointed, has been shed for our redemption and salvation. Therefore, we can render this clause in Moses' law (to not partake of animal blood) null and void because the blood of animals no longer represents the forgiveness of humanity's sins.

Even though I find the idea of a black pudding disgusting, I don't think it is wrong to eat it as a Christian. I may choose to not eat pork because there are healthier forms of meat to consume, but from a spiritual point of view, I have no problem eating a generous serving of crackle once a year during Christmas lunch. When I have a medium rare steak and the blood oozes out, my conscience is not in any way convicted as a lawbreaker.

The final ruling of the Jerusalem council was not a list of binding laws that place Christians under slavery to ritualistic religion. The apostles' motive was actually to make it *as easy as possible* for the Gentiles who were turning to God (Acts 15:19). This godly compromise promoted peace; continuing to be sympathetic towards the vastness of the Jewish culture, but also determined with boldness and clarity that the Judaizers were illegal heralds who, from this point onward, had to be disregarded.

When the Gentile believers at Antioch read the letter, they were *'glad for its encouraging message'* (Acts 15:31). They had been liberated from bondage to a ridiculous number of religious rules and were free to follow Jesus by walking in the Spirit with the least amount of hindrances possible.

For in Christ Jesus neither circumcision nor uncircumcision has any value. ***The only thing that counts** is faith expressing itself through love*. (Gal. 5:6)

*Neither circumcision nor uncircumcision means anything; **what counts is the new creation**.* (Gal. 6:15)

*¹⁸Was a man already circumcised when he was called? He should not become uncircumcised. Was a man uncircumcised when he was called? He should not be circumcised. Circumcision is nothing and uncircumcision is nothing. Keeping God's commands is **what counts**.* (1 Cor. 7:18-19)

~ Chapter 5 ~

'TRUE' CIRCUMCISION

²⁸For a person is not a Jew who is one outwardly, and <u>true circumcision is not something visible in the flesh</u>. (Rom. 2:28 CSB) *²⁹Rather, a person is a Jew who is one inwardly, and <u>real circumcision is circumcision of the heart, by the Spirit</u>, not by the written code.* (Rom. 2:29a NRSV, 29b NIV)

The authentic version of circumcision is a spiritual circumcision of a person's innermost being, performed not by the hands of men, but by the Spirit of the Living God. The physical circumcision found in the Old Testament was merely a shadow of this reality. When the appropriate time came, God sent His Son to the earth, born of a woman, born under law, *to free those under the law* (Gal. 4:4). Through Christ's sacrificial atonement, God can now perform true circumcision in the hearts of men, rendering the shadow obsolete.

The Lord revealed the purpose for this in Deuteronomy 30:6;

⁶The LORD your God will circumcise your hearts and the hearts of your descendants, so that you may love him with all your heart and with all your soul, and live.

In Romans 2:25a, Paul states that physical circumcision only has value if someone is able to observe the law perfectly. If this were achievable, Deuteronomy 30:6 would become a reality, leading to the fulfilment of the first and greatest commandment and equate to being circumcised in heart, leading to life. Unfortunately, this holy endeavour was impossible to achieve under the old system of Mosaic Law, and the prophet Jeremiah confirmed this sad reality;

*²⁵"The days are coming," declares the Lord, "when I will punish all who are circumcised **<u>only in the flesh</u>**—²⁶... for all the nations are uncircumcised, and all the house of Israel <u>are uncircumcised in heart</u>."* (Jer. 9:25-26 NIV, ASV)

Through Jeremiah, we can identify that God viewed the house of Israel as uncircumcised, even though all the males had been physically circumcised when they were eight days old. In His eyes, they were no better off than all the other pagan nations surrounding them; their behaviour was no different. In Romans 2:25b, Paul completes the verse by stating that if you break the law (don't observe it perfectly) you have become as though you were uncircumcised. In Galatians, he showed us that this failure was still occurring in his day;

> *[12]Those who want to impress people by means of the flesh are trying to compel you to be circumcised. The only reason they do this is to avoid being persecuted for the cross of Christ. <u>Not even those who are circumcised keep the law,</u> yet they want you to be circumcised that they may boast about your circumcision in the flesh.* (Gal. 6:13)

Because of their inability to obey, the Israelites were circumcised *only in the flesh*. This ended up being merely a physical attribute they could boast about. By compelling Gentile converts to be circumcised, the Judaizers took this boasting with them into their version of Christianity to prevent their unsaved Jewish compatriots from persecuting them for the cross of Christ. For Paul reveals that physical circumcision gave the Jews no spiritual advantage over the Gentiles because the power of sin held everyone captive, circumcised and uncircumcised alike (Rom. 3:9). Unlike the Judaizers, Paul would never boast in anything except the cross of Christ, through which the world had been crucified to him, and he to the world (Gal. 6:14). God was looking forward to a greater form of circumcision, one that would bring the Lord's people close to His heart through intimacy. Therefore, the only way to be truly circumcised in heart is by coming to know the Lord through the born again experience. This is why Paul told the Philippian church that '*it is **we who are the circumcision,** we who <u>worship by the Spirit of God</u>, who glory in Christ Jesus, and who <u>put no confidence in the flesh</u>.*' (Phil. 3:3)

The Seal of Two vastly different Covenants

The rite of circumcision began with Abraham way back in Genesis 17. Immediately after changing his name from Abram to Abraham, God said to him;

> *"As for you, you must keep my covenant, you and your descendants after you for the generations to come. [10]This is my covenant with you and your descendants after you, the covenant you are to keep: Every male among you shall be circumcised. [11]You are to undergo circumcision, <u>and it will be the sign of the covenant between me and you</u>... [14]Any uncircumcised male, who has not been circumcised in the flesh, will be cut off from his people; he has broken my covenant."* (Gen. 17:9-11, 14)

The first person Abraham circumcised was his son Ishmael. When God sealed the covenant agreement with the sign, or 'distinguishing mark' of circumcision, Abraham was already 99 years old and Ishmael 13. Yet God first instituted this covenant with Abraham back in Genesis 15, well before Ishmael was born to him at the age of 86. While the sign of the covenant would be given here at Abraham's introduction to circumcision, the promises, terms and blood were established way back then, and it is said that the moment Abraham believed God it was instantly credited to his account as righteousness (Gen. 15:6).

What did Abram believe? He believed that a son of his own flesh and blood would be his heir, not his servant Eliezer of Damascus, and that through this promised son, his offspring would be as numerous as the stars in the sky. God hadn't given Abraham a *physical* mark of the covenant when He spoke these promises to Abraham, even though he was already viewed by God as righteous.

In-between the instigation of this covenant and the giving of this sign, Abram and Sarai would by their own human effort (works of the flesh) attempt to fulfil God's promise, conjuring up a plan to birth Ishmael through their slave girl, Hagar. (Gal. 4:22-23)

Only after re-appearing to Abram, changing his name and speaking about the imminent birth of Isaac - the genuine child of promise - does God introduce Abraham to circumcision. From this time forward, circumcision was the distinguishing mark *displaying outwardly* that a male had been sealed *by birth* into the Abrahamic Covenant. {If a baby was not circumcised on the eighth day, he had broken the covenant (Gen. 17:14). You can't break something you don't possess. That means they had already been sealed into it on the day they were born}

Even after being circumcised, Ishmael, along with his mother Hagar, would eventually be cast out of Abraham's presence when Ishmael began mocking Isaac. The son of the slave woman would not be permitted to share in the inheritance with the free woman (Gal. 4:21-31). For it was through Isaac that Abraham's offspring would be traced (Rom. 9:7, Gen. 21:8-12). Galatians 4:28 tells us that as saints of God, we are like Isaac, children of promise. That's makes us Abraham's true offspring! We have been grafted into this covenant of promise by faith through our relationship to Jesus Christ; the promised Son of God who is Abraham's ultimate seed (Gal. 3:16). For it is now through Him that all of Abraham's descendants are counted. This is how the Lord fulfilled the primary promise He gave Abraham; "you will be the Father of *many* nations", for while Abram means 'exalted father', Abraham means 'father of a multitude' (Gen. 17:4-7). Paul testifies concerning this;

>*⁵So again I ask, does God give you his Spirit and work miracles among you by the works of the law, or because you believe what you heard? ⁶Consider Abraham: "He believed God, and it was credited to him as righteousness." ⁷Understand, then, that those who **have faith** are children of Abraham. ⁸Scripture foresaw that God would justify the Gentiles **by faith**, and announced **the gospel** in advance to Abraham: "All nations will be blessed through you." ⁹So those who **rely on faith** are blessed along with Abraham, **the man of faith**…¹⁶The promises were spoken to Abraham and to his seed. Scripture does not say "and to seeds," meaning many people, but "and to your seed," **meaning one person, who is Christ.*** (Gal. 3:5-9, 16)

The Scripture is clear: Those who have faith *in the gospel about Jesus Christ* are the promised children of Abraham.

◊◊◊◊◊

When Moses went up Mount Sinai and received the law, something strange occurred. The initiation rite of circumcision got transferred across to the Law of Moses. It reverted away from the Abrahamic Covenant and got incorporated into the Mosaic. All of a sudden, a baby was not circumcised on the 8th day as a sign they had been born into the faith covenant of promise, but sealed into all the religious obligations contained within the law. This is explained in Leviticus chapter 12, alongside the purification for women after childbirth.

We see these Levitical laws playing out in the life of baby Jesus. He was 'born under the law' as Galatians 4:4 reveals. In Luke chapter 2, Mary gives birth to Jesus and is therefore unclean for the first seven days. Then on the eighth day, Jesus was circumcised, according to Leviticus 12:3 (Luke 2:21). After this, 'when the time came for the purification rites required by the Law of Moses, Joseph and Mary took Jesus to be presented to the Lord' (Luke 2:22). Jesus was 40 days old when His parents took Him to the temple, as Leviticus 12:4 states that after being unclean for the first 7 days, the mother must wait an additional 33 days to be purified from her bleeding.

To purify the mother, the parents were to offer a one-year-old lamb and a dove or pigeon. But if the family was too poor to afford a lamb, they could simply offer a pair of doves or two young pigeons. This is what Joseph and Mary did, for Jesus was the Lamb (Luke 2:24). They were still poor at this time, but after the Magi came from the east and visited Jesus as a toddler, they were amply supplied with plenty of gold. This infusion of wealth enabled them to escape to Egypt before Herod killed all the children two years old and under! Herod did this because he had learned from the Magi that the timing of the star indicated Jesus would most likely be 1-2 years old at the time they arrived in Jerusalem. (Matt 2:1-16)

When He was older, Jesus confirmed that circumcision, though originating with the Patriarchs, had been hijacked by Moses (come under the law). He also shows us how highly rated circumcision was. If the day conflicted with the Sabbath Day, circumcision would override it and the rite of initiation would still go ahead anyway! Speaking to the Jewish leaders, He remarked;

> *"I did one miracle, and you are all amazed. [22]Yet, because Moses gave you circumcision (though actually it did not come from Moses, but from the patriarchs), you circumcise a boy on the Sabbath. [23]Now if a boy can be* circumcised on the Sabbath so that the law of Moses may not be broken, *why are you angry with me for healing a man's whole body on the Sabbath?"* (John 7:21-23)

Jesus makes it clear: If someone did not circumcise their newborn male on the eighth day, they would be breaking *the Law of Moses*, not the Abrahamic Covenant! For a season, the LOM took precedence over the promises given by God to Abraham. Paul picks up on this also, showing us the futility of what circumcision had become since the Law of Moses had been introduced;

> *[1]It is for freedom that Christ has set us free. Stand firm, then, and do not let yourselves be burdened again by a yoke of slavery. [2]Mark my words! I, Paul, tell you that if you let yourselves be circumcised, Christ will be of no value to you at all. [3]Again I declare to* every man who lets himself be circumcised that he is obligated to obey the whole law. (Gal. 5:1-3)

From the moment Moses ratified the Mosaic Covenant, circumcision was now a lifelong obligation to obey every law contained within. Just one failure and you were done for! *Jesus Christ came to set us free from this Mosaic circumcision,* but after being saved and beginning their new life in the Spirit, the Galatians were being burdened again by a yoke of slavery, drawing back into religious works because the Judaizers were telling them they needed to get physically circumcised!

The Believers Circumcision

As previously discussed in chapter 2; Ephesians 2:11-13 clearly states that through faith in Jesus, believers are integrated into the covenants *of promise*. This is how we connect with God; through the faith modelled by Noah, Abraham and David. We have *not* been included in the covenant of law.

In Galatians 3:17-19, Paul shows us that the law introduced 430 years later did not set aside the Abrahamic Covenant previously established or do away with the promise. No, because it was impossible for fallen man to adhere to its stringent demands, the law was merely a schoolmaster to lead everyone to Christ. It held humanity in protective custody until the Messiah was revealed, showing us our need for a Saviour in the process. The futility of the law causes mankind to break free from flesh-driven works and embrace Jesus' act of sacrifice on their behalf, leading them *back* into the faith exhibited by Abraham. Once the guardian (the law) has done its work, it is no longer necessary (Gal. 3:23-25, 4:1-7). If the inheritance depended on works of the law, then it no longer depended on God's promise. If the law was the way to obtain the Lord's inheritance, it would be impossible to attain, for it requires perfect adherence. Fortunately for us, God, in His grace, gave it to Abraham as a promise, accessible through faith to those who believe. God will never go back on a promise, but He can abolish an inferior system of rule-keeping.

> *²¹Is the law therefore contrary to God's promises? Absolutely not! For if the law had been granted with the ability to give life, then righteousness would certainly be on the basis of the law. ²²But the Scripture imprisoned everything under sin's power, so that <u>the promise might be given on the basis of faith in Jesus Christ to those who believe</u>.* (Gal. 3:21-22 CSB)

It is abundantly clear then that the *spiritual* circumcision of the Christian has nothing to do with the Mosaic form of circumcision. It is patterned after the typology of the rite of circumcision given by the Lord to Abraham. Paul discusses the nature of our circumcision here;

> *¹¹When you came to Christ, you were "circumcised," but not by a physical procedure. Christ performed <u>a spiritual circumcision—the cutting away of your sinful nature</u>. ¹²For you were buried with Christ when you were baptized. And with him you were raised to new life because you trusted the mighty power of God, who raised Christ from the dead.* (Col. 2:11-12 NLT)

We are spiritually circumcised via water baptism in the same manner Abraham was physically circumcised in Genesis 17. Yet it is not the cutting away of the flesh of our foreskin that is in view. The focus is on the cutting away of our fleshly nature; the dominion of sin has been broken!

◊◊◊◊◊

The link between Abrahamic circumcision and our faith in Christ is thoroughly explained by Paul in Romans 4, where he links the Abrahamic Covenant to the reality of the New Eternal Covenant in Christ's blood. Throughout his writings, Paul continually *contrasts* the Mosaic Covenant with the New Covenant, but always *relates* it to the Abrahamic;

> *What then shall we say that Abraham, our forefather according to the flesh, discovered in this matter? [2]If, in fact, Abraham was justified by works, he had something to boast about—but not before God. [3]What does Scripture say? "Abraham believed God, and it was credited to him as righteousness."*
>
> *[4]Now to the one who works, wages are not credited as a gift but as an obligation. [5]However, to the one who does not work but trusts God who justifies the ungodly, **their faith** is credited as righteousness.* (Rom 4:1-5)

Here Paul begins a dialogue culminating in the reality that people exhibiting faith are regarded as the children of Abraham. He is the father of us all (v16); the father of all **who believe** but have not been circumcised, and also the father of the circumcised *as long as they **follow in the footsteps of the faith** Abraham had before he was circumcised (Rom 4:11b-12). The focus here is always on faith, not any subsequent action performed after the initial seed of faith has been germinated. All of us obtain our right-standing with God through the same mechanism as Abraham; faith, aside from additional works. This is how all of us enter the family of God; not by any righteous deeds we have done, but through His mercy (Tit. 3:5a). **Upon believing**, our account is credited with an 'imputed' righteousness; the holy sinlessness of Christ.

But now here's where it gets interesting. After quoting King David speaking of the blessedness of the one to whom God credits righteousness apart from works, Paul now injects circumcision into the equation;

> *[9]Is this blessedness only for the circumcised, or also for the uncircumcised? We have been saying that Abraham's faith was credited*

*to him as righteousness. [10]Under what circumstances was it credited? Was it after he was circumcised, or before? **It was not after, but before!** [11]And he received circumcision as a sign of the seal of righteousness that he had by faith while he was still uncircumcised. So then, he is the father of all who believe but have not been circumcised, in order that righteousness might be credited to them.* (Rom. 4:9-11)

In Colossians 2:11-12, Paul told us that water baptism was representative of our spiritual circumcision. Keeping this in mind, we must now consider what he says here;

1. The right standing with God came *before* Abraham was circumcised, and

2. He received circumcision as a tangible sign (Gen. 17:11) of the inner seal of righteousness *he had already obtained by faith* while uncircumcised. (Gen. 15:6)

This becomes vitally important when it comes to soteriology; the study of salvation. Is a person saved only after water baptism, or are they saved when they first believe? Paul asks the question in Romans 4:10; under what circumstances was righteousness credited to Abraham? Was it after circumcision or before? The answer he gave was BEFORE. Relating this to water baptism, of which Abraham's circumcision is the type and shadow, it is clear that we are saved not at our water baptism, but at the moment we believed God and were credited with righteousness; the day we were born again. Another confirmation of this truth is Jesus' response to the thief on the cross. He told him; "today you will be with me in paradise" (Luke 23:43). This thief was going to be with Jesus for eternity after he died, but there was definitely no opportunity for him to get water baptised.

Just like in Romans 4:11, we read in Genesis 17:11 how God gave Abraham circumcision as a sign, or 'distinguishing mark', that they were in covenant; a witness for the people to see and acknowledge! But Paul adds extra detail here. He states that this mark was given as a witness to 'the seal of righteousness' Abraham already possessed from the moment he believed. Likewise, our water baptism is a sign or distinguishing mark that we have been sealed into the New Covenant by the Holy Spirit, and this sealing (along with its imputed righteousness) is also something we possessed prior to that glorious occasion. Baptism, then, is our public declaration displaying outwardly what God *has already done inwardly.*

This is confirmed by the timing of when Scripture says we were sealed;

> **_When you believed_**, _you were marked in him with a seal, the promised Holy Spirit_, [14]*who is a deposit guaranteeing our inheritance until the redemption of those who are God's possession—to the praise of his glory.* (Eph. 1:13b-14)

When we believe, the blood of Christ washes away all our sins through rebirth and renewal by the Holy Spirit (Tit. 3:5b). As a result, we receive eternal life, being immediately welcomed into God's presence to stand before Him as holy and blameless without a single fault (Col. 1:22). At that moment, faith comes alive and the Lord immediately performs the circumcision of our heart and the cutting away of our sinful nature by His Spirit. God takes ownership over us by marking us *spiritually* with the Holy Spirit as His down-payment. We instantly become His prized possession. We do not have to wait till our water baptism for this sealing to occur.

Water Baptism, therefore, is symbolic of all these things. We are re-enacting what took place to unashamedly demonstrate the inward transformation to those present and display our commitment to seeing our salvation through to the end. The Holy Spirit coming into our heart seals us into the New Covenant, and while water baptism confirms this, it does not instigate it. (2 Cor. 1:22, Eph. 4:30)

Baptised into a New Creation

The holiness God bestows upon us is far more than just a position of 'right-standing'; it is a completely new way of life! We read in Colossians 2:12 that *'you were buried with Christ when you were baptized. And with him _you were raised to new life_ because you trusted the mighty power of God, who raised Christ from the dead.'* Water Baptism represents the death of our old man (nature); and rising up out of the water represents our new man (nature) entering resurrection life alive in the Spirit. Paul goes even deeper into this in his letter to the Romans;

> [1]*What shall we say, then? Shall we go on sinning so that grace may increase?* [2]*By no means! We are those who have died to sin; how can we live in it any longer?* [3]*Or don't you know that all of us _who were_ **_baptized into Christ_** Jesus were baptized into his death?* [4]*We were therefore buried with him through baptism into death in order that, just*

*as Christ was raised from the dead through the glory of the Father, **we too may live a new life**.*

⁵For if we have been united with him in a death like his, we will certainly also be <u>united with him in his resurrection</u>. ⁶For we know that our old self was crucified with him so that <u>the body ruled by sin might be done away with, that we should no longer be slaves to sin</u>—⁷because anyone who has died has been set free from sin. (Rom. 6:1-7)

Theologians debate whether the baptism into Christ mentioned here by Paul refers to water baptism, or being born again of water and the Spirit. But once you realise that water baptism is simply representative of what occurred at salvation, the argument becomes irrelevant. It can clearly refer to both. One is the outward symbolism, the other the inward reality. The point Paul is making is that there is a new resurrection life available for everyone found in Christ. Our sinful nature has been cut away through spiritual circumcision. Therefore, the old version of us ruled by sin can be done away with. We don't have to live by its dictates any longer. By dying with Christ, we shall also be raised to live in victory with Him: We no longer have to be slaves to sin, for death no longer has mastery over Him, nor shall it over us. We have been transformed into a new creation; the old has passed, the new is here! (2 Cor. 5:17)

The Pledge of a Clear Conscience

Does the Apostle Peter have any critical input to add regarding this subject? Yes, he does;

This water symbolises baptism that now saves you—not the removal of dirt from the body but <u>the pledge of a clear conscience towards God</u> through the resurrection of Jesus Christ (1 Pet. 3:21 NIV, CSB)

During water baptism, not only did you re-enact the symbology of what occurred when you were saved, but alongside this public declaration you also *signed yourself up to an ongoing commitment.* The latter is the most vital facet of baptism, which results in us 'standing firm to the end and being saved' (Matt 10:22). Whether you realised it or not, when you were water baptised you entered into a lifelong pledge *to maintain a clear conscience before God.* A pledge is a promise or agreement *that must be kept.* The Greek word (eperōtēma) denotes a 'demand given' along with a 'craving or intense desire'. Having thoroughly cleaned them, the Lord Jesus places upon us the demand of keeping our consciences clear from defilement, and we willingly respond with an intense desire to obey.

Water baptism is the moment when we make this wholehearted commitment, but neither it nor the baptism ceremony is the catalyst that produces our salvation. Though it might seem otherwise, Peter is actually in agreement with this, stating above that our pledge saves us *through the resurrection of Jesus Christ*. For we know from Romans 10:9 that if we confess with our mouths that "Jesus is Lord," and believe in our heart *that God raised him from the dead*; we will be saved (Rom. 10:9). This is all that is required to bring a soul into eternal life, but without sustaining this belief and confession in Christ through repentance, no one can remain continually saved. For it is only by faith in Jesus' finished work and an ongoing application of His blood that we find forgiveness and maintain our right-standing in His sight. If we remain in Him, He will remain in us. (John 15:4)

Peter is not saying that we were 'saved' (past tense) at the baptism ceremony. We are *being* saved 'now' by maintaining our pledge through faith in His resurrection. When Peter speaks of the waters of baptism 'saving us' (present-continuous tense), he is talking about remaining steadfast *in* our salvation till the end, in which keeping our pledge is key. *This is the only part of baptism that is not symbolic.* Our vow originates on this day, propelling us into the new way of resurrection life described in Romans 6:4-14. As we descend into the precious waters, we are renouncing sin, renouncing the world, renouncing the devil, and we are coming up liberated from the death-grip of this present evil age to embrace Jesus' offer of abundant life.

The symbolic nature of water baptism does not insinuate that God is absent from moving during the sacrament: {a visible sign of an inward grace (seal) accompanied by an oath or solemn pledge.} The power of the Holy Spirit is always present, working mightily; breaking chains of bondage to further lift the weight of sin and guilt off His children's shoulders *as we honour Him by making this pledge.* Deliverance from demons and baptism in the Holy Spirit may be experienced here as well. Make no mistake about it! We progress towards the full freedom Jesus won for us through a process, so the Holy Spirit can use the day of baptism as a catapult, launching a believer into a new stratosphere of intimacy with Jesus.

◊◊◊◊◊

On the day of our salvation, the blood of Jesus also cleansed our guilty, defiled consciences, restoring our innocence (Heb. 10:22). Maintaining our baptismal oath keeps our consciences clear through a lifestyle of repentance. That's why the New Testament water of immersion is a baptism *of repentance* <u>for</u> the forgiveness of our sins (Mark 1:4). This is a promise to live with no deliberate, habitual, intentional sin. If we go on committing sins we are not yet aware of, our innocence is affected, but our conscience remains clear as we continue to receive God's mercy (1 Tim 1:13). When we do accidentally miss the mark during moments of weakness, we must be deeply sorrowful and quick to repent. As our bodies are washed in the sacred waters of repentance, the sprinkled blood of Christ cleanses our guilty consciences, reinstating pure innocence in that area. This lifestyle of repentance enables us to 'fight the battle well, holding onto faith and a good conscience' (1 Tim. 1:18b-19a).

We cannot *knowingly* practice evil because the blood of Jesus does not cover a repetitive pattern of purposeful sin. That's why Hebrews 10:26 tells us that if we deliberately continue sinning after the knowledge of the truth, no expiatory sacrifice is left. Even more importantly, the scriptures concerning baptism give us the keys on how to live free from these sins. For we know that anyone born of God does not continue to sin; the One begotten of God at His resurrection keeps them safe, and the evil one cannot harm them. (1 John 5:18)

> *How much more, then, will the blood of Christ, who through the eternal Spirit offered himself unblemished to God, <u>cleanse our consciences from acts that lead to death</u>, so that we may serve the living God!* (Heb. 9:14 NIV)

> *And so it is written, that the Christ (the Messiah, the Anointed) would suffer and rise from the dead on the third day, [47]and that <u>repentance [necessary] for forgiveness of sins</u> would be preached in His name to all the nations, beginning from Jerusalem.* (Luke 24:46-47 AMP)

SECTION II:

TABERNACLE OF MOSES

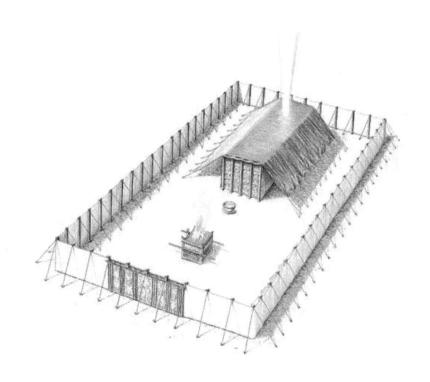

~ Chapter 6 ~

THE OUTER COURT

As previously stated, everything pertaining to the tabernacle of Moses (except the moral law, which is still in place under Christ's law) has passed away and been nailed to the cross. The true spiritual realities hidden within these natural regulations were fulfilled through Christ's life, sacrificial death, burial and resurrection. All the elements within the Mosaic system were mere '*shadows* of law'; the coming of the Saviour brought the *actual substance*.

When we look back on any of these; the festivals, the sacrificial system with its offerings, or the divine service inside the Holy Place, we do so for only one goal; to find revelation about God's Anointed One. Whilst Jesus is hidden prophetically through the Mosaic Covenant, we never have to practically apply any of it to our lives, thinking that if we do, we find some kind of extra favour with God. This is 'works-based' earning, not 'grace-based' favour. We will not find extra blessings by attempting to follow any of these rituals. Instead, simply discover more about Who the Saviour of the world is through these sacred writings, and then praise Him for His flawless character and unrelenting, compassion-filled love.

The Apostle Paul, who was previously the strictest adherent to all these customs (Phil. 3:4-6), told us in Colossians;

> *16Don't let anyone condemn you for what you eat or drink, or for not celebrating certain holy days or new moon ceremonies or Sabbaths. 17These are a shadow of the things that were to come; the reality, however, is found in Christ.* (Col. 2:16 NLT, 17 NIV)

Jesus is the *perpetual* fulfilment of every ordinance, sacrifice and holy day. We do not have to wait for certain dates on the Jewish calendar to observe the reality of what Christ has achieved in fulfilling them. Nor does an offering given on one of these days have any more power to bless than an offering given on any other day. 'Perpetual' means; 'enduring *forever,* lasting indefinitely *without intermission or interruption,* blooming continuously throughout *all seasons of the year*'. Pause and reflect on that.

In Romans 15:5, Paul also said;

One person considers one day more sacred than another; another considers every day alike. Each of them should be fully convinced in their own mind.

If there was a distinct advantage in certain days of the year, Paul would have stated that people who 'consider every day alike' were at a disadvantage to the ones who regarded certain days as more sacred. If this were the case, he would have given us a list of the 'special days' where God is more willing to move than on others.

A 'type' or 'shadow' is like having a picture of someone, but the 'reality' or 'substance' is ongoing access into the actual presence of that person. If you had the option to look at a picture of Jesus, or meet Him in Person, which one would you choose? I understand it's a no brainer, but think about what you are doing when you incorporate Old Testament types and shadows into your Christian experience. Isn't that the same as choosing to look at a picture of Jesus on the shelf, instead of accepting the invitation to dine with Him, and He with you? You have direct access to your Redeemer. Don't get distracted by the allure of the fancy picture frames and come to the table!

What's in the front yard?

Outside Moses' Tent there was a fenced courtyard with a front gate. The fence was made from curtains of finely woven linen, held up by silver rings connected to posts that were securely anchored in bronze bases. The gate was a curtain that was 30 feet long, decorated with beautiful embroidery in blue, purple, and scarlet thread, situated on the east side. (Exod. 27:9-19)

When you walk through this gate, the first thing you'd come across was a bronze 'altar of burnt offering' where many types of prescribed animals would be sacrificed. These sacrifices on the altar represent the blood of Jesus shed on the cross for the forgiveness of *known sin*. These sins are not the sins from the 'hidden-faults' category mentioned in Psalm 19:12. In other words, they are not committed in ignorance by the transgressor and can be directly acknowledged and repented of. This leads us to the spiritual application of 'the laver'...

In-between the entrance to the Tabernacle and this bronze altar was a bronze laver or 'washbasin'. Here the priests would wash their hands and feet prior to and after the animal sacrifices. The priests would wash their hands and feet, not only before performing animal sacrifice, but also prior to entry inside the Holy place of the Tabernacle. Failure to do so would result in death! (Exod. 30:19-21)

What is interesting about the bronze laver is that in Exodus 30:17-18 God gave Moses the blueprint. Then in Exodus 35 the people were encouraged to donate raw materials toward the building of the tabernacle, including its furnishings and equipment. But when it came to the time of constructing the washbasin, they used items that were not in the donation list compiled by Moses in Exodus 35:22-28.

Exodus 38:8 tells us;

> *Bezalel made the bronze washbasin and its bronze stand from <u>bronze mirrors</u> donated by the women who served at the entrance of the Tabernacle.* (NLT)

The bronze washbasin was constructed by beating together (or perhaps melting down) all the brass mirrors given by the women who ministered at the entrance to the tabernacle. These women were stationed right next to the laver in their service to God, which is probably why they were so keen to donate the materials to be used in its design.

In what ways were these women ministering? Perhaps cleaning or sweeping? Fixing up tears and blemishes in the tabernacle's fabric? Maybe they sewed together new priestly garments by spinning goat's hair into yarn? (Exod. 35:25-26) No one knows for sure, but these women re-appear several centuries later in 1 Samuel 2:22 when the TOM was stationed in Shiloh, proving that on a regular basis certain women were appointed to this service. Although there are no specific details given in Scripture, these women were given certain ministerial tasks *(tsâbâ' in Hebrew)* that were of equal importance to the rituals given to the Levite men.

The washbasin ended up being a large mirror where the priests could see their reflection clearly. If there was no water in it, they saw their reflection, and if there was water in it, they still saw their reflection in the water. This was quite important for a priest, because he needed to have everything in perfect order to be accepted before the Lord upon entrance into the Holy Place.

Washbasin of Repentance

The water in the bronze laver represents baptism: washing in the waters of repentance. The altar of burnt offering is the blood sprinkled for the forgiveness of sins, while the water is our correct response of repentance from a lifestyle of habitual sin. Hebrews 10:22 says;

> *let us draw near to God with a sincere heart and with the full assurance that faith brings, having our hearts <u>sprinkled</u> to cleanse us from a guilty conscience and having our <u>bodies washed</u> with pure water.*

When the blood of Christ is sprinkled on us, His forgiveness cleanses us from a *guilty* conscience. But for this to be effective we must also have our bodies washed with pure water. This is where the dirt of our unholy lifestyle and compromise is washed away so that we may live new lives that honour the sacrifice of Christ. While the blood cleanses our guilty conscience, we are then commanded to *keep a clear* conscience (1 Pet. 3:16, 1 Tim 3:9), and we do this through the water of the laver. If we fail to keep a clear conscience (by falling back into our old disobedient lifestyle), our guilty conscience returns and a re-application of the blood is necessary to bring it back to a 'clean' state. (1 John 1:9)

◊◊◊◊◊

With this in mind, let's re-examine what Peter said regarding Water Baptism;

> *This water symbolises baptism that now saves you—not the removal of dirt from the body but <u>the pledge of a clear conscience towards God</u> through the resurrection of Jesus Christ* (1 Pet. 3:21 NIV, CSB)

Let me re-iterate. It is not water baptism that saves you. You are saved *'by the resurrection of Jesus Christ'*. However, you *maintain* your salvation by remaining loyal to the pledge you made *at baptism,* which was to keep a clear conscience toward God. This pledge is a promise to maintain 'a lifestyle of repentance', which is what water baptism really is: 'a baptism *of repentance* for the forgiveness of your sins' (Luke 3:3). What you may not have realised until you read this book, however, is that this pledge was not a once-off commitment; it was the beginning of a lifelong vow. Day after day, the priests would continually wash themselves afresh, and so should we, in the waters of repentance.

Water baptism was your spiritual circumcision when your fleshly nature was cut away (Col. 2:11-12 NLT). You were baptised into His death when you went under the water, and your old self was crucified with Him. You then came up united with Him in His resurrection; your body of sin was done away with, that you should no longer be a slave to sin! (Rom. 6:1-7)

Therefore, from this time onward, you should count yourselves dead to sin and alive to God. You should not let sin reign in your mortal body, obeying its evil desires. You should not offer any part of yourself as an instrument of wickedness, but offer *every part* of yourself as an instrument of righteousness! Please don't get mad at me, I'm simply quoting straight out of the Bible (Rom. 6:11-13). This is how you maintain a clear conscience before God.

When you fail, you must be deeply sorrowful and quickly repent. Head straight back to the bronze altar and get sprinkled (apply the blood of Jesus) from a guilty conscience, then be washed clean, making a fresh pledge of allegiance at the laver. Proceed forth in true righteousness, holiness and truth once more. You have no other choice! This is the narrow way, the only way. (Matt 7:13-14)

◊◊◊◊◊

James gives us the most vital key on how to keep our 'baptismal vow', clearly defining what the mirror of the washbasin signifies;

> [22]*Do not merely listen to the word, and so deceive yourselves. Do what it says.* [23]*Anyone who listens to the word but does not do what it says is like someone who looks at his face in a mirror* [24]*and, after looking at himself, goes away and immediately forgets what he looks like.* (Jam. 1:22-24)

The Word of God is the mirror that examines our heart motives. As we open up our spirit to God's truth we find it reflecting back to us what we actually look like. Through *James' mirror* we see ourselves as we really are. In *Paul's mirror* mentioned in 2 Corinthians 3:18, we see Jesus; the One to whom we are striving in the Spirit to imitate. At Paul's mirror, we behold and then reflect His glory as we are changed into His image.

The comparison between the two reflections highlights our shortcomings. From here we can make the necessary adjustments, just as you would if you looked in the mirror and saw your hair messed up, make-up smudged, or clothes out of place. In such instances, you wouldn't walk away without fixing yourself up.

Yet God says that if we are not doers of the word, but hearers only, then 'spiritually speaking' we do this very thing! We have immediately forgotten the image of ourselves reflected back to us and gone on as if nothing needed adjusting. The problem I find is that many people only want to gaze into one mirror and not the other. They love to look into the mirror that enables them to behold the image of Jesus, but shy away from ever looking into the mirror that reflects back the current state of their own image. To truly succeed in our Christian walk we must strike a perfect balance between the two.

This fixing up process mentioned by James is what the Bible calls *'being cleansed by the washing of water through the Word'* (Eph. 5:26), which makes the spirit we carry more beautiful to God and to those around us. As 'priests unto our God', we are to come back daily and gaze into James' mirror (the 'bronze washbasin') before entering the Holy Place of His presence. When the Word of God convicts us, we can commit to change. Through prayer and introspection we can also ask God to reveal anything that is preventing Him from creating in us a clean heart and a right spirit (Ps. 51:10). He will never rebuke us for asking (Jam. 1:6). Our immediate response should be to clean ourselves up as we would when looking into a natural mirror, not by trusting in human effort and willpower, but through reliance on the grace of the Holy Spirit (Phil. 2:13). This is a pure heart; the broken and contrite spirit which God does not despise. It is the lifestyle of repentance that fulfils our holy promise and pledge.

It is the heart of David, whose life was defined by verses such as these;

> *"Examine me, O LORD, and try me; Test my mind and my heart."* (Ps. 26:2)

> *"Search me, O God, and know my heart; test me and know my anxious thoughts. Point out anything in me that offends you, and lead me along the path of everlasting life."* (Ps. 139:23-24)

Now we will venture through the tabernacle entrance and focus our attention on the sanctuary inside the tent.

Chapter 7

AN 'EARTHLY' SANCTUARY

Tabernacle of the First Covenant

We have already touched on the heavenly sanctuary described in Hebrews 8:1-2, but now we will briefly skip across to Hebrews 9:1-7 where the writer gives us a brief summary of Moses' Tabernacle and what was found inside. In the same way that the writer of Hebrews was focusing primarily on the true tabernacle patterned after David's tent, so we have the same intention.

With the eyes of our heart enlightened, let's now look to Hebrews 9;

> *Now the first covenant had regulations of divine worship and the **earthly sanctuary**. [2]A tabernacle was set up.* (Heb. 9:1 NASB, 2a NIV)

There are two key features mentioned regarding the setup of the Tabernacle of Moses. First, we find it was an *earthly* sanctuary, which, although being a copy and shadow of heavenly things (Heb. 8:5), is in stark contrast to the post-resurrection sanctuary mentioned in Hebrews 8:2. At the time of Jesus' ascension, there had to be an upgrade to the heavenly tabernacle in order to match the covenantal change on earth. When Jesus entered true Zion as our 'new and improved' High Priest, He placed His blood on the mercy seat. When this occurred, the heavenly archetype unveiled to Moses was renovated, bringing into fullness the futuristic vision David had of the New Testament Age. Everything found within the courtyard and the Holy Place was now wrapped up inside Him who sits permanently in the Most Holy Place.

Moses' tabernacle is described as 'earthly', not only to distinguish it from the prototype located in heaven at the time, but primarily because the ministry performed there was 'naturalistic' or 'material' in nature. **None of it entered the spirit of man at the heart level.** It was mere 'outward' activity. Now let's examine the second feature mentioned in Hebrews 9:1 which further highlights the nature of *these activities* contained within the Mosaic function.

◊◊◊◊◊

> *Now the first covenant had **regulations of divine worship** and the earthly sanctuary. [2]A tabernacle was set up.* (Heb. 9:1 NASB, 2a NIV)

The true nature of the activities in Moses' tabernacle is confirmed by the second feature found in Hebrews 9:1. This describes the liturgy attached to this earthly tabernacle. The NASB calls them **'regulations of divine worship'**. (*dikaiōma latreia* in Greek)

The Greek word for 'divine worship' is *latreia*. Its general definition is *'service rendered for hire'*. Every time it's used in the Bible, however, it denotes *'any service or ministry done unto the Lord'*. The word *divine* is therefore placed in front of it, because the tasks have been ordained by God. Good, so the divine part is correct, but this does not automatically infer that every act of *latreia* expresses 'worship'. The way *latreia* should be translated depends on the context of the other Greek words surrounding it. If it is linked to something spiritual, connecting with God, or a matter of the heart, it is undoubtedly a form of worship. Otherwise, it may be simply a work of divine *service*.

The unique characteristic about this form of *latreia* in Hebrews 9:1 is the attached word; *dikaiōma* translated 'regulations'. It means *'a judicial decision, an ordinance of law; a regulation.'* The activity of the priests in the TOM were 'regulations' or 'ordinances', of either divine *service* or *worship*. To come to our solution, we need to find out the nature of these regulations.

Hebrews 9:10 gives us the answer by revealing the true nature of these ordinances (or regulations). The *dikaiōma* is described in the NASB as;

> **'external regulations (sarx** *dikaiōma) applying until the time of the new order.'*

The KJV states the reality even more bluntly, summing up the Mosaic rituals as; **'carnal ordinances (sarx** *dikaiōma) imposed on them until the time of reformation.'*

The regulations *(dikaiōma)* of the Mosaic priestly service were 'external, fleshly or carnal'. This is because it has the Greek word *sarx* in front of it, which is the same word for 'the flesh' or 'sinful nature'. The type of *latreia* in the Tabernacle of Moses was a flesh-driven, *regulation-based* service unto the Lord. These works of the law were '*imposed* on them' via obligation rather than free-willing cheerfulness. Therefore, the NASB translation of 'divine *worship*' in Hebrews 9:1 does not fit well in this instance, for the *latreia* at the Tabernacle of Moses was *not spiritual* at its core, nor did it bring the priests any closer to God at the heart level. They were not worshiping the Lord, they were serving Him only. Thank God this is not the blueprint we live by in the New Covenant.

To get the accurate interpretation of Hebrews 9:1, we'll transplant the word 'carnal' (*sarx*) found in Hebrews 9:10 and incorporating it into the verse, and we'll also adopt the more accurate KJV rendering of 'divine service' for latreia;

> The first covenant had *'carnal ordinances of divine service'* (*sarx dikaiōma latreia*)

The statement above encapsulates the nature of the priestly service at Moses tabernacle. We now have a clearer understanding as to the overall nature of the ministry of the Levitical Priesthood. There wasn't any 'true worship' going on, only earthly service (works of the flesh/law).

◊◊◊◊◊

> "The first covenant had *'carnal* ordinances of divine service' and a *worldly sanctuary*"

Now we can re-focus on the sanctuary itself, which was a '*kosmikos hagion'*; a worldly sanctuary entirely connected to the cosmos – this broken, fallen world. This stands in obvious dissimilarity to the *ouranos hagion* (heavenly sanctuary) described in Hebrews 8:1-2 where Jesus currently serves as Great High Priest; the New Covenant sanctuary David's Tabernacle is patterned after.

The sanctuary inside the Tabernacle of Moses was more than simply 'earthly' (situated in this earth realm), it was '*worldly'*. The Tabernacle of David would never be described in such a fashion because the worship going on there was a perfect replication of what is now occurring during the age where believers express true divine worship in Spirit and in truth.

In stark contrast to David's tent, the religious service at Moses' Tent was completely 'of this world'; none of these sacrifices were connecting with heaven. The transactions of the blood sacrifices were not getting the job done, that would require the blood of the Saviour. John tells us; '*do not love the world (kosmos) or anything in the world*' (1 John 2:15), and according to the only other time *kosmikos* is found in the Bible, Titus 2:12, we discover that this word is associated with the *worldly* passions of this present, corrupt age.

Everything the broken world offers us leads to lust and pride (1 John 2:16). No wonder these regulations of service were by their very nature, 'fleshly'.

The priest's mindsets were only engaged in carnality and worldliness; there was nothing spiritually wholesome with respect to the tasks they religiously repeated (Rom. 8:5-9 KJV). This does not imply, however, that none of these priests had a humble disposition toward God. John the Baptist's father, Zechariah, is a good example of someone who possessed that (Luke 1:5-6). I'm simply saying that the *tasks* they were commanded to perform would not have contributed to this humility.

We must conclude then that the Mosaic covenant had 'ordinances of divine **service**', and being administered at a worldly sanctuary meant these were nothing more than **carnal regulations**. There was NO SPIRITUAL COMPONENT to them and therefore a *lack of genuine substance* behind the activity at the Tabernacle of Moses. The Greek word *latreia* in Hebrews 9:1 should be translated 'service' instead of worship because Jesus said in John 4 that; "worship is in Spirit". This is extremely important to grasp.

When you remove the spiritual aspect out of *latreia* you get nothing more than religious works *of the flesh*; the 'carnal ordinances of divine service' of Hebrews 9:1 & v10 combined. We do not want even a skerrick of this in our walk with the Lord. Even though we have been liberated from such burdens, our flesh will constantly attempt to seduce us into 'works of religious law'. Every time we attempt to gain God's favour through a religious work aside from Holy Spirit relationship, God categorises it as 'carnality'.

Now let's continue with Hebrews 9;

> *²A tabernacle was set up. In its first room were the lampstand and the table with its consecrated bread; this was called the Holy Place.*
>
> *³Behind the second curtain was a room called the Most Holy Place, ⁴which had the golden altar of incense and the gold-covered Ark of the Covenant. This ark contained the gold jar of manna, Aaron's staff that had budded, and the stone tablets of the covenant. ⁵Above the ark were the cherubim of the Glory, overshadowing the atonement cover.* (Heb. 9:2-5a)

In the tabernacle of Moses there were *two* rooms, unlike David's tent, which only had one. The first room of the Tabernacle of Moses was 'the Holy Place'.

This was a room where only the priests (the male descendants of Aaron) could enter. Levites were not allowed in this room, although they helped to transport the tabernacle and all its furnishings from one place to the next (Num. 4:1-33). Hebrews 9:2 describes two pieces of furniture contained within the Holy Place. These were a 7-wick oil lampstand, and a table with consecrated bread.

An Apparent Discrepancy in the Furniture Layout

[2]A tabernacle was set up. In its first room were the lampstand and the table with its consecrated bread; this was called the Holy Place. [3]Behind the second curtain was a room called the Most Holy Place, [4]which had the golden altar of incense and the gold-covered Ark of the Covenant.
(Heb. 9:2-4a)

According to the Law of Moses in the Old Testament, we find that there were actually *three pieces* of furniture in this first room, and this is where a contradiction seems to arise between the writer of Hebrews above and the Torah (1st 5 books of the Bible).

When God gave Moses the pattern for the tabernacle on Mount Sinai, He told Moses to have a golden lampstand on the left-hand side and a golden table on the right. Then straight ahead, directly in front of the veil that separated the two rooms, he was to place *a golden altar for burning incense.* This was not in the second room, as stated above, but the first. The Ark of the Covenant alone was in the second.

Exodus 30:6 and 40:26 give us a scriptural basis as to the placement of this altar;

> *Place the incense altar just <u>outside</u> the inner curtain that shields the Ark of the Covenant* (NLT)

> *He also placed the gold incense altar in the Tabernacle, <u>in the Holy Place</u> in front of the inner curtain.* (NLT)

In Moses' tent the incense altar was placed directly *before* the Ark, but the veil stood in-between them. **1 Kings 6:22 says that King Solomon; *'overlaid with gold the altar <u>that belonged to the inner sanctuary</u>'.*** In the Temple of Solomon there was a *sacred* connection (special relationship) between the Altar of Incense and the Most Holy Place. Yet it wasn't a physical belonging;

for in the time of Herod's Temple we find confirmation that the golden altar *physically* resided in the Holy Place. When Zechariah, John the Baptist's father, was chosen by lot to go and burn incense in this Temple, the Angel Gabriel came and stood on the right hand side of the altar of incense (Luke 1:11, 19). Zechariah was a priest from the division of Abijah. He was not the High Priest. Therefore, he could not have been burning incense in the Holy of Holies; he was in the 'first room'.

Those of you who are cluey might be asking this question right about now; "Why then, does Hebrews 9 say that the altar of Incense was inside the Holy of Holies with the Ark?"

> *In its first room were the lampstand and the table with its consecrated bread; this was called the Holy Place. ³Behind the second curtain was a room called the Most Holy Place, ⁴which had the golden **altar of incense (thymiatērion)** and the gold-covered Ark of the Covenant.* (Heb. 9:2-4a)

In the story of Zechariah, the altar of incense mentioned in Luke 1:11 is in Greek, **'thysiastērion'** (altar) **'thymiama'** (incense). Don't get me to pronounce that, but what is of paramount importance is the Greek translated 'Altar of Incense' in Hebrews 9:4 (quoted above) is not that of Luke 1:11. It is simply *one* Greek word, **'thymiatērion'**. If you look carefully, this word is a combination of the two found in Luke 1:11. The last six letters are identical to the last six letters in the word for altar, and the first six are identical to the first six in the word for incense. In light of these similarities, I can see why the assumption could be made that because the Altar of Incense is not mentioned in the contents of the first room (listed in Hebrews 9:2), the writer of Hebrews must be referring to it here in Hebrews 9:4.

However, *thymiatērion* is more accurately translated as 'a *utensil* for fumigating or burning incense'. While being vitally linked to the Altar of Incense, the actual item being referred to in Hebrews 9:4 is more likely a golden censer used in the process of applying incense smoke over the mercy seat once a year. In fact, the Septuagint (the Greek Old Testament), only uses *thymiatērion* twice, and both times it is in reference to *a censer*, not the Altar of Incense (Ezek. 8:11 & 2 Chr. 26:19). Even of greater significance is that in 2 Chronicles 26:19 there is not only a censer mentioned but also a reference to the Altar of Incense in the very same verse. The Altar of Incense is translated in Greek exactly the same way that it is in Luke 1:11; *'thysiastērion thymiama'*. King Uzziah is holding a censer (thymiatērion) in his hand, and the judgment of God (leprosy) broke out on his forehead from beside the Altar of Incense.

Whoever wrote Hebrews had this version of the Old Testament. The Septuagint (or LXX) was the primary translation of the Word of God in circulation at the time. Therefore, the author would have known the correct Greek word to use for exactly what he was describing, having a direct Old Testament reference in the same language he was writing in. The Greek word in Hebrews 9:4 is *thymiatērion*. We must conclude, therefore, that it is *not* the Altar of Incense being referred to, but most likely a special golden censer used on the Day of Atonement.

Although there is no mention in the Torah about a censer reserved for such use, writings such as the Mishna describe later laws being added which not only prescribed a censer of gold, but even specified a particular kind of gold. This was not one of the ordinary censers used from day to day which were made of silver. Everything in the Most Holy Place had to be golden.

> *⁶When everything had been arranged like this, the priests entered regularly into the outer room to carry on their ministry. ⁷But only the high priest entered the inner room, and that only once a year, and never without blood, which he offered for himself and for the sins the people had committed in ignorance.* (Heb. 9:6-7)

Hebrews 9:1-4 was written in context with the Day of Atonement, spoken about above in verse 7. The Apostle Paul, the writer of Hebrews (in my opinion), was stressing the vital link between the Altar of Incense and the Ark in the Holy of Holies *on that particular day*. Because the veil was lifted only on this one day of the year, the Altar of Incense was beholding the Ark, poetically speaking of course (1 Kings 6:22). For this was the High Priest's command on that day;

> *¹¹ "Aaron shall bring the bull for his own sin offering to make atonement for himself and his household, and he is to slaughter the bull for his own sin offering. ¹²He is to take a censer (firepan, incense burner) full of burning coals from the altar before the Lord and two handfuls of finely ground fragrant incense and take them behind the curtain. ¹³He is to put*

*the incense on the fire before the Lord, and the smoke of the incense will
conceal the atonement cover (mercy seat) above the tablets of the
covenant law, so that he will not die."* (Lev. 16:12-13)

We can see here the use of a censer to carry the burning hot coals into the Holy
of Holies. To do this the curtain had to be folded back. The incense would
cover the mercy seat so that when Aaron sprinkled the blood of the bull on it
(and then later the goat) he would not die. Thus, the Altar of Incense and the
Ark were intimately associated on this holy day in achieving atonement for the
people, one beholding the other (*'before'* each other) because the veil was
removed. They were paired up on this day, and that's why on the Day of
Atonement we find both articles being purified by the blood of a bull and goat
(Lev. 16:14-18). In fact, because of this annual act we see in Exodus 30:10 the
Lord referring to the altar as *'Most* Holy to the Lord', or literally in Hebrew
'Holy of Holies to the Lord', which is along the same lines as what 1 Kings
6:22 is talking about when it states that the golden altar *belonged to* the Most
Holy Place. This does not insinuate that it was physically placed in that room,
but it shows the connection of 'most holiness' between the Ark and the Altar.
This is something the showbread and the lampstand did not possess.

In Hebrews 9, Paul deliberately did not mention the altar of incense in the Holy
Place, but rather the golden censor taken into the Holy of Holies, because it
was to be used in conjunction with the altar of incense during the High Priests
ceremonial duties. The mention of the gold censer automatically implied the
existence of the golden altar to anyone who had knowledge of these Mosaic
arrangements. It also puts greater emphasis on the 'Most Holy' nature of the
incense altar, rather than its actual location; for the burning coals that came
from it were taken through the veil.

Most commentators have suggested that it would be impossible for this censer
to be stored inside the Most Holy Place, because in order to fetch it, the High
Priest would have died, which I tend to agree with. This seems most likely,
especially when you consider God's warning to Aaron in Leviticus 16:1-3. My
conclusion is that the censer, kept in a separate storeroom every other day of
the year, could still be referred to as being *in* the Holy of Holies in Hebrews
9:4, because on the Day of Atonement the censer was taken in there.

Now we have solved the mystery of Hebrews 9:4: Even though it may seem to indicate otherwise, there had always been three pieces of furniture in the first room with only the Ark behind the second curtain. This never changed from its original layout given to Moses all the way up until Jesus' birth (except that there was no Ark in the 2nd Temple).

I will now share some alternate translations that bring clarity to what we have concluded;

> [2]*A tent was set up. The first part of this tent was called the holy place. The lamp stand, the table, and the bread of the presence were in this part of the tent.* [3]*Behind the second curtain was the part of the tent called the most holy place.* [4]*It contained **the gold incense burner** and the ark of the Lord's promise. The ark was completely covered with gold.* (Heb. 9:2-4 GW)

The NKJV in Hebrews 9:3-4a says;

> [3]*and behind the second veil, the part of the tabernacle which is called the Holiest of All,* [4]*which had **the golden censer** and the ark of the covenant overlaid on all sides with gold.*

~ Chapter 8 ~

ALTAR OF INCENSE

As we have just discovered, the Altar of Incense was located in the first room directly in front of the veil; *'before the veil that is before the ark of the Testimony, before the mercy seat that is over the Testimony'* as the NKJV puts it (Exod. 30:6).

This altar was the tallest piece of furniture in the Holy Place, standing at approximately 36 inches, or 3 feet tall. Like the Ark, it was made of acacia wood, then overlaid with gold. It had four horns, one on each corner in the same fashion as the altar of burnt offering, which was just outside the entrance to the Tabernacle. This is significant, because the burning coals that were laid upon the *golden* altar of incense were taken out from the *bronze* altar of burnt offering (Lev. 16:11-12). The bronze altar was the place of animal sacrifice, a fire that burned perpetually. The priests were commanded in Leviticus 6:13 to never let this fire go out!

Twice a day, incense would be burned on the golden altar by placing a specific combination of spices and frankincense mixed together with salt upon these burning coals. This was God's special recipe, a pure and holy concoction, and He made it abundantly clear that no other formula should ever be used (Exod. 30:7-9). Nor was anyone allowed to duplicate God's recipe for their own private use. This was a terrible sin in the Lord's sight, so much so that those who transgressed would be cut off from among God's people! (Exod. 30:34-38)

The incense could be placed directly onto the coals upon the golden altar, or as we have already learnt, the burning coals could be transported with a censer to another location and then the holy incense would be placed on top to create the sweet smelling smoke.

The horns on the altar are important for another reason. They reveal the atoning power of the Altar of Incense, linking it strongly to the Atonement Cover on top of the Ark. On three separate occasions, the blood of an animal would be applied to its four horns to cleanse the defilement of the people. One of these occasions was when the blood of the bull and the goat were administered by the High Priest on the Day of Atonement (Lev. 16:18-19). The other two occasions are found in Leviticus 4:3-21. First was any time the High Priest sinned unintentionally and it became known. Second was any time the entire congregation of Israel sinned corporately in an unintentional manner and they were made aware.

Not just the altar, but even the incense itself had atoning power. After Korah's rebellion in Numbers 16, a deadly plague broke out against the Israelites because they continued to mutter against Moses' leadership. When God began destroying them, Moses commanded Aaron to grab a censer and take some hot coals outside (from the golden altar of incense) where he was to stand amidst the congregation and burn holy incense. This atoned for the people's sin, satisfying God's wrath and the plague stopped! (Num. 16:41-48)

◊◊◊◊◊

King David unlocked the true spiritual substance in the TOD through worship. It was a pleasing aroma of incense in God's nostrils. He declared;

May my prayer be set before you like incense; may the lifting up of my hands be like the evening sacrifice. (Ps. 141:2)

Because they did not have any of these furnishings in the 'TOD layout', the worshipers were always on a quest to find out the true spiritual reality of what these things represented. Otherwise, shouldn't they have had these articles integrated back in? King David was fully convinced of what he saw when he partook of the powers of the coming age, and he was determined not to buckle under any form of pressure that would push him into a compromise between God's new blueprint and the old way of doing things.

By revelation of the Spirit, David saw that 'the prayers of the saints are counted by the Lord as true incense'. Then he also declared that lifting up our hands represents 'the true evening sacrifice'. Paul even mentioned in the New Testament that as we spread the knowledge of Jesus, our lives become 'a Christ-like fragrance rising to God'. (2 Cor. 2:14-15)

The Altar of Incense is intimately associated with prayer. Our prayers ascend to God just like the smoke of the incense ascended in the Holy Place. Aaron was commanded to burn incense first in the morning and again at twilight (Exod. 30:7-8), and this is a reminder that we are to offer prayer without ceasing day and night before the throne of God in heaven (Luke 18:1, 1 Thess. 5:17). The allotted times for Aaron were exactly in line with the morning and evening sacrifice, hence David mentioning that we are to lift our hands in reverential submission as the evening sacrifice (Heb. 5:7 NIV). Our prayer life is a vital part of laying down our lives in living sacrifice, where we symbolically lay our body down on the altar of burnt offering each and every day. (Rom. 12:1)

In his vision of heaven, John saw that the elders around the throne *'were holding golden bowls full of incense, which are the prayers of God's people'* (Rev. 5:8). Unlike smoke on the earth that eventually disappears, we find that when we *'pray in the Spirit on all occasions with all kinds of prayers and requests'* (Eph. 6:18), they reach up to heaven and are stored in bowls. Once again, we symbolically see 'an evaporation' or a 'fading away' of the Mosaic Covenant, in complete juxtaposition to the everlasting covenant in Jesus' blood, which will remain forever. (2 Cor. 3:7, Heb. 13:20)

As Zechariah the priest was offering incense in the temple, *'all the assembled worshipers were praying outside'* (Luke 1:10). The Greek text indicates that these worshipers were actually 'a multitude of ordinary people'. This group were not specially ordained priests or even prophets. They were a large team of passionate prayer warriors who came to intercede for Zechariah, not because they were commanded by law, but because of the willingness of their heart. I believe these prayers dispatched the angel Gabriel to visit Zechariah, rather than his burning of tangible incense.

Look at the reality of heaven's activity regarding this truth;

> *[3]"And another angel came and stood at the altar with a <u>golden censer,</u> and he was given <u>much incense to offer with the prayers of all the saints</u> <u>on the golden altar before the throne,</u> [4]and the smoke of the incense, with the prayers of the saints, rose before God from the hand of the angel. [5]Then the angel took the censer and filled it with fire from the altar and threw it on the earth, and there were peals of thunder, rumblings, flashes of lightning, and an earthquake."* (Rev. 8:3-5 ESV)

What power we the saints of God walk in, especially those who partner with God as end-time intercessors during the unfolding of the end of this age! The impact of 'Yahweh's watchmen' is even more extreme than the result of the prayers of Daniel or Elijah! Just like the Altar of Incense stands before the Ark, there is a golden altar before the heavenly throne. This altar represents the place where the prayers of those who stand in the gap come before the Almighty and His Heavenly Host. The answers to these prayers are hurled back onto the earth by an angel holding a similar transportation device as we see in Hebrews 9:4, a golden censer. This could be another reason why in Hebrews

9:4 God wanted the writer to emphasise the golden censer instead of the golden altar. This Greek word used for censer in Revelation 8:5 (libanōtos) is also translated 'frankincense'; the primary scent of the incense that flows upward into heaven from the prayers of the saints below.

Jesus: Mediator of a Superior Covenant

The Altar of Incense must also be recognised as a picture of the intercession of Christ. Just as the Altar of Sacrifice in the courtyard is a type of Christ's *earthly* mediation, the Altar of Incense in the Holy Place is a type of Christ's *heavenly* mediation, which is constant intercession before the Father (Heb. 7:25). He is still interceding for us in heaven right now, just as He mediated on earth through His death on the cross.

We know that the Altar of Incense was situated *before* the mercy-seat of the Ark—and this is a picture of Jesus' ongoing mediation on our behalf. 1 John 2:1 states that Jesus is our *'Advocate with the Father.'* He is our defence lawyer who stands before the Father, pleading our case; the golden altar of intercession standing before the Ark, the Judge's seat (Exod. 40:5). This is why Jesus Christ is Mediator of the New Covenant (Heb. 9:15). All He has to do is point towards His blood sprinkled upon the throne of the Righteous Judge and He instantly wins every case!

The Greek word for mediator (mesitēs) means: 'one who intervenes between two, in order to make or restore peace and friendship'. Jesus is the 'middle-man' or the 'go-between'. He settles the legal case against us and continues to maintain our direct access to the Father. From heaven, Jesus is constantly pleading His once-for-all, continually effective act of mediation completed on earth. This intercession on our behalf is a sweet smelling fragrance to the Father. (Eph. 5:2)

God the Father is love, and because of this He longs to connect intimately with His children. But He is also holy, just and entirely righteous. To maintain these qualities, He must have righteous anger toward things that defame and undermine His character. The mediation of Christ pacifies God's wrath by satisfying His need for justice, restoring us to right standing with the Father. Seeing us as perfectly righteous, the Holy Spirit comes inside to empower us to live out the righteous life the Father requires. This enables us to abide in His love instead of being separated from it. (John 15:9-10)

Because of Christ's mediation, we can also enter a posture of intercession, partnering with Him in the affairs on earth. A huge percentage of Jesus' intercession is actually mediation. We, on the other hand, are 100% intercession and 0% mediation. We do not have any right to become mediators between anyone else and God, and we should never assume such a position over another believer's life. 1 Timothy 2:5 says; *"there is only one mediator between God and man, the man Christ Jesus."* We have the privilege of interceding on behalf of others for God to move in their lives. That is our role. It is not to abuse the ignorant and unstable by attempting to control and manipulate through exalting ourselves into a mediatory position over them.

Even though God commanded Aaron to burn incense only twice a day, He still referred to it as; *'a perpetual incense before the Lord throughout your generations'* (Exod. 30:8b KJV). Thus, Christ's mediation and intercession is constant; just as His sacrifice continually takes away the sin of the world. *His death* is the antitype of the morning and evening *sacrifice*; therefore, His blood continually speaks of peace and pardon, and it contains within it every blessing of grace for His people. *We* are an antitype of the morning and evening *incense*; for Jesus ever lives to make intercession *for us*, thus His mediation is ongoing and our access to the Father maintained. Because of this, the prayers of the saints can be directed to the Father both morning and evening, and we do not cease in prayer as long as we live.

> *"For Christ did not enter into <u>a holy place (hagion)</u> made with human hands, which was only a copy of the true one in heaven. He entered into heaven itself <u>to appear now before God on our behalf</u> (mediation)."* [25]*Nor did he enter heaven to offer himself again and again, the way the high priest enters <u>the Most Holy Place (hagion)</u> every year with blood that is not his own.* [26]*Otherwise Christ would have had to suffer many times since the creation of the world. But he has appeared **<u>once for all</u>** at the culmination of the ages to do away with sin by the sacrifice of himself.* (Heb. 9:24 NLT 25-26 NIV)

Here the cornerstone of Christ's mediation is contrasted with the Day of Atonement. Jesus paid our debt of sin 'once for all' on Calvary's cross. Every year, when the High Priest scanned his *'bulls and goats'* debit card, it kept declining due to 'insufficient funds'. That's why he had to keep coming back year after year to 'scan again'. (Heb. 9:27-10:4, John 1:29)

After many fruitless attempts by the High Priest to 'pay the price', 'God sent His Son, born of a woman, born under law to redeem those stranded under the legal indebtedness caused by the law' (Gal. 4:4, Col. 2:13-14 NIV). *'The body of the Lord Jesus'* debit card was accepted by the Father on the very first swipe; the debt of man's sin was instantly removed as the transaction was accepted (Heb. 10:5-6). Jesus didn't need to come back and swipe His card a second and third time; man's redemption had been 'paid in full', good for all time. That's how precious and pricy the blood of Jesus really is. Where sin has been forgiven, sacrifice for sin is no longer necessary. (Heb. 10:18)

The 'type' and 'shadow' kept coming up empty, having no power to cleanse the conscience of the worshiper and remove the power of sin from their heart (Heb. 9:9, 14-15). Those in attendance still felt guilty each and every year; their sin-consciousness being heightened on this particular day because, according to Hebrews 10:3, the Day of Atonement was the annual reminder that they were still under sin's dominion and control. (Rom 6:14)

Spiritual Significance of the Altar on the Day of Atonement

We have previously discussed how the Altar of Incense was 'most holy to the Lord' because, just like the mercy seat, it was atoned for with the blood of the bull and goat. It is therefore the blood of Christ applied to our hearts that makes our prayers acceptable. Our prayers become a pleasing aroma because of Jesus' sacrifice, and therefore they are satisfactory to the Father, providing they come from a pure heart and a faithfully renewed spirit.

Now let's narrow our focus to the specific role the Altar of Incense had in this solemn festival (full details in Leviticus 16). We previously discovered that the High Priest had to collect burning hot coals from the golden altar in a golden censer. After this he took them, along with two handfuls of holy incense mixture, into the Holy of Holies. These hot coals that were placed onto the golden altar came from the bronze altar, where the animals had just been sacrificed outside the tabernacle entrance. When he burned the incense, the sweet smelling smoke would cover the mercy seat, so that when Aaron applied the blood of the bull (to purify himself and his family), and the blood of the goat (to purify the Holy of Holies and whole congregation of Israel), he would not die. *The High Priest could not behold the glory of the Lord emanating out from the Ark and live!* That's why the incense was used as a holy smokescreen.

After the purification of the Most Holy Place was completed, the High Priest would proceed back to the Holy Place and apply the blood of the bull and goat to the four horns of the Altar of Incense, purifying it and making it holy. The Ark and the Altar had to be cleansed because '*of the defiling sin and rebellion of the Israelites*' which had accumulated since the previous year. (Lev. 16:16, 18-19)

The burning coals, which came from the bronze Altar of Sacrifice, signify the great sufferings of Christ which He bore for us on the cross. Not only the physical suffering of His body, being extremely painful, but also the spiritual suffering of His righteous soul when the wrath or 'raging displeasure' of God was poured out upon His innermost being. These coals, after being transferred onto the golden Altar of Incense, remained *before the Lord*. This communicates to us that the sufferings of Christ, according to the will of the Father, were satisfying to Him because the blood of the animal *sacrificed on the coals* was applied to the throne between the Cherubim while the incense was being burned (Ps. 99:1).

The coals being brought *through the veil* does not denote that Christ is still in a suffering state. He is currently in the midst of the throne as a Lamb that *had* been slain (Heb. 8:1-2, Rev. 5:6). The continuing virtue and efficacy of his *previous* sufferings, on which we place our faith and hope, are forever in operation on behalf of His chosen people because after the victory of the resurrection, Jesus carried the blood of His sacrifice through the curtain and applied it. (Heb. 9:11-12)

The two handfuls of incense carried in with those coals typified the intercession of Jesus in heaven, pure, holy, sweet, delightfully fragrant and perpetual. Having his hands *full* of the mixture, the High Priest expresses the fullness of Christ's intercession for His elect. As a perfect High Priest, He makes requests about *all things* concerning His beloved. He cares about every detail of our lives, and through His redemptive work, has full ability to plead on a continual basis for the betterment of our eternal destinies.

The incense being placed upon the burning coals in the golden censer shows us that Christ's intercession relies upon the foundation of His blood and sacrifice, His sufferings and death. Therefore, it becomes favourable to the receiver and has abounding influence. Why? Because the smoke from the incense covers the mercy seat; the place now revealed as 'the throne of grace'. Christ has made it accessible to 'whosoever wills'.

'Therefore, let us draw near with confidence to the throne of grace, so that we may receive mercy and find grace to help in time of need.' (Heb. 4:16 NASB)

Just as the Priest, washed and dressed in his sacred garments (Lev. 16:4), never dies when offering the holy incense as a smokescreen, so those for whom Jesus intercedes will never be turned away from the manifest presence of God. Jesus' intercession enables us to approach God with full confidence: *His mediation is the protective canopy of incense,* enabling us to approach the mercy seat and receive forgiveness for our past mistakes without incurring judgment. By bathing ourselves in the pure waters of repentance and putting on the sacred garments of humility, brokenness and contrition, we obtain bold access into His throne room without any fear of rejection, no matter how badly we have 'missed the mark' since our last visit.

[24]because Jesus lives for ever, he has a permanent priesthood. [25]Therefore he is able to save completely those who come to God through him, because <u>he always lives to intercede for them</u>. (Heb. 7:24-25)

Holy Incense

When God gave Moses the precise recipe for the incense mixture, He commanded that no other type of incense or other offering ever be placed on the altar (Exod. 30:9). This was an admonition to pray *only* to the *one* true God, not to angels, or any other false deity. When He commanded that the recipe never be duplicated for private use (Exod. 30:37-38), He was warning us that we should never use the ministry of God to glorify ourselves by turning the attention away from Him. This is a major abuse of the priestly calling on our lives. The Pharisees and teachers of the law were doing this in the time of Jesus. He rebuked them, saying;

[5]Everything <u>they do is done for people to see</u>: they make their phylacteries wide and the tassels on their garments long; [6]they love the place of honour at banquets and the most important seats in the synagogues; [7]they love to be greeted with respect in the market-places and to be called "Rabbi" by others. (Matt 23:5-7)

In the Sermon on the Mount, Jesus labelled them hypocrites who *"love to pray standing in the synagogues and on the street corners <u>to be seen by others</u>."* (Matt. 6:5)

When a priest went to burn incense inside the Holy Place, he could not be seen by outsiders. But if someone burned the incense in their own home, they could use it to 'show off'. That's why our private prayer-life should be predominant over our public-prayer life. If this is the wrong way around, our spiritual life is out of balance and we are in danger of falling from grace. The strength of our private times of devotion will always fuel the effectiveness of our public ministry.

The Sad Story of King Uzziah

Uzziah was made king at the ripe old age of 16. Fortunately, this young upstart had an excellent mentor to guide him in the early years. He sought God during the days of Zechariah, who instructed him in the fear of God. As long as he sought the Lord, God gave him success. (2 Chr. 26:5)

But later in life Uzziah stopped seeking the Lord and became proud of the many achievements and accolades that he had accomplished during the times when he *was* seeking the Lord. In his insolence, he took up the role of priest by entering Solomon's Temple and burning incense at the golden altar. As an old covenant king, Uzziah was forbidden from doing this. He required a priest from the family line of Aaron as a human mediator.

King David and his son Solomon were able to partake of priestly exemptions inside the Tabernacle of David because it was a brief season of 'experiencing the powers of the coming age'. Unlike Uzziah, they never presumed they could go into Moses' tabernacle and do such a thing. Because of his irreverent presumption, King Uzziah broke out in leprosy and hid away in seclusion until the day he died. (2 Chr. 26:21)

But praise God! Because of Jesus' mediation, *we* are well assured that as we approach the golden altar through prayer, we will suffer no ill effects. Even so, we must be careful not to presume upon the grace of God, either. There will be consequences if we parade arrogantly up to God in prayer while living in a brazenly unrepentant lifestyle. It is only a broken and contrite spirit that enables us to enter the heavenly tabernacle with bold confidence. Without these garments of humility on we should be greatly afraid, because as in King Uzziah's case, *'it is a dreadful thing to fall into the hands of the living God.'* (Heb. 10:31)

~ Chapter 9 ~

TABLE OF SHOWBREAD

The table of showbread was twelve loaves of wheat bread baked fresh each Sabbath, corresponding to the twelve tribes of Israel. They were set in two piles of six upon a pure gold table (Lev. 24:5-9). When entering the tabernacle, this article of furniture was situated 45 degrees to the priest's right.

The loaves represent Jesus, the bread of life, Who is the true bread that came down from heaven in similar fashion to the daily manna that fell in the wilderness (John 6:32-33, 49-51). The table therefore represents a place of covenant, fellowship and feasting with the Lord.

God describes the bread that was on display as *lechem pânîym*, the 'Bread of the Presence' or 'bread of His face' (Exod. 25:30). To be in God's presence is to have His face shine upon you and His gaze directed toward you. The terminology of God 'looking upon' us or 'turning toward' us is found many times in the Bible, and it is always referring to those who have obtained a privileged place of favour in His sight (Lev. 26:9, Ps. 84:9, Isa. 66:2b, Ezek. 36:9, 1 Pet. 3:12). It essentially means that you have captured God's attention! Entrance into this level of 'face-to-face companionship' is unlocked through consuming the bread on the table.

Jesus said, 'whoever comes to eat of the bread I provide will never hunger' (John 6:35). According to John 1:14, Jesus is 'the Word who became flesh', and His name in Revelation 19:13 is 'the Word of God.' When we approach the Bread of the Presence, we are coming to experience His affection whilst feeding on the sustenance of Christ. He nourishes us by revealing who He is, the magnitude of what He won for us, how much He loves us and the authority He has given us over all the power of the enemy. (Luke 10:19)

When Satan came in the wilderness, he tried to tempt Jesus into breaking His God-ordained fast by turning a stone into bread. Jesus replied with a dynamic weapon from Deuteronomy 8:3; *"Man shall not live by bread alone, but every <u>word</u> which proceeds from the mouth of God."* (Matt 4:4 NKJV)

Jesus is not only stating this scripture to overcome His immediate temptation. He is also alerting us to the important truth that physical bread is not all that humanity needs in order to sustain a healthy life. Human beings need to partake of a spiritual form of bread as well. Like Jesus, we need to be daily consumers of the living and powerful Word of God to survive in this fallen world of temptation and trial.

In the Greek language there are two variances of our English term, 'word'. This distinction, found in Matthew 4:4, must be understood. Jesus is highlighting that "man lives off every *rhēma word* that proceeds from the mouth of God." Therefore it is the **rhēma** Word of God that is man's spiritual diet, and not the **logos**, which is the 'written word'. In John 1:1, Jesus is referred to in the beginning as 'the logos'.

'The Reason Why'

A brief look into history will help explain why John referred to Jesus as the Logos. This concept had particular meaning in Ephesus, where John was writing. Six hundred years earlier there lived in Ephesus a man called Heraclitus, widely acknowledged as the founder of science. He believed in the necessity of scientific enquiry; probing the natural world by asking how and why things were the way they were.

From this new scientific point of view, he would explore the deep philosophical questions of his day. He looked for patterns or 'laws' to see if he could deduce some logic behind the operations of the natural world. He used the word logos to stand for 'the reason why'; the purpose behind what took place. When he looked at life (bios) he looked for the logos; when he studied the weather (meteor) he repeated the process. This concept now appears in our vocabulary for the study of different areas of science: biology, meteorology, geology, psychology, sociology, etc.

Every branch of science is looking for the logos, the reason why things are as they are. John, realizing that Jesus is 'the ultimate reason why', embraced this idea and called Jesus the 'Logos Word'. John skilfully presents that the Son of God was already named the Logos before any of the sciences had been created; 'in the beginning' when there was no one to communicate with except the Father and Holy Spirit. The entire universe was made through Him and for Him and He is the reason why we are here. All creation exists because of Him and is summed up in Him. Jesus Christ is the 'Reason for everything'.

Look at how John 1:1 reads when you apply this meaning to the text;

In the beginning was 'the Reason why', and 'the Reason why' was with God, and 'the Reason why' was God.

How powerful is that!

Weaponizing the Word

A *rhēma* word is direct, first hand revelation from the Master. It is alive and presently active in you and serves as a weapon in your mouth for your current situation. *Logos* is the written Word in its entirety; *rhēma* is when God illuminates a *certain passage* within the Word. *Rhēma* words are deposited in us by reading the *logos* Word.

The meaning of *rhēma* is illustrated well in Ephesians 6:17, where *'the sword of the Spirit; the* (rhēma) *word of God',* is not referring to the Scriptures as a whole, but to a strategic portion which the believer wields as a sword in the time of need.

Your fancy, leather-bound Bible with gold embroidery sitting on your coffee table for *good looks* contains the *logos* word inside, but unless you place your sticky paw prints on it, risk getting a few creases, and perhaps even a tea stain—God forbid, it will never do you any good.

In order to receive *rhēma* words from the Lord, we must take time-out from the hustle and bustle of modern-day life and *meditate* on the Scripture. We cannot 'speed-read' with countless notifications going off on our phones at the same time. I'm sure if mobile phones were invented in the time of Moses, God would have said; "Thou shalt not bring thy cell phone into the Holy Place." Maybe just turn aeroplane mode on for a while, and you'll be right!

Every Sabbath the High Priest would bake twelve new loaves to be set in place for the next week, and the priests got to eat the 12 old loaves that were being replaced. This was only once a week, and even though it was a Sabbath day of rest for the whole of Israel, the priests could not even eat the bread sitting down, for there was no provision for rest inside Moses' tabernacle (Lev. 24:8-9, Matt 12:5). You, on the other hand, can eat of the Bread of Life *every single day*, and you can do it from a position of rest, 'seated with Jesus in heavenly places' (Eph. 2:6). Hebrews 10:11-12 says;

*[11]Day after day every priest **stands** and performs his religious duties; again and again he offers the same sacrifices, which can never take away sins. [12]But when this priest had offered for all time one sacrifice for sins, he **sat down** at the right hand of God.*

If we meditate deeply on God's word day and night, we will always have faith to defeat the flaming missiles of the evil one. Not only that, we will become *like a tree planted along a riverbank, bearing fruit every season. Our leaves will not wither, and whatever we do shall prosper.* (Ps. 1:3)

In Joshua 1:8 we find this promise;

"This Book of the Law shall not depart from your mouth, but you shall meditate in it day and night, that you may observe to do according to all that is written in it. For then you will make your way prosperous, and then you will have good success." (NKJV)

To meditate means 'to reflect upon, to ponder and mutter over and over again.' Or 'to contemplate something as one *repeats* the words.' The best worldly analogy is to regurgitate Scripture in our mouths and minds in the same way that a cow regurgitates grass when chewing the cud: A cow grazes through the pasture, finds an abundance of tasty grass, chews it, and finally swallows it. Later, up comes the chewed grass to be re-chewed and re-digested. Each time the cow brings up the old cud and chews it, she is refining it and making it more and more a part of her system. She chews until all the nutrients are extracted out of it. As a part of this process, the stems and stalk are also removed, making it fit for consumption into her body.

Likewise, feed on a scripture over and over: Chew on it, swallow it, and then bring it back up again. Each time you regurgitate, you are demanding all the nutrients out of it. As you ponder over its life-giving message, useless baggage begins to separate itself from you. Meditation is the process of chewing on the Word and communing with Jesus. We take a scripture, speak it, think on it, and repeat the process until it becomes a part of our spiritual DNA. Having been awakened in our innermost being, logos metamorphoses into rhēma revelation, rather than remaining as letters of ink printed on a page.

Just like the Israelites had to go out routinely to collect their supply of manna, so we must get our spiritual dose of 'daily bread'. If they tried to keep any overnight, they awoke in the morning to a foul odour and manna full of maggots (Exod. 16:19-20). Labouring after food was to be a daily discipline to ensure they maintained physical health and nourishment.

Jesus told us; *"Do not <u>labour</u> for the food which perishes, but for the food which endures to everlasting life, which the Son of Man will give you."* (John 6:27 NKJV)

Labour is not always easy. Ask any mother about that. But I'm sure the majority will tell you it is worth it! At times Bible-study will feel like labour, especially when you first start out. But just you wait and persevere, for it won't be long until you enter the Spirit of wisdom and revelation and begin to soar with wings as eagles! Like the two disciples on the road to Emmaus, you will exclaim;

> *"Were not our hearts burning within us while he talked with us and opened the Scriptures to us?"* (Luke 24:32)

God said to us through Isaiah;

> *"Why do you spend money for what is not bread, And your wages for what does not satisfy? Listen carefully to Me, and eat what is good, And let your soul delight itself in abundance."* (Isa. 55:2 NKJV)

And Jeremiah exclaimed;

> *"Your words were found, and I ate them, And Your word was to me the rejoicing of my heart."* (Jer. 15:16 NKJV)

The Crown Moulding

[23]*"Make a table of acacia wood – two cubits long, a cubit wide and a cubit and a half high.*[24]*Overlay it with pure gold and make a <u>gold moulding</u> around it."* (Exod. 25:23-24)

We have already discovered how intimately associated the Golden Altar is with the Ark in comparison to the Table of Showbread and the Lampstand, which do not share such honour. But there is one feature on the Table of Gold that it shares with both the Golden Altar and the Ark of Testimony. All three articles of furniture were ornamented with a 'gold moulding' (Exod. 25:11, 30:3). The KJV translates the Hebrew '*zêr zâhâb*' as a '**crown** of gold'. Practically, this was moulded into the design to form a border so that items laid on them would not fall off. **'Zêr' in Hebrew is simply a 'border' or 'circlet'**.

But when you examine the actual design, the way they ornamented this moulding is very similar to a golden wreath. The pattern resembled leaves and foliage. **Another definition of 'zêr' is 'border, edge, *wreathed* work'**, and we see this brought out in Young's literal Translation in Exodus 37 where the crown moulding in verses 2, 11-12 and 26 (Ark, Table and Altar of Incense) is translated **'wreath of gold'**. This is correct, because 'zer' is not used anywhere in the Old Testament of a king's diadem.

If you read verses 11-12, you also find that the table actually had *two* golden wreaths in its make-up. One was a *decorative design* for the entire table, and the other for the rim as a *practical border*. This golden moulding or 'wreath' represented 'the crown of the priesthood'. God was already revealing His desire that His people be a royal priesthood; kings and priests unto our God (Rev. 1:6).

According to Exodus 19:5-6, God's overwhelming desire, even from the inception of the Mosaic Covenant, was that the Israelites would become to Him, *"a kingdom of priests and a holy nation"*. Unfortunately this did not occur, because in their own human frailty, the Israelites were unable to keep the terms of that Covenant. Fortunately for us, this privilege has now been passed onto us who *'serve in the new way of the Spirit, and not in the old way of the written code.'* (Rom. 7:6, 1 Pet. 2:9)

Go the Distance, Win the Marathon

*[24]"Do you not know that in a race all the runners run, but only one gets the prize? Run in such a way as to get the prize. [25]Everyone who competes in the games goes into strict training. <u>They do it to get a **crown** that will not last; but we do it to get a **crown** that will last for ever</u>. [26]Therefore I do not run like someone running aimlessly; I do not fight like a boxer beating the air. [27]No, I beat my body and make it my slave so that after I have preached to others, I myself will not be disqualified for the prize."* (1 Cor. 9:24-27)

We can see here that Paul is after a prize, an 'incorruptible crown' as he puts it. This is the crown of righteousness which the Lord, the righteous judge, will award us on that Day (2 Tim 4:8). But this crown is not like that of a sovereignly crowned ruler. This is a victory wreath! The Greek word for crown here is 'stephanos', derived from the primary word stéphō, meaning 'to twine or wreathe'. It is a laurel garland like those which the victorious fighters and runners would receive as winners in the Ancient Olympics. Being akin to the gold medal of modern times, it exemplified someone of 'exalted rank'.

A laurel wreath is a round wreath made of connected branches and leaves of the Bay Laurel, an aromatic broadleaf evergreen. In Greek mythology, Apollo is usually represented wearing one of these laurel wreaths. In the ancient Olympics, they designed the wreath from a wild olive tree known as 'kotinos'. This is where the saying "resting on your laurels" comes from, meaning 'to settle down and rest in your achievements.'

Paul was determined (like those who go into strict training to become world champion) to beat his body into such a spiritually fit condition, that he would be assured of receiving the incorruptible wreath at the end of his 'lifelong' event.

We are all competing in this same lifelong event, but remember, we are engaged in our own separate fight and our own separate race. You don't have to worry about competing against other people, like those in the Olympics do. The only competitors are 'you vs the devil'. It's an easy win when you have the Spirit of grace on your side to assist you in your spiritual disciplines. Yet we must heed Paul's warning to beat our flesh into submission to God's Spirit every day. We are always more than conquerors when we yield our body over to Christ's love.

Jesus, our Exalted King

You may not realise this until now, but Jesus also has quite a lot of experience with 'stephanos' wreathes. His first experience was not a very pleasant one. Remember what the Roman soldiers did to Him on the day of his crucifixion? In mock worship, they placed a nasty 'crown of thorns' upon His head. This was actually a "*stephanos akanthinos,*" that is, 'a wreathe of thornbush twigs woven together' (Mark 15:17). It is a wreath because it was made from a thornbush, just like all other wreathes or garlands, which are woven together from some kind of plant material.

Whenever you meditate on the everlasting crown that you will one day receive, make it a time of reflection to remember the crown of thorns Jesus wore for you. He had to suffer *in the natural* with a crown, before you could rule *in the spirit* with a crown.

If we delve deeper into the definition of *stephanos,* we find it is 'the victor's crown'; a reward or prize given as the symbol of triumph in the games or another similar contest. Along with the bay laurel and olive, it could also be woven as a garland of oak, ivy, parsley, myrtle, or *in imitation of these, gold.*

> *Then I saw a white cloud, and seated on the cloud was one like the Son of Man, a golden wreath atop His head and a sharp sickle in His hand*
> (Rev. 14:14 VOICE)

In Revelation 14:14 we find Jesus wearing *the gold version* of this 'victor's wreath', a prize for conquering death when He rose out of Hades completely unscathed. Rising from the grave, He returned with this replacement whilst still carrying the 'honour marks' from the nails and spear as mementos of His remarkable achievement. The wreath of thorns that dug into His skull is now a thornless golden wreath. At this very moment, Jesus is wearing this crown.

At a future time described in Revelation 14:14, Jesus is holding a sharp sickle in His hand in order to reap the final end-time ingathering of souls across the whole earth! This is the harvest, which is the end of the age (Matt 13:39). I believe the swinging of the sickle equates to at least a tithe of the earth's population; that's now upwards of one billion new kingdom citizens (doesn't hurt to aim high). This is the primary reason the Tabernacle of David must be rebuilt! Jesus is wearing His victory wreath, and as you are about to find out, you have been crowned for your role in this coming harvest as well!

In the Greek there are two primary words that are translated 'crown'. The other Greek word translated crown (aside from *stephanos*) is *diadēma*, from which we derive the English word 'diadem'.

When we arrive at Revelation 19:12, we find an amazing prophecy. Just before Jesus mounts His white horse to return and rule the nations with a rod of iron (Ps. 2:9, Rev 2:27), He exchanges His golden wreath for a diadem crown! While *stephanos* is a mark of 'exalted rank', the *diadēma* is the crown of 'kingly and imperial dignity.' It is the crown worn by a *Sovereign* Ruler.

In Revelation 12:3 and 13:1, the dragon, and then the beast, attempt to displace God by also wearing a diadem crown. Yet we find that the beast (antichrist) is *only* given a wreath (stephanos) when he comes on his white horse in Revelation 6:2. The antichrist might think he can rule by His own sovereign might and power, but in reality, he only has a measure of rule limited to that which God has granted him. Only Jesus can successfully transfer His wreath for a diadem because as God, He is our only Sovereign and Lord (Jude 4). The devil and the antichrist can attempt to wear one, but they will not prevail. Jesus will defeat them *'with the breath of His mouth and the splendour of His coming'* (2 Thess. 2:8), showing the world that the diadem crown is reserved for Him alone.

So you see, the eternal crown granted to believers is in the form of a *stephanos*, a wreath. James refers to it as the wreath of life (Jam. 1:12), Paul, the wreath of righteousness (2 Tim 4:8), and Peter calls it the wreath of glory that will never fade away (1 Pet. 5:4). I believe these apostles were all talking about the same crown, only each of them had a unique name for it. Every one of us shall cast this wreathe down at the feet of Jesus (Rev. 4:10). For by then it will be abundantly clear that it was His grace alone that empowered us to *'endure to the end and be saved'*. (Matt 24:13)

This is the same *'incorruptible crown'* that Paul mentions in 1 Corinthians 9:25, stating how 'he would beat his body into submission to God's will, so that after toiling in God's work he would not find himself disqualified from receiving it.'

Wreath of Salvation

On top of all this, we are all granted a 'free wreath' as born again believers:

> *I am coming quickly; hold fast <u>what you have</u>, so that no one will take your crown.* (Rev. 3:11 NASB)

Unlike the incorruptible crown in 1 Corinthians 9:25, this is not a crown that we will be awarded *after* we exit this earthly body. It is one we wear *during* our earthly life. According to this verse, we have it in our possession *before* Jesus comes back. But we must be vigilant, so that we don't allow anyone to take it away from us. This wreath is actually the most important one, because it sets us up for success in *this* life. It is only by prevailing that we qualify for the upgrade to the everlasting victory wreath, our incorruptible crown of gold.

Out of the seven churches Jesus addressed in the book of Revelation, this church at Philadelphia (which Jesus was addressing in Rev. 3:11) was one of only two churches that Christ did not rebuke. Known as 'the faithful Church', they seemed to have no faults, or at least recorded faults either in morals or doctrine. That's why they were told to 'hold fast' to their crowns, because up until this point there had been no stumbling that would place their crowns in jeopardy. There was no blatant rebellion that would cause their names to be blotted out of the Book of Life, neither any misdemeanours that would warrant the threat of lampstand removal. (Rev. 2:5, 3:5)

The faithfulness of the church at Philadelphia is a vital clue on how we prevent our crown from being stolen. This requires standing steadfast on the Word, perseverance through all things, and a relentless pursuit toward the prize of the high calling of God. We must hold strong in the grace given in Christ Jesus and walk through this life as uncompromising, unwavering, faith-filled overcomers. (Phil. 3:14, 2 Tim. 2:1, Rev. 3:10-12)

To be knighted with such a prestigious honour is a wonderful privilege, but we must consider that Jesus is the *'One'* who *'won'* the victors prize. When He wore the crown of thorns and *"for the joy set before Him endured the cross, scorning its shame"* He won the greatest 'one-off' Olympic event ever conducted. By the blood on His brow and His triumph on the tree, we are counted worthy to wear such a wreath. It is not something we could have ever earned, but a free gift from Jesus at salvation. We could easily equate our wreath with 'the helmet of salvation'.

This special endowment gives us a sound mind and divine power to demolish strongholds, protecting our thoughts from the attack of the enemy. It is also a statement to the devil of our inheritance in God. We are His prized possession! The moment we were born again was the moment we were crowned. That's why when a woman in labour is fully dilated and the baby first becomes visible, it is called 'the crowning of a baby's head'. It is time for the baby to be born, and when our head was *spiritually crowned*, it was our time to be 'born again!' At this point, the mother has just gone through transition. On the day of our salvation, we transitioned out of the dominion of darkness into the kingdom of His dear Son. (Col. 1:13)

I encourage you to imagine yourself wearing this victory wreath upon your head. You have been born of royal descent and are already crowned king over the adversary. Start to actively engage in the race Jesus has mapped out for you and target the enemy with purposeful blows. God has not given you a spirit that shrinks back in timidity, but a spirit that is full of power, overflowing with love for people, and protected by a soundly crowned mind. (2 Tim. 1:7)

Hold your head up high, take every thought captive to the obedience of Christ, and counter all the schemes of the enemy with bold and courageous faith! He has already been defeated by the One who went ahead of us as our Fore-*runner*. All we need to do is follow in His footsteps (Heb. 6:19, 1 Pet 2:21, Job 23:11). So continue to punch with accuracy, advance with tenacity in every stride, and complete your course with enthusiasm and resolve!

> *"I have fought the good fight, I have finished the race, I have kept the faith. [8]Now there is in store for me the <u>crown of righteousness</u>, which the Lord, the righteous Judge, will award to me on that day – and <u>not only to me, but also to all who have longed for his appearing.</u>"* (1 Tim. 4:7-8)

~ Chapter 10 ~

GOLDEN LAMPSTAND

Directly across from the Table of Showbread (45 degrees left when entering) there was a golden lampstand; 'menorah' in Hebrew. It was purposefully designed to look like an almond tree in blossom. There was a central trunk or stem, then coming off the main stem were six branches, three on each side. The central trunk was slightly taller than the other six branches, because it had an extra decorative almond blossom combination crafted into it (Exod. 25:31-40). It was an oil lamp, with seven wicks, one for each branch and one for the stem. In the night watches, the priests were commanded to keep the lamps burning. They had to continue pouring oil through the centre stem. The design enabled the oil to flow down the trunk and through into the branches, keeping all seven lamps burning. Jesus said;

> *I am the light of the world. Whoever follows me will never walk in darkness, but will have the light of life.* (John 8:12)

As previously established, Jesus is THE WORD of GOD. The Bible promises us; *'Your word is a lamp for my feet, a light on my path.'* Through the illumination of the Word of God, Jesus imparts direction for our lives: what to do, where to go and how to walk faithfully in His sight. This propels us to imitate the One we have given up our life to follow. For He also said;

> *[14]__You__ are the light of the world. A city situated on a hill cannot be hidden. [15]No one lights a lamp and puts it under a basket, but rather on a __lampstand__, and it gives light to all who are in the house. [16]In the same way, let your light shine before others, so that they may see your good works and give glory to your Father in heaven.* (Matt 5:14-16 CSB)

In Numbers 8:2, Moses was commanded to face the lamps forward. This would ensure that they would illuminate the Bread of the Presence on the other side, which is the *rhēma* Word of God. Worship is the light-source that assists our ability to meditate on His Word and gather first-hand revelation from God's table of blessings. That is why it is always beneficial to have deep times of worship and adoration before hearing the spoken Word, or studying the written Word. The combination of the two is a sure-fire way to experience the abundance of the Lord.

There was no other light in the Holy Place, and no windows for moonlight to shine in. That's the reason God commanded the priests to keep the lamps burning all night (Exod. 27:21). If they did not fill the oil up and the seven lamps went out, the priests would be in complete darkness. That is what happens to us if we stop worshiping, praising and honouring our marvellous Saviour and Maker: We will enter such gross darkness that we will no longer find any guidance or illumination from His Word. In this dark setting, even the living and energetic *logos* of God seems dry and lifeless. It becomes to us like 'manna', which means 'what is it?' As the manna was unknown to the Israelites, so Christ becomes unknown to us when the oil lamps of worship run dry. Worship is a key to a healthy relationship with Jesus. He longs to reveal the deep things of His heart, and worship is how we 'connect in'.

The lampstand represents Jesus' exhortation to *"Be dressed ready for service and keep your lamps burning, [36]like servants waiting for their master to return"* (Luke 12:35-36). We must maintain the oil of the Holy Spirit in our lamps, keeping the flames of intimacy blazing, that we may be always ready to obey. Jesus wants us to be prepared for His return like faithful servants who He can trust to put in charge of His household while He is absent. Jesus also tells us in John 15:14-15 that if we faithfully obey His commands, we will receive an upgrade from servant to friendship status!

The last thing we want is to end up like the foolish virgins who did not buy extra oil for their lamps. When the bridegroom tarried longer than they expected, they were caught out without the 'Light of the world' in their lamps at the critical moment of His return. They were locked out of the wedding supper of the Lamb, and the Bridegroom went even further; saying, 'I don't even know you!' If a person no longer has the light of Jesus burning in their heart, then it stands to reason that He wouldn't be in relationship with them. Don't let that be you. Don't put your trust in a 'left behind' second-chance scenario either, because this parable seems to indicate that there isn't one (Matt 25:1-13). *You* be the judge, but I wouldn't want to risk it!

Sevenfold Spirit of God

In the book of Revelation, we see strong ties between the golden lampstand and the seven spirits of God. The seven spirits of God are the sevenfold operation of the *one* Holy Spirit. He is One Spirit with seven unique elements or virtues within His character or 'make-up'. God is a Trinity: One God in three Personages. The Holy Spirit is one Personage in seven 'expressions'. These seven spirits picture the Holy Spirit in His manifold, dynamic activity; seven distinct ministries of God's Spirit that exalt Christ's rule, producing a rapid increase of His government whenever they are unleashed.

In Revelation 4:5 we read;

> *From the throne came flashes of lightning, rumblings and peals of thunder. In front of the throne, <u>seven lamps were blazing. These are the seven spirits of God</u>*

In the heavenly throne room we see that the lampstand actually resembles this sevenfold Spirit of God. In light of Christ's resurrection, this is now a fully functioning spiritual reality;

> *Grace and peace to you from him who is, and who was, and who is to come, and from <u>the seven spirits before his throne</u>* (Rev. 1:4)

According to Revelation, the seven spirits of this heavenly lampstand are before Jesus' throne. This means that they are at His disposal; ready to be utilised in His ongoing plan of redemption.

If you read Revelation 3:1, you will find confirmation that Jesus has the seven spirits firmly in His possession. The Holy Spirit's fullness is *His* to keep, and the Spirit is *His* to distribute (John 1:33). This makes sense, for when the Spirit descended like a dove and remained on Him, the Spirit of the Lord rested upon His ministry from that day forward (John 1:32). The Son of God operated out of the sevenfold workings of the Holy Spirit during His three-and-a-half year ministry on earth, and He still holds this mantle up in heaven.

Isaiah further confirms this truth by listing for us what the seven spirits of God actually are;

> *There shall come forth a shoot from the stump of Jesse, and a branch from his roots shall bear fruit. ²And the Spirit of the Lord <u>shall rest upon him</u>, the Spirit of wisdom and understanding, the Spirit of counsel and might, the Spirit of knowledge and the fear of the Lord.* (Isa. 11:1-2 ESV)

If you count them, you will find that there are seven spirits mentioned here, and they rested on the new Shoot that came out of the stump of Jesse. The stump of

Jesse is David's dilapidated kingdom, which at the time of Christ's first coming had been symbolically 'chopped down' so that only a stump and a root system were left intact. Christ was sent into the world from the lineage of David to restore it and include the rest of humanity, as we previously studied in Acts 15. *Verse 10* of Isaiah 11 says; *"In that day there shall be a Root of Jesse, Who shall stand as a banner to the people. <u>For the Gentiles shall seek Him</u>."* (NKJV)

◊◊◊◊◊

> *[33]Behold, the Lord God of hosts will lop the boughs with terrifying power; the great in height will be hewn down, and the lofty will be brought low. [34]<u>He will cut down the thickets of the forest with an axe, and Lebanon will fall by the Majestic One</u>. There shall come forth a shoot from the stump of Jesse, and a branch from his roots shall bear fruit.* (Isa. 10:33-11:1 ESV)

In the two verses prior to the Promise in Isaiah 11:1-2, we find the prophecy of the fall of the Assyrians beyond any hope of recovery (Isa. 10:33-34). It is depicted as the felling of the cedars of Lebanon by the axe, swung allegorically by God's own hand. Once a cedar is cut down it cannot grow new shoots; and so the might of Assyria, when it fell, would be destroyed forever.

This metaphor is carried on with surpassing beauty in the first part of this prophecy, (Isa. 11:1 above) contrasting the indestructible vitality of the Davidic kingdom (through the promise of Messiah) with irreparable destruction; the fate of the northern kingdom's most formidable antagonist. The enemy is a cedar; its stump rots slowly but never recovers. God's kingdom is an oak, which every woodsman or forester knows will put out new growth from the 'stool.'

There is a traditional method of woodland management called 'coppicing' which exploits the capacity of many species of trees to put out new shoots from their stump or roots if cut down. In a coppiced wood, young tree stems are repeatedly cut down to near ground level, resulting in such a stool. In this instance, the prophet Isaiah does not see a crowd of little suckers: He sees only One. This single Shoot would eventually outgrow the previously chopped down tree in both size and fruitfulness. The prophecy is distinctly of One Person, in whom the Davidic monarchy is re-established into a prosperous kingdom which experiences increase that has no end! (Isa. 9:6-7) He has incorporated the Gentiles into His kingdom populace and is now going about the fulfilment of Acts 15:16; 'the rebuilding of the tabernacle of David which had previously fallen down.'

The small Offshoot that grew into a Branch is Jesus Christ, and the seven spirits of God rested upon Him enabling Him to restore the entire oak, according to Isaiah 11:2. He has done this by branching out further in His new covenant people. For He said; *"I am the vine, you all are the branches. Whoever lives in Me, and I in them, will produce much fruit"* fulfilling Isaiah 11:1, which boldly declares that the Branch will bear fruit out of a dead stump that hadn't produced anything in such a long time. The oak is regrowing, and the kingdom of God is as strong as ever, even though it may not always look that way from our worldly perspective. For Jesus said;

> *The kingdom of heaven is like a grain of mustard seed that a man took and sowed in his field. [32]It is the smallest of all seeds, but when it has grown it is larger than all the garden plants and becomes a tree, so that the birds of the air come and make nests <u>in its branches</u>.* (Matt 13:31-32 ESV)

We have been crafted as almond blossoms into the branches of the Menorah. In the same way we, as wild olive shoots, are grafted into the nourishing sap of the olive root (Rom. 11:17). The Lamb of God is not possessive concerning the Spirit of God. Revelation 5:6 tells us that the sevenfold Spirit under His control has been 'sent out' into all the earth. The seven expressions of the Holy Spirit have been released upon His sons and daughters. Jesus said; *"As you sent me into the world, so I have sent them into the world."* (John 17:18 CSB)

When Jesus was sent into the world the *'Spirit of the Lord was upon Him because God had anointed Him to preach Good news to the poor'* (Luke 4:18). Jesus boldly declared that He is sending us out in exactly the same way He was sent, giving us the same access to 'Holy Spirit fullness'. For as John the Baptist declared; *"the Lord gives Him the Spirit without limit"* (John 3:34). As we integrate ourselves into the revelation of the golden lampstand, we are positioning ourselves to catch Jesus' 'seven Spirits of God' mantle. Wearing this mantle activates us to operate in the realm of the Father's glory!

Glory Awaits

We could go on forever, delving deeper into the prophetic symbolism of the High Priests garments (the ephod and breastplate), the spiritual application of all the feast days, the anointing oil, and the varying sacrifices on the altar of burnt offering (Lev. 1-7), which reveal all the multi-dimensional facets of Christ's propitiation. You can even find revelation in the type of materials used and the exact dimensions of the courtyard, tabernacle and furniture. But as the writer of Hebrews states emphatically in Hebrews 9:5, *"we cannot discuss these things in any more detail now"*.

The Lord Jesus is the antitype of all these things. He is the Tabernacle of Moses and all its furnishings 'Personified'. Thus, His rending of the veil has brought these types and shadows into the Most Holy Place. They are now found 'in Christ', the One permanently seated in the heavenly Holy of Holies.

From our New Covenant perspective, the physical furnishings and the ceremonial service are out of date and have been discontinued. Their only remaining purpose is to direct our gaze toward Him. The first covenant only ever represented pictures compiled in the 'Jesus Christ photo album'. We have had a decent scan through the album, but we have been invited to meet with the actual Person, the Son of Man; Jesus Christ.

How to 'accept' the invitation and the details of His residential address can be found within the new agency discovered by King David. The spiritual reality of all these 'external regulations' are contained within the TOD lifestyle of worship, prayer, and intimacy with God through His Word. We now have the genuine fulfilment; the 'real deal' pertaining to the condition of the human heart, rather than an outward, fleshly foreshadowing which brings no meaningful change to the person performing the divine service.

◊◊◊◊◊

To wrap up this section, let's progress forward to Hebrews 9:6;

> *⁶When everything had been arranged like this, the priests entered regularly into the outer room to carry on* <u>*their ministry*</u> (the divine service, 'latreia') (Heb. 9:6)

Here we discover the second mention of the Greek word *latreia* within Hebrews 9. The RSV Bible translates *latreia* here as 'ritual duties'. I think this hits the nail on the head. Earlier in our examination of Hebrews 9:1, we discussed how the work of the Old Testament priests in the Holy Place was a strictly religious form of *latreia*; none of it affected their heart.

What is most intriguing is that according to Romans 12:1, New Covenant saints are called to outwork *latreia* in its new radical design. For us, *latreia* should always be defined as *worship*, but as mentioned previously; in the case of these priests, the lack of a spiritual dimension makes it inappropriate to attribute it as such. In their case, 'divine service' or 'service unto God' is a more accurate term, for these priests were merely performing religious obligations without understanding the spiritual significance behind them. It was simply baking loaves of bread, keeping incense burning and oil lamps flickering, washing their hands and feet with water, killing animals and sprinkling blood. To them, they were practical duties, and if you completed the task using the correct method, it kept you in God's 'good books'.

We have a superior covenant based on better promises (Heb. 8:6). As born again believers, every thought, word and action has a spiritual element that can be clearly understood and acknowledged by the one carrying out the *latreia*. But that's all I will say regarding this hugely significant point until later on… stay tuned!

Verse 7-9 of Hebrews chapter 9 caps off this chapter;

> *[7]But only the high priest entered the inner room, and that only once a year, and never without blood, which he offered for himself and for the sins the people had committed in ignorance. [8]The Holy Spirit was showing by this that the **way into the Most Holy Place had not yet been disclosed** as long as the first tabernacle was still functioning. [9]This is an illustration for the present time, indicating that the gifts and sacrifices being offered were not able to **clear the conscience*** (didn't impact the heart) *of the worshiper.*

When the High Priest came out of the Most Holy Place after sprinkling the blood of bulls and goats on the mercy seat, he would close up the veil for another year because the way into the Most Holy Place still had not yet been disclosed. If the sacrifices had effectively cleansed the conscience of the people through the actual 'taking away' of their sins, he would have said, *"It's worked! The sacrifices were effective! Everybody welcome inside the Holy of Holies: Queue up here to encounter the manifest glory of God!"* But that never happened. The Day of Atonement was only an annual reminder that sin still bound them, and that the animal sacrifices were ill-equipped to do for them what they so desperately required.

> [1]*The law is **only a shadow** of the good things that are coming—not the realities themselves. For this reason it can never, by the same sacrifices repeated endlessly year after year, make perfect those who draw near…* [2]*Otherwise, would they not have stopped being offered? For the worshipers would have been cleansed once for all, and would no longer have felt guilty for their sins.* [3]**But those sacrifices are an annual reminder of sins.** [4]*It is impossible for the blood of bulls and goats to take away sins.* (Heb. 10:1-4)

Let's now examine the purpose of the Ark and then we'll retrace its travels prior to it being brought into Jerusalem by King David.

SECTION III:

THE ARK OF HIS GLORY

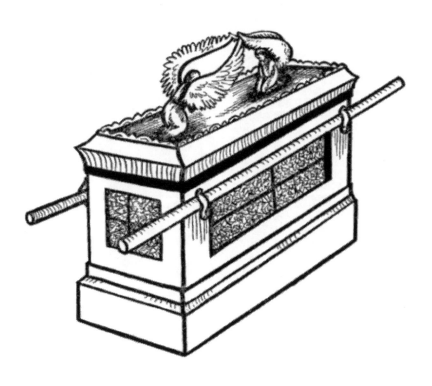

~ Chapter 11 ~

ARK OF THE COVENANT

Israel camped at the base of Mount Sinai for about a year, and in that time Moses climbed up and down the holy mountain numerous times. But it was during his first of two 'long stays' on the mountain (forty days and forty nights) that God began talking to Moses about the tabernacle and its furnishings. They were to be built on earth according to the exact specifications of the heavenly pattern: the architectural design or blueprint (Exod. 25:9, 40, Heb. 8:5). God's purpose for this is found in Exodus 25:8;

> "Have the people of Israel build me a holy sanctuary <u>so I can live among them</u>". (NLT)

Under Moses' Tabernacle, there were many restrictions and barriers between God and fallen humanity. Even so, we see that God's 'heart desire' has always been the same. **His deepest longing is to dwell among men.** The ultimate fulfilment of this will occur in Revelation 21:2-3 when the heavenly Jerusalem descends onto the earth so that the Father's permanent dwelling place can be among His children.

While we might not be at this glorious point in time yet, the great news is that now, in the New Covenant, God doesn't merely dwell among us; He dwells in us! (John 14:15-17) We are His habitation. This means full access beyond the veil into the throne room, Tabernacle of David style.

In the days of Moses, the closest an Israelite outside of the priesthood could get to God was when they brought their animal sacrifices to the altar of burnt offering, just outside the tabernacle entrance. Even though access to the inner sanctuary was a long way off, this was still better than nothing! (Exod. 29:42-44)

Moses' first forty-day stay on top of Mount Sinai was his second climb overall. This ascent begins in Exodus 24:15, shortly after the children of Israel accepted the Lord's covenant (Exod. 24:3-8). It ends abruptly all the way down in Exodus 32 with the golden calf incident.

Concerning the Ark, God made a precious and most fascinating promise to Moses, and its significance is often overlooked. *Immediately* after laying out the plans, God begins to open up *the number one reason why* Moses is building such an article;

"I will meet with you there and talk to you from above the atonement cover (mercy seat) between the gold cherubim that hover over the Ark of the Covenant. From there I will give you my commands for the people of Israel." (Exod. 25:22 NLT)

God told Moses that once this item was built and then installed inside the tabernacle, it would be the location where God would speak to Moses from that point onwards. Moses would have a permanent place to come and inquire of Yahweh from within *His Divine Glory*! Most people would say that the number one purpose for the Ark and the Holy of Holies was the Day of Atonement, but God doesn't start talking about that until Leviticus 16.

There are three important truths the Ark of the Covenant symbolises;

1) The Ark is a representation of God's throne, both on earth and in heaven: He is Lord of heaven and earth (Acts 17:24). When David went to retrieve the Ark from the small forest-village of Kiriath-jearim he was actually bringing back *"the Ark of God which bears the name of the Lord, who is enthroned between the Cherubim"* (1 Chr. 13:6). This is exactly where God told Moses to come and speak with Him. Moses was actually given divine permission to approach the King of Glory at the footstool of His throne, much like Esther, who had the King of Persia extend his royal sceptre, that she may approach his throne without incurring the death penalty. (Est. 4:11, 5:1-2)

Psalm 99:1-2 re-iterates this truth;

"The Lord is king! Let the nations tremble! He sits on his throne between the cherubim. Let the whole earth quake! (NLT) *The Lord is great in Zion; he is exalted above all the peoples."* (CSB)

Psalm 99 elaborates further by giving us *a locational address* for God's throne. It is up on the top of a mountain called *Zion*. King David was bringing the Ark up to Mount Zion in natural Jerusalem, fulfilling this heavenly reality. The true Mount Zion is located in the heavenly Jerusalem: the City of the Living God, according to Hebrews 12:22. When the heavenly Jerusalem descends to become a permanent fixture on earth, Mount Zion makes her return and the entire Godhead will take up residency on the newly renovated earth. From that time on, the literal throne of God will be with us forever! (Rev. 21:2-4)

For us currently living in the New Covenant, Mount Zion refers to 'life in the Spirit'. Whenever we abide in the Holy Spirit, we enter heavenly Mount Zion in the spiritual realm. When we come across Mount Zion in the Scriptures and replace it with 'life in the Spirit', it will bring us a far greater depth of meaning, rather than skimming across it without a second thought.

God promised King David that one of his descendants would sit on His throne as an everlasting dynasty (2 Sam 7:12-13), and the ultimate fulfilment is none other than our Lord and Saviour Jesus Christ. He is going to rule the nations with an iron sceptre (Ps. 2:9). This reign of Jesus actually begins at His second coming, 1000 years before the heavenly throne descends. He will sit on the throne of David in Mount Zion, natural Jerusalem. This leads us to the Ark's second symbolism…

2) The Ark is a type of our Lord Jesus Christ, the Son of God: But more specifically, the Ark represents the Anointed One as *'the fullness of the Godhead bodily'* (Col 2:9), implying that the Trinity is also in focus here. This is highlighted by the three items kept inside the Ark according to Hebrews 9:4: The Ten Commandments, a golden pot of manna which supernaturally *did not decay*, and Aaron's staff that miraculously budded. These represent the Father's Law, the Son as our Heavenly Manna, and the fruitfulness of the Holy Spirit.

Exodus 25:10-11 states that the Ark was to be built of acacia wood and then overlaid with pure gold inside and out. The 70 translators of the Septuagint (Greek Old Testament) translated the Hebrew for 'acacia wood' into 'incorruptible wood'. Wood is symbolic of Jesus Christ's perfect, sinless and incorruptible *humanity* (1 John 3:5, Ps. 16:10). The pure gold (which overlaid the wood) is symbolic of *deity*, or *divine nature*. Therefore, incorporated within the gold and the wood, we have the revelation of the two natures in the One Person.

Once all the designing and building work had been completed, they brought the entire tabernacle to Moses for inspection. After Moses had vetted that everything was precisely completed according to the pattern shown him on the mountain, he blessed them. (Exod. 39:42-43)

The very moment Moses finished implementing the last feature of the setup (which was the fence and outer gate forming the courtyard), the cloud of glory burst forth *from on top of the Ark*: A cloud so dazzling, so dense and so weighty that no priest, or even Moses, could initially enter because of its brightness and thickness. This was the first close-up encounter for the entire nation with the *kâbôwd Yĕhovah*, the glory of the Lord. It had shifted down from the top of the mountain and entered into the midst of the camp! (Exodus 40:34-35) With this in mind, we can begin to grasp the magnitude of what Paul wrote to the church at Colossae;

> To them God chose to make known how great among the Gentiles are the *riches of the glory* of this mystery, *which is Christ in you, the hope of glory.* (Col. 1:27 ESV)

And

> [9]*For the entire fullness of* the Godhead *dwells bodily in Christ,* [10]*and you have been filled by him, who is the head over every ruler and authority.* (Col. 2:9-10 CSB)

We have been filled with this magnificent Glory!

All this pertains to the third element, which is most profound.

3) At that time, the Ark was the only place on the planet where the glory of God dwelt in an ongoing manifestation: It was the solitary location where you were *guaranteed* to experience His *weighty presence*. But there was *one small problem*: In order for the Ark to radiate the Majestic Glory in this manner, it had to be *housed* in a *Tabernacle* or *Temple*. To be specific, this dazzling glory was only found when the Ark was placed within a *Most Holy* Place. King David said;

> "Lord, I love *the house* where you dwell, the place *where your glory resides.*" (Ps. 26:8 CSB)

The Ark would not emanate with the same glory while being transported because the cloud of glory had already moved ahead of the Israelite camp to direct them where to go (Exod. 40:36-38, Num. 9:15-23). Also, in Numbers 4:4-6 the Kohathite clan of the Levites, who were commanded to carry the Ark, had to wait for the priests to cover the Ark with three protective layers, thus veiling any residual glory. Numbers 4:20 states that the Kohathites would drop dead even if they simply went into the Holy Place to *watch any* the holy objects being covered!

Now for *the major problem*: Under the Mosaic Covenant, no one was allowed to go into the Most Holy Place and experience the Majestic Glory. The people were permitted to 'enter his gates with thanksgiving and His courts with praise' (Ps. 100:4) as they brought their animals to the priests at the brazen altar, but here you could only sense a fraction of the full weightiness. The only person who was allowed to continually commune with God by venturing uninhibited into the Most Holy Place was Moses! Everyone else was locked out of the Glory-realm. Having access to the newly created outer court meant the glory was now close-at-hand, which was better than the distant gloom upon the mountain, but they still couldn't be intimately acquainted with the Lord like Moses could.

This problem has been removed for us under *the New Testament version* of the Davidic order of worship. We are all portable tabernacles of the Holy Spirit! According to the two verses we previously examined in Colossians, New Covenant believers have been filled to overflowing with the glory of the fullness of the entire Godhead! Did you catch that? Now, the problem for us is not inviting the glory in, but reflecting it out! That is the commission of His end-time army of believers. The manifestation of this weight of glory is going to fill the whole earth to the same degree that the waters cover the sea (Hab. 2:14). If you didn't grasp the analogy, that means *the entire planet* will witness this *through* a chosen body of people. What a glorious calling we have been born into for such a time as this, but it is also one we should revere and take seriously.

Free from his own Law: A man of Unique Privileges

Let's backtrack to Moses: He was a 'special case' you could say. For he was not placed under the same laws and obligations contained within the very Covenant he inaugurated. Why was this so? Moses was the mediator of the Covenant *between the two parties:* God and the children of Israel. He was not actually a party in the Covenant.

Now this may shock you, but in many ways Moses, like David, also lived in the New Covenant before his time. Remember Exodus 25:22? God told Moses that once the Ark had been placed behind the veil in the tabernacle, he could go in there and commune with God *at his own convenience*. For Moses, there was no 'once-a-year' high priestly reservation to be concerned about; it was an *open invitation, any day, any time*. Doesn't that sound more like the experience David brought to Israel on Mount Zion? The only difference between Moses and David is that Moses didn't bring anyone else into this reality, except for perhaps Joshua to a certain extent. David, on the other hand, opened it up for whosoever desired.

This might shed some light on why Moses encountered certain hardships. His 'open access to the Father' was most likely the catalyst for Korah's rebellion in Numbers 16. Korah was a Levite who was coveting the Priesthood of Aaron, but we can see from what Moses said in verse 28 that he was also jealous of the special privileges God gave Moses as well.

On another occasion, even his own biological siblings—Miriam and Aaron—criticised him! God immediately called the three of them to the Tent of Meeting, and as they approached, the Lord descended in the glory cloud and stood at the entrance of the tabernacle. The sad part is, the majority of times when God ventured out of the Holy of Holies and stood at the entrance was when there was disciplinary action required, as was the case with Aaron and Miriam. Moments of disobedience are not the time you would want to approach this depth of Glory, just ask Ananias and Sapphira. (Acts 5:1-11)

When Aaron and Miriam had been summoned, God said to them;

> *"If there were prophets among you, I, the Lord, would reveal myself in visions. I would speak to them in dreams. ⁷But not with my servant Moses. Of all my house, he is the one I trust. ⁸I speak to him face to face, clearly, and not in riddles!* ***He sees the Lord as he is** (beholds the form of the Lord).* *So why were you not afraid to criticize my servant Moses?"* (Num. 12:6-8 NLT)

Did you read that? Moses has a higher level of intimacy with God than a prophet! He doesn't even require God to give him visions or dreams. He can waltz right in and talk with Him face to face! Not only that, but HE SEES THE LORD AS HE IS: He tangibly beholds the form of the Lord! What Moses experienced was nothing short of monumental! No wonder even his own family members were jealous of him. Sounds a bit like entering *boldly* into the throne of grace, doesn't it? I hope you are grasping the level of intimacy God wants to have with *you*. Are you 'champing at the bit' to enter in? Look, the same cloud of glory is promised to us;

> *"then the LORD will create over the whole area <u>of Mount Zion and over her assemblies</u> a <u>cloud by day</u>, even smoke, and the brightness of a <u>flaming fire by night</u>; for over all the <u>glory will be a canopy</u>. [6]There will be a shelter to give shade from the heat by day, and refuge and protection from the storm and the rain."* (Isa. 4:5-6 NASB)

Lord Jesus, bring us under the canopy of your glory! For it is our end-time mandate;

> *Arise, shine, for your light has come, and the <u>glory of the Lord</u> (kâbôwd Yĕhovah) has risen upon you. For behold, darkness will cover the earth, and deep darkness the peoples; But the <u>LORD will rise upon you And His glory will appear upon you</u>.* (Isa. 60:1-2 NASB)

~ Chapter 12 ~

BEHOLDING THE FORM OF THE LORD

Moses was the mediator of the Mosaic Covenant, which meant he was not required to live under it. He was *another* Old Testament character operating in New Covenant revelation! We discovered in the previous chapter that Moses SEES THE LORD AS HE IS or 'beholds the form of the Lord', as it is more readily translated. Let's unpack the statement...

In his first letter, the Apostle John tells us that;

> <u>When Christ appears</u>, we shall be like him, for we <u>shall see him as he is</u>.
> (1 John 3:2)

Jesus is the full expression of the Father in human form, for He stated; *"Don't you know me, Philip, even after I have been among you such a long time? Anyone who has seen me has seen the Father"* (John 14:9). I pray that the time when Christ first appears to you in this way would be prior to His second coming. Jesus has *already* given us an invitation to see His glory: That's why He also prayed;

> ²²<u>I have given them the glory that you gave me</u>, that they may be one as we are one...²⁴*"Father, I want those you have given me to be with me where I am, and **to see my glory**, the glory you have given me because you loved me before the creation of the world."* (John 17:22, 24)

This glory was the same glory that caused Isaiah to become undone in Isaiah 6 (John 12:41). Through His manifested glory, we can see the Lord as He is and be transformed into His likeness *in the here and now!* If Moses continually 'saw the Lord as he is' in the Old Testament, how much more should we?

> *Of all my house, he is the one I trust. ⁸I speak to him face to face, clearly, and not in riddles! He sees <u>the Lord</u> as he is.* (Num. 12:7b-8 NLT)

A funny observation about the way God addressing Miriam and Aaron is that the Lord, who is three Persons, talks about Himself in the '3rd person'. Notice that Moses 'sees' or 'beholds' the Lord as He is. It doesn't say he 'saw', or 'beheld' past tense, for He beheld the form of the Lord on a continual basis. He had unbridled access to this glory realm while on the earth. Once Moses had been 'lit up' with the bright rays of the Lord's glory, he was forever welcome inside the Holy of Holies. God can never reverse such an encounter. Access was granted for life!

◊◊◊◊◊

But prior to Numbers 12:8, there was a time in Moses' life where he would speak to the Lord face to face, but He had *not yet* SEEN THE FORM OF THE LORD. The latter is a higher level of manifestation. There is the presence of God, but *then* there is the glory of God. A most fascinating discovery is that Jesus elaborated on these two levels of the *experiential* knowledge of God. Get a hold of this;

> [37] *"And **the Father** who sent me has himself testified concerning me. <u>You have never heard his voice nor seen his form,</u>* [38]*nor does his word dwell in you, for you do not believe the one he sent."* (John 5:37-38)

While speaking to the Jewish leadership, Jesus states that they have neither **heard the Father's voice** (that's speaking face-to-face/Holy Place) nor **seen the Father's form** (that's seeing the Lord as He is/beholding His glory/Holy of Holies). Due to their stubborn unbelief, they didn't even have His Word dwelling in their hearts. In this scripture, Jesus Christ specifically points out that it is specifically the form *of the FATHER* that we behold while engulfed in the Majestic Glory!

Everyone who believes in the One whom the Father sent is invited to have the same experience Moses had. *We* are able to have the Father's reflected glory on our countenance. **When we see the Lord as He is, we will come to know the fullness of His name: the full depth of His nature and divine attributes.** While beholding His form, we receive an impartation of 'the Father's love' that can be taken with us and shared abroad.

As we examine the life-transforming experience Moses had, we will recognise what to aim for in our own relationship with God.

The Glory of the Father

The first reference in Scripture of the Glory of Yahweh is found in Exodus 16:10. In Hebrew it is the *kâbôwd Yĕhovah*: the full weight of the glory of the entire Godhead. There are multiple elements that make up the glory of the Lord. In this encounter, the Israelites had not yet reached Mount Sinai, so they are less than two months into their exodus journey. The 'glory of the Lord' appeared in the cloud for the very first time. Following this encounter with the Glory, they were provided with quail to eat and a daily supply of manna from heaven.

The *pillar of cloud by day*, and *the pillar of fire by night*, was the means by which the Father would appear to His Old Testament people during the time of their wilderness wanderings. Almighty God would speak to them from within the cloud; the cloud of the Holy Spirit that directed them on all their travels.

To the church, the Holy Spirit is the pillar of cloud and the pillar of fire through which the Father communicates. The *'fire of His Spirit'* consumes anything in us that is not of Him, while *'the cloud of His Spirit'* is His covering of protection over us. But the only way to get *inside* the cloud is by entering the Most Holy Place where the incandescent brilliance emanating from the mercy seat can be experienced in blissful wonder. This is the Father's glory.

In Exodus 24:15-17, the second mention of the glory of the Lord appears. This time it was on top of Mount Sinai inside *the same* cloud, now hovering on its peak. On Moses' first trip to the top of Mount Sinai (recorded earlier in Exodus 19-20), this 'dark, gloomy, stormy and burning' cloud was a terrifying sight to those who stood below (Heb. 12:18-21, Deut. 4:11-12). However, we must recognise that at this time, Moses was not yet *intimately acquainted* with the Father's glory, even though He travelled up into the midst of it.

Moses' First Hike

God's intention in this first mountaintop visitation was to reveal to Moses that He was going to put on a fearful display of His glory, all the way down to the foot of the mountain. After only a short stint at the peak, God told Moses to descend, promising that He would follow Him down in the form of fire and speak to Moses in the hearing of the people. He said;

> *"I will come to you in a thick cloud, Moses, so the people themselves can hear me when I speak with you. <u>Then they will always trust you.</u>"*
> (Exod. 19:9 NLT)

In Deuteronomy 4, Moses recounts this incident;

> [10]*"Never forget the day when you stood before the Lord your God at Mount Sinai, where he told me, 'Summon the people before me, and I will personally instruct them. Then they will <u>learn to fear me as long as they live</u>, and they will teach their children to fear me also.'*
>
> [11]*You came near and stood at the foot of the mountain, while flames from the mountain shot into the sky. The mountain was <u>shrouded in black clouds and deep darkness</u>. [12]<u>And the Lord spoke to you from the heart of</u>*

*the fire. **You heard the sound of his words but didn't see his form;
there was only a voice**. [13]He proclaimed his covenant—the Ten
Commandments—which he commanded you to keep, and which he wrote
on two stone tablets."* (Deut. 4:10-13 NLT)

The name 'Deuteronomy' literally means 'second law'. The bulk of its content
is Moses repeating the law (including events from the book of Exodus) a
second time (Deut. 1:3). Take note here that Moses carefully mentions the fact
that in this encounter they *did not see his form*. THERE WAS ONLY A
VOICE! Like the people, Moses had not yet seen God's form when this fearful
event occurred, but by the time he spoke these words above (looking back forty
years in hindsight), he had beheld the Father's form many times.

Before God inscribed the Ten Commandments on stone tablets and gave them
to Moses, He proclaimed them audibly in the hearing of the people. His voice
reverberated like thunder, and the long loud blast of a ram's horn made them
tremble in their boots. There was a volcanic-like eruption from the top and
lightning flashed inside the molten smoke (Exod. 19:16-20).

They heard God speak, but by reading Exodus 19:9 & 20:19, we can decipher
that they were actually overhearing a dialogue between the Lord and Moses.
After this terrifying event, the people told Moses;

> *"You speak to us, and we will listen. But don't let God speak directly to
> us, or we will die!"* (Exod. 20:19 NLT)

God knew this would be their response. Nevertheless, it achieved His purpose;
that they would learn to trust Moses (Exod. 19:9) and understand the fear of the
Lord (Deut. 4:10). The Israelites request was the catalyst for Moses going up the
mountain a second time. The conversation was now just between Moses and
God in seclusion, the people having shunned their open invitation to eavesdrop.

> *[20]Moses said to the people, "Do not be afraid. God has come to test you,
> so that the fear of God will be with you to keep you from sinning." [21]The
> people remained at a distance, while Moses approached the thick
> darkness where God was.* (Exod. 20:20-21)

Moses' Second Hike

The glory which travelled with them as a cloud by day and a fire by night had
now parked itself on top of the Lord's lofty mountain. The account of the glory
cloud *(kâbôwd Yĕhovah)* found in Exodus 24:15-17 is from Moses' second

ascent. On both *the first and second* trip, there was no tangible transformation to Moses' countenance when he came back down. This is vitally important to grasp.

The first climb was a short stint, but the second time God called Moses up for *forty days and forty nights.*

> *[15]When Moses went up on the mountain, the cloud covered it, [16]and the **glory of the Lord** settled on Mount Sinai. For six days the cloud covered the mountain, and on the seventh day the Lord called to Moses from within the cloud. [17]To the Israelites the <u>glory of the Lord looked like a consuming fire</u> on top of the mountain. [18]<u>Then Moses disappeared into the cloud</u> as he climbed higher up the mountain. He remained on the mountain forty days and forty nights."* (Exod. 24:16-17 NIV, 18 NLT)

Moses ascended cautiously for six days and then, on the Sabbath Day, God beckoned him to come inside the cloud. Notice that He told Moses *not to rest* on the Sabbath. He was to labour in entering closer to the Lord, where he would find rest for his troubled soul (Heb. 4:11). For over a month they talked *face to face*, yet in all that time Moses didn't SEE HIM. The gloomy manifestation of God's glory (likened to 'a consuming fire') had overtaken him, rather than the bright and illuminated rays of glory that were soon to enter the newly constructed sanctuary. This is where we must heed the scripture;

> *Consider, then, the kindness and severity of God: his severity toward those who fell, but God's kindness toward you—if you continue receiving his kindness. Otherwise, you too will be cut off.* (Rom. 11:22 ISV)

God wants us to strike an equal balance between His kindness and His severity. The Divine Glory contains two basic properties: the ability to destroy and the ability to preserve. After criticising her brother, Miriam experienced the 'destructive' or 'judgment' side of the glory when she broke out in leprosy (Num. 12:10). This is not just restricted to Old Testament times, for in the New Testament, Ananias and Sapphira experienced 'judgment by glory' when they lied to the Holy Spirit and were instantly struck dead (Acts 5:1-11). No one can mess around and get away with it when the atmosphere is charged with the manifest glory. Sin that is tolerated in the outer court causes destruction in the Most Holy Place.

We must love the Lord our God with all our heart, and fear Him just the same. If you examine the resurrected Christ who appeared to John in Revelation 1:13-

16, you will find He perfectly combines both sides of the glory: Mighty Judge of Brass and Gentle Light-Bearer, Lion and Lamb.

Hebrews 12:21 says that when the consuming fire and billows of smoke came down to the foot of the mountain, the sight was so terrifying that even Moses was trembling in fear! This produced a holy fear in Moses that protected him whenever he ascended into it. The people, on the other hand, were just plain scared. Not having a revelation of the love of God to balance this fear out, they ran *away* from God instead of the reaction a healthy fear of the Lord produces; running *to* Him. Moses was drawn to God because he had a sufficient blend of both.

◊◊◊◊◊

The Lord had two major objectives to fulfil through Moses on his second journey to the summit. The first was giving Moses the tablets of stone containing the Ten Commandments, personally inscribed by His divine signature. Through these tablets of stone, God revealed the 'permanency' of the Moral Law; His righteous standards will never be done away with and find their perfect fulfilment through the Royal Law of love, the basis and foundation of Christ's New Covenant law. (Jam. 2:8, Lev. 19:18)

The second purpose was to give Moses the architectural design for the Tabernacle's framework, its furnishings, and details concerning the priestly garments required to properly institute all its sacrifices and ceremonies. He further explained how to dedicate the priests, elaborated on Sabbath rules, gave the recipes for the anointing oil and incense, and summed everything up by showing Moses the craftsmen *who were skilled and anointed* to construct. With no modern conveniences such as computers, or even a ballpoint pen, this must have taken Moses a long time to dictate.

The People Disappoint

Now we're in Exodus 32: Forty days have come and gone, and Moses is still upon the summit. He has taken *so* long that the Israelites presumed he had perished, perhaps by a volcanic eruption consuming him. With Moses seemingly out of the picture, it only takes them a split second to forget about the terrifying display of God's glory only a month earlier. The fear of God had already deserted them (Prov. 8:13). *"We're free from Moses, and we're free from the God of Moses as well!"* [Be careful what you call *freedom:* To be free from the Lord is to be a slave to sin. And to be freed from sin is to be the Lord's slave (Rom. 6:22)].

In their folly, they approached Aaron, [who is supposed to be the responsible caretaker in Moses' absence (Exod. 24:14)], and asked him to build a golden calf for them to worship. They desire to worship something they can *see with their eyes and touch with their hands:* something 'tangible'. Being unable to see the *form* of the Lord caused them to *form* an idol instead. We should not form idols; according to Paul the Apostolic travail is that *'Christ be formed in us'* (Gal. 4:19). As we behold the form of the Lord, He is formed in us.

In celebration of their new 'god', Aaron of all people organises a pagan festival to indulge in all varieties of sin and debauchery. This lewdness seems to have cut short Moses' stay on the mountain. In Exodus 32:7-10 God tells Moses;

> *"Quick! Go down the mountain!* <u>*Your people*</u> *whom you brought from the land of Egypt have corrupted themselves. How quickly they have turned away from the way I commanded them to live! They have melted down gold and made a calf, and they have bowed down and sacrificed to it...I have seen how stubborn and rebellious these people are. Now leave me alone so my fierce anger can blaze against them, and I will destroy them. Then I will make you, Moses, into a great nation."* (NLT)

Here God actually tells Moses to 'leave Him alone'. But Moses is gutsy and extremely bold. First of all, he wants to address one of the finer details with God;

> *"Hang on a minute Jehovah sneaky, why did you call them 'my' people, I thought they were 'Your' people. How come all of a sudden you flipped them onto my shoulders? I'm not going to bear the responsibility of these rebels! Let me make one thing clear before we move on; they're not mine, they're Yours."* (Refer Exod. 32:11)

In His own mind, God had already discarded them as His people because of their blatant paganism, but thank goodness for Moses' intercession. Carefully note what Moses tells God in verses 12-13. He has two points of defence for the people.

First, Moses tells God (in verse 12) that He will ruin *His own* reputation among the Egyptians and other surrounding nations, because they will say, *"the God of Israel delivered his people from Egypt only to slaughter them in the desert".* In other words: *"God, you're gonna look bad!"*

Second, he intercedes for them regarding the promises made to Abraham, Isaac and Jacob (verse 13). God must remember His promise to them, because He is 'not the God of the dead, but of the living' (Matt 22:32). The Promised Land was guaranteed to all the descendants of Jacob. Moses is essentially quoting Romans 11:28 to God before it had even been written:

> "As far as their behaviour is concerned, they are Your enemies, but as far as election is concerned, You must love them *on account of the Patriarchs.*"

God can't deny His own Word, so in Exodus 32:14, He relents and changes His mind.

The only other Israelite who did not partake of this pagan revelry was Joshua, who faithfully stationed himself halfway up the mountain. When Moses came down to meet him, Joshua presumed war had broken out in the camp. But Moses corrected Joshua's evaluation with the intel God had shown him (Exod. 24:13, 32:17-18). Moses got so angry when he laid eyes on the camp and saw all that was happening he threw the two stone tablets on the ground, smashing them to pieces!

After handing out stern rebukes and vengeful judgement, Moses headed up the mountain a third time to plead forgiveness for the people (Exod. 32:30-35, Deut. 9:18-21). God still holds the unrepentant sinner accountable, stating He will erase them from the Book of Life (v32-33). Moses may be able to intercede in stopping God from destroying Aaron and the Israelites from the face of the earth, but personal forgiveness cannot be granted via Moses. Turning back to God and leaving behind their life of blatant rebellion could only be a heart decision made by each individual. Jude confirms this by warning us as New Covenant believers; *"Though you already know all this, I want to remind you that the Lord at one time delivered his people out of Egypt, but later destroyed those who did not believe."* (Jude 1:5)

~ Chapter 13 ~

MOSES IN THE TABERNACLE OF DAVID?

A remarkable thing happens in Exodus 33: God begins to speak with Moses *at the foot* of Mount Sinai instead of on the top, alerting Moses to the fact that their stay at Horeb is coming to an end. They must prepare to go forth and take the Promised Land. Most alarmingly, God made it clear that he would *not* be going with them. If he did, He would likely destroy them along the way. The best God can offer is to send an angel ahead of them to drive out the inhabitants of the land. (Exod. 33:1-3)

For Moses to even cope with the thought of this, he seeks clarification by partaking in serious correspondence with God. But before we go any further, I want to ask: Why does Moses suddenly have a communication line with the Lord somewhere other than the summit?

Exodus 33:7 states that it was Moses' practice to *pitch a tent* outside the camp which he would enter to talk with the Lord. The Hebrew for 'pitch a tent' ('ôhel nâṭâh) is exactly the same phrase used when King David 'pitched a tent' on Mount Zion in 1 Chronicles 15:1.

Moses pitched *his own* tent *some distance* from the camp. This was to escape the grumblings of the people and all their compromise *inside the camp*. Moses desired a place to commune with God at the base of the mountain. That way, he wouldn't have to wait till the next time he was summoned to climb. God had previously shown Moses that once the tabernacle was completed, he would be able to talk with the Lord from between the Cherubim, but Moses just couldn't wait that long. He was so desperate for fellowship that he erected a temporary 'Tabernacle of David' in the interim.

God honoured Moses in this, even though He never commanded him to do it. He saw Moses' heart to connect with Him. In fact, when Moses approached this tent, the pillar of cloud would come down off the mountain and hover over the entrance of the tent, mimicking what He would do many times later at the Tabernacle of Moses. (Exod. 33:10a)

A puzzling aspect of this set-up was that the people would petition Moses to ask God questions on their behalf, and the Lord would answer them, even though God was calling them stubborn and rebellious (Exod. 33:7b). There was a relationship of sorts going on between God and the people during this brief period. Even crazier to fathom was that when the people saw the pillar of cloud hovering at the entrance of Moses' tent, they would stand at the entrance of their own tents and *bow down in worship!* These were the same people who had just worshiped a golden calf! (Exod. 33:10b)

This is the only time the Hebrew word for 'bow down' (*shâchâh*) is ever used of the Israelites concerning *action toward God*. Sadly, once they were placed under the LOM along with the official Mosaic Tabernacle, they never worshiped in this way again. Being locked out of any genuine connection with the Lord, the focus became religious works instead of heartfelt worship. The only time *shâchâh* is used in conjunction with the people after Exodus 33:10 is in the form 'you shall NOT worship'. 'You shall NOT worship any other god'. 'You shall NOT form an idol and worship it' etc. What did this command-based system end up producing the majority of the time? Worship of false gods and the formation of idols, the very thing they were commanded not to do (Rom. 7:10-11). This is what 'the curse of the law' really is; being weakened by the flesh, the law gave sin its power. (Rom. 8:3, 1 Cor. 15:56)

Missing the Critical Piece

The only difference between this temporary tent and David's tabernacle was *the absence of the Ark*, which is our focus for the rest of this chapter. Moses knew he was lacking something, and we shall examine what that was. He was deficient in the critical element promised to him by God.

> *"The Lord would speak with Moses <u>face-to-face</u>, just as someone speaks with a friend. Then Moses would return to the camp. But the young man who was his helper, Joshua son of Nun, stayed in the Tent."* (Exod. 33:11 GNT)

Here Moses could talk to the Lord 'face to face', yet He had not yet SEEN THE LORD AS HE IS. It seems like Moses had the highest level of intimacy possible: speaking face to face with God as a man with his friend! Surely Moses had reached the pinnacle! No, he hadn't. Remember that the Ark was missing; at this point, it hadn't been built. Yet it was destined to be the only place on the planet where the weighty *kâbôwd* could manifest in an uninterrupted, ongoing fashion. *(Kâbôwd* comes from the Hebrew root word *kabad*, which means 'to be heavy or weighty')

Moses had not yet entered 'the realm of the Father's glory' in his experience with God. What he had experienced was face-to-face *conversation*, the Hebrew word '*pânîym*'; the *presence* of God. It is equivalent to the Bread of the Presence on the table of Showbread. This is 'Holy place' apprehension, not 'Most Holy Place' habitation (a far deeper expression of God). In this level of relationship Moses didn't actually *see God* face to face, he *talked* face to face. How do I know this? Two reasons 1. Because the Lord says later to Moses, '*no one can see My face and live*' (Exod. 33:20) and 2. When Moses recollected the time God came down off the mountain to speak with him in front of the Israelites he said that they *heard the sound of His words but didn't see His form; there was only a voice* (Deut. 4:12 NLT). The current communion Moses had with the Lord was relationship on the conversation level, which is good and most essential, yet it is only the base level relationship for a born-again believer. God was still invisible to Moses during these encounters. He could not behold His form. There is the presence of the Holy Spirit, the anointing of the Anointed One, but what about the glory of the Father? That, my friend, is the pinnacle! Progressing through these three levels is our primary quest.

Moses had received friendship with God through face-to-face conversation. He had been anointed with power to perform signs and wonders at the burning bush. Being acquainted with the presence and anointing of God did not satisfy him. There was more to apprehend, and he knew it. Access to God's glory was the missing element.

In the Glory realm, you actually SEE THE LORD AS HE IS: you don't just have conversations; you BEHOLD THE OUTLINE CONTAINING THE <u>SUBSTANCE OF HIS CHARACTER</u>, resulting in all kinds of supernatural manifestations. This is where we get to know the Father's heart through and through. We begin to sense what He senses, feel what He feels and desire what He desires. We become acquainted with His deepest longings and affections, and are captured and overwhelmed by the immensity of His love. Moses longed to enter this place of relationship, though He had not yet obtained it.

◊◊◊◊◊

A few days later, Moses discusses serious matters with the Lord. We can assume that this was back in his special temporary prayer tent, because Moses was not up the mountain. His desire to behold the outline of the invisible God is now insatiable. He no longer wants to talk with an invisible Friend. He wants to experience the One, *"who alone is immortal and who lives in unapproachable light, whom no one has seen or can see"* (1 Tim 6:16). Hebrews 11:27 says that Moses; *'persevered as one who **saw Him who is invisible'**.* How would this be possible for a man possessing the fallen flesh of humanity? Even with glorified bodies, we cannot behold the full features of the Father, let alone in this earthly vessel. The glory of the Father *is so bright* that when combined with the lamp of the Lamb it illuminates the whole of heaven so that there is no need for sun or moon; there is not even a casting of a shadow. (Rev. 21:23)

We'll pick up in Exodus 33:12-14;

> *"Moses said to the Lord; "You have been telling me, 'Take these people up to the Promised Land.' But you haven't told me whom you will send with me. You have told me, 'I know you by name, and I look favourably on you.' ¹³If it is true that you look favourably on me, let me know your ways so I may understand you more fully and continue to enjoy your favour. And remember that this nation is your very own people."* (NLT)

Moses explains the situation to God; *"Ok Lord, you've told me you cannot go with the people, but you haven't told me who you will send with me."*

Moses then attempts to convince God to go with him; *"remember that you know me by name, and you promised to look favourably upon me..."*

Straight after this, Moses puts out an additional request that will launch him into the next level of intimacy with God. He says, *"I don't want to merely hear your commands and see your mighty acts, I want to know your ways."*

King David shows us that God granted Moses this request;

> *'He made known His ways to Moses, His acts to the children of Israel.'*
> (Ps. 103:7 NKJV)

The Israelites only ever knew God by His outward actions, but Moses came to know His character and vital attributes. Then Moses throws in a quick reminder to God, *"Don't forget they are <u>Your</u> people, not mine."* Moses doesn't want a repeat of what happened during the golden calf incident, where God attempted to flip ownership of the people onto his shoulders. Moses knew he couldn't bear that kind of weight.

The Lord replied, *"My Presence shall go with you, and I will give you rest."* (Exod. 33:14)

Here the Lord assures Moses that He will go with him. The word for Presence here is one again *pânîym*, so what God is saying to Moses is;

"The very same Presence that you experience when I speak with you 'face to face' ('pânîym pânîym'—Exod. 33:11) in this tent will travel personally with you Moses. Don't despair; everything is going to be ay-okay."

[15]Then Moses said to him, "If your Presence does not go with __us__, do not send __us__ up from here. [16]How will anyone know that you are pleased with me and with your people unless you go with __us__? (Exod. 33:15-16a NIV) *For your presence among us sets your people and me apart from all other people on the earth." [17]"The Lord replied to Moses, "I will indeed do what __you__ have asked, for I look favourably on __you__, and I know __you__ by name."* (Exod. 33:16b-17 NLT)

Notice the distinctions here when Moses talks compared with the Lord. Moses continually states "us", while the Lord replies with "you". This is what God is essentially saying;

"look Moses, I can't make any promises about the nation as a collective, but I will certainly go with you. When the other nations see My presence with you as the leader, they will certainly fear you all collectively."

By now the insatiable desire inside Moses' heart to experience the next level with God has reached fever pitch. Before his mind could catch up with what his mouth was saying, he blurts out;

*"If all of this is true, as a confirmation please 'show Me **your glory.**'"* (Exod. 33:18)

Think about this: Moses has already been up the mountain numerous times speaking with the Lord from within the pillar of fire. He speaks with God in this tent face-to-face as a man talks with his friend, and He has even seen the actual finger of God come down and engrave the Ten Commandments on the two tablets of stone (Deut. 9:10), yet he still says; "show me Your glory"! Haven't you seen enough of God, Moses?

Here's my take on the thinking behind his request;

*"Lord, I appreciate that you'll always be with me, even until the end of the age, but I am desperate to partake of Your **weightier presence**. Thank you for your pânîym (ordinary presence), but I need to see your kâbôwd (glory). **I need to taste the 'Greater Glory' now** so I can experience a glimpse of the promise you have for me when the Ark and Holy of Holies are completed. Such an encounter will give me the courage and fortitude to complete the build and make preparations to move the people onward."*

God does not even hesitate for a second; He is always in the business of allowing people to partake early of what is later to come because faith is always at the heart of these requests. The Lord gives us glimpses of our future to keep us standing firm and steadfast as we await His Promises. As in Moses' case, there was no harm in asking, was there? Moses reaped bountifully from this bold petition, and we will see the gravity of this encounter through Exodus 34 and beyond. He opened the door into the glory for us too!

His Glory reveals His Name

The Lord, being the Father of unapproachable light, has some conditions to discuss with Moses as to how he can effectively see 'the One who is invisible' without being utterly destroyed (Heb. 11:27);

[19]*The Lord replied, "<u>I will make all my goodness pass before you, **and I will call out my name, Yahweh, before you.**</u> For I will show mercy to anyone I choose, and I will show compassion to anyone I choose.* [20]*<u>But you may not look directly at my face, for no one may see me and live."</u>* [21]*The Lord continued, "There is a place near me where you can stand on a rock.* [22]*As my **glory (kâbôwd)** passes by, I will hide you in the crevice of the rock and cover you with my hand until I have passed by.* [23]*Then I will remove my hand and let you see me from behind. But my face will not be seen."* (Exod. 33:19-23 NLT)

The first point to consider is that seeing His Glory (goodness passing before him) will occur simultaneously with *the Lord announcing His name* to Moses. This reveals the *timing* of the encounter; it ends up occurring in Exodus 34:5-7. The passage above is a description of what God was going to do to enable it to happen: There was a rock on top of the mountain, close to where the Lord was dwelling. Moses could stand on this rock hidden between a perfectly sized crevice, enabling the Father to cover Moses with His hand as He approached from the front.

What Moses was about to experience, for his consolation and encouragement, was his first encounter with the splendour in an open display of the Divine Majesty. Not in His *absolute* shining forth, but as much as the weakness of his humanity would allow.

The hand covering and the placement in the crevice of the rock reveals that God toned the glory down to the perfect level of brilliance. The amount Moses was able to witness and still live was the form of the Lord *from behind*. In other words, he could only make out the *outline* of the Father. That is the major facet of beholding His form: to see an outline of His dazzling radiance. This bright glow would stop Moses from seeing specific features clearly, most prominently, His face. The Father's form is illuminated in a garment of pure, uncreated light. In heaven, the features that are most easily distinguishable are those outside of that garment, primarily His hands and feet. Regarding the Father, His mere outline is the greatest weight of glory frail humanity can endure without imploding. Thus beholding His form, like Moses, should be every believer's primary pursuit.

This is what Moses had been waiting for, and he knew that this same *kâbôwd Yĕhovah* (glory of the Lord) would be freely accessible to him once the Ark was set in the Holy of Holies. After this encounter, he would have ample motivation to see this tabernacle project through to completion!

Moses had previously experienced the severity of God within the *dark cloud of glory* on the summit of Sinai, but this only propelled him to pursue something far weightier: *the incandescent cloud of glory*. He had been enveloped in the glory cloud multiple times, yet even after these mighty encounters he was still prompted to ask the Lord: 'show Me your glory'. Moses had become well acquainted with the terror of the Lord, but in this new experience, he was going to be forever changed by beholding the kindness of God as His goodness passed by. From this manifestation of glory there is no turning back! You just want to know Him more and more.

~ Chapter 14 ~

MOSES' DEFINING MOMENT

Moses is now heading up the mountain a fourth time. His first task was to *'chisel out two stone tablets like the first ones'* (Exod. 34:1). He was going to have to carry these heavy stones all the way up the mountain. His 80-year-old muscles must have been bulging by the end of it. Although Moses was busily carving out the tablets, his mind was preoccupied with the thought of reaching that special rock where God would call out His name and pass by in full glory. This intense anticipation must have propelled Moses up the mountain, lugging those burdensome stones.

It didn't take God long to position Moses and then arrive in glorious splendour. The Father had desired this meeting just as much as Moses, if not more.

> *⁵Then the Lord came down in a cloud and stood there with him; and he called out his own name, Yahweh. ⁶The Lord passed in front of Moses* (Exod. 34:5-6a NLT)

God came down in the midst of the cloud, toning down the glory to the level Moses could physically bear. Then He passed by, calling out His name: "Yahweh!"

Moses thought: *"What an unbelievable encounter."* Every fibre of his being was reverberating with the Spirit of the Living God! But Moses got more than he bargained for; the Lord threw a bonus in: the *extended version* of His mighty name:

> *"Yahweh! The Lord! The God of compassion and mercy! I am slow to anger* (longsuffering) *and filled with goodness* (unwavering loyalty) *and truth* (faithfulness). *⁷I lavish unfailing love to a thousand generations. I forgive iniquity, rebellion, and sin* (of the ones who repent). *But I do not excuse the guilty* (those who don't repent). *I lay the sins of the parents upon their children and grandchildren; the entire family is affected— even children in the third and fourth generations."* (Exod. 34:6b-7)

Even to this day, this description is still regarded among the Jews as the 'extended name of God'. The fact that this 'long name' was proclaimed to Moses at the exact same moment he first beheld the glory, reveals the Lord's long name is vitally linked with beholding the form of the Lord. By beholding the aspects that make up WHO HE IS, we see Him AS HE IS. (1 John 3:2)

Therefore, encountering the glory reveals the vital attributes, character and *ways* of God, encapsulated within the kingdom culture we are called to imitate. Through this experience, Moses had two requests fulfilled at the same time. He was shown God's glory (Exod. 33:18), and within the glory he came to an experiential knowledge of *His ways*. This would enable Moses to apprehend the intricacies of the Father's Personality and continue to increase in His favour. (Exod. 33:13)

Thus a figurative definition of 'seeing the Father's outline' or 'beholding the form of the Lord' is; **"Contemplating the depth of His character, becoming tethered to His heartbeat and intimately acquainted with His modes of operation."** This is far more than simply hearing His commands and seeing His actions: It is grasping the 'heart intention' behind His words and the motivation behind everything He does. To use modern terminology, the divine glory is the place where we come to know the Father inside and out, back-to-front.

In response to this, Moses *'Immediately threw himself to the ground and worshiped'* (Exod. 34:8). This brought him to a new level of desperation. This wasn't merely the *shâchâh*, a 'gentle bowing down' as the Israelites had done at the entrance to their tents [when Moses entered His temporary tent of Meeting (Exod. 33:10)]. Moses 'threw himself toward the earth' in worship (*qâdad shâchâh).*

Glistening Glory

When Moses first 'saw the Lord as He is', he encountered 'THE IMMENSE WEIGHT of God's glory'. What were the outward results of entering this realm?

> *"When Moses came down from Mount Sinai with the two tablets of the Testimony in his hand, he did not know that the skin of his face was shining [with a unique radiance] because he had been speaking with God."* (Exod. 34:29 AMP)

After Moses saw the Lord in His incandescent glory, his face was lit-up like a light bulb!

This time 'speaking with God' was different from all previous ones. God was now speaking with Moses out of His *kâbôwd*, not merely His *pânîym*. When Moses came down the mountain for the fourth time, His face was glistening with glory! On every other occasion no such situation had transpired, even though God had been speaking with Moses just as much.

The glory dimension Moses entered impacted those around him through the reflected glory emanating from him. Time spent in the glory will place a glow on us where people, even strangers, can tangibly sense the glory of God emitting out from us. It will embolden them to say; "There's something different about you". Others may fall under the conviction of sin within a certain radius of our physical location. If we want to be light bearers to the world around us, we must experience the Lord as He is.

When Moses came down the mountain, he was not even aware that he was glowing. The response of Aaron and the rest of Israel was to cower backwards in fear (Exod. 34:30). They could not look steadily at the face of Moses. In their stubborn and rebellious heart condition, they rejected the brightness of God's perfect and wholesome radiation. This prevented them from receiving His agape love.

I love Moses' boldness in Exodus 34:31-33. With an unveiled face, he forced Aaron and all the leaders to come over to him while he talked with them. Eventually, they got up the guts to approach. Then Moses listed all the instructions the Lord had given him on Mount Sinai.

Immediately after he finished, Moses then covered his face with a veil to give them some relief from the outstandingly brilliant Majesty of God: What a deplorable situation! Instead of drawing them *into* fellowship, the glory upon Moses was *to them* like insect repellent, pushing them *away* from their heavenly Father. We must ensure we don't develop a sinful, unbelieving heart that turns away from the living God. (Heb. 3:12)

The Apostle Paul wrote in 2 Corinthians 3:7-8

> [7]*if the ministry that brought death, engraved in letters on stone, came with glory, so that the Israelites could not look steadily at the face of Moses because of its glory, fading though it was,* [8]*will not the ministry of the Spirit be even more glorious?*

The ministry Moses brought down from the mountain that day was the 'letter of the law' carved on the stones, and while the letter kills, the Spirit gives life. Shouldn't the ministry of the Holy Spirit given *to us* come with far greater glory?

Therefore, since we have such a hope, we are very bold. We are *not like Moses* who put a veil over his face. On the contrary, as in a mirror we behold and then reflect the Lord's glory (the kâbôwd Yĕhovah) as we are transformed with ever-increasing glory into His image. The Holy Spirit accomplishes this, not our own 'works of human striving' contained within the Mosaic system of Law. (2 Cor. 3:12-18)

You cannot be transformed into the image of one you don't see. In the glory, while beholding the form of the Lord, we are metamorphosed as we become partakers of His divine nature (2 Pet. 1:4). Let me be clear: We are not divine *in* nature; we partake *of* the divine nature. This does not refer to becoming a god or somehow graduating to 'god-status'. It is harmonising with the character of God through the fruits of the Spirit; becoming holy as He is holy (1 Pet. 1:16). When we see Him, we shall become like Him. The divine nature is the antithesis of the sinful nature. Therefore, as we walk in the Spirit, we partake of the divine nature and will not fulfil the lusts of our flesh. That's how we reflect His glory. Through this lifestyle of ever-increasing glory, people see an ambassadorial witness of the attributes of God.

[33]When Moses finished speaking with them, he covered his face with a veil. [34]But whenever he went into the Tent of Meeting to speak with the Lord, he would remove the veil until he came out again. Then he would give the people whatever instructions the Lord had given him, [35]and the people of Israel would see the radiant glow of his face. So he would put the veil over his face until he returned to speak with the Lord. (Exod. 34:33-35 NLT)

The Tent of Meeting mentioned here is still Moses' personal tent set up outside the camp; the one that would prompt the Israelites to stand at the entrances of their own tents and worship the Lord. But check out the radical change that has taken place since Moses saw God's glory. Last time he was in this tent he was pleading with the Lord; "Show me Your Glory!" Now he has it resonating out from his very own face!

Moses could now enter into *his own* 'Tabernacle of David arrangement' and remove the veil from his face, enabling the glory of the Lord to emanate inside. This created a 'Holy of Holies' because Moses' face was being utilised as a substitute for the 'soon to be designed' Ark of the Covenant! At this stage the Ark had not been constructed, so prior to this there had been a vital element missing from Moses' Tent: the Majestic glory of the Lord. Previously Moses only had the dark shroud of the glory (the cloud; the fear of the Lord) with him in the tent, now he also had the incandescent brightness of the Lord's goodness and mercy. By yielding himself as a holy vessel, Moses had personally filled this void through radical devotion. *He was the Ark*; His life shone as a carrier of the glory! This is our mandate in the last days.

For this short transitionary time, Moses' face radiated the glory of the Lord until the actual Tabernacle was built. Moses could live in the Most Holy Place despite the absence of the Ark, and because the glory upon his face was slowly dissipating, this fuelled His desire to complete the epic build in quick time! Now that the glory was resident in Moses' personal tent, we can confidently assert that this was an early foreshadowing of the Tabernacle of David.

Take note, however, that from this time onwards the glory on Moses' face is never mentioned again, as if by perfect divine timing it would fade to nothing just as the Ark was set in place. The fading glory shows us that the Mosaic arrangements were contained within an obsolete covenant destined to disappear with the coming of a much superior one; one that had already been previously established as a promise to Abraham. (Gal. 3:17-18, Heb. 8:13)

The Glory fills the Tabernacle

Throughout Exodus 40, Moses meticulously sets up every detail specifically according to the pattern shown him on the mountain. His final task is found in verse 33: Moses set up the outer courtyard, forming a border around the tabernacle and the Bronze altar of sacrifice. This included a curtain fence held up by posts set in bronze bases, and silver hooks and rings to attach the material. Then there was an outer gate;

> [18]*He made the curtain for the entrance to the courtyard of finely woven linen, and he decorated it with beautiful embroidery in blue, purple, and scarlet thread. It was 30 feet long, and its height was 7 1/2 feet, just like the curtains of the courtyard walls.* (Exod. 38:18 NLT)

Everything was now set in its rightful place; *'So at last Moses finished the work.'* (Exod. 40:33 NLT)

Next is the fulfilment of the Lord's promise given to Moses;

> [34] *Then <u>the cloud</u> covered the Tabernacle, and the <u>glory of the Lord</u> filled the Tabernacle.* [35] *Moses could no longer enter the Tabernacle because **<u>the cloud had settled</u>** down over it, and the <u>glory of the Lord</u> filled the Tabernacle.* (Exod. 40:34-35 NLT)

Bursting forth from the top of the Ark was the glory of the Lord, the very same *kâbôwd Yĕhovah* Moses had encountered on the mountaintop. The cloud also came in and *settled.* Nestled between the shadows of the winged Cherubim, and the Atonement Cover became the *permanent* dwelling of the divine glory of God! After a short while, the cloudy element lifted, leaving only bright illumination. Then what God had promised Moses way back in Exodus 25:22 became a reality;

> *Whenever Moses went into the Tabernacle to speak with the Lord, he heard the voice speaking to him from between the two cherubim above the Ark's cover—the place of atonement—that rests on the Ark of the Covenant. The Lord spoke to him from there.* (Num. 7:89 NLT)

Moses had his dream fulfilled; obtaining access behind the veil to commune with the Father between the Cherubim at the footstool of His mercy seat. Just like King David, full access to the *kâbôwd Yĕhovah* was at his disposal any time he pleased. There was a stark contrast, however. Under Moses' leadership, God locked everyone else out of the glory and sadly, they would never worship Him again (Exod. 33:10). They no longer worshiped at the entrances of their tents, exchanging this life-giving practice for the dead ritualistic duties of the Law. The only person who benefited from the Mosaic Covenant being officially set up and ratified was the only one *not placed under it.* Moses the mediator, had life and life more abundantly while the rest were installed into the ministry of condemnation (2 Cor. 3:9, John 10:10). Thanks be to Jesus Christ our Lord: He has redeemed us from the curse of the latter and grafted us into the former.

~ Chapter 15 ~

GLORY IN THE WILDERNESS WANDERINGS

The Divine Glory next appears in Leviticus 9: It ventures outside the Holy of Holies in the form of fire that came from the presence of the Lord and burned up the animal sacrifices presented to Aaron (v23-24). This showed God's approval of all the various offerings he had explained in the previous chapters of Leviticus. This momentous event occurred on the 8th day subsequent to Aaron's inauguration as High Priest, the seven days of his consecration were now over. To show everyone that this new divine service was acceptable to Him, God once again produced a 'tangible sign' on the eighth day as a witness to the people. The fire was another appearance of the consuming element of God's glory, representing His divine wrath against sin; the same fire that Elijah called down on top of Mount Carmel (1 Kings 18:38). There can be no doubt: Our God is a consuming fire! (Exod. 24:17, Heb. 12:29)

Glory in the Midst of Rebellion

Even though the Israelites had complained and grumbled many times prior, the first *major* rebellion was the golden calf incident. After Moses sprung them amid their pagan revelry, he had to intercede for the people because God was going to wipe them out! You may recall that he used two points of intercession: The first was that God would be made a laughingstock among the nations if He did all those miracles to free them as slaves from Egypt, only to annihilate them in the desert. Second, Moses called upon the Covenant oath sworn to the Patriarchs, who were long dead. God would be breaking his promise to them.

The second major rebellion against God and Moses was the incident with Miriam and Aaron from Numbers 12. The glory came to the entrance of the tabernacle and the 'judgement side' of glory fell on Miriam in the form of leprosy. God told Miriam that Moses beheld the form of the Lord, so she should be very careful in criticising him. If Moses was displeasing the Lord, he would have dropped dead in the midst of the glory long ago.

In the third major rebellion against God and his servant Moses, found in Numbers 14, the *kâbôwd Yĕhovah* is mentioned again. This occurred during the fallout in the aftermath of the twelve tribal elders being sent to spy out the Promised Land. After ten of the spies brought back a negative scouting report, the people staged a mass protest against Moses and Aaron. They decided to choose a new leader and go back to slavery in Egypt. Joshua and Caleb, the other two spies, tried to deter the people from their plan by speaking positively about their chances of taking the land with the Lord's help. But when the people heard their advice, they decided they would stone them to death!

In this moment, God became enraged, utterly fed up with their impenetrable stubbornness and blatant unbelief. The instant the stone collecting began, *the glory of the Lord* appeared around the Tabernacle in a manner they could all perceive. As Moses set off toward the glory, everything else immediately came to a grinding halt and you could hear a pin drop.

> *[11]And the Lord said to Moses, "How long will these people treat me with contempt? Will they never believe me, even after all the miraculous signs I have done among them? [12]I will disown them and destroy them with a plague. Then I will make you into a nation greater and mightier than they are!* (Num. 14:11-12 NLT)

This is the second time God is about to destroy Israel and make a new nation out of Moses! Once again, the servant of all God's house (Heb. 3:5) will have to stand in the gap and intercede, but he'd better come up with a more compelling argument than last time. God is even more ticked off on this occasion. Fortunately for Moses, he has new ammunition in his belt. He'll use that last, but first he'll stick to his previous formula. Moses objected;

> *"What will the Egyptians think when they hear about it?" he asked the Lord. "They know full well the power you displayed in rescuing your people from Egypt. [14]Now if you destroy them, the Egyptians will send a report to the inhabitants of this land, who have already heard that you live among your people. They know, Lord, that you have appeared to your people face to face and that your pillar of cloud hovers over them. They know that you go before them in the pillar of cloud by day and the pillar of fire by night. [15]Now if you slaughter all these people with a single blow, the nations that have heard of your fame will say, [16]"The Lord was not able to bring them into the land he swore to give them, so he killed them in the wilderness."* (Num. 14:13-16 NLT)

It is sad to comprehend what Moses says to the Lord here. He reminds God that He appeared to *all of Israel* face-to-face. If you recall, this incident occurred straight after Moses' first ascent when God descended the mountain in Exodus 19 and 20. But this was not the *pâniym* 'face to face' that Moses encountered on a daily basis. This is more accurately translated 'eye to eye' (`*ayin*) which is entry-level exposure to God. It leads towards face-to-face, if we desire to go deeper. 'Eye to eye' represents an initial contact or initial greeting, so to speak. They all *figuratively* made 'first eye contact' with God, and once their eyes had met, they immediately ran the other way. The people didn't want to hear God anymore, and told Moses to speak with God on their behalf. How heartbreaking for God that all but two people (Moses and Joshua) rejected face-to-face conversation with the Lord? (Exod. 20:18-19)

In Moses' opening argument, he implements a repeat of the; 'you're gonna look bad' strategy that he used back at Mount Sinai. This was a reasonable start; a good sounding argument that had been previously effective, but he needs even more evidence to avert the Lord's fury. Now, in this second attempt at convincing God to relent from destroying the people, Moses musters up a new appeal. This time, he does not mention God's promises to the Patriarchs. This had probably worn thin on God, who requires *obedience* to the Covenant, not mere lip-service.

A covenant agreement contains terms that have to be met in order to activate the Promises found within them. Had Moses tried the 'promises made to the Patriarchs' strategy a second time God probably would have echoed the words of John the Baptist years later, *"Produce fruit in keeping with repentance. <u>And do not think that by saying, 'We have Abraham as our father',</u> that makes everything ok. Out of these stones I can raise up children for Abraham. The axe is laid at the root of the trees, and every tree that does not produce good fruit will be cut down and thrown into the fire."* (Matt. 3:9-10)

Thankfully, Moses is one step ahead of last time. As he brings his new proposal to the Lord, he appeals to God's very own attributes; the character he has come to know all too well. Below is my paraphrase;

> *"Lord, when you passed by and showed me Your glory, you revealed to me your 'long name'. Now I am intimately acquainted with your ways, nature and attributes, and this course of action does not line up with them! Remember that you contain love that cannot fail? That you are long-suffering, slow to anger, full of tender-loving mercy, and willing to*

forgive sin and iniquity? Therefore, based on Your own declaration, you can't do this!" (Num. 14:18-19)

Moses essentially quotes back to God His long name word-for-word, and this actually backs God into a corner. He says, "Prove that your Name is as great as you have claimed by holding to the integrity of Who you are" (V17). Moses had seen God in all His glory, and he now knew His ways. This depth of relationship gave him *extra leverage in prayer*! God is no respecter of persons: It will be no different with any of us. Do you want to have the ability to move God in the secret place? Then pursue Him until you see Him in all His glory, then be transformed into the image of that glory. This is what God means when He says;

> *To those who by persistence in doing good <u>seek glory</u>, honour and immortality, he will give eternal life.* (Rom. 2:7)

This is not seeking to take the glory away from God and receive it unto ourselves. It is seeking to be changed into his glorious image, to be carriers and reflectors of His glory. It is the cry of Moses; "Show me your glory!" Such people will glorify the Lord, not themselves.

The Lord can do nothing but respond with; "I will pardon them as you have requested". God cannot send the plague to kill everyone and stay consistent with Who He is. Isn't that comforting? He is the soothing Balm of Gilead; restorative mercy poured like warm oil upon the wounds of disobedient, obstinate people. In His long-suffering nature, it takes a mighty amount of stubbornness on our part before God ceases His relentless pursuit for the allegiance of our heart. But let us never forget to thank the Lord for His intercessors, the faithful warriors who cry out for our souls day and night!

Having said all that, we should consider that the Lord also clarifies that their rebellion comes with a severe price-tag. Although not destroyed, none of them will set foot inside the Promised Land. They will all die scattered over the wilderness. They won't be struck dead, but they will die never attaining the promises of God for their lives. If they never repent of their wickedness and turn back to God, they will end up being thrown into the fire. No one ever gets away with deliberate disobedience scot-free.

²⁰Then the Lord said, "I will pardon them as you have requested. ²¹But as surely as I live, and as surely as the earth is filled <u>with the Lord's glory</u>, ²²not one of these people will ever enter that land. <u>They have all seen my glorious presence and the miraculous signs I performed both in Egypt and in the wilderness,</u> but again and again they have tested me by refusing to listen to my voice. ²³They will never even see the land I swore to give their ancestors. None of those who have treated me with contempt will ever see it." (Num. 14:20-23 NLT)

Experiencing proximity to the glory of God and seeing all His miracles actually increased their level of accountability for their actions. Those who have never known God or seen Him move are given greater mercy because they are acting in ignorance and unbelief. (1 Tim 1:13)

Two chapters later the glory of the Lord appears to judge the tents of Korah, Dathan and Abiram in their attempt to take over the priesthood from Aaron. This was the fourth rebellion against Moses' leadership. In another vengeful display of God's glory, the earth swallowed the men involved, and they fell directly into the pit of hell under the earth. (Num. 16)

◊◊◊◊◊

The last time Moses experiences the *kâbôwd Yĕhovah* in public is a sad occasion. Miriam had just died, and Moses was probably grieving her loss. Now there was a water shortage for the second time (Num. 20:1-13). Even though Moses had struck a rock back at Mount Sinai with miraculous results (Exod. 17), the people once again complain and grumble against him. They come up with their usual gripes, stating that the food and water they had back in Egypt gave them a better quality of life. Longing to return, they conveniently forget about the intense oppression, crushing labour, and excruciating whippings they were subjected to under conditions of extreme slavery.

In the midst of the glory, Moses is commanded to *speak* to the Rock, but in an act of direct disobedience he *struck* the Rock a second time. 1 Corinthians 10:4 reveals that the Rock that travelled with them was Christ. Moses struck Christ twice prophetically, when Jesus was only to be struck dead once, never to die again. The death He died, He died to sin 'once for all'; but the life He now lives, he lives to God (Rom. 6:10). Here is God's reply;

¹²But the Lord said to Moses and Aaron, "Because you did not trust me enough to demonstrate my holiness to the people of Israel, you will not lead them into the land I am giving them! (Num. 20:12 NLT)

Because of his presumptuous actions, Moses, along with his brother Aaron, were not permitted to enter the Promised Land. They would perish just outside the boundary of Israel's promise! Be careful how you respond when the glory shows up. No presumption will be tolerated, not even for the 'head-honcho'. We want the glory, but *do we really* want the glory? I know I do, I will pay whatever price is necessary. Will you?

~ Chapter 16 ~

POST TABERNACLE GLORY

When King Solomon completed the epic task of constructing the first temple, the Lord Almighty finally had a permanent house where His glory could abide. Solomon built the Temple according to the specific plans laid out by His father David. It had been *David's* heart-desire from his youth to find the specific geographical location where God destined the Ark to rest and remain. (Ps. 132:1-5)

King David had longed to see this monumental task completed during his lifetime. Even after bringing the Ark into Zion, David felt a sense of unworthiness because he was living inside a majestic palace while the Ark of the Covenant sat outside in a humble tent (2 Sam 7:2). But God didn't seem to mind at all;

> *Are you the one to build a house for me to live in?* *⁶I have never lived in a house, from the day I brought the Israelites out of Egypt until this very day. I have always moved from one place to another with a tent and a Tabernacle as my dwelling. ⁷Yet no matter where I have gone with the Israelites, I have never once complained to Israel's tribal leaders, the shepherds of my people Israel. I have never asked them, "Why haven't you built me a beautiful cedar house?"* (2 Sam 7:5b-7 NLT)

> *From the time I brought Israel out of Egypt until today I have not lived in a house; instead, I have moved from tent to tent and from tabernacle to tabernacle.* (1 Chr. 17:5 HCSB)

There were no complaints from God here. He was delighted with the unhindered access He had to the people while stationed in David's Tabernacle. The Lord knew that when a permanent house was built, access to His glory would be denied once again because the Ark would return *behind the veil*. For that reason, God was making the most of this remarkable season of 'the coming New Covenant Age' that David was operating under.

What David thought was offending God actually pleased Him! In Psalm 132, we find out that David's desire as a young boy had been to find a dwelling place for the Mighty One of Jacob: the God of Israel. Little did he know, by installing the tent on Zion, he had fulfilled this vow in God's sight. The oath

David swore was to provide a 'dwelling place' (Hebrew: mishkân) for the Lord (Psalm 132:2), not a 'house' (Hebrew: bayith). The tent David set up by God's direction had actualised the promise without him even realising it. Mount Zion, the mountain of the Lord, will always be known as God's chosen 'dwelling place' (Ps. 132:13). He proved this to David by acknowledging through the prophet Nathan that He was more than happy with the current setup. It is clear; although God is the lofty One of Heaven, He doesn't mind camping with the lowly upon the earth.

But God wasn't finished there. Not only did He deny David the honour of setting Him up in a majestically adorned Temple, He went on to promise David an even higher blessing than his current palace arrangement;

> *"I took you from tending sheep in the pasture and selected you to be the leader of my people Israel. [9]I have been with you wherever you have gone, and I have destroyed all your enemies before your eyes. Now I will make your name as famous as anyone who has ever lived on the earth...""Furthermore, the LORD declares that <u>he will make a house for you—a dynasty of kings!</u>"* (2 Sam 7:8b-9,11b NLT)

Hang on a minute: David already lives in a luxurious cedar palace, and yet God is promising Him *another house?* King David thought living in the palace was already far too elaborate considering the state of the Ark's humble surroundings, but now God says; *"Forget the palace, that's only the beginning of my blessings. I have even more favour to pour out on you than that: <u>a royal throne that will live on for endless generations!</u>"* The ultimate fulfilment of this promise would come when One of David's own descendants would come to earth as Messiah and be crowned to sit upon His throne eternally, never to be removed.

> *"Furthermore, the Lord declares that he will make a house for you—a dynasty of kings! [12]For when you die and are buried with your ancestors, I will raise up one of your descendants, your own offspring, and I will make his kingdom strong. [13]He is the one who will build a house—a temple—for my name. And I will secure his royal throne forever. [14]<u>I will be his father, and he will be my son</u>. If he sins, I will correct and discipline him with the rod, like any father would do. [15]But my favour will not be taken from him as I took it from Saul, whom I removed from*

your sight. [16]Your house and your kingdom will continue before me for all time, and your throne will be secure forever." (2 Sam 7:11b-16 NLT)

The underlined section above is quoted in Hebrews 1:5b, proving Nathan is referring prophetically to Jesus. Then we find the pivotal moment of the coronation ceremony in Psalm 2:6-7;

[6]"As for me, I have <u>set my King on Zion</u>, my holy hill." [7]I will tell of the decree: The Lord said to me, "You are my Son; today I have begotten you." (ESV)

There is a double application to what God told David in 2 Samuel 7 above, just as there is for the passage in Psalm 2. Both sets of scripture refer to Jesus Christ, but also to David's son Solomon, who would take the throne after David's death. He would be the one to build a *permanent house* for God to dwell in. Once God's Temple was completed, temporary earthly tabernacles would be a thing of the past. From this moment on, the Ark would no longer travel. In fact, God's intention was for the Ark to remain in this Holy of Holies, never to be taken out again. It would not be like the days in the wilderness or the early conquests in the Promised Land, where the Ark would be removed from the tabernacle to lead a procession causing the walls of a fortified city to crash to the ground. Nor would it be used to supernaturally cross the overflowing banks of a rushing river (Josh 3:11-16). It was intended that the Ark would remain a fixed object inside the Oracle; the Most Holy Place built by Solomon.

The Temple is built on Mount Moriah

King Solomon brought the Ark of the Lord's Covenant from its location in the City of David, placing it in the Temple of God built on the threshing floor of Araunah the Jebusite on Mount Moriah (1 Chr. 21:18-22:1, 1 Kin. 8:1-10). In 1 Kings 7:51, the Bible says;

So King Solomon finished all his work on the Temple of the Lord. Then he brought all the gifts his father, David, had dedicated—the silver, the gold, and the various articles—and he stored them in the treasuries of the Lord's Temple. (NLT)

From here, the final step was to transport the Ark across from Mount Zion to Mount Moriah.

⁶Then the priests carried the Ark of the Lord's Covenant into the inner sanctuary of the Temple—the Most Holy Place—and placed it beneath the wings of the cherubim. ⁷The cherubim spread their wings over the Ark, forming a canopy over the Ark and its carrying poles...¹⁰When the priests came out of the Holy Place, <u>a thick cloud</u> filled the Temple of the Lord, so that the priests could not <u>stand</u> to minister because of the cloud, for the <u>glory of the Lord</u> filled the house of the Lord. (1 Kin. 8:6-7, 10-11 NLT, NASB)

When King Solomon placed the Ark inside the Holiest of All, the *kâbôwd Yĕhovah* came and enveloped the Temple as a glory cloud in almost identical fashion to what had occurred for Moses when he placed the Ark inside his tabernacle back in Exodus 40:34-35. But there is one extra detail at Solomon's Temple that was not mentioned back in Moses' tent. The Scripture says that the priests could not *stand* to minister. In Hebrew, this word means 'to take a stand', or 'to remain standing'. The priests could not remain in a standing position; they fell to the ground under the intensity of the glory of the Lord! This is proof that being slain in the Spirit is in the Bible. While I don't condone people falling down for anything and everything, I believe there are times when our knees will bend and our legs will buckle under the weight of His glory. Sometimes God needs to do a deep work that requires us to be knocked out in the Spirit, so that our fleshly appetites, carnal minds and human logic doesn't fight against or block the transformative work the Lord wants to perform. Once again, we must take the Bible at face value. Our mortal flesh cannot stand up under the weight of the magnificent splendour of the Glory of God.

Solomon's response to this powerful display of God's majesty is startling. He prayed;

"O LORD, you have said that you would live in a thick <u>cloud of darkness</u>. ¹³Now I have built a glorious Temple for you, a place where you can live forever!" (1 Kin. 8:12-13 NLT)

Solomon declares that the cloud he was seeing was a *dark cloud*. The brightness of the *kâbôwd Yĕhovah* was shielded by the darkness of the cloud surrounding it. Just like at Mount Sinai, where Moses first passed through the dark cloud of glory, before experiencing the Father's bright glory *inside* the cloud. The International Standard Version translates Solomon's prayer this way; *"The Lord has said that he lives <u>shrouded in darkness</u>."* This is the truth: To get to God's *incandescent rays of glory* we must first penetrate the *dark shroud of His glory.*

Double Glory

From here, King Solomon spoke a blessing over the entire congregation of Israel. Then he stood up on a bronze platform he had constructed in the centre of the outer courtyard to give the official prayer of dedication. Before he could utter a word, he found himself on his knees in adoration toward God. This is the conclusion of his Holy Spirit inspired prayer;

> [40] *"O my God, may your eyes be open and your ears attentive to all the prayers made to you in this place.* [41] *"And now arise, O Lord God, and enter your resting place, along with the Ark, the symbol of your power. May your priests, O Lord God, be clothed with salvation; may your loyal servants rejoice in your goodness.* [42] *O Lord God, do not reject the king you have anointed. Remember your unfailing love for your servant David."* (2 Chr. 6:40:42 NLT)

When Solomon finished praying, this time 'fire flashed down from heaven and burned up the burnt offerings and sacrifices, and the glory of the Lord filled the Temple *again,* so that the Priests could not enter once more because the *kâbôwd Yĕhovah* had filled it.' (2 Chr. 7:1-3)

The fire which burned up the offerings and sacrifices was the same as Leviticus 9, where the Lord's Divine Glory appeared outside the tabernacle in blazing fire to burn up the animal sacrifices presented by Aaron. This is the fire that, along with the dark cloud, brings the fear of the Lord through the consideration of His severity and His wrath against sin. It is the holy fire of His disciplinary love; a fire that purges and purifies the saints, refining them for faithful devotion unto the Lord. This process makes us acceptable to enter through the shroud into the brightness, experiencing Him in fullness.

Thus the post-tabernacle, pre-Messiah era of glory had arrived. God affirmed the Temple as a vital and necessary advancement under the dispensation of law that was to remain in operation till the coming of the Chosen One. The Mosaic Covenant had to continue as a guardian of the infant human race, functioning as a tutor or schoolmaster, leading us into the grace of Christ at His appointed time. (Gal. 3:24-25, 4:4, John 1:17)

We do see prophetic signs, however, of the limited scope of this new arrangement. Access behind the veil was now denied to the everyday commoner among Israel. The tabernacle of David had now fallen down, waiting to be rebuilt in these last days. It wouldn't be long before the king and all the people with him would drift away from intimacy with God and the prosperity garnered under the kingship of David would slowly disintegrate. The barring of access from the Holy of Holies would affect Solomon in a greater measure than he ever imagined.

There are signs of this in 1 Kings 8:9. It states:

"Nothing was in the Ark except the two stone tablets that Moses had placed in it at Mount Sinai, where the Lord made a covenant with the people of Israel when they left the land of Egypt." (NLT)

The only thing that remained in the Ark was the item that symbolised the Law of Moses and all its arrangements. Where did the other two items go which we find mentioned in Hebrews 9:5? Solomon seemed pretty confident in the decision to leave them out;

"I have built this Temple to honour the name of the Lord, the God of Israel. [21]And I have prepared a place there for the Ark, which contains the covenant that the Lord made with our ancestors when he brought them out of Egypt." (1 Kin. 8:20b-21 NLT)

First, the Rod of Aaron that budded was not in there. This was prophetic of the fact that the fruitfulness of the Holy Spirit under David's Tabernacle had now been removed from the people's grasp.

Second, the gold jar containing the supernaturally preserved manna was missing. The lack of daily manna signified the lack of the prophetic rhēma of God. They had preserved the written Scriptures of the Torah, but the flow of rhēma revelation found on Mount Zion was immediately halted. The Word of God was no longer alive and active in them, except for a few prophecies here and there. For the majority, experiential worship and hearing His voice from an intimate closeness had been abolished. Being banished from His glorious presence, they were escorted once again into the dead religion of distant onlookers.

◇◇◇◇◇

The Spirit of prophecy testifies of Jesus (Rev. 19:10). Now you can see why the Jewish people lacked pure prophetic anticipation for the true form of their Coming Messiah. They began to operate out of their own humanistic ideas according to their natural reasoning, comprehension and logic. On the whole there was a lack of Spirit-inspired insight into who He was designated to be and why He was to come. There were however, a few exceptions such as Isaiah the prophet and Simeon, a devout man of prayer. Both of these men knew the Messiah had to come first as a suffering servant (Is 52:13-53:12, Luke 2:25-35).

Jesus Christ, the embodiment of the Ark in human form, was soon to announce Himself on the world stage. The Ark was nearing its final days of relevance. Less than 400 years after Solomon's death, the Babylonians would come to ransack Jerusalem and pillage the temple. The Lord raised up the prophet Jeremiah during these final generations of the first temple period, and he spoke the word of the Lord, saying;

> *When you multiply and increase in the land, in those days—this is the Lord's declaration—no one will say again, "The ark of the Lord's covenant." It will never come to mind, and no one will remember or miss it. Another one will not be made.* (Jer. 3:16 CSB)

Jeremiah prophesied that a time was coming when no one would mourn the loss of the Ark, for the true Ark of God would be set in true holy places: the hearts of men and women in the New Covenant! There would be no sad feelings; no one would regret its loss! Neither would a new one ever be made.

Nebuchadnezzar took all the furnishings, articles and treasures from the Temple of God, yet he never got his hands on the Ark. It had strangely gone missing before his armies arrived. In the Apocrypha, 2 Maccabees 2:4-5 indicates that Jeremiah, knowing that the Babylonians were coming soon to destroy Jerusalem, took the Ark along with the tent and the Altar of Incense and hid them in a cave dug into a mountain. The Ark has never been seen since. Whether there is any end-time significance of the original Ark being discovered as a sign and wonder to the world, we don't know. One thing is for sure; according to Jeremiah, a new one will certainly not be made!

The removal of the Ark from the public eye does not insinuate that the glory disappeared with it. On the contrary, with the tearing of the veil, the glory has now been released upon us: His children; regenerated and renewed by the Holy Spirit. We are portable Tabernacles of God's glory, spread across the entire planet to reflect the glory of the Lord in the face of Jesus Christ. (2 Cor. 4:6)

A New Temple for Jerusalem

After 70 years of exile in Babylon, it was hard for the Jewish people to believe that the former glory of Solomon's Temple would ever be restored in fullness. In fact, when the returning exiles completed the foundation of the *second* temple, many of the older Priests, Levites and other leaders who had seen Solomon's Temple wept out loud. The drabness and sparsity of this site did not compare with the wealth and grandeur of the original (Ezra 3:12, Hag. 2:3).

Immediately after this foundation was laid, the builders caved in to opposition, abandoning the project. So God sent the prophets Haggai and Zechariah to give them a holy 'kick in the butt', encouraging them to get back to the task at hand. Haggai told them they were putting their wages into pockets with holes because they were building fine houses for themselves while saying; *"The time has not yet come to rebuild the house of the Lord"*. They were prioritising their own houses over God's Temple, so they were suffering with lacklustre harvests. (Hag. 1:5-6 NLT)

But along with this rebuke came a most glorious promise to those who would divert their attention back to the Temple and finish the divine project. Haggai said, by God's Spirit;

> [6] *"For this is what the Lord of Heaven's Armies says: In just a little while I will again shake the heavens and the earth, the oceans and the dry land.* [7] *I will shake all the nations, and the <u>treasures of all the nations will be brought to this Temple</u>. I will fill this place with glory, says the Lord of Heaven's Armies.* [8] *The silver is mine, and the gold is mine, says the Lord of Heaven's Armies.* [9] *<u>The future glory of this Temple will be greater than its past glory</u>, says the Lord of Heaven's Armies. And in this*

place I will bring peace. I, the Lord of Heaven's Armies, have spoken!"
(Hag. 2:6-9 NLT)

Haggai promises that *the glory* of the latter house will be greater than the former. But it was not the glory of the materials and the expensive commodities used. History tells us that no building in Jerusalem has ever come close to comparing with the expenditure utilised by Solomon on the first temple. The glory *inside* the second temple would be greater than the first one, not the outer glory of the physical structure itself. Material opulence is no match for majestic glory. For surely the glory Haggai is referring to is the *kâbôwd Yĕhovah.*

If there was no Ark ever placed inside the second Temple, how then could there ever be greater glory than the previous structure which had the glory shining forth from the mercy seat? This prophecy was fulfilled by none other than Jesus Himself: As a twelve-year-old boy He remained back at the temple, sitting with the scribes and asking them questions. He also confounded them with the depth of His insight and answers. (Luke 2:46-47)

◊◊◊◊◊

Later in His adult years, the Son of God would *teach* inside the temple complex. You couldn't get greater glory than that! Now One greater than Solomon's Temple was here! (Matt 12:6, 42) Jesus would also clear the temple grounds of the defilement that was preventing this Haggai prophecy from being fully accomplished. *The 'treasures of all nations' being brought into the Temple* in Haggai 2:7 represented all the different ethnic groups who were meant to come and participate in 'the house of prayer *for all nations*.' (Isa. 56:6-7)

> *Jesus would not allow anyone to <u>carry merchandise</u> through the temple courts. [17]And as he taught them, he said, 'Is it not written: "My house will be called a house of prayer for all nations"? But you have made it "a den of robbers".* (Mark 11:17)

The 'treasure' in Haggai's prophecy was supposed to be the Gentiles and their prayers, yet at this time the ground plan of Herod's Temple restricted the Gentiles from approaching anywhere near the temple. The place where they were supposed to be allowed to come and pray was occupied by moneychangers who had turned the Father's house into a marketplace (John 2:16, 2 Cor. 2:17). They were preventing the true treasures; people created in God's image, from coming into the Temple grounds. Instead, they used this area to peddle profit off of their own people through inflated exchange rates and ridiculously expensive merchandise, which they forced their Jewish brothers and sisters to purchase for sacrifice. They did not allow them to bring their own animals to the Lord, even though this was clearly permitted in the LOM.

Haggai 2:9 is a promise for us individually as well. The glory of our latter days in life will be greater than our former days of youth. If we progress faithfully towards maturity in the Lord we are guaranteed to see this come to pass in our own personal lives.

But the corporate, end-time application for the Body of Christ is even more exciting! The glory upon believers at the time of the end will exceed that of the church in the Book of Acts. Sounds too good to be true, but here it is, prophesied in Habakkuk 2:14;

> *For the earth shall be filled with the knowledge of the glory of the Lord,*
> *as the waters cover the sea* (KJV)

There has never been such a widespread display of God's glory prepared for people on earth. This will happen right before the end of the age as *"the gospel of the kingdom is preached as a testimony to all nations!"* (Matt 24:14)

The glory of the Lord will spread further and wider than ever before because the gospel will penetrate society *beyond the four walls of the churches*, passing through the market square into all spheres of influence.

No longer will we rely on dragging people into an official church gathering to see them encounter the Lord. There will be God-encounters in the midst of all the mind-moulders of culture; the very same places where Mystery Babylon is attempting to take her seat (Rev. 17:9). The Lord will show up through His people with a demonstration of the superiority of *His* kingdom over the world system. This will build a platform conducive to evangelism: the gospel of salvation.

This is how the masses will enter the kingdom in the final great ingathering of souls. It is revival at the grassroots level. No longer will the select few at the top do all the heavy lifting, such as the mega-evangelist, or healing crusader. It will be everyday Christians each engaged in their own kingdom calling, strategically partnering together where necessary. No one will be a dormant spectator. There will be spot fires of revival breaking forth everywhere, and they will culminate and join into one big bushfire by the winds of the Holy Spirit.

A Word of Warning

Some people are drawn to the 'seven mountain message' (spreading the gospel throughout all spheres of society) with wrong motives. It can entice and draw people who have an idol of fame or greed. Therefore, it gets a bad name. Itching ears love the message, but it is the elect (the pure and undefiled remnant) who will be successful; those who seek the Lord and not a name for themselves. When you are invited to a wedding feast, take the *lowest place*, and if God wants to promote you to a higher seat, He will. (Luke 14:7-11)

The pure of heart, the humble and the lowly will be used in mighty ways. Too many fall off course by pursuing a title. Jesus said; *"The kings of the Gentiles Lord it over them, and those who exercise authority love to be called by a special title of honour. But you are not to be like that."* (Luke 22:25)

When it's truly God's time to send people out into the mountains of influence, they will have been through the fiery furnace and matured enough to know that this world can give them nothing. Following after what the world can offer is nothing more than an unsatisfying letdown. Without this balance in our teaching, we are setting people up for failure.

~ Chapter 17 ~

SYNONYMS FOR THE GLORY OF YAHWEH

We don't actually find the word Shekinah in our Holy Bible; it appears only in later Rabbinic literature. The Semitic root from which Shekinah is derived means "to settle, inhabit, or dwell". That's why the Rabbi's added this word to *kâbôwd* to describe the glory that dwelt permanently upon the Ark of the Covenant when it lay in the Holy of Holies. The Shekinah, then, is the place of God's *habitation.* While in proximity to the Shekinah, the connection to God is more readily perceivable. This is the pinnacle of the New Covenant, cohabiting with the Father. This glory realm is not merely a visitation from God; it is the Lord 'settling in' as He makes his home among us. Jesus said;

> *If anyone [really] loves Me, he will keep My word (teaching); and My Father will love him, and We will come to him and make <u>Our dwelling place</u> with him.* (John 14:23 AMP)

Like Shekinah, this is a 'permanent abode'. We are invited to become the habitation of the Father and the Son. The Spirit of God wants to settle on us just as the dove settled on Jesus *and remained* from the point of His water baptism onwards. This is the sevenfold Spirit of God, the fullness of the Holy Spirit, which can only operate from within the confines of the glory of the Father. The Lamb embodies these seven spirits, and the Holy Spirit takes from what is His (John 16:15). This is a powerful example of the Godhead working in perfect synchronisation.

The presence of the Holy Spirit is what we all receive at salvation when He takes up residence *inside us*. This is the Spirit which abides *in us* forever. From this place we can enter a face-to-face relationship with the Lord, where the Holy Spirit as our Teacher, Comforter and Counsellor leads us into all truth (John 14:15-17, 16:13). As stated previously, it is face to face relationship on the *conversation* level, not the visual level. Beholding only occurs in the glory-level.

The next level comes in receiving the baptism of the Holy Spirit, which is the anointing or 'power' of the Spirit *upon us*. Christ means Anointed One, and that's why Jesus is the baptizer in the Holy Spirit (John 1:33). Through this equipping God empowers us with gifts of the Spirit, and these come upon us for a reason and for a season. The anointing of the Spirit comes onto us and then lifts off until it is required next. In these times of co-labouring with God, He is using us as a vessel; we are pouring out from ourselves and exerting effort.

The glory of the Father is the *settling* of the fullness of the Holy Spirit *in our midst*: the operation of the seven spirits of God. This is experienced when the Divine Glory envelops and 'inhabits' a certain location. When the glory shows up, the Father and His angelic host take over! You have surely heard of the saying; "all hell is breaking loose". When the Father's Glory invades a setting and transforms it into His habitation "all heaven breaks loose!" Instead of everything bad happening, everything good happens! When the father arrives in glory, must yield to Him, laying down our own plans and agendas, allowing the fullness of God's Spirit to flow as we surrender to the weight of the magnificent glory.

Unlike operating under the anointing, when the glory falls we don't have to do anything. This can happen during times of worship, prayer, or even during the preaching of the Word. In this realm, we may still be used as a mouthpiece to convey what God is doing in the atmosphere *as He moves sovereignly*. A preacher or teacher may continue to speak their message while the glory of the Father arrives in unusual and enthralling demonstrations; or even as He moves throughout the congregation, unveiling Himself to individuals and imparting according to His will. The important thing is to flow with what God wants to do.

In the glory, we must be prepared to experience varying kinds of weird and wonderful manifestations, for they are arriving express post from the heavenly realm. It is the invasion of the heaven's atmosphere with slices of heaven touching down on earth. Those who carry a religious spirit will find it hard to accept some of these intriguing phenomena, but we must embrace what originates from the glory of God, irrespective of how it challenges our logical mindsets.

Having said all that, we should always fix our eyes on the Father rather than seeking manifestations themselves. This type of dangerous behaviour is why many moves of God begin to dissipate just as they are gaining momentum. By yielding to the fickleness of human nature, people take their eyes off of the

Lord and get caught up pursuing mystical phenomena instead of the Father. This gives access to deceiving spirits who will pollute the supernatural move of the Spirit. God forbid we convert the manifestations of His glory into a tourist attraction!

Building upon One Another

It is important to note that these three levels of relationship with God do not replace each other. Like a three story building, each floor builds upon the previous. We all begin our journey with salvation level *pânîym*—the presence of the Holy Spirit. But when we are endued with power from on high (Luke 24:47) the presence of the Holy Spirit is not subtracted; the Lord simply adds the anointing of the Son onto us. As we seek Him at a deeper level by dying to self and making Him and His calling our major focus in life, we build up to the top level; the habitation of the Father manifested through the magnificence of His Glory.

This is not experiencing the Father *only*: In His glory, we have the *entire* Godhead in active fellowship with us! In the midst of His weighty presence or 'kâbôwd', we enter all three manifestations and become enamoured, captivated, and perhaps even undone by the illustriousness of all three Persons in the Trinity.

Initially, we are given the *presence* of the Holy Spirit, followed by the *anointing* of the Holy Spirit, but in the glory we partake of 'Holy Spirit fullness'. In the first realm, the Holy Spirit is predominant. In the second, the Spirit and the Son are active participants. And whilst abiding in the third, we discover the full majesty: the Spirit, the Son, *and the Father*. This is why the Ark, 'the seat of His glory', is a type of Christ, whom Paul refers to in Colossians 2:9 as: "the fullness of the Godhead bodily".

The Magnificent Glory

Distinguishing ordinary earthly glory such as the 'splendour of clothing' or 'earthly positions of honour', from the 'glory of the Lord' by using the word Shekinah is helpful and has its place, but found within the New Testament is an official term straight from God's own mouth.

In his second letter, the Apostle Peter shares his personal testimony of encountering this Glory;

> [16] *"For we did not follow cleverly devised stories when we told you about the coming of our Lord Jesus Christ in power, but we were <u>eyewitnesses of his majesty</u>. [17] He received honour and glory from God the Father when the voice came to him from **<u>the Majestic Glory</u>**, saying, "This is my Son, whom I love; with him I am well pleased." [18] We ourselves heard this voice that came from heaven when we were with him on the sacred mountain."* (2 Pet. 1:16-18)

Peter was an eyewitness of Jesus' transfiguration. After waking from his slumber, he was enveloped in a powerful display of the 'divine majesty' or 'glory of the Lord'. In this encounter Jesus' *'face shone like the sun'* (Matt 17:2) and His *'clothes became dazzling white, as bright as a flash of lightning'* (Luke 9:29).

When reading Luke's account, we find that Moses and Elijah also 'appeared *in glory*' and were talking with Jesus (Luke 9:30-31). However, *they* only appeared in *doxa*; the Greek word for glory, which when stated alone refers to the ordinary form of glory.

After the resurrection of Christ, Peter, having finally come to grips with what he saw on the Mount of Transfiguration, adds a special adjective to describe the glory that was upon Jesus.

> [17] *He received honour and glory from <u>God the Father</u> when the voice came to him from the <u>Majestic Glory</u>* (2 Pet. 1:17)

Peter defines it as MAJESTIC glory, the 'megaloprepēs doxa'. This is the official biblical name for God's glory, in contrast to 'shekinah' from the Jewish Talmud. It can also be defined as 'magnificent', 'excellent' or 'splendid' and this is the only time this Greek word appears in the New Testament. It is reserved for God's glory alone.

We can therefore derive many synonyms that describe the glory realm of God. You can name it straight out of the Old Testament as the **"Glory of Yahweh"**, also referred to by some as the **Shekinah Glory**. Peter calls it the **Majestic or Magnificent Glory**. Another appropriate term is the **"weighty or glorious presence"**. Although the word *presence* is used here, it is actually still a reference to the glory, not the <u>ordinary 'presence' (*pânîym* in Hebrew, *prosōpon* in Greek)</u>. These are just a variety of labels to help us define the same property, the **"dwelling or settling of the Divine Glory of God"**.

Although Peter did not understand what was happening at that time, Jesus was revealing to Him that He was the embodiment of the *kâbôwd Yĕhovah* that dwelt permanently upon the Ark in Old Testament times. Jesus was showing Peter, along with James and John, that He was the antitype of the Ark of Glory. Found in Him, 'the fullness of the Godhead in bodily form', was access to Father, Son and Spirit in wondrous magnificence;

> *While he was still speaking, <u>a bright cloud</u> overshadowed them, and behold, a voice out of the cloud said, "This is My beloved Son, with whom I am well-pleased; listen to Him!"* (Matt 17:5 NASB)

The Father spoke from the Majestic Glory, His voice came from inside the Holy Spirit pillar of cloud that overshadowed Peter, James and John. Jesus was transformed to a degree into the dazzling appearance of His Father, enabling the disciples to gaze upon Him without being utterly consumed.

The call to rebuild David's Tabernacle is the world-wide mandate for us, as a body of believers, to enter through *the silver lining* into this glory realm in the last days. That's why David wrote;

> *"As for me, I shall behold <u>thy face</u> in righteousness; I shall be satisfied, when I awake, with <u>beholding thy form</u>."* (Ps. 17:15 ASV)

David had face-to-face interaction with God *and also beheld the form of His Divine Majesty* as he ventured daily into His tent. This is where the true remnant of the Body of Christ is heading. When I say remnant, I am referring to those who will not partake in the great apostasy: the great falling away of the church (Matt 24:12-13, 2 Thess. 2:3). This remnant; the 'faithful elect', shall see the greatest ingathering of new believers added to the body of Christ. This will occur at the same time the lukewarm are falling away at a similarly alarming rate.

Is it still Noble to 'Confine' the Glory of God?

When Peter woke up on the Mount of Transfiguration, in his fright his first impulse was to blurt out;

Lord, it is good for us to be here; if You wish, I will make three tabernacles here, one for You, and one for Moses, and one for Elijah. (Matt 17:4 NASB)

Did Peter want to tone down the glory upon Jesus, or was he attempting to memorialise the encounter? He was probably just trying to be hospitable. The Bible says that he didn't really know what he was saying.

What is most important is that whether he knew it or not, Peter was actually obeying Old Testament regulations regarding the fact that the Divine Glory always had to be *housed in a physical dwelling* to settle and remain accessible to men on earth. But look what happens next;

[34]While he was speaking, <u>a cloud appeared</u> and covered them, <u>and they were afraid</u> as they entered the cloud. [35]A voice came from the cloud, saying, "This is my Son, whom I have chosen; listen to him." [36]When the voice had spoken, they found that Jesus was alone. (Luke 9:34-36)

When the cloud enveloped them, it caused fear and trembling. It was the Father who spoke to them from within the cloud. Inside this cloud was the glory of the fear of the Lord: the sternness or seriousness of the Father. This was yet another appearance of the dark cloud that was up on Mount Sinai, yet it was lit up brightly by the incandescent glory radiating from Jesus (Matt 17:5). Like in the natural, it is the 'sun' that lights up the clouds. Once again we see the two properties of the Majestic Glory working together; the radiance of God's glory upon Jesus, and the darkness of God's glory in the Holy Spirit cloud.

The Father said;

"This is My Son, whom I have chosen. *Listen to Him*". (Luke 9:35)

In requesting tabernacles for all three, Peter was placing Moses and Elijah as equals with Jesus. Moses represents the Law, Elijah the Prophets, but Jesus is the entire Word of God! The Law and the Prophets point to Him, are fulfilled in Him, and are summed up in Him. That's why Moses and Elijah disappeared with only Jesus left standing. Out of the three, the Father singled out Jesus! He is our sole focus.

By leaving Peter's question unanswered, the Father revealed to us that there is no longer a requirement to house the glory of the Lord *in any worldly*

structure. *He did not want the Majestic Glory tabernacled!* No longer was the glory of the Lord to be confined or veiled in any capacity.

In Psalm 26:8, David shows us that *in the Old Testament,* the glory had to be 'housed'. Now, through Jesus, the weighty *kâbôwd* has broken out of 'tabernacle confinement'. Our bodies, as members of Christ's body, are now the temples of the Holy Spirit; He is housed within us. Despite this, we are directed by the Lord to become pipelines where His glory can be released from heaven into earth. We are not called to keep the glory *contained on the inside*; we are called to *reflect* the glory *out*!

Even after His ascension, Jesus gives us real-life testimony that His glory is still out and about; for this was the SAME brightness that blinded Saul when he was knocked off his donkey on the road to Damascus (Acts 9:1-8, 22:11). At this time in his life, Saul was not going to be found inside a meeting where God's glory was manifesting. He spent all his time out on terrorist missions against the saints! The brilliance of God's majestic splendour could even bring immediate transformation to a violent persecutor of the Lord Jesus Himself, and the manifestation of His glory occurred on a road in-between two towns. There were no buildings in the vicinity.

It is encouraging to note that when we graduate from this life (into our glorified bodies) we will look straight into the full Excellency of His Glory without being blinded like Saul was. Although no one will ever see the Father's face because of the immense brightness (Exod. 33:20, 1 Tim 6:16) or be able to make out any specific features except His outer members, our new bodies will adequately handle the power emanating through us as we draw close to the Father's throne.

In this current body of flesh, we have many limitations to the degrees by which God's glory can impact us (like Moses being positioned in the cleft of the rock). God will give us all we can handle without bringing us to ruin, so we can pursue His glory without trepidation. When the Father visits earth during this age, it is not possible for Him to come in the same form which we can approach Him in heaven. If our spirit-man is taken to the third heaven, then that is a different story.

The Most Intimate Place

We have learnt that the presence of God is described as 'face to face conversation', and that the glory realm is likened to seeing the outline or form of the Father. When experienced in our earthly life, this is *more spiritual than literal*. But this realm is more than just gazing upon Him in awe and wonder, although that is definitely our initial response. It is a call to come and sit in the Father's lap: Nestled inside the security of His loving embrace, we find repose and comfort, just as Lazarus did alongside Abraham in Luke 16:22-23.

When we approach the Ark and dwell in the midst of the cherubim, we come into contact with Jesus. According to John 1:18, Jesus is found in the loving embrace of *His* Father (John 1:18). Jesus is fully pleasing to the Father in every way, abiding as a mature Son in perfect union. As we learn of Jesus Christ and follow His example we can, by becoming more like Him, be escorted also into the Father's loving arms (Matt 11:29). It is a place for *all* His sons and daughters, not only His firstborn. This will become a literal reality in heaven, but here on earth it is figurative; a place of spiritual positioning as our Father embraces us via His Spirit and angelic host to experience His divine love.

In order to sit in our heavenly Father's lap we must first, like Moses, gain access through the dark cloud that surrounds Him. The darkness is designed to bring us into a disposition of holy fear. Remaining anchored in this place, we can experience the outpouring of His immense love many times over. Hidden within the dark cloud is His true resplendence, and as the fire of His love burns through the density of the dark oily substance, it breaks up the cloud so we can penetrate through, revealing the Father in His quintessential form. It is a fire that purifies, a fire that purges; a fire of perfect holiness. It burns up anything that is wood, hay or straw, exposing the true motives of the heart. His love and holiness cannot be separated: They are one and the same fire. Once we have passed through this fire, the dark cloud re-materialises, surrounding us as a protective covering.

Resplendence is 'a quality of almost unbelievably majestic beauty, gorgeous in both grandeur and brilliance'. As we draw closer to the final generation, the Father desires to remove what has veiled Him and fully disclose His resplendence. Amid this incandescent glory, the devil is completely immobilised. Surrounded by the dark shroud of His glory, we are shielded *from* the enemy's reach.

In this generation, the Spirit of Elijah has been released to turn the hearts TOWARD THE FATHER, bringing them into the glory of His loving embrace. This is how the Lord is setting apart a company of forerunners who will prepare for the Lord's second coming (Mal. 4:6). As a result, the hearts of the Fathers will be turned back to the children, and the disobedient to the attitude of the righteous, which is to seek and submit to the will of God (Luke 1:17).

These forerunners will lead by example, laying out a template for abiding in the loving embrace of their Heavenly Father, and presenting themselves as a spotless bride to their Betrothed. God's invitation to enter the fullness of His glory has been sent out to all humanity. The chosen remnant of His children, earnestly desiring to be set apart, will willingly endure whatever disciplinary love is necessary and enter the closest proximity available. Ear pressed upon His chest, they will tune themselves in to His very heartbeat, just as David did when he pressed up between the Cherubim of Divine Glory.

SECTION IV:

~ THE ARK ~

AWAY FROM HOME

~ Chapter 18 ~

CAST YOUR MIND BACK TO SHILOH

In light of the previous seven chapters (concerning the Ark of God's Glory), let's briefly summarise what the Ark of the Covenant represents;

First, it is where the throne of God is located. According to Isaiah 16:5, this throne is established in God's mercy. This mercy is married with truth as Jesus sits on it *in the Tabernacle of David*. No wonder God's overwhelming pursuit is to resurrect David's fallen tent in these last days.

We have also learnt that the Ark is symbolic of Jesus Christ Himself, the fullness of the Godhead in bodily form. But most importantly, it is humanity's *contact point* with the Majestic Glory of the Father. That is the consummating factor behind all that is purposed in the rebuilding of the Davidic order of 'worship-based encounter' with the Lord.

Now, having thoroughly examined the purpose of the Ark, let's trace its travels prior to it being brought into Jerusalem by King David…

In order to do this we must cast our minds back to a place called Shiloh. This was the only fixed location the Tabernacle of Moses ever had after coming into the Promised Land from the wilderness wanderings. This is where every citizen of Israel was commanded to sacrifice their burnt offerings to the Lord (Deut. 12:5-7, Josh 22). It had such permanency that in 1 Samuel 1:9 and 3:3, it is referred to as *hêykâl*, which is a Hebrew word used for something fixed in place, such as a palace or temple.

In Joshua 18:1, the Tabernacle of Moses was initially set up in Shiloh by Joshua. When we fast forward to Judges 18:31, we find it is still located there. Although there may be an instance or two where the TOM was temporarily shifted away from Shiloh, (such as the national convention held in Joshua 24 at Shechem, and perhaps Bethel in Judges 20:27), it was the inaugural site and primary place of Mosaic worship in the land of Canaan. Even after the multiple backslidings of the Israelites throughout the Book of Judges [a season categorised as a time where: *'the people did what was right in their own eyes'* (Jud. 17:6)], the TOM survived all the way to the beginning of 1ˢᵗ Samuel.

◊◊◊◊◊

Sometime later Jeremiah, who lived during the final era of Solomon's Temple, refers back to the tabernacle at Shiloh as he prophesied to the people of Judah;

*The Lord gave another message to Jeremiah. He said, [2]"Go to the entrance of the Lord's Temple, and give this message to the people: 'O Judah, listen to this message from the Lord! Listen to it, all of you who worship here! [3]This is what the Lord of Heaven's Armies, the God of Israel, says: "'Even now, if you quit your evil ways, I will let you stay in your own land. [4]But don't be fooled by those who promise you safety simply because the Lord's Temple is here. They chant, "The Lord's Temple is here! The Lord's Temple is here!"' [5]But I will be merciful **only** if you stop your evil thoughts and deeds and start treating each other with justice; [6]**only** if you stop exploiting foreigners, orphans, and widows; **only** if you stop your murdering; and **only** if you stop harming yourselves by worshiping idols. [7]Then I will let you stay in this land that I gave to your ancestors to keep forever.*

[8]*"'Don't be fooled into thinking that you will never suffer because the Temple is here. It's a lie! [9]Do you really think you can steal, murder, commit adultery, lie, and burn incense to Baal and all those other new gods of yours, [10]and then come here and stand before me in my Temple and chant, "We are safe!"—only to go right back to all those evils again? [11]Don't you yourselves admit that this Temple, which bears my name, has become a den of thieves? Surely I see all the evil going on there. I, the Lord, have spoken!*

[12]*"'**But return to my place that was at Shiloh, where I made my name dwell at first. See what I did to it because of the evil of my people Israel.** [13]Now, because you have done all these things—this is the LORD's declaration—and because I have spoken to you time and time again but you wouldn't listen, and I have called to you, but you wouldn't answer, [14]what I did to Shiloh I will do to the house that bears my name—the house in which you trust—the place that I gave you and your ancestors. [15]I will banish you from my presence, just as I banished all of your brothers, all the descendants of Ephraim.'"* (Jer. 7:1-11 NLT, 12-15 CSB)

Jeremiah's prophetic warning came to Judah because they were trusting in the physical temple on Mount Moriah to keep them safe from divine punishment while continuing to live in ways contrary to the Lord's decrees. They were doing whatever pleased their flesh, then they used the physical structure of the Temple in their midst as false reassurance that there would be no consequences for their disobedience. This was a similar thing to what was happening in the days of John the Baptist: The people were declaring; *"we have Abraham as our Father"*, reasoning that this ancestral connection would automatically exempt them from the repercussions of a habitual lifestyle of sin.

Why would this time period in Israel's history be brought back to their remembrance centuries later as part of God's stern admonition concerning the impending judgement of Babylonian captivity along with the destruction of the Temple? What devastating events could possibly have occurred back at Shiloh to warrant this?

Eli and his sons

Although there were many seasons of compromise and apostasy in Israel throughout the time of the Judges, with respect to the Tabernacle at Shiloh we find the issues arising at the beginning of 1st Samuel. When Jeremiah tells the people of Judah to refer back to what happened at Shiloh, he is pointing specifically to the events that occurred in 1 Samuel chapters 1-4.

The story centres on a man named Eli, who was the second-last judge of Israel and High Priest over the Tabernacle of Moses in Shiloh. When we first come across Eli in the Scripture, he seems to have a severe lack of spiritual discernment; a quality that a High priest of God should excel in. When a young woman named Hannah is crying out to God in great anguish and sorrow, Eli mistakes her for a drunk!

Hannah was barren and had borne no children for her husband, Elkanah, while his other wife, Peninnah, had many children. Every year when Elkanah's family would travel to Shiloh to sacrifice to the Lord, Peninnah would taunt Hannah and make fun of her because she could not conceive. This would send Hannah into total despair, to the point where she would not even eat! (1 Sam 1:7)

On one of these occasions, after the sacrificial meal was over, Hannah ventured across to the prayer compartment connected to the Tabernacle and went into intense travail before the Lord. That is when Eli mistook her for a drunk as he sat in the entryway of the *hêykâl Yĕhovah* (1 Sam 1:9). Hannah promised God that if He opened her womb and gave her a son, she would dedicate him to serve of the Lord all the days of his life.

Once Hannah clarified the source of her agony, Eli said; *"In that case, go in peace! And may the God of Israel grant your request."* Hannah was so filled with expectation and faith that she jumped up and exclaimed, "Oh thank you sir!" Then she was no longer sad and began to eat. (1 Sam 1:17-18)

◊◊◊◊◊

The divine judgements that occurred at Shiloh are not accredited to Eli alone, but also to his two sons, Hophni and Phinehas. They served as priests of God under the leadership of their father. The spiritual condition of the priesthood is quite often indicative of the nation as a whole. We have already seen the lack of discernment on the part of Eli, but it gets far worse than that!

Throughout the times of the Judges, the spiritual condition of Israel was up and down like a Yo-Yo. Now, at the time of Eli, God's firstborn nation is once again at a low-ebb spiritually. The lamp of the Lord was almost completely snuffed out, and because of this *'the word of the Lord was rare and prophetic visions were not widespread.'* (1 Sam 3:1b CSB)

Here we have a High Priest who is spiritually indifferent: While not living in complete disobedience, he lacks any genuine interest or concern about the statutes of the Lord. Though not an absolute apostate, he is deficient in passion for God's house. It was said of Jesus; *"Zeal for my Father's house has eaten me up"* (John 2:17). This definitely was not the case for Eli; he was mediocre. He was 'in the middle', as close as an Old Testament example of what it means to be lukewarm; the type of person God vomits out of His mouth. (Rev. 3:16)

Eli's sons, on the other hand, are utter apostates. They were scoundrels who had no respect for the Lord whatsoever. They are referred to in 1 Samuel 2:12 as 'sons of Belial'. Belial means *'worthless, good-for-nothing and unprofitable'*, but we can also define it as *'wicked, lawless and reckless'*. If you look in the New Testament, the Apostle Paul says;

"What harmony can there be between Christ and Belial [the devil]?"
(1 Cor. 6:15 AMPC)

Hophni and Phinehas were literally 'sons of the devil', or as Jesus put it when elaborating on the tares; *"sons of the evil one"* sown into the world by the devil (Matt 13:38-39). They were like Simon Bar-Jesus, whom Paul referred to as *'a child of the devil and an enemy of everything that is right'* (Acts 13:10), or the Jewish Leaders, of whom Jesus said;

> *"You belong to your father, the devil, and you want to carry out your father's desires."* (John 8:44)

It was the corruption of Eli's sons that precipitated the rise of the prophetic ministry of Samuel, who was the miracle child born to Hannah in response to her desperate prayer at the Tabernacle. Little did Eli know that when he spoke the blessing over Hannah's prayer, this little baby would end up pronouncing God's judgements on him and his own family! What evil could Hophni and Phinehas be committing that would cause God to view them as sons of Satan?

Brazen Behaviour

Two major sins are mentioned regarding the indecent behaviour of these two rebellious rascals. The first concern was their abuse of animal sacrifices brought to the Altar of Burnt Offering.

In 1 Samuel 2:12-17, we see that when the people came to sacrifice their animal, Hophni and Phinehas would demand a greater portion of the meat than was allocated according to the Laws found in Leviticus 7:22-38 and Deut. 18:3. Hophni and Phinehas would steal the offerings by force before the full process had been completed, and they were so cowardly that they wouldn't even do it themselves: They sent a poor servant to break God's commandments for them!

At certain times, the servant would arrive while the meat was still being boiled in the pot. The priests were supposed to wait until the boiling process was complete before they could take what was rightfully theirs. But the servant would come with a massive fork and plunge it into the pot, and whatever meat attached itself to the three prongs, he would confiscate. In this way, the priests did not allow the people to complete the animal sacrifices they brought to the Lord. Because of this, the Scripture says *'they abhorred the offering of the Lord'*. The people despised the atonement because of the way these sons behaved. (2 Sam 2:12-17)

On other occasions, it was far worse. The servant would demand the raw meat before it had even been boiled. That way the priestly family could use it for roasting. This was even prior to the fat being rendered down. In this way, they could roast it in the fat and make it more flavoursome. The fat in particular was the Lord's portion; it had to be entirely burned away upon the altar to God (Lev. 3:16). So not only did the priests fail to administer the people's sacrifices, but in these moments of gluttony, they would even confiscate the Lord's portion as well! This was sacrilegious behaviour of the highest order! (2 Sam 2:29)

In the New Covenant, the fat of the offering refers to the 'excesses of the flesh' or 'indulging the flesh'. Just like when we eat too much fat in our physical diet and we see the excess of indulging our fleshly appetites affecting our skin folds, so it is spiritually. God wants us to deny the flesh and be led by His Spirit. If we walk in the Spirit, we will not fulfil these lusts (Gal. 5:18). If we abide in Jesus, and His Word abides in us, we will produce much fruit (John 15:5). The Lord wants our spiritual life fit and in good shape. He does not condone indulging the cravings of our sinful nature whenever they arise, for that is equivalent to the priests yielding to the temptation of indulging themselves with the fat of the animal sacrifice.

If eating God's portion of the sacrifices is blasphemy of the highest order, then what they did next was desecration of the highest, highest order. Do you recall back in chapter eight how we discovered there were women who donated their mirrors for the construction of the bronze washbasin in Exodus 38:8? These same women served at the tabernacle entrance, doing what exactly, we don't know. Well, they make a re-appearance here in 1 Samuel chapter 2, only this time it is not an honourable mention. Here we find them doing *something*, but it is definitely not 'serving the Lord'. 1 Samuel 2:22 says that Hophni and Phinehas would seduce these women as they performed their duties at the entrance, resulting in sexual relations right outside God's throne room!

In the midst of all this defiance, the young boy Samuel was growing up alongside Eli in the Tabernacle. Wearing a linen ephod, he served the Lord faithfully as he spiritually developed (1 Sam 2:18). The linen ephod is the garment of a priest; a replica of the garment worn by King David when he stripped himself of his royal robes and danced before the Lord. When Samuel grew older, he would be the one who was used by God to anoint David as King.

God was raising up His faithful priest and righteous replacement amid those who were ripe for the judgment of the winepress. Having lost all sensitivity, they were totally oblivious to the horrible fate that shortly awaited them. (Eph. 4:18-19)

Is Eli really to blame?

You might be thinking; *"what's the problem with Eli? He's not the one committing these abominations before the Lord. What crimes has he committed to be included with his sons in these divine judgments?"*

Here's the truth: Spiritual indifference can often land us in the same danger as outright blasphemy. Eli was in a position of authority, and he had been made aware of the transgressions against the Lord by those underneath his covering. He had all power to ensure that the evil behaviour of his sons stopped immediately; otherwise, he could have kicked them out of the job. Instead, he made a feeble attempt at disciplining his sons: Like a beggar, Eli basically pleads with them to stop instead of demanding obedience. He wants to be his children's friends more than their father-figure. After pleading with them to stop and giving them some hard truth about the dangers of sinning directly against the Lord, he simply lets them go on their way with no more follow up and hopes for the best. (1 Sam 2:22-25)

But there is even more to it than that: Eli was partaking in minor aspects of their ungodly conduct. Because of this, Eli figured that if he took the hard-line against the 'bigger' sins, he would by necessity also have to make them stop everything that was abhorrent to the Lord. This would include the smaller sins that *he* enjoyed. Thus he dwelt in a place of compromise. Even though certain sins are worse than others (Luke 7:41-47), it is dangerous to rank transgressions into 'big ones' and 'little ones'. You may well end up giving yourself permission to commit minor infringements against the Lord.

One day an unknown, unnamed man of God came up to Eli. This man was a hidden but faithful servant of the Lord. He was nameless and faceless to other human beings, but both his name and face were well recognised by God and all of heaven, for he had died to his flesh and to self.

God always has His hidden remnant amongst the spiritually indifferent within any nation. In the time of Elijah, he thought *he* was the only prophet left in Israel, but God had hidden 7,000 more who had not bowed the knee to Baal (1 Kin. 19:18). Elijah thought he was alone because in times of apostasy the true bondservants of God have to be hidden away from the public eye. Like Elijah, when required they are summoned by the Lord to make sudden and shock appearances with significant power, accuracy and impact.

This was such a time: Messages from the Lord were very rare and prophetic visions were quite uncommon. This man was hidden away from the 'mainstream', hearing clearly from God. Below is his message to Eli from the Lord;

> *"I revealed myself to your ancestors when they were Pharaoh's slaves in Egypt. [28]I chose your ancestor Aaron from among all the tribes of Israel to be my priest, to offer sacrifices on my altar, to burn incense, and to wear the priestly vest as he served me. And I assigned the sacrificial offerings to you priests. [29]So why do you scorn my sacrifices and offerings? Why do you give your sons more honour than you give me— for **you and they** have become fat from the best offerings of my people Israel!"* (1 Sam 2:27-29 NLT)

Aha! *You* and they (*Eli* and his sons) have become fat from the best offerings of my people Israel! Here we find the compromise that caused Eli to cave in when stern discipline was required. He was *taking part* with his sons in the fat of the offerings! He indulged his flesh along with his sons in this supposedly minor misdemeanour. But no, it was not minor at all; he was eating *the Lord's portion* and was getting fat from the offerings given to God. This is rampant today among Christianity; ministers of the gospel are getting financially fat from the offerings of God's people. They are the moneychangers who convert God's house into a place of merchandise! (John 2:16) It was just like this in the time of Jeremiah, when he warned the people to look back to Shiloh;

> [11]*Don't you yourselves admit that this Temple, which bears my name, has become a den of thieves?* (Jer. 7:11 NLT)

We must not make God's house of prayer for all nations a hideout for robbers. Rather, as Paul suggests, let us also commit to this declaration: *"Unlike so many, I do not peddle, market, or trade the word of God for profit. On the contrary, in Christ I speak before God with sincerity, as one sent from God."* (2 Cor. 2:17)

Faithfulness amongst Evil and Indifference

The Lord preserved Samuel, protecting him from demonic influence in the midst of the corrupt conditions brought about by Eli and his family. Once Samuel matured, he was known for two noble attributes. The Bible says that *'none of his words fell to the ground, nor did he ever beg for bread from the people.'* (1 Sam 3:19, 1 Sam 2:35-36) Everything Samuel uttered *in God's name* was true. He did not deviate to the right or to the left, but spoke the pure, undiluted revelation of Jesus Christ.

Samuel also relied upon God to provide his daily necessities; he did not beg the people for money. The man of God who prophesied to Eli spoke of Samuel by saying 'Eli's surviving family members would constantly beg for silver and food from his family' (1 Sam 2:36). In other words, Samuel would trust in the supernatural supply of the Lord, whilst Eli's family would be under a continual curse of poverty. On this issue, Samuel's character is proven in a showdown with the people in 1 Samuel chapter 12. Samuel says;

> *"I have walked before you from my youth even to this day. ³Here I am; bear witness against me before the LORD and His anointed. Whose ox have I taken, or whose donkey have I taken, or whom have I defrauded? Whom have I oppressed, or from whose hand have I taken a bribe to blind my eyes with it? I will restore it to you." ⁴They said, "You have not defrauded us or oppressed us or taken anything from any man's hand."*
> (1 Sam 12:2-4 NASB)

What a contradiction we find between the conduct of Eli and his sons and Samuel. It was chalk and cheese. There was not even one occasion where Samuel used the Lord's ministry for personal gain, but Eli's family did it repeatedly. As the man of God continued his prophetic message to Eli, we discover the consequences of their unrepentant lifestyles. The Lord would have no other choice but to release judgement on Eli's house or 'family line':

> *"Therefore, the Lord, the God of Israel, says: I promised that your branch of the tribe of Levi would always be my priests. But I will honour those who honour me, and I will despise those who think lightly of me.*

[31] The time is coming when I will put an end to your family, so it will no longer serve as my priests. All the members of your family will die before their time. None will reach old age. [32] You will watch with envy as I pour out prosperity on the people of Israel. But no members of your family will ever live out their days. [33] The few not cut off from serving at my altar will survive, but only so their eyes can go blind and their hearts break, and their children will die a violent death. [34] And to prove that what I have said will come true, I will cause your two sons, Hophni and Phinehas, to die on the same day!" (1 Sam 2:30-34 NLT)

The family line of Eli, divinely positioned to be God's High Priestly family for endless generations, will now see the priesthood stripped from them in the near future. This is yet another example where we learn that things such as our Temple (church), family line, or *even the Promise of God* cannot save us from God's wrath if they are being presumptuously traded in place of obedience. God is not obliged to keep His promises if we refrain from serving Him as Lord. Always remember; *'You cannot mock the justice of God'* (Gal. 6:7).

God gave a sign that the demise of Eli's family would eventually occur; Eli's two sons will die on the very same day! Even though Hophni and Phinehas perished via divine retribution, Eli's priestly line continued on for a few more generations (1 Sam 14:3). Then it came to an abrupt end...

~ Chapter 19 ~
ABIATHAR AND ZADOK

Abiathar was the tenth high priest of Israel and fourth in descent from Eli. He was the son of a man named *Ahimelech*. Abiathar was the first High Priest under the reign of King David.

When King Saul was still alive, a man named Ahijah the priest would travel with him wearing the ephod, the priestly vest. Therefore, Ahijah was technically the High Priest, for he consulted the Lord wearing the priestly garments [1 Sam 14:3, 18 (To dismiss confusion: 1 Samuel 14:18 in LXX (Septuagint) correctly reads 'ephod', not 'Ark of God')]. But strangely enough, Ahijah was *not* stationed at the tabernacle of Moses, as the high priest should have been…

Ahijah was the brother of *Ahimelech*. Ahijah stayed alongside the King wherever he went, but Ahimelech was set up as caretaker of the tabernacle of Moses at a place called Nob. He was in charge of the Levites and also oversaw the sacrifices and ritual duties enacted by the priesthood. In differing ways he too was operating like the high priest, whilst not officially holding the title. The father of these two priests was Ahitub, and he was the eldest son of Phinehas, the scoundrel son of Eli. Thus Ahitub, a descendant of Eli, had two sons in high-level priestly positions under Saul.

King Saul didn't care too much for the tabernacle, nor did he bother to follow the proper protocols set up by Moses. After all, the Ark wasn't present, and there were no attempts by Saul to move the Ark back into its rightful place whatsoever. David even stated himself that the Ark of God was neglected during the reign of Saul (1 Chr. 13:3). Saul left it hidden away at Abinadab's house, which probably explains why he established such an unorthodox setup: He cared more about what suited him than what suited God.

Saul Rejected

Worse problems arose for Saul immediately after Israel defeated the Amalekites. Following the victory, King Saul did not completely obey the voice of the Lord through Samuel, and the Lord rejected him as king of Israel (1 Sam 15). From this point on, instead of being under the influence of the Holy Spirit, an evil spirit tormented Saul (1 Sam 16:14). The only time he had a brief reprieve from the depression, paranoia, and fear was when David came into his court to play the harp for him. (1 Sam 16:23)

After David killed Goliath, he became the commander of Israel's army. Saul then became jealous even of David, his number one asset. The women throughout Israel were singing; *"Saul has killed his thousands, but David his tens of thousands"* (1 Sam 18:7-8). The next time David came in to play his harp, instead of being relieved by the songs, Saul was so overcome with rage he hurled his spear at David while he was still in the middle of playing a tune (1 Sam 19:8-9). The more David succeeded, the more Saul became afraid of him. In his delusional mindset, Saul became certain that David would soon dethrone him as king and take his place.

Eventually, David was driven out of the king's palace altogether, banished into the wilderness. He was now on the run with Saul determined to kill him. Eventually David would escape his grasp, making his hideout in the cave of Adullam. When other discontented, impoverished and troubled souls heard where David was, they joined him there (1 Sam 22:2). In quick time David became the captain of 400 men.

But prior to this, while David was fleeing from Saul, he stopped by the Tabernacle of Moses in Nob, where he met with Ahimelech, father of Abiathar. David didn't actually tell Ahimelech why he was in such a hurry. In fact, to cover up what was really going on, David told Ahimelech that he had been sent on an errand *by King Saul* (1 Sam 21:2). David (and the men he had arranged to meet up with later) needed food desperately. He had fled abruptly, without even taking a weapon. When David asked if there was any food, Ahimelech did not hesitate. He said;

> *"We don't have regular bread, but there is the holy bread which you can have if your young men have not slept with any women recently"* (1 Sam 21:4 NLT)

Since there was no other food available, Ahimelech gave David the holy bread—the Bread of the Presence that was placed before the Lord in the Tabernacle. In the gospels, Jesus Himself admitted that this bread was lawful only for priests to eat, yet David, as a future king-priest in the same likeness as Melchizedek, was not judged for eating it; neither were his companions. Ahimelech also gave David the sword of Goliath, the giant from Gath whom David had killed many years earlier. Then he sent him on his way, believing that he had helped both David and King Saul, for he was unaware David was actually running away from Saul.

Everything would have been just fine, if not for the appearance of a mysterious character at the tabernacle that day. Doeg the Edomite, Saul's chief herdsmen, witnessed the whole encounter! Why Saul would have a descendant of Esau as his number one shepherd is yet another strange decision. Doeg was not a man of godly character, to say the least. He had no conscience about harming God's anointed, and he also got a real kick out of being a spy and talebearer.

After staying in the cave for a little while, David was commanded by the prophet Gad to leave the stronghold and return to the land of Judah. By this time, King Saul's paranoia had reached the pinnacle. He no longer had the anointing of David's Spirit-filled harp playing to relieve his tormented soul. Saul thought everything was a conspiracy; to him, every single human being on the planet was out to get him. To make things worse, Saul believed David was the one spearheading the entire campaign! This was, however, the outright opposite of the truth; for the demonic spirits controlling Saul's mind came directly from the father of lies.

Convening under the Tamarisk Tree

When Saul found out that David had returned to his kingdom territory, he exploded with rage against the Benjamites, claiming that they were 'all in' on the conspiracy with David to have him dethroned as king. Saul was fully convinced they had joined in a solemn pact with David to finish him off! Doeg the Edomite was standing there with Saul's men, and at that moment he decided to step up with his piece of vital information. In the presence of all, he told Saul about the favours Ahimelech did for David at the TOM in Nob. This enraged Saul beyond the point of sound thinking. He immediately sent for Ahimelech and the members of his family, all who were old enough to serve as priests. When Saul confronted him, Ahimelech swore he knew nothing about a plot against him, nor did he assist David by helping him escape. (1 Sam 22:7-15)

Saul wouldn't have a bar of it. Right there, under the tamarisk tree on the hill at Gibeah, he ordered his bodyguards to kill all the priests standing in front of them. The bodyguards, being convicted in their conscience, refused to do it. So Saul said; *"Doeg, you do it"*. (1 Sam 22:16-18)

Doeg murdered all the serving priests in Ahimelech's family—85 in all. If that wasn't enough, he also ran off to Nob and killed all the priest's families as well—men and women, children and babies, even their livestock! (1 Sam 22:19)

With these orders, King Saul effectively eliminated his own priesthood. Clearly, this was not a smart thing to do. From now on, he would operate with no priestly blessing. Spiritually, he would be all alone. In fact, the lack of access to the Lord granted through the priesthood would eventually cause him to do something he vowed he would never do: He went and sought God's counsel from a medium out of the occult. (1 Sam 28)

The End of the Family of Eli?

With the slaughter of all these priests, you would assume this was the fulfilment of the prophetic word given to Eli by the man of God (1 Sam 2:27-36). All of these slaughtered priests were his descendants, coming from the seed of his grandson Ahitub. But one young boy escaped the slaughter and fled to David. *It was Abiathar, the son of Ahimelech!* David was sorely grieved to hear that he had indirectly caused the deaths of Abiathar's entire family, so he promised to protect him and look after him, for he said; *"The same person wants to kill us both."* (1 Sam 22:23)

When Abiathar escaped the slaughter of the priests, he had quickly confiscated the priestly vest and brought it with him to David. In this way David was able to receive divine communication through Abiathar's ministry that ended up being crucial to David overcoming major trials and fulfilling his God-ordained destiny. What was Saul's loss had become David's gain.

Abiathar remained loyal to David through the wilderness wanderings, abiding faithfully alongside David (the anointed yet rejected heir). Upon Saul's death, David began his reign over Judah in Hebron, then after 7.5 years, he was anointed King over all Israel. Abiathar, who had grown into the role, was appropriately placed as high priest over the nation.

Zadok: Warrior turned Priest

Zadok appears first as a warrior who joined David's army shortly after he was anointed king of Israel at Hebron (1 Chr. 12:28). Even the Levites, who were ultimately destined to become tabernacle assistants, had conscripted men in the army of the Lord. Zadok was one of these; and he was not only related to Levi but also to Aaron. This made him a powerful combination: priest of God Most High *and* a mighty man of valour!

The first time Zadok is directly mentioned is in 2 Samuel 8:17, where he suddenly appears alongside Abiathar as a leader among the priesthood. Both Zadok and Abiathar were given honorary roles in the inauguration ceremony for David's tabernacle (1 Chr. 15:11). After this, David assigned Zadok the responsibility of high priest over the Tabernacle *of Moses* on Mount Gibeon. This left Abiathar as high priest over the Tabernacle *of David* (1 Chr. 16:39-40). This explains why there were suddenly two high priests on the scene. Prior to this Abiathar had been the sole high priest.

Zadok definitely pulled the short straw in this arrangement, for he had to remain faithful far away from the Ark amid dead religious activity. There was no glory of God anywhere near his vicinity.

Abiathar: Living the Dream

Abiathar had it made: There was barely anything for him to do at David's tabernacle except join in with the worship and enjoy the manifest glory of Jehovah. You would think that remaining faithful to the Lord would be easy in this environment, yet Abiathar became progressively familiar with his role and began harbouring disloyalty toward David, and by extension, God Himself.

Being positioned around worship and glory doesn't automatically make you faithful to God's will. You can be just as easily deceived in the midst of a move of God as you can in the mundaneness of a religiously contrived environment. Faithfulness to Jesus Christ is personal, not corporate. We all have an individual responsibility to maintain our intimacy one on one, away from the assembly. This is where it is won or lost: time alone with God! When the Lord sees what is done *in secret,* He begins to reward *openly;* that is, in the public eye. (Matt 6:4, 6, 18 NKJV)

Zadok had come on board *after* David was crowned king, which is probably why he was given the short straw of high priest at the Tabernacle of Moses. Abiathar had been faithful as priest alongside David during the *entire time* he suffered in the desert, hiding in caves and holes in the ground. That's why when David became king Abiathar received the highest honorary position during the period of David's reign: inaugural high priest at the Tabernacle of David.

Zadok: Faithful till the Very End

In 1 Chronicles 24:6, Zadok *and Abiathar* were also given upcoming assignments when preparations were being made for Solomon's Temple. David had a place for *both of them* to continue ministering together in the temple era under Solomon. This, however, never eventuated...

When Absalom rose up and attempted to usurp the throne, both of David's high priests remained loyally steadfast to their king (2 Sam 15:24-36). But it was near the time of David's death that Abiathar caved in to rebellion. He sided with Adonijah (the son born to David directly after Absalom), when he self-proclaimed as king in David's place. (1 Kin. 1:11-19)

But Zadok, compelled by David to preside over a dead religious system, remained faithful to the very end! He sided with King David in this royal contest. David had declared that his son Solomon was God's choice to be the next king. (1 Kin. 1:8)

Although Abiathar had been completely faithful throughout so much of David's life, this single act of disobedience *right at the end* caused him to be thrown out of the priesthood. *This* is where the prophetic word given to Eli by the man of God finally came to pass: Eli's priestly line was now destroyed from the face of the earth. From the time of the inauguration of Solomon's Temple onwards, the role of high priest was given exclusively to Zadok and his descendants. (1 Kings 1:34, 4:2)

Obedience leads to Legacy

Later on in history we witness a remarkable legacy originating all the way back to Zadok's unrelenting obedience. In chapter 44, Ezekiel mentions Zadok's descendants at the time of Solomon's Temple. When all the other Levitical Priests abandoned the Lord by straying toward idol worship, those descended from Zadok were the only priests who remained undefiled. They fulfilled Leviticus 10:10, distinguishing between *'what is holy and what is profane, discerning what is clean and unclean'*. (Ezek. 44:23)

Because of this, the Zadokites are promised an eternal position as priests unto God, while the others missed out, facing stern consequences. They forfeited their position before the Lord forever, and will bear the shame of all the detestable sins they have committed. (Ezek. 44:10-14)

> ¹⁵*However, the Levitical priests of the family of Zadok continued to minister faithfully in the Temple when Israel abandoned me for idols. These men will serve as my ministers. They will <u>stand in my presence and offer the **fat and blood** of the sacrifices</u>, says the Sovereign Lord.* ¹⁶<u>*They alone*</u> *will enter my sanctuary and approach my table to serve me. They will fulfill all my requirements.* (Ezek. 44:15-16 NLT)

As partakers of the New Covenant, I believe we can be counted among the priesthood of Zadok provided we remain loyal to the Lord as they did. They represent the faithful remnant of the Lord's people, those who qualify to approach the altar in the millennial Temple (Ezek. 40:46, 48:9-12). Notice also (emphasis underlined above) that they stand in God's presence and offer the *fat and the blood* of the sacrifices. There is no stealing of the Lord's portion here, unlike Eli and his sons.

Zadok came from the lineage of Aaron's son, Eleazar (1 Chr. 6:4-8). Eli and Abiathar were descended from Aaron's other son, Ithamar. Thus Ithamar's family line was done and dusted with regard to the priesthood. It was sealed by Abiathar's actions, but the family curse originated back with Eli four generations before Abiathar committed treason against God's anointed (1 Kings 2:26-27). It was inevitable because of the disgraceful actions of Eli, along with his two sons, Hophni and Phinehas; Abiathar's great grandfather. What they did was so serious that God spoke through Samuel's lips; *"I have vowed that the iniquity of Eli's family will never be wiped out either by sacrifice or offering."* (1 Sam 3:14)

What a difficult introduction Samuel had to the prophetic office. The first prophecy he ever received was to tell Eli that there was nothing left for him and his descendants but judgement! Thank God, by the blood of Jesus, we can break generational curses placed over us by our ancestors. We do not have to live under the curses they placed on us, but can transform the legacy of our posterity from curses to blessings.

God had given Eli and his sons an ample grace period to repent, but eventually it got to the point where they essentially became the equivalent of those who commit the unpardonable sin in the New Testament. According to Samuel, the blood of sacrifice could no longer cover their sins. Sadly, this curse would also pass down the family line without remedy. It had become impossible to bring Eli, Hophni or Phinehas back to repentance because *being once enlightened*, they were intentionally: 'holding the Lord up for public disgrace.' (Heb. 6:4-6)

~ Chapter 20 ~

THE LORD ABANDONS SHILOH

The nameless, faceless man of God had spoken. Eli and his sons had scorned God's sacrifices by consuming the fat from the best offerings of His people, Israel. The branch of his family tree (regarding the priesthood) would be effectively cut down. God would now raise up a faithful priest that would do all He desired, and that was Samuel (1 Sam 2:35). As stated earlier, Samuel was so surrendered to God's will throughout his life that he operated in an unprecedented level of accuracy where *'every word he spoke proved to be reliable'*. (1 Sam 3:19 NLT)

The releasing of this prophecy from the man of God seems to have brought an impartation which activated Samuel's prophetic gift. Though not yet manifest in the natural, the transition of priestly authority from Eli to Samuel had now begun in the spiritual realm. Shortly after the man of God disappeared back into his place of 'hiddenness', Samuel had a defining encounter that commissioned him forever into the public eye. From this day onward he was confirmed as the prophet of the Lord. As he grew in stature, all the people acknowledged this unanimously (1 Sam 3:20).

Many of us know this story: The lamp of God, which represented God's presence among His people, had almost gone out. Samuel was sleeping in the tabernacle near the Ark of God. Suddenly the Lord called out, "Samuel!" The breath of the Lord Almighty instantly fanned the lamp of God back into flame! God called out three times to Samuel, and each time he thought it was Eli, the priest. When Samuel approached Eli for the third time, Eli finally caught on to what was happening. He replied to Samuel, "Next time you hear your name, answer with 'Speak Lord, your servant is listening'". (1 Sam 3:9)

This time, because of Samuel's response, God downloaded His first prophecy into his heart;

> *[11]The LORD said to Samuel, "I am about to do something in Israel that everyone who hears about it will shudder. [12]On that day I will carry out against Eli everything I said about his family, from beginning to end. [13]I told him that I am going to judge his family forever because of the iniquity he knows about: his sons are cursing God, and he has not stopped them.*

[14]Therefore, I have sworn to Eli's family: The iniquity of Eli's family will never be wiped out by either sacrifice or offering." (1 Sam 3:11-14 CSB)

Here is the next progression in Eli's judgment process. The man of God had previously stated that Eli and his sons were getting fat off the offerings. Because of this, the family line was cursed. To prove this, Hophni and Phinehas would die on the same day.

To this point, there was not yet any eternal condemnation. This meant that just like with Jonah and Nineveh, the prophetic word could still be overturned if there was swift repentance. This is one of only a few situations, such as Jonah's, where we should *not* label a prophet as false when their word does not eventuate.

Now, with Samuel's word the stakes rise to a whole new level: This time the focus is on the fact that "Eli did not *discipline his sons because of their contemptible behaviour* (most likely committing fornication at the tabernacle), nor did he heed the warning of judgement given by the man of God." There had obviously still been time (after the prophecy from the man of God) for Eli to take corrective action. But he was so lukewarm and indifferent that he just accepted the man of God's prophecy as inevitable and gave up.

This now meant, (according to the fresh, updated word given to Samuel) not only would his sons die, but God vowed through Samuel that *"the sins of Eli and his sons would never be forgiven either by sacrifice or offering"* (1 Sam 3:14). There was no more time for repentance; it was all over. Every judgment that the man of God pronounced, plus the extras spoken later by Samuel, would now befall the family, even for generations to come.

Eli's Strange Response

When I read about the weird, overly religious response Eli gave to Samuel's prophecy, I was bewildered. When Samuel finally gets up the guts to spit it out, Eli replies; *"It is the Lord's will. Let God do what He thinks is best"* (1 Sam 3:18). If you've just been told you're eternally condemned, accursed, and cut off from God's forgiveness forever, surely that kind of answer cannot come from your mouth? Wouldn't you be pleading upon the mercy of God? This shows that Eli had little or no conscience left at all. He was merely existing as a zombie in religious garments.

This is just like people who have committed the unpardonable sin in the gospel age. Those who have truly committed this sin have their 'consciences seared as with a hot iron' leaving them incapable of ethical functioning (1 Tim 4:2 AMP). There is no desire for God left in them; not a skerrick of conviction remains in their heart. You can appeal to such people all you like: You can show them their sin as plain as day, but no matter what you say, they won't listen. They want nothing to do with God ever again!

I trust that is not you, my friend. If it were, you would not be reading this book. The deep sorrow over your past sin and the conviction that led you back to repentance means you CANNOT HAVE BLASPHEMED THE HOLY SPIRIT. The Lord is clearly working in your life and has not abandoned you, so don't be disheartened; rather, be encouraged.

The whole way through the disciplinary process Eli had no reaction of remorse or godly sorrow that would lead him to repentance (2 Cor. 7:10). His conscience was totally dead; it was not 'cognitively connected'.

We could liken Eli to the unbelievers Paul talks about in Ephesians 4 who are so hardened in their hearts they 'lose all sensitivity'. By this stage Eli was 'past feeling, full of greed, with a continual lust for more' (Eph. 4:19). This caused him to live in a perpetual state of apathy, where all hope was drained away. We don't need to let the devil oppress us in this way. By the power vested in Christ, we can rise out of this victim mentality, turn the tables on the devil and make him the victim by putting him under our feet where he belongs!

At War with the Philistines

At that time Israel was at war with the Philistines. The Israelite army was camped near Ebenezer, and the Philistines were at Aphek. ²The Philistines attacked and defeated the army of Israel, killing 4,000 men. ³After the battle was over, the troops retreated to their camp, and the elders of Israel asked, "Why did the Lord allow us to be defeated by the Philistines?" Then they said, "Let's bring the Ark of the Covenant of the Lord from Shiloh. If we carry it into battle with us, it will save us from our enemies." (1 Sam 4:1a-3 NLT)

Israel's enemies started prevailing once again, as had happened many times before during the period of the Judges. The people of God had relapsed into idolatry, wickedness, and immorality. They had heard stories about the Ark and how it had brought favour to Israel in times gone by. One example was when the walls of Jericho came crashing down as they marched around the city with the Ark at the head of the procession. They also recalled how powerful the Ark was in drying up the Jordan River, even though it was flowing so rapidly that it was overflowing its banks. This enabled Israel to cross over into the Promised Land on dry ground! Surely, bringing the Ark into a battle situation would produce similar results. The words of Moses from Numbers 10:35 may also have been on their minds;

Whenever the Ark set out, Moses would shout, "Arise, O Lord, and let your enemies be scattered! Let them flee before you!" (NLT)

The children of Israel failed to realise that the power upon the Ark was Immanuel 'God with them', not the physical piece of furniture. Jesus' hand of favour and protection was only upon them if they were living in obedience to His commands. Instead, they thought of the Ark as a magic formula and lucky charm. Their faith in God had degenerated into a superstitious belief in the *material* Ark of the Covenant, which in reality, was nothing more than a modern-day coffin!

This is yet another example of presumption by Israel. At different times throughout their history, they trusted in their Abrahamic ancestry, the Temple of Solomon, the promise of God, and on this occasion it was the physical presence of a wooden box overlaid with gold. If they had truly believed the God of the universe was dwelling upon the box, they would have revered Him and obeyed Him with fear and trembling. Hophni and Phinehas did no such thing: They were contemptible to God in their blatant blasphemy. They brought the holy priesthood of Yahweh into disrepute through their detestable deeds committed inside God's holy courtyard. Now these two brothers think they can just haul off the Ark into battle and everything will be fine and dandy? *"Let's just ignore God all day, every day and then when we get into trouble, let's call on His name to help us out."* Sorry folks, it doesn't work that way.

When you are not living right, bringing the glory of God into a situation can actually cause judgment to fall instead of blessing. This is exactly what happened in this instance;

⁴So they sent men to Shiloh to bring the Ark of the Covenant of the Lord of Heaven's Armies, who is enthroned between the cherubim. Hophni and Phinehas, the sons of Eli, were also there with the Ark of the Covenant of God. ⁵When all the Israelites saw the Ark of the Covenant of the Lord coming into the camp, their shout of joy was so loud it made the ground shake!

⁶"What's going on?" the Philistines asked. "What's all the shouting about in the Hebrew camp?" When they were told it was because the Ark of the Lord had arrived, ⁷they panicked. "The gods have come into their camp!" they cried. "This is a disaster! We have never had to face anything like this before! ⁸Help! Who can save us from these mighty gods of Israel? They are the same gods who destroyed the Egyptians with plagues when Israel was in the wilderness. ⁹Fight as never before, Philistines! If you don't, we will become the Hebrews' slaves just as they have been ours! Stand up like men and fight!" (1 Sam 4:4-9 NLT)

At first, the Ark's presence seemed to have the desired effect. The Philistines were panicked at the thought of facing the same God who sent the plagues to Egypt and parted the Red Sea. The Israelites thought if they imitated the loud shout which brought the walls of Jericho down, they would once again experience a supernatural victory. But the plan quickly backfired on them. The presence of the Ark actually emboldened the Philistines to fight all the more resiliently; they knew now that their only hope was to put in a 110% effort. On top of all this, Israel had no supernatural help, because the favour of the Lord was no longer on them.

¹⁰So the Philistines fought, and Israel was defeated, and each man fled to his tent. The slaughter was severe—thirty thousand of the Israelite foot soldiers fell. ¹¹The ark of God was captured, and Eli's two sons, Hophni and Phinehas, died. (1 Sam 4:10-12 CSB)

Oh dear! That wasn't the desired result. Israel had 4,000 casualties the first time. Now, due to their presumption, it had cost them a further 30,000! Not only that, the sign of judgment upon Eli's house was fulfilled. As prophesied by the man of God, Hophni and Phinehas died on the same day on the battlefield. They had taken the Ark out into transit when it was not commanded by the Lord. The sons of Belial actually signed their death warrant by agreeing with the people to take the Ark to war. For the first time in Israel's history, the Ark of God fell into enemy hands. This terrible event is reflected upon in Psalm 78:60-61;

> *He forsook the tabernacle at Shiloh, the tent in which He had dwelt among men [never to return to it again], ⁶¹And delivered His strength and power (the ark of the covenant) into captivity, and His glory into the hands of the foe (the Philistines).* (AMPC)

This is what Jeremiah was speaking about when he told those trusting in the existence of Solomon's Temple to 'cast their minds back to Shiloh' and see what God did (Jer. 7:12-14). Did they end up listening to Jeremiah? Absolutely not! Now we can see why he is known as the 'weeping prophet'. Jeremiah would have preferred a Jonah-like turnaround, earnestly desiring that his warnings of Babylonian judgment would never eventuate. Jonah, on the other hand, was angry when God relented concerning Nineveh's destruction. He preferred that his prophetic word be vindicated, rather than caring for the 120,000 people that were going to be destroyed. (Jon. 4)

"No Glory"

While the battle was raging, Eli had an 'uneasiness' come over him. While he was waiting for news of the outcome, his heart trembled for the safety of the Ark of God (1 Sam 4:13). All of a sudden, under such a tense situation, his calloused heart gained some feeling back. Had Samuel's word slowly penetrated through as he meditated over it? Potentially so, but maybe the Ark being removed from its safe confines reminded Eli of the emotions that came with the immense responsibility of being anointed as high priest: His number one role was to keep the Ark of the Covenant safe.

You would think Eli would be at least slightly worried about his sons carrying a box unarmed into a war-zone, but he wasn't. His mind was totally fixated upon the Ark; he sensed something was wrong, very wrong. The nervousness and tension pulsating through his body must have been so hard to bear for an old man who had barely felt any genuine emotion in a very long time.

A man from the tribe of Benjamin ran from the battlefield and arrived at Shiloh later that same day. He had torn his clothes and put dust on his head to show his grief, but the 98-year-old Eli could not see this because by this time he was blind (1 Sam 4:12). He had no vision, and without vision, people cast off restraint and then perish. (Prov. 19:18)

As the man relayed events to the people, Eli overheard the loud outcry resounding throughout the land. So he yelled out; "What's all this noise about?" The messenger ran towards Eli to tell him the news. (1 Sam 4:14)

First, he said; "Israel has been defeated by the Philistines". But even considering this news, there was no emotional response from Eli. Next he said; "The people have been slaughtered, and your two sons, Hophni and Phinehas, were also killed." Still, Eli was completely unmoved. Third, the messenger said; "The Ark of God has been captured!" (1 Sam 4:17)

This immediately struck a nerve in Eli. His worst fear had become a reality. Out of intense shock, Eli fell backwards off his chair. Because he was overweight, the impact of the fall broke his neck and he died instantly. His forty-year leadership role as judge over Israel came crashing to an abrupt end! (1 Sam 4:18)

Not only did Eli lack vision. The fat of the animal sacrifices he had consumed (his disobedience/feeding of the flesh) had caused an in-balance which he could not recover from. He could not remain upright according to God's plumb-line. He had fallen backwards (backslided) to his destruction.

Becoming overweight from God's sacred offerings came back to bite him big time (pardon the pun). A string of supposedly small compromises eventually ballooned out into a major catastrophe. Always remember, *a little yeast spreads through the whole batch of dough.'* (Gal. 5:9)

The fact that Eli broke his neck reveals he was 'stiff-necked' towards the things of God. He was full of pride and stubbornness. Therefore, we have in Eli a man who is stiff-necked, living in the flesh and lacking vision. It's little wonder things ended up the way they did.

God had abandoned the very place where the land of Israel had been divided up by Joshua after prevailing over their enemies (Josh 18). Now, the complete opposite of victory was occurring. I don't think anyone present when Joshua divided up the people's inheritance could have ever fathomed that something like this would ever occur in Shiloh.

Eli's daughter-in-law, the wife of Phinehas, was pregnant and near her time of delivery. She had previously given birth to her firstborn son named Ahitub, who as we have already studied, later became the grandfather of Abiathar, David's inaugural high priest.

When Ahitub's mother heard of the news about her husband's death and the capture of the Ark, the shock waves sent her into premature labour and she gave birth. It was such a traumatic delivery that she was nearly dead by the end of it. The midwives tried to reassure her that everything would be alright, but she wouldn't listen to them. In her final act before passing away, she called her son "Ichabod". Then she said with one final breath; *"The glory has departed from Israel, for the Ark of God has been captured."* (1 Sam 4:20-22 NLT)

Ichabod in Hebrew is *"Iy- kâbôwd"; literally translated "NO GLORY".*

The glory of Yahweh (***kâbôwd Yĕhovah***) first bestowed upon Moses' countenance and then upon the Ark he constructed, had left Israel. The very Substance that set them above all other nations had been extracted into a foreign land. Thus the Holy of Holies in the Tabernacle of Moses was left vacant, and the Ark would *never* return there again…

~ Chapter 21 ~

THE ARK IN PHILISTIA

Ashdod

The Philistines seized the Ark out of Israeli hands on the battleground at Ebenezer and took it immediately to the town of Ashdod. They did this because the temple of their chief god Dagon was located there. Dagon, which means 'a fish', had the head and hands of a man but the tail of a fish. He was like a male version of a mermaid (1 Sam 5:1-2). The Philistines were thinking along these lines; *"If we combine the power of our fertility god with the power of the God of Israel, then our nation will have multiplied power and no other nation will ever be able to defeat us"*. So they took the Ark into the Temple of Dagon and placed it beside his statue.

The philosophy of combining a false god with the one true God was a huge mistake. While you might get this multiplied effect by combining two or more false gods, it would not work with El Shaddai involved: A house divided cannot stand (Mark 3:25). When combining two false gods you are essentially combining demons with more demons, so the counterfeit power of the devil increases. They were yet to discover the real God was not on the same team. They were adding light into darkness; the Holy Spirit into a demonically engineered environment;

> *[19]Do I mean then that food sacrificed to an idol is anything, or that an idol is anything? [20]No, but the sacrifices of pagans are offered to demons, not to God, and I do not want you to be participants with demons. [21]You cannot drink the cup of the Lord and the cup of demons too; you cannot have a part in both the Lord's table and the table of demons.* (1 Cor. 10:19-21)

You see, it is impossible to combine 'the cup of the Lord' and 'the cup of demons' into one super concoction. They are opposing forces that do not mix: just like oil and water. The moment the Ark was placed in the temple, God began contending with and overpowering Dagon. The demonic entities who had attached themselves to Dagon were no match for God's Glory.

The next morning, the citizens of Ashdod went into the temple to admire their spoils of victory and to marvel at their newly established supernatural power-combo. But to their dismay, the statue of Dagon had fallen with his face to the ground in front of the Ark of the Covenant. They quickly stood Dagon back up on his fish tail, pretending like it never happened. (1 Sam 5:3)

On the following morning, to the people's horror, it was even worse: Dagon had crashed to the ground once again, but this time his hands and his head had broken off and were lying in the doorway. The body of a fish was all that was left intact! (1 Sam 5:4-5)

No human being or false god can stand in the presence of the great 'I AM'. In the Garden of Gethsemane, when Judas guided a detachment of soldiers with swords and clubs to capture Jesus, all the Lord had to say was 'I AM'. Just like Dagon, the soldiers and everyone with them were knocked to the ground at the mention of His name! (John 18:2-6)

What was occurring in the Temple of Dagon was the least of their concerns. By taking the Ark into their land, the Philistines unknowingly signed themselves up for the legal requirements of the Mosaic Covenant. In that dispensation, the Ark came attached with all the requirements God instituted when he created the Ark *of the Covenant.* As implied within the name, there was a *covenant* attached to possession of the Ark. The Philistines did not carry the sign of the covenant via circumcision, and because they didn't adhere to any of the moral, hygienic, sacrificial, or ceremonial requirements, they had set themselves up for the curses of disobedience written in Deuteronomy 28. The Lord afflicted the Ashdodites with a fulfilment of Deuteronomy 28 verses 27 and 61.

The hand of the Lord was heavy upon them. A highly contagious plague of tumours and boils broke out amongst the population, along with an innumerable number of rats who swarmed their ships and then descended upon the township, bringing death and destruction wherever they went. Eventually, the people put two and two together. They realised it was the Ark of God among them that was causing all this disaster. They concluded rightly, *"the God of Israel is against us. Dagon is destroyed, and if we don't get the Ark out of here, we will be next!"* (1 Sam 5:6-7)

Gath & Ekron

The rulers of Philistia decided to send the Ark to Gath; the Philistine town that would become most well known as the birthplace of Goliath in the near future.

These same two plagues happened to the people of Gath, and in their panic they sent it across to Ekron, another Philistine town. By this time the people were catching on to the inevitability of what would happen next. Even before the Ark arrived at Ekron, its entire populace were begging the Philistine rulers not to send the Ark their way: For the deadly plague had already begun and great fear was sweeping across the town. Those who didn't drop dead were still afflicted with the tumours, but amazingly the cry from the town rose up to God in heaven. They started aiming their prayers toward the one true God, pleading upon His mercy. In their desperation, they forsook their weak idols and cried out to Yahweh for deliverance. (1 Sam 5:9-12)

Strangely, the Philistines tried to keep hold of the Ark a *full* seven months, even amidst such horrible judgment. Finally, the *five* rulers of the Philistines called upon their own priests and diviners, asking them what they should do to end this disaster. Possession of the Ark no longer mattered to them; they just wanted to be 'plague free'. In the end, all *five* of the major towns in Philistia were affected by the plague, not only the three towns where the Ark had been taken. By this time it had spread into a nation-wide pandemic! (1 Sam 6:17)

The Philistine rulers declared; *"We want to give the Ark back to Israel. Please explain to us how to return it in a manner which their God will accept, so that He will relent of His fierce anger."*

The priests and diviners replied; *"Whatever you do, make sure you do not send it back empty! You must give Him some kind of gift. In this case, we recommend a guilt offering to show your remorse. Hopefully, this will bring restitution for your wrongdoing. Then our people shall be healed, and you will know for certain that it was His hand that caused you all this trouble."*

The five rulers agreed to this, but then challenged them further; *"What sort of guilt offering should we send?"*

The priests of the Philistines were priests of the occult, and the diviners got their predictions from demonic sources. They did not have any grid of reference for what the God of Light would require to remove guilt. So they came up with the best idea they could think of, for they knew that consulting their usual omens or utilising demonic fortune telling techniques was not going to give them a correct answer. What they suggested was actually quite logical;

"Since the plague has struck both you and your five rulers, make five gold tumours and five gold rats, just like those that have ravaged your land. [5]Make these things to show honour to the God of Israel. Perhaps then he will stop afflicting you, your gods, and your land. [6]Don't be stubborn and rebellious as Pharaoh and the Egyptians were. By the time God was finished with them, they were eager to let Israel go." (1 Sam 6:4b-6 NLT)

There was still a mighty fear of Yahweh stemming back centuries to the time when God delivered Israel from the stubborn Pharaoh in Egypt. The reputation of God's mighty arm had been passed down through the generations, so that even those who practiced the dark arts were still aware that the Lord was the ultimate source of power. A simple formula was used for the guilt offering; five major towns afflicted with rats and tumours = five gold rats and five gold tumours. The use of gold showed a generosity that brought honour to God.

Back to Israel on a New Cart

From here, the Philistines needed to formulate a plan of how to *transport* the Ark and these gifts back into the Land of Judah. Note in the forthcoming passage how the Philistine priests refer to God as 'the Lord', Yahweh in Hebrew. They are now using the name of God, a name which is usually only spoken by those who are in a covenant relationship with Him. This shows us that the fear of God brought by these plagues caused them to speak of God Almighty as if He truly was the One and only God of the universe. They were acknowledging that there were no other gods in the world but He. (1 Cor. 8:4-6)

[7]*"Now build a new cart, and find two cows that have just given birth to calves. Make sure the cows have never been yoked to a cart. Hitch the cows to the cart, but shut their calves away from them in a pen. [8]Put the Ark of the Lord on the cart, and beside it place a chest containing the gold rats and gold tumours you are sending as a guilt offering. Then let the cows go wherever they want. [9]If they cross the border of our land and go to Beth-shemesh, we will know it was the Lord who brought this great disaster upon us. If they don't, we will know it was not his hand that caused the plague. It came simply by chance."*

[10]*So these instructions were carried out. Two cows were hitched to the cart, and their newborn calves were shut up in a pen. [11]Then the Ark of*

the Lord and the chest containing the gold rats and gold tumours were placed on the cart. [12]And sure enough, without veering off in other directions, the cows went straight along the road toward Beth-shemesh, lowing as they went. The Philistine rulers followed them as far as the border of Beth-shemesh. (1 Sam 6:7-12 NLT)

The Philistine priests believed so greatly in the supernatural ability of Yahweh that they set Him up to perform an extraordinary miracle. They wanted to make it 100% certain that it was the presence of the Ark stolen from Israel that was causing all this chaos, and they didn't make it easy for God either: They attached a yoke upon the shoulders of two milk cows that had just given birth to calves. As first-time 'yoke bearers', they would have to pull the Ark along on a new cart *with no human aid.*

These mother cows had never been trained how to walk in unison, nor did they know how to keep to paths. They were untamed and apt to wandering. Contrary to nature, they would also have to walk away from their newly born calves, something mother cows rarely do. God would have to supernaturally direct these cows away from the natural instincts He placed within them. They concluded that if God truly is Creator of all things, surely He could manipulate these animals into following His will.

Without deviating to the left or to the right, the mother cows walked in one accord *away* from their newly born calves, keeping the most direct path toward the Jewish border town of Beth-shemesh. They kept to the highway all the way into the land of Judah like fully trained oxen. Even more miraculous was the fact that they did it without the help of a human driver. The five Philistine rulers (following until they reached the border) must have been awe-struck at what they had just witnessed. Even greater adulation must have erupted later that day when they returned home to find the towns which they ruled totally plague-free! It had lifted the heavy hand of the Lord off the nation, at least for the time being.

While God was definitely in the business of receiving guilt offerings back in those days, He would usually require the blood of a *clean* animal, in this particular case, a ram (Lev. 5:14-16). The guilt offering of the Philistines didn't come with the shedding of innocent blood, and to make matters worse, the animal they presented in gold was an unclean one. Despite this, God saw that the offerings stemmed from their *belief* that He had sent the plague of rats and boils, and *this faith* moved His hand on their behalf. Godly faith springing forth from the heart always trumps perfect protocol or performance, and this is still true today.

God made an exception to the rule because the Philistines had never heard the commandments of the Lord. He accepted the unusual offerings from them because He looked deep into the heart motive behind their generous gift, rather than strict adherence to the carnal ordinances He had imposed upon Israel (Heb. 9:10). The five golden rats and five golden tumours showed the Lord that they were truly remorseful. God also originally intended for the Ark to be carried with poles on the shoulders of the Levites, yet even the use of a cart to transport the Ark was excusable due to their ignorance. (Exod. 25:13-15, 1 Chr. 15:13-15, Num. 4:15)

The Ark's arrival at Beth-shemesh

The Bible says that the people of Beth-shemesh were out harvesting wheat during the season of Pentecost. They were in a field owned by a man named Joshua. When they saw the Ark coming their way, they were overjoyed with excitement. It was the most unexpected, incomprehensible sight!

> *"Why are the Philistines sending back the Ark without the slightest qualm? Not only have they returned it without receiving payment; they have given us gifts of gold! And how strange? They gave the immense responsibility of transporting the most precious item in the world to two unsupervised, untrained animals! This doesn't make any sense..."*

The cows brought the Ark right into Joshua's field and stopped by a large rock. The first reaction of the Jewish harvesters was to set things in proper order, and that meant disposing of the animals and the brand new cart. They knew that method was not God's prescribed way of doing things. Breaking up the cart to make firewood, they kindled a fire. Then they killed the cows and sacrificed them on the fire as a burnt offering, pleasing to the Lord.

I believe this burnt offering administered by the Jews was actually a blood sacrifice on behalf of the Philistines, who didn't know how to appease God properly. For *their cart* produced the fire and *their cows* went up as a pleasing aroma to the Lord. This is only conjecture, but this may have been the precise moment when the plagues stopped (1 Sam 6:10-14). *At least the Philistines had sent clean animals to transport the Ark!*

Now that the cart and animals had been removed from the scene, they decided the best cause of action would be to use the large rock as an altar to place the Ark upon. Like the Ark, the Rock also represents Jesus Christ; the solid rock on which we stand. They rounded up some Levites who were familiar with how to carry the Ark properly to come and insert wooden poles so they could lift it up onto the rock. Then the Ark, along with the chest containing the gold rats and tumours, were placed there. (1 Sam 6:15-18)

So far, so good: The Israelites had been extremely reverential, carefully obeying the lord's decrees blamelessly. As the Philistines had already found out, the Ark was not something to fool around with. But after many more sacrifices and burnt offerings had been given to God, curiosity got the better of some of them. Seventy men had profane thoughts. They whispered to one another; *"You know the Ten Commandments are inside the Ark? How awesome would it be to take a quick peek? They were written by the finger of God, you know!"* So after the festivities died down these men snuck up on top of the rock and lifted the atonement cover off the Ark, peering inside. They symbolically took away the blood upon the mercy seat which covered their sins and beheld the Ten Commandments which condemned them. After they had all taken their turn, the entire group dropped dead! (1 Sam 6:19)

Great fear and alarm swept the town as news of the tragedy quickly spread amongst the inhabitants. They mourned greatly for the loss of such a high percentage of their population and were now more scared of God than the Philistines had been;

> *"Who is able to stand in the presence of the Lord, this holy God? Where can we send the Ark from here?"* (1 Sam 6:20 NLT)

Off to Abinadab's House

A cry rang out across the entire town of Beth-shemesh; *"Get this thing out of here pronto!"* Messengers were immediately dispatched to the people of Kiriath-jearim, telling them; *"The Philistines have returned the Ark of the Lord. Come over here and get it!"* So the men of Kiriath-jearim came to fetch the Ark, taking it to a house on the hillside belonging to a man named Abinadab. He ordained his son Eleazar with the tremendous responsibility of being in charge of its safe-keeping. (1 Sam 6:19-7:1)

> [2]And the ark remained in Kiriath-jearim a very long time [nearly 100 years, through Samuel's entire judgeship, Saul's reign, and well into David's, when it was brought to Jerusalem]. For twenty years all the house of Israel lamented after the Lord. (1 Sam 7:2 AMPC)

There at Kiriath-jearim, the Ark was left in this small, secluded forest-village for the rest of Samuel's life, through the entire reign of King Saul and a further 7.5 years under his son Ishbosheth—a time period somewhere in the vicinity of 80 to 100 years. After the initial wave of fear swept Israel (as a reaction to the wrath of God at Beth-shemesh), there were twenty years of subsequent mourning as they lamented the fact that the Lord had abandoned them. As time went on, the Ark, being hidden away, lost its vital importance as it faded from the forefront of the Jewish psyche.

Hearts begins to Turn

During this twenty-year period, there was a slow but steady 'turning of the tide' as the Israelites developed a renewed hunger for Jehovah. This progression towards surrender was mostly because of Samuel's positive example and tireless efforts. Slowly but surely, he turned the hearts of the people, awakening them through his loving yet stern appeals.

The major reason for this positive turnaround is found in the remainder of 1 Samuel 7. After this 20-year period was over, Samuel exhorted the Israelites to get serious about returning to the Lord, so they repented of their idolatry and got rid of all their false gods. Mourning ceased and hope returned. Israel went out onto the battlefield to face the Philistines once more, and this time, instead of having an inactive priest sitting on a chair trembling in fear, they requested that Samuel actively intercede for them as they went into battle.

This time the roles were reversed; the Israelites were afraid of the Philistines, and the Philistines were overly confident they would win. Through Samuel's prayers and a crucial burnt offering of a lamb, the Lord spoke with a mighty voice of thunder, sending the Philistines into confusion and mayhem, allowing Israel to defeat them. Samuel had brought victory to Israel because the priesthood was no longer corrupt. There was no need for the physical presence of the Ark amongst the army. God's favour and blessing had returned to Israel because the priest had been active in his intercessory role and had called for nation-wide repentance back to pure, undiluted worship.

The Philistines were subdued for the rest of Samuel's days. The Jewish villages that the Philistines had seized were returned to Israel. Even the Amorites stayed away! Life went back to normal, and the land of Israel was safe and secure. Yet despite these victories, the Ark remained greatly neglected, and even the thought of its existence was the furthest thing from their minds. It was treated like an artefact from a bygone era that was no longer relevant. God's blessing had returned without the Ark, so they reasoned in their hearts; *"Is it even necessary? Do we really need it? Surely having our own king like other nations would be far more beneficial than some wooden box."* This was the overall attitude of the post-Eli generation, for he had tarnished the Ark's sacred reputation in the eyes of the people. But an unwavering passion within the heart of one young man made him an exception…

SECTION V:

THE MAKING OF A KING

~ Chapter 22 ~

DAVID'S LOYAL ENDURANCE

"Lord, remember David and all his afflictions" (Psalm 132:1 KJV)

Before the thought of becoming a king had ever entered David's mind, he was already living as a 'young boy after God's own heart'. He was devoted to the worship of Yahweh out of pure motives; not for what he would get out of it, but to celebrate God's presence in his life as he experienced intimate fellowship with his heavenly Father.

Out of a desire planted in his heart at a young age, David made a vow to God. Fulfilling this vow would become David's major pursuit for the rest of his days on earth. For many years, it was the sole purpose that got him out of bed in the morning. His heart would erupt with inspiration from its mandate; the noblest of desires birthed out of the very heart of God Himself.

Even after being anointed as the future king of Israel by Samuel, David did not err from this lifelong commission. The vow he made to God never fell from the 'number one' position. For David knew that the promise of sustained success in royalty would always be contingent upon fulfilling, *and then continuing to live out* this monumental oath. It is one thing to see a promise initialised in our life, but are we determined to see it outworked by *living in the promise* after God has released it to us?

When David killed Goliath, he did a strange thing. After cutting off the head of the giant, he grabbed it and ran straight for Jerusalem, dropping it off there (1 Sam 17:54a). At this time, Jerusalem was still under the control of the Jebusites, so it seemed peculiar that David would take the head and leave it in a city inhabited by foreigners. But David had received divine foresight. He knew that one day (perhaps a decade or two into the future) there would be a mighty fulfilment of the vow he had made, and God had already revealed to David the place where it would come to pass. This city of Jerusalem would also be the very place where the head of the greater giant, Satan himself, would be spiritually cut off through the greatest act of love the world will ever witness. What would eventuate upon the stronghold of Zion would strip the devil of his authority as 'prince of this world'. (John 12:31)

Although this vow is not directly recorded in the scriptural history of David's life, it has been written down for us by an unknown author in Psalm 132.

1. Remember David's Afflictions

Just prior to the introduction of David's vow, the psalmist states this;

"Lord, remember David and all the hardships he endured" (Ps. 132:1 CSB)

"Remember, O Lord, on David's behalf, all his affliction" (Ps. 132:1 NASB)

Here the song-writer is imploring God to remember David on behalf of a future generation who are currently not living in the sincere devotion and obedience their forefather exhibited. He wants to ensure that God will be merciful enough to fulfil His covenant promises *to David,* even though his descendants are walking in ways contrary to the Lord. The Psalmist sincerely hopes that the dismal behaviour of David's royal posterity during the 'in-between time' will not affect the covenant promise of the coming Messiah, David's ultimate Son. The Apostle Peter said;

[30]David was a prophet and knew that God had promised him on oath that he would place one of his descendants on his throne. [31]Seeing what was to come, he spoke of the resurrection of the Messiah, that he was not abandoned to the realm of the dead, nor did his body see decay. [32]God has raised this Jesus to life, and we are all witnesses of it. (Acts 2:30-32)

Fortunately, the coming of the Messiah through David's lineage had already been guaranteed by oath, regardless of the behaviour of the 'in-between' generations.

The ESV renders verse 1 this way;

"Remember, O Lord, in David's favour, all the hardships he endured" (ESV)

'The hardships of David' are the sufferings he endured because he made a stand for God and His righteousness. These difficulties were brought upon him through no fault of his own; being inflicted because, as a godly man, his endeavour was to maintain true worship to the Lord. Included within these were the painful trials he undertook in order to provide a place where everyone

200

could celebrate Him corporately. The afflictions mentioned here in Psalm 132:1 are all the tribulations David underwent; the trouble and opposition he experienced in his lifetime for the cause of God, especially in establishing a sanctuary in Jerusalem.

There was always an ungodly presence in the nation and abroad, and these evil forces were never slow to slander, hinder, and molest the servant of the Lord. Although David had his faults, he kept true to the Lord Almighty because of his broken and contrite heart. In repayment for this unwavering devotion, he was the black sheep among his family, most of the common people and even later, the monarchs. Because he zealously delighted in the worship of Yahweh both before and after he was made king, he was constantly despised and ridiculed by those who could not understand the reason for his enthusiasm. They had not experienced the same hunger for the Lord that had been cultivated by David during the days of his youth while he worshiped on his harp as he took care of his father's sheep.

Through this psalm, God is reckoning the endurance of godly suffering in David's favour for the sake of the future promises given to his lineage. David will be rewarded for these sufferings in this way; the generational blessing would never be utterly destroyed or removed from his legacy, even though some of his descendants would not partake.

◊◊◊◊◊

What were some of the afflictions thrust upon David because he earnestly sought God in his generation?

Firstly, we see a glimpse in 1 Samuel 20:1 where David exclaimed to his close friend Jonathon;

> *"What have I done? What crime have I committed? I have done nothing to harm your father. So why is he trying to kill me?"* (NIRV)

This verse incorporates all the persecution inflicted upon David by King Saul. David is beseeching Jonathon as to why he has to go through such intense persecution from his father when he has never harmed him. He has only ever served, obeyed and blessed Saul, yet all he receives in return are death threats. What David doesn't realise at this point is that he is in a greater spiritual battle. All the powers of hell have been gathered against God's beloved in an attempt to make him fail in his heart's desire concerning the Ark of God. Ever since David made this vow, the favour and anointing of God had come mightily upon him, yet at the same time, he also became a marked man in the cross-hairs of the enemy. All the days he spent on the run in exile were due to the fact that the devil inside Saul didn't want David to survive to complete the oath he swore unto the Lord.

Second, in Psalm 69 we find even greater detail of many of the hardships thrust upon David because of righteousness. In this psalm David writes about all the crazy stuff he has had to overcome thus far;

First of all he states in verse 4;

> *"Those who <u>hate me without reason</u> outnumber the hairs of my head; many are my <u>enemies without cause</u>, those who <u>seek to destroy me</u>. I am forced to restore what I did not steal."*

If that wasn't bad enough, look what happens from verse 7 onwards;

> *"For Your sake I have borne reproach; Shame has covered my face. [8]I have become a stranger to my brothers, And an alien to my mother's children; [9]Because zeal for Your house has eaten me up and the reproaches of those who reproach You have fallen on me."* (Ps. 69:7-9 NKJV)

David had to bear reproach and disgrace for the sake of being loyal to God. Because of this, intense shame overwhelmed his countenance. Like Jesus, who had to endure the cross, *scorning its shame*, so is the case with us when we are shamed for the sake of taking up our cross and following Him. We must despise the shame by throwing it off. This means we are not to entertain shame or become intimately acquainted with it, but must courageously face up to others even in our humiliation, and continue pressing boldly ahead. If God truly is our portion, how can we allow the opinions of human beings to have any sway over us?

David also explained that he had become a stranger, even to the members of his own family. His intense pursuit of God had made him an alien in the sight of his own siblings. A similar thing happened to Joseph in the book of Genesis. Like Joseph, David didn't fit the traditional mould. We saw evidence of this when David was excluded from the family meeting organised by Samuel. Jesse left David out in the field tending the sheep, considering only his other sons worthy of becoming Israel's next king. Later on, David's older brother, Eliab, scolded him for being inquisitive about the taunts of the Philistine giant billowing out from the other side of the valley of Elah. David got on his brother's nerves because he was so full of faith in the ability of his God. His brothers were soldiers in the army, yet they were so terrified of Goliath they trembled in their boots. *In their minds,* David was the little runt who thought he could play with the big dogs. David became like a foreigner to his mother's children *because of zeal!* Zeal for God's house had eaten him up, and the flaunting of such a passionate lifestyle offended his lukewarm brothers. (Ps. 69:9)

What does it mean to be 'zealous for God's house?'

Whenever you see the word 'house' in the Bible, it is beneficial to substitute the word 'vision' in its place. This is because our individual visions build God's *true* house, which is the Mountain of the Lord's Temple located in the heavenly Mount Zion (Isa. 2:2, 1 Pet. 2:5-6). This Temple comprises the church of the Living God, the pillar and foundation of the truth; the universal body of believers joined together into a holy dwelling in which God lives by His Spirit (1 Tim 1:15, Eph. 2:19-22).

When Jesus was twelve years old, He was asked why He stayed back at the Temple; *God's house.* He replied, *"didn't you know, I had to be about My Father's business?"* (Luke 2:49). This means that the Father's business (the vision He has given you) is the extension you are to build onto God's house. God is in the contracting business, and every calling in every sphere of society builds the diversity of His house upon the mountain of the Lord. The Father is 'the jack of all trades' and desires to train you as an apprentice to take over a certain aspect of the family business. Therefore, what David is expressing in this Psalm is; "Passion for *the vision God has given me* has eaten me up; fervour for His mandate upon my life has totally and utterly consumed me!"

In the second half of Psalm 69:9, we get down to the nitty gritty. David reveals the actual reason he is up against this constant opposition and ridicule. It is because 'the reproaches that *should be directed at God* end up falling on him.' Those who despise David are actually offended at God, even though they don't even know it. In their agitation against the Lord they see no other target but His loyal servant who has caught favour in His eyes. They are heaping their abuse on the messenger instead of the Sender. The real issue is that they are disappointed at God because they dislike the way He wants to take lordship over their lives. This makes them irritated at any display of raw passion: Everything that has zeal towards God offends them because they are against building God's house. David says; "My brothers reproach me because they don't like the zealous approach to my life. It challenges and disturbs their lukewarm, compromised, 'comfort zone' existence." (Ps. 69:9b)

We see even more detail of David's ongoing afflictions in verses 10-12;

> *10 "When I weep and fast, I must endure scorn; 11 when I put on sackcloth, people make sport of me. 12 Those who sit at the gate mock me, and I am the song of the drunkards."*

David says that his acquaintances even scorn him *for praying and fasting*. When he puts on the clothes of mourning and cries out in intercession for people's souls, their response is to make fun of him. He is the mockery of the entire community; the butt of everyone's jokes. If that wasn't enough, the singing drunks in the taverns even joined in on the act! What we must realise in these times is that if we are capturing the attention of so many people, we must be doing something right. Let us not be deterred by the free advertising resulting from the mockery and ridicule Satan gives us in the public square.

2. Remember David's Meekness

In the Greek Septuagint version of Psalm 132:1, it reads, 'Lord, remember David and his *humility or meekness'*. Even the Hebrew word for 'affliction' in the Masoretic Text ('ânâh) can be translated 'to bow low in humility'. The NIV translates it; *"remember David and all his self-denial."* This shows us that the type of afflictions David endured came from yielding his will to God's Lordship. He truly did deny himself, take up his cross and follow.

Through enduring the humiliation, David became fully submitted and broken in to God's will, no matter the cost. He was 'sold out' to the calling of God, and the vow he made was a lifelong 'until'. He had a broken spirit, which God could never despise. Obedience to God's will was not optional, for he had determined to discipline himself and 'endure hardship like a good soldier of

Christ Jesus' (2 Tim 2:3). There was no out-clause in David's contractual obligations made before God, and that's what we must replicate as well.

The Greek word found in the Septuagint is *praÿtēs*, and just like the root word *praus*, it means *'mildness of disposition, gentleness of spirit, meekness.'* We have to understand that this does not mean we are weaklings who can be thrown around like a rag-doll. A person can display this mild disposition while also being as bold as a lion and as steadfast as an ox in their declaration regarding the truth of God.

What meekness truly entails is 'absolute power under perfect control'. It is staying calm in the heat of the battle: not giving up in defeat or becoming a punching bag. We are to be kind and gentle even to those who disagree and mock us, but we are not to give in to them by allowing them to compromise our confident stand for the truth. We can be bold and candid in a delicate and considerate manner that keeps the power of God under perfect control. The absolute power is *of* God, and the perfect control we exhibit comes *from* God. It is the final fruit in the list of 'the fruits of the Spirit': self-control or temperance. This godly characteristic enables us to keep our temper in the intensity of the moment.

> *Always be prepared to give an answer to everyone who asks you to give the reason for the hope that you have.* <u>*But do this with gentleness and respect,*</u> *[16]keeping a clear conscience, so that those who speak maliciously against your good behaviour in Christ may be ashamed of their slander.* (1 Pet. 3:14-16)

We are never to back down nor retract our position, but we can back away from an aggressive altercation if that appears to be the likely result. When we are not provoked, our good behaviour in Christ causes those who want to pick a fight to be ashamed of their slander.

David's ongoing humility is seen in his response after Nathan the prophet reveals God's desire to bestow upon his lineage an everlasting kingdom;

> *"<u>Who am I</u>, O Sovereign Lord, <u>and what is my family</u>, that you have brought me this far? [19]And now, Sovereign Lord, in addition to everything else, you speak of giving your servant a lasting dynasty! Do you deal with everyone this way, O Sovereign Lord? [20]"What more can I*

say to you? You know what your servant is really like..." (1 Sam 7:18-20 NLT)

David never deviated from a posture of humility, even after God exalted him as the most powerful king on the face of the earth.

3. Remember David's Declarations

We can determine that the infinitive plural of the word 'ânâh in its first sense means 'to declare or tell'. If this interpretation is utilised, the verse could easily read, 'Lord, remember David and all his *declarations'*.

David's vow was a declaration he made out loud with his mouth. It was a decree of anointed utterance spoken with authority into the realm of the Spirit: so much so that it attracted the favour of God and sent demons on assignment right to his doorstep. We know he released it because it seems like many people in Israel knew about it, even generations after David had died. He did not leave it residing only in his mind; he must have verbalised it numerous times. His bold declaration of faith activated the vow, opening up a portal establishing a pathway for delivery from heaven to earth. The demonic agenda of the principalities and powers was to block this pathway at all costs!

When we partake in 'declaration prayer', we are speaking those things that be not, as though they are an actual substance that will materialise soon (Rom. 4:17, Heb. 11:1 KJV). What is loosed on earth has already been loosed in heaven, because God has told us so. We are to declare God's will as He reveals it to us in prayer, and see it come to pass in due time. Only through intimacy and relationship will Jesus reveal the sequence of the puzzle pieces. Then we can declare the correct things in the correct order and see the full picture come together. This is not just some 'name it and claim it' type of thing.

Put your Energy where your Mouth is

David made bold and daring declarations, but he also backed them up with dedicational effort on his own behalf. Not 'human' effort, but 'Spirit-empowered' effort. This was also how the Apostle Paul operated;

But by the grace of God I am what I am, and his grace to me was not without effect. No, I worked harder than all of them – yet not I, but the grace of God that was with me. (1 Cor. 15:10)

Here Paul reveals that if we neglect to present ourselves as honourable vessels, we cause the grace of God to be 'without effect'. We can stifle the grace of God if we are not willing to cooperate with the declaration through *corresponding hard work!* Grace kicks in as we *move* in faith. In Colossians 1:29, Paul also said;

> To this end *I labour, struggling with all His energy* that works *powerfully within me.*

We have all heard the saying; 'put your money where your mouth is'. But like Paul, let's 'put our *energy* where our mouth is'. People love the declaration part, but not the labour of toil that comes on the other side of it. Although by His grace God did the bulk of the heavy lifting, Paul did all within his power to ensure His will came to pass. Like David, Paul was always willing to go through whatever it took to see God's mandate fulfilled;

> Now I rejoice in what *I am suffering for you,* and I fill up in my flesh what is still lacking in regard to *Christ's afflictions,* for the sake of his body, which is the church. (Col. 1:24)

David proved himself faithful through the midst of affliction: Jesus Christ was obedient to His Father even to death on a cross; the Apostle Paul was not afraid to partake of what remained in regard to Christ's afflictions for the sake of His body, the church. It is time to go ALL OUT for the cause of Christ, no matter the earthly cost. Our treasure and reward is an eternal one stored up in heaven.

> Many are the afflictions of the righteous, but the Lord delivers him out of them all. (Ps. 34:19 ESV)

~ Chapter 23 ~

DAVID'S SOLEMN VOW

Remember, O Lord, in David's favour, all the hardships he endured, *²how <u>he swore to the Lord and vowed to the Mighty One of Jacob,</u>* ³**"I will not enter my house or get into my bed,** ⁴**I will not give sleep to my eyes or slumber to my eyelids,** ⁵**until I find a place for the Lord, a dwelling place for the Mighty One of Jacob."** (Ps. 132:1b-5 ESV)

Here in Psalm 132:1-5, we begin to find out specific details about the solemn vow David made to the Lord. While this promise unleashed many hardships upon David, it also set him up for divine favour and promotion as he overcame opposition through steadfast endurance.

Jesus said in the Sermon on the Mount that we shouldn't swear by things, like heaven, earth, Jerusalem or even our own heads (Matt 5:33-37). According to Jesus, a simple 'yes when we mean yes' or a 'no when we mean no' is sufficient.

I believe the vow David took was actually a fulfilment of 'simply letting yes be yes' rather than an unethical oath. David was not swearing *by something*, He was swearing *to Someone*. In effect, David was replying "Yes" to what God had already told him. The Lord placed a yearning inside David to see the Ark of God positioned centre stage so that the manifest Glory could be experienced by all. David was simply responding to this God-given mandate. His response was, "I'm all in!"

Swearing to the Lord (not by Him) in this manner is a sincere pledge of lifelong commitment, making the Lord our refuge: the Most High our dwelling, and from this place we pursue His will whatever the cost. In other words, we will never give up UNTIL we see the fulfilment and the realisation of 'His kingdom come' in the area God has promised. Every Christian should make this generic commitment to the Lord out of a pure and sincere heart. Surely it is God's desire that all His followers come on an adventure with Him by living a sacrificially laid-down life. There is nothing more invigorating and exciting than forfeiting your own feeble plans and yielding wholeheartedly to the journey with the Lord. Every day is an experience of enthralling, unexpected twists and turns. What a ride!

The end of verse 5 says David vowed to the 'Mighty God *of Jacob*'. The specific mention of Jacob here shows us that David's vow originated from his knowledge of the first vow to God ever recorded (made by his forefather Jacob back in Genesis 28:18-22). God had looked upon this vow favourably: Jacob had encountered the Lord at Bethel in a profound way, and he was ready to turn from his supplanting ways and commit the rest of his life to following Yahweh.

> [33]*"Again, you have heard that it was said to our ancestors, 'You must not break your oath, but you must keep your oaths to the Lord.'* [34]*But I tell you, don't take an oath at all: either **by** heaven, because it is God's throne;* [35]*or by the earth, because it is his footstool; or **by** Jerusalem, because it is the city of the great King.* [36]*Do not swear **by** your head, because you cannot make a single hair white or black.* [37]*But let your 'yes' mean 'yes,' and your 'no' mean 'no.' Anything more than this is from the evil one.* (Matt 5:33-37 CSB)

The oaths Jesus alludes to above are targeted more at vows permitted under the LOM (Lev. 19:12, Num. 30:2, Deut. 23:21). Some of the laws Moses implemented were not God's perfect plan or original design: Moses had to add them because the people's hearts were hard (Mark 10:5-8). By the time of Jesus, the Jews had a culture of swearing by everything and for every little thing. They no longer swore in response to the Lord's utterance, but with respect to their own selfish endeavours. Not only that, but the main emphasis is that they did not swear to the Lord Himself, but by lesser things, minimising the impact of breaking them. It had become so trivialised that vows no longer meant anything. This was causing them more harm than good.

These laws concerning oaths also established two differing standards for faithful speech. If you vowed it, you had to keep it, but if you didn't vow it, it justified you breaking it. We see this today in modern courts of law when 'put under oath'. It makes us think that when we are 'under oath' we must tell the truth, but it doesn't really matter if we lie any other time. Everything Jesus talked about in this section of His sermon was about grace *outdoing* the standards of the law. Therefore, the essence of what Jesus was telling us in Matthew 5:33-37 is; *"make your whole life, everything you do in word and corresponding deed, full of integrity."* Jesus is showing us that it's not only perjury that God frowns upon; it is any time your actions don't line up with your words, *period*. *"Let your yes mean yes and your no mean no"* means *'keep your word all the time'*. In God's eyes, you're *always 'under oath'*. According to Jesus, any lowering of this standard originates with the evil one.

Therefore, the righteous commitments made by Jacob and David are pure vows undefiled by Moses' law. These are true heartfelt responses to God's goodness in a person's life up to that point, causing them to further define their future in accordance with His plan and purpose. I believe that if we find righteous vows such as these in Scripture, we should heed them, rather than denounce them. Which one of us hasn't felt prompted by the Holy Spirit to recommit our lives to Him afresh with a renewed sense of reverential obedience? Surely this is a healthy thing.

"I will not enter my House"

Studying David's level of commitment is most astounding! It was one of fully fledged determination.

> [3]*"I will not enter my house or get into my bed, [4]I will not give sleep to my eyes or slumber to my eyelids, [5]until I find a place for the Lord, a dwelling place for the Mighty One of Jacob."* (Ps. 132:3-5 ESV)

Obviously, David is using poetic language here. He didn't literally mean that he would not sleep until this vow was fulfilled. That would have been humanly impossible. So what, then, is David saying? He is articulating;

"I am not going to REST until I find a RESTING PLACE for God in my life. I will not be satisfied until there is a place where I can find God *personally*. Only after I can consistently locate the Lord, can I truly rest *in Him*. Therefore, I will not settle down, chill out, or rest easy UNTIL this all-consuming focus becomes an established, true and present reality."

This was not a casual, happy-go-lucky approach on David's part. Weariness, disappointment, or bitterness was not going to cause him to quit. There was no 'plan B' to fall back on. This was it, the be-all and end-all: David was going to find the place where God desired to take up permanent residency and dwell. In David's life, the place the Sovereign Lord had ordained was Mount Zion.

When David said: *"I will not enter my house"* he was referring to his domestic life and personal resources. In his list of priorities, David would not put either of these above the fulfilment of the vow. Sure, he was going to attend to these matters and be a wise and responsible steward, but they would never usurp first place. David was putting God's house (His abiding presence and vision) above his own house.

In Haggai 1, we see the results of what happens when we put our own desires (the lust of our flesh, the lust of our eyes, and the pride of life) higher than worship and the vision God has given us;

⁴Why are you living in luxurious houses while my house lies in ruins? ⁵This is what the LORD of Heaven's Armies says: "Look at what's happening to you! ⁶You have planted much but harvest little. You eat but are not satisfied. You drink but are still thirsty. You put on clothes but cannot keep warm. <u>Your wages disappear as though you were putting them in pockets filled with holes!</u>" (Hag. 1:4-6 NLT)

"I will not go into my Bed"

When David said; *"I will not go up into my bed"* he was referring to personal comfort. This didn't mean that David never took a vacation or had a day off. It meant he never settled down into a 'comfort zone'. On the whole, he didn't entertain laziness. In fact, the one time he gave in to laziness, he fell into the gravest sin he committed in his lifetime. When he should have been out fighting his enemies, he was taking a midday nap! (If you don't know the rest of this story, you can read about it in 2 Samuel 11).

Often in the proverbs, we see the link between too much slumber and laziness.

⁶Take a lesson from the ants, you lazybones. Learn from their ways and become wise! ⁷Though they have no prince or governor or ruler to make them work, ⁸they labour hard all summer, gathering food for the winter. ⁹But you, lazybones, <u>how long will you sleep? When will you wake up?</u> ¹⁰<u>A little extra sleep, a little more slumber, a little folding of the hands to rest</u>—¹¹then poverty will pounce on you like a bandit; scarcity will attack you like an armed robber. (Prov. 6:6-11 NLT)

"I will not give sleep to my Eyes"

When David said; *"I will not give sleep to my eyes or slumber to my eyelids"* he was referring to exerting full effort, even to the point—God forbid—of feeling tired. David put all his strength into his daily tasks, so much so that he had nothing left to give by the end of the day. Now obviously, we don't want to overdo it and burnout, but sometimes we are so concerned about becoming 'tired' that we never wholeheartedly pursue anything.

On certain days, maintaining the *disciplines of the Lord* whilst also completing the *work of the Lord* will require significant time and uncompromising dedication. But always remember that God gives rest to the ones He loves (Ps 127:2). God's rest (consisting of: 'peace of mind, reassurance and comfort') is a major part of the reward of following the disciplines of the Lord if we approach them with the right motive (relationship instead of religious legalism).

This is the reason we set up a dwelling place for the Lord in the first place; to establish a retreat where we can find rest for our souls in times of weariness. That being said, we will never find the place of fruitfulness or God's rest by being a sluggard. Lying on the couch in front of the TV aimlessly flicking channels or spending endless hours scrolling down our never-ending social-media feed just won't cut it. While I have done my fair share of channel surfing in times gone by, I have come to realise that my life is worth far more than that, and my time on earth is too short for that!

All of these factors are elements of David's self-denial. This humility enabled him to fulfil the promise he made to the Lord: establishing a central hub for the open manifestation of the Glory of God to the multitudes.

Designating a 'Place'

*⁵Until I find out a **place** for the Lord, a <u>habitation</u> for the mighty God of Jacob.* (GNV)

*⁵Until I find a **place** for the Lord, a <u>dwelling place</u> for the Mighty One of Jacob.* (ESV)

David said he would not be satisfied until he had provided God with a 'place'. The Hebrew word here for place is 'mâqôwm' and the corresponding Greek word is 'topos'. These words both refer to 'a portion of space marked off'; any type of fixed location, such as a village, town, or city. It is somewhere a person can call home-base.

More specifically, both words refer to a *'standing* place'; a place of *occupation*, such as being stationed at a post or on watch-duty in a tower or on a wall. In such a place of safety and fortified protection, you can 'take a stand' against incoming enemies. This is why, metaphorically speaking, *topos* can be used for 'an opportunity or occasion for action', as it has been by Luke in Acts 25:16. Therefore, finding the 'secret place of God' in our lives is vitally necessary on multiple fronts: It even strengthens and empowers us to *'occupy till He comes'*. (Luke 19:13 KJV)

It is interesting to note that prior to David's takeover, Mount Zion was known as 'The Stronghold' or 'Fortress'. David found a weakness through the water tunnel, which was how he took the city as his own. After taking the city from the Jebusites, David re-consolidated all the breaches and fortified it further (1 Chr. 11:5-8). When David set up the Tabernacle on Mount Zion, it truly was a *mâqôwm*; a fixed location inside a city (the City of David) that was securely guarded from the attack of the adversary. (1 Sam 5:7-9)

> *Now David built <u>houses</u> for himself in the city of David; and he **prepared a place** (mâqôwm/topos) for the ark of God and pitched **a tent** ('ōhel/skēnē) for it.* (1 Chr. 15:1 NASB)

> *⁵Until I find out a **place** (mâqôwm/topos) for the Lord, a **habitation** (mishkân/skēnōma) for the mighty God of Jacob.* (GNV)

> *⁵Until I find a **place** (mâqôwm/topos) for the Lord, a **dwelling place** (mishkân/skēnōma) for the Mighty One of Jacob.* (ESV)

A geographical, fixed location of security is what 'place' *(mâqôwm/topos)* highlights, but what is of even greater importance is the word used in Psalm 132:5b for 'habitation' or 'dwelling place'. It emphasises the *type of dwelling* the Lord will be housed in. In 1 Chronicles 15:1, the scripture tells us that David built *houses* for himself. In Psalm 132:3, David said that he would not enter his 'house'. On both occasions, the word for 'house is *bayith*. Throughout the Bible, we find that *bayith* directly corresponds to the Temple of Solomon. But the word for the Lord's habitation in verse 5b is not *bayith*, but *mishkân*, which always refers to a tent-like construction; the structure implemented for the Tabernacle of Moses and the Tabernacle of David.

A second aspect of the word *mishkân* is that the occupant of the tabernacle fully 'inhabits' the place, dwelling there *on a permanent basis*. Rest assured, you will always find them there. They are never 'away from home'. When Jesus came down and tabernacled among us, He stayed on earth permanently. He didn't come and go between heaven and earth, but remained here to live out a fully human life. In the same way, we can always find God in *His* dwelling place upon heavenly Mount Zion. The Father is permanently seated there with Jesus at His right hand. To use bad English, "they ain't goin' no-where." This is reassuring, but what we must do is find our own 'secret place'; the unique, custom designed 'prayer closet' whereby we gain access to this heavenly tabernacle and throne of grace.

Bethlehem Ephrathah

*⁵Until I find out a place for the Lord, a habitation for the mighty God of Jacob. ⁶Lo, we heard of it in **Ephrathah**, and found it in the fields of the forest.* (Ps. 132:5-6 GNV)

We *heard of the ark in Ephrathah;* **_we_** *found it in the fields of Jaar.* (Ps. 132:6 CSB)

In verse 6, David suddenly shifts in the middle of his vow from singular to plural format. Instead of 'I' he now says 'we'. David tells us he *heard about* the Ark *in a group setting* from a place called Ephrathah. Sometime later, he went with a group and *retrieved the Ark* in the fields of the forest, or in Hebrew, Jaar.

First, we must understand more about these two places: 'Ephrathah' and 'the fields of Jaar'.

We know from Genesis 35:19 and 48:7 that the place where Rachel was buried was called Ephrathah, *also known as Bethlehem*. When Boaz took Ruth as his wife, the people exclaimed;

"We are witnesses. May the LORD make the woman who is coming into your home like Rachel and Leah, both of whom built the house of Israel; and may you achieve wealth in Ephrathah and become famous in Bethlehem." (Ruth 4:11 NASB)

Boaz and Ruth became the grandparents of Jesse, which makes them great grandparents of King David. In 1 Sam 17:12 it says;

Now David was the son of the Ephrathite of Bethlehem in Judah, whose name was Jesse. (NASB)

This gives us the clear link that King David grew up in Ephrathah (Bethlehem). We also know from the book of Matthew that Caesar Augustus called a census of the entire Roman world at the time when Mary was to give birth to Jesus. To partake in the census, Joseph was forced to take his heavily pregnant wife back to the destination where his lineage was traced. Since he was a descendant of King David, he had to go to Bethlehem. This fulfilled the prophecy in Micah 5:2, which states;

But you, Bethlehem Ephrathah, though you are small among the clans of Judah, out of you will come for me one who will be ruler over Israel, whose origins are from of old, from ancient times.

So the full name of Bethlehem is 'Bethlehem Ephrathah'; where David grew up as a young boy before being drafted into Saul's army and moved into the palace headquarters.

When David was at school in Ephrathah, the teacher taught Jewish history. Among the subject matter was the Ark of the Covenant. They would learn about Moses and the weightiness of God's glory upon the mercy seat. They studied about how the *kâbôwd* radiated out from inside the Tabernacle of Moses and how it caused entire nations to tremble at the sight of His power.

By included this within *history* class, the teacher was telling tales of folklore, misrepresenting the Ark as some long, lost relic of a bygone era. Yet at this very same time, it was sitting in a man's house no more than 10 miles down the road!

I can see young David, who had been experiencing the very same glory while out playing his harp tending the sheep, sitting in class slightly bewildered. He knows from personal experience that God still wants to reveal Himself and dwell amongst His people. Eventually, the religious nature of the curriculum became too much for him. Before he even realised, his hand flung up in the air.

Teacher: *"David, do you have a question?"*

David: *"Well yes I do: I know you've been telling us about the history of the Ark, but isn't it just over there in the fields of the forest-village?"*

Teacher: *"Oh umm, yes, well, that is true."*

David: *"Then why are we sitting in the classroom listening to the tales of old? Let's go on an excursion and experience the reality in our own generation!"*

Teacher: *"Ah well, sorry we can't. It doesn't fit within the occupational health and safety guidelines."*

David is convinced that the subject of the Ark should be taught as a part of geography class, not history. Throughout Israel, it seemed that everyone except David was content to reminisce over the revival stories of antiquity. Having their minds fixated on monuments of the past gave them enough of a thrill to satisfy their religiosity.

David, on the other hand, wants to start a new movement in the 'here and now'. He knows that access to God's glory had not been forever forfeited. Truth be told, a personal encounter was only a matter of walking distance away. The scripture: *"God did this so that men would seek him and perhaps reach out for him and find him, though he is not far from any one of us"* definitely springs to mind (Acts 17:27). David is desperate to acquire a testimony to call his own; after all, they didn't call it the 'Ark of the Testimony' for nothing. It quickly becomes his life's passionate pursuit, eventually leading him to the formation of the solemn vow found in Psalm 132.

In David's vow, the Psalmist is quoting David from a time after its fulfilment. In verse 6, he begins to speak about how the vow was fulfilled: *'we found (retrieved) it in the fields of the forest'*.

The 'fields of Jaar' are none other than Kiriath-jearim, which means 'forest town' or 'forest village'. 'Jear' means forest or woods, and 'the fields' denote that Abinadab's house was probably out in the surrounds of the countryside rather than inside the centre of town. This may be why David said they had to 'find' the Ark. A certain amount of searching would have been required to locate its exact whereabouts. The Ark had been neglected in the time of King Saul's reign, so David may not have known whether the Ark was still at its original destination or had been moved elsewhere. When Mount Zion was prepared and ready, he sent for intelligence to make certain that the Ark was still where it had been initially stored almost a century earlier. Having confirmed the Ark's exact location, a large group went and fetched the Ark from Abinadab's house in the countryside of Kiriath-jearim (1 Chr. 13:1-7).

David had to wait until he was 37 years old before he had the opportunity to fulfil the vow of his youth. Think about the major obstacles David had already overcome to get to this point. Surely it was this promise that kept him going through the hard times.

~ Chapter 24 ~

ENTRANCE OPEN

*⁵Until I find out a place for the Lord, a <u>habitation</u> (mishkân) for the mighty God of Jacob. ⁶Lo, we heard of it in Ephrathah, and found it in the fields of the forest. ⁷<u>We will enter into his **Tabernacles** (**mishkân**), and worship before his footstool.</u>* (Ps. 132:5-7 GNV)

The words in verse 7 do not, as in verse 6, recall an incident of the past. They express David's determination *in the present*. Verse 7 is David's tenacity to *live in the promise* from the moment of its initial fulfilment until the day he departed the earth.

It wasn't enough to simply establish a habitation for encounters with the Lord. David was bound by his oath to live in the midst of *daily God-encounters*, and the tent he pitched on Zion enabled this to be a living reality. On one of these occasions, as he poured out his heart to God in the Tabernacle, he exclaimed;

*⁴"One thing I have asked from the Lord, that I shall seek: That I may dwell in the house of the Lord <u>all the days of my life</u>; to behold the beauty of the Lord and to meditate in His temple. ⁵For in the day of trouble He will conceal me <u>in His **tabernacle**; In the secret place of His **tent**</u> He will hide me; He will lift me up on a rock."* (Ps. 27:4-5 NASB)

The 'house of the Lord' David is referring to in verse 4 is the tent *('ōhel)* he pitched on Zion (1 Chr. 16:1), which he clarifies in verse 5. In Psalm 76:2, the same word for tabernacle *(sōk)* is used in this context;

His <u>tabernacle</u> is in Salem; His dwelling place also <u>is in Zion</u>. (NASB)

The words 'house' and 'temple' in Psalm 27:4 are poetic language which would later have a future meaning. But in the literal sense, David was referring to his Tabernacle on Zion.

*"One thing I have asked from the Lord, that I shall seek: That I may dwell in the house of the Lord **<u>all the days of my life</u>**"* (Ps. 27:4a NASB)

The vow David made in Psalm 132 was *lifelong* according to Psalm 27; something he would never retire from. He longed to behold the magnificence and splendour of the Lord every single day. Stationing the Ark in Jerusalem was only the beginning for David. From here, he committed to day-by-day fellowship in his tent. Being concealed in God's tabernacle, David was assured that when the day of trouble came along, he would be protected in the secret place; hidden under the shadows of His wings.

It was only in David's Tabernacle that such a lifestyle would be achievable. The new temple arrangement was going to block entry to anyone outside the priesthood. Later, when David requested to build God a temple, he didn't realise that this petition was actually going *against* his vow. For if David had constructed the temple in his lifetime, he would no longer have been able to be 'enter into His tabernacle' nor 'dwell in the house of the Lord all the days of his life'.

Tabernacles 'Plural'

[7]We will enter into his <u>Tabernacles</u>, and worship before his footstool. (Ps. 132:7 GNV)

[7]Let us go to his <u>dwelling place</u>; let us worship at his footstool. (Ps. 132:7 CSB)

The Hebrew word for tabernacles here is *mishkân mishkân*, which is the same double emphasis the Psalmist used inside David's vow in verse 5; *"until I find a place for the Lord, a <u>tabernacle</u> for the Mighty One of Jacob."* (ASV)

In 1 Chronicles 17:5, God spoke to David through the prophet Nathan. He told David that He had lived among Israel until that point from *'ôhel* to *'ôhel*, and mishkân to mishkân. In other words, the Lord had gone from one tent or tabernacle to another, but had not yet resided in a permanent house (temple). As we already covered in chapter 13, God was more than happy with this living arrangement; the unhindered access to the people He currently had in David's Tent on Zion brought Him immense joy. To cut this season short would have disappointed the Lord just as much as it would have disappointed His people.

In Psalm 132:7: 'let us go into his *tabernacles,*' we see mishkân; ('dwelling place', 'habitation' or 'tabernacle') in the plural. Like in verse 5, translating it 'tabernacle' is more accurate than 'dwelling place' because a dwelling place could be any type of structure. David is not talking about a *bayith*; a house like structure such as Solomon's Temple. He is referring exclusively to TENT-LIKE STRUCTURES and in the case of both verse 5 & 7, there has to be *more than one* because mishkân is plural.

The first thought that springs to mind is that the two structures David is referring to must be the TOM and the TOD. But upon closer observation, this doesn't fit the context; 'we shall **enter into** his tabernacles.' In previous chapters, we thoroughly covered that no one outside the priesthood was allowed to go *into* Moses' Tabernacle. David was from the tribe of Judah; he could not be referring to the TOM because he was never allowed into that tent.

There are only two tabernacles mentioned in Scripture which David could be referring to. In this way, he is speaking both literally and prophetically. One of the Tabernacles was the earthly fulfilment through David's literal tent, but the other was the heavenly tabernacle that this tent was patterned after all along. David speaks of the literal tent which he dwelt in daily, but also of the heavenly *hagion* (Holy of Holies) from Hebrews 8:2, where Jesus, the Son *of David* and eternal King-Priest, now dwells forever!

> *[1]Now the main point in what has been said is this: we have such a high priest, who has taken His seat at the right hand of the throne of the Majesty <u>in the heavens, [2]a minister in the sanctuary (hagion) and in the true tabernacle, which the Lord pitched, not man</u>.* (Heb. 8:1-2 NASB)

> *[1]What I mean is that we have a high priest who sits at the right side of God's great throne in heaven. [2]<u>He serves as the priest in the most holy place inside **the real tent there in heaven**</u>. This tent of worship was set up by the Lord, not by humans.* (Heb. 8:1-2 CEV)

Being filled with the Spirit, David not only saw the New Covenant foreshadowing (which he was permitted to experience and live under), but also the complete fulfilment of the coming age; the gospel age we now are part of. He knew *his* tabernacle was only a *pattern* of the 'real tent in heaven'. He saw every believer having access onto the throne of grace to sit with Jesus in heavenly places (Eph. 2:6, Heb. 4:16). We can *go into* His tabernacle any time, free of charge. By His blood, Jesus has paid our way in.

Yet we have something even greater to look forward to: a coming Kingdom Age where these two tabernacles will be combined into one. This is the fulfilment of the Covenant God made with David in 1 Chronicles 17:11-13, the re-establishment of the Davidic kingdom throughout the natural earth-realm! The King's name is the King of all kings, Jesus Christ.

The prophet Ezekiel prophesied about this extremely special time in history in Ezekiel 37;

*23They will no longer defile themselves with their idols, or with their detestable things, or with any of their transgressions; but I will deliver them from all their **dwelling places (môwshâb)** in which they have sinned, and will cleanse them. And they will be My people, and I will be their God.* (NASB)

Ezekiel 37:23 refers to the historic nation of Israel. The people of God were caught up in 'dwelling places' of sin. 'Dwelling places' here in Hebrew is the double emphasis; 'môwshâb, môwshâb'. This word will be important later, but put simply; while *môwshâb* in general terms means 'dwelling', it specifically refers to a jurisdiction where assemblies of people gather around a table in seats of authority. The behaviour of the people gathered within that dwelling or jurisdiction establishes the source of that authority. Ezekiel saw these 'seats of Satan' torn down with the re-emergence of the Davidic kingdom in the millennium. This is the fulfilment of the promises in the Davidic Covenant, which we will touch upon throughout the remaining verses of Psalm 132.

Let's continue with Ezekiel;

*24My servant David (prophetically the Jewish Messiah; Jesus) will be king over them, and they will all have one shepherd; and they will walk in My ordinances and keep My statutes and observe them. 25They will live on the land that I gave to Jacob My servant, in which your fathers lived; and they will live on it, they, and their sons and their sons' sons, forever; and **David My servant** will be their prince forever. 26I will make a covenant of peace with them; it will be an everlasting covenant with them. And I will place them and multiply them, and will set My sanctuary in their midst forever. 27My dwelling place (mishkân, mishkân) also will be with them; and I will be their God, and they will be My people. 28And the nations will know that I am the Lord who sanctifies Israel, when My sanctuary is in their midst forever.* (Ezek. 37:24-28 NASB)

The restoration of Israel to their native soil (Ezek. 37:11-22) paves the way for the second coming of the promised King, the Son of God descended from David. He will gather into His kingdom the true Israel; all who shall by faith be acknowledged as the Israel of God (Gal. 6:16), Jew and Gentile alike. As 'one new man' in Messiah, they shall be His people, and He their God, (Ezek. 37:23, Heb. 8:10). Gentiles are *also* included, because we have been grafted in. Hallelujah!

The reign of the Ultimate King David is the eternal reign of Christ beginning with His millennial kingdom. This is part of the everlasting covenant of peace ratified by the precious blood of Christ shed on the cross (Luke 2:14, Heb. 13:20). The culminating factor setting His people apart from everyone else (survivors of the great tribulation) is that His 'mishkân mishkân' (dwelling place/tabernacle) will be in the midst of them. The tabernacle of the Lord's Majesty Glory will once again be set in place upon the *physical* location called Zion in Jerusalem. The two tabernacles mentioned by David in Psalm 132:7 (natural and heavenly) will be effectively merged into one!

During this 1,000 year period, the Tabernacle in Heavenly Jerusalem will be vacated, but not removed from its place. It will come back into prominence after the millennium. Mankind will not have to go into the spiritual realm to visit the heavenly tabernacle any longer. The re-established TOD will be the central meeting place of all the sons and daughters of the kingdom. From there, the Lord Jesus will reign upon David's throne, and the land of Israel will once again be the praise of the earth.

Though this is for a future time, God is calling all of us *right now* to 'go into His heavenly tabernacle' (described in Hebrews 8:2) as a foreshadowing to demonstrate the reality of this coming Davidic kingdom to a lost and dying world. We *do not* have to wait until the millennium. God has given us permission to 'experience the powers of the coming Kingdom Age', and we do this, not merely for our own comfort and repose, but also to extend the invitation of citizenship to unbelievers who the Lord has placed around us.

Positioned at His Footstool

[7]We will go into his tabernacles: we will worship at his footstool.
(Ps. 132:7 KJV)

The footstool is 'the ground immediately surrounding the Ark', or 'the platform on which it stands'. In order to sprinkle the blood on the mercy seat, the High Priest would have approached this footstool. Use of the word 'footstool' proves that we must go INTO the tabernacles, not merely 'get within eyesight' of them.

David says that an integral part of entering His tabernacle is worshiping at His footstool. King David would have approached the Tabernacle using this protocol. The word for worship here speaks of 'bowing down, or bowing low', prostrating ourselves at His feet. We must not stand haughtily before Him, but must bend the knee, lowering ourselves in our own estimation to give Him the honour due His name. In this way, we first minister to Him before He ministers to us.

Let's re-examine Psalm 99;

> The Lord reigns! Let the peoples tremble. <u>He is enthroned between the cherubim.</u> Let the earth quake. [2]The Lord is great <u>in Zion;</u> he is exalted above all the peoples. [3]Let them praise your great and awe-inspiring name. He is holy. [4]The mighty King loves justice. You have established fairness; you have administered justice and righteousness in Jacob. [5]Exalt the Lord our God; <u>bow in worship at his footstool.</u> He is holy. (Ps. 99:1-5 CSB)

The only way to come under the shadow of His wings is through lordship. Metaphorically speaking, true worship is 'bowing down' at the foot of the Ark. Hebrews 4:16 shows us we can approach his throne with bold confidence because we know He will welcome us with open arms. But as we enter, we MUST BOW LOW in reverential worship as we draw near to Jesus. Coming 'boldly' is not arrogance or presumption, but thankfulness and contrition springing forth from the abundance of mercy we received upon entry.

By falling at his feet in gratitude (like the woman with the alabaster box of expensive perfume), Jesus will then bid us to come and sit alongside Him on His throne. By first kissing His feet, we can now place our feet upon His footstool. According to Psalm 110:1, Jesus' enemies are His footstool. So as we sit in fellowship (abide in the Spirit), Jesus places Satan and all his princes *under our feet*. Jesus is seated far above all principality, power, might and dominion, and He wants us to abide in that same authority. (Eph. 1:20-21)

Finding a Tent vs Building a House

The only way to *'enter into God's tabernacle and worship at His footstool'* in the Old Testament was via the Tabernacle of David. In the New Covenant, this can be experienced in Spirit via the heavenly Holy of Holies; the true tabernacle set up by the Lord in heavenly Jerusalem. According to Hebrews 12:22, it is 'the city of the living God'. Footstool-worship could not be attained or achieved in either the Tabernacle of Moses or the Temple of Solomon, because access inside the Most Holy Place was denied. Keep this in mind as we skip across to powerful revelations from Stephen in Acts 7.

It may be beneficial to go back and review the first half of chapter 13; 'Post-Tabernacle Glory' as a quick refresher which will make it easier to apprehend the following information...

Stephen explains to us;

> [46]*David found favour in God's sight, and asked that he might find a dwelling place for the God of Jacob. [47]But it was Solomon who built a house for Him.* (Acts 7:46-47 NASB)

On face value, this does not look like a big deal: This was my original presumption as a young believer;

> *"David wanted to build the Temple (the dwelling place for the God of Jacob), but Solomon was the one who was allowed to actually build it."*

For years I thought this was the case, but that IS NOT what Stephen is saying here. I had been reading the NIV84 version which says; *'David asked that he might provide a dwelling place for the God of Jacob, but it was Solomon who built **the** house for him'.* This portrays the Temple as 'the dwelling place for the God of Jacob'.

The translation should say that Solomon 'built **a** house for Him'. In the NIV 2011 they have corrected it now to 'a'. The subtle use of the word 'the' drew me to the wrong conclusion; that the house Solomon ended up building *was* the dwelling place David desired to build but never attained. But if you look more closely at the verse, that couldn't be further from the truth. David desired 'to find a *dwelling place* for the God of Jacob', which is taken straight out of Psalm 132:5! *On the other hand,* Solomon built him a *house*! There is a massive difference between 'finding a dwelling place' and 'building a house'. If the verse had said 'David asked to build a house', the use of the word 'the' in Acts 7:47 would be justified. But Stephen is actually distinguishing between two totally different achievements here.

The word for dwelling place in Greek is *skēnōma,* which is the corresponding word for *mishkân* in the Hebrew. It is the word used for *'let us enter his TABERNACLE.'* David's 'original' desire was to raise up a tent where men could enter, not to build a house where they would be barred from entry. In fact, if you look at the Greek Septuagint for Psalm 132:v5 and v7 you will find it uses *skēnōma* in their translation of the word *mishkân.* When James quoted Amos 9 in Acts 15, stating God's desire to rebuild the tabernacle of David, he used the word *skēnē,* of the same family as *skēnōma* (Acts 15:16). Let's examine what Stephen really said. It is translated correctly in the 'New Testament for Everyone' translation;

> [46]*David found favour with God, and requested permission to <u>establish a Tabernacle</u> for the house of Jacob.* [47]*But it was Solomon who <u>built him a house</u>.* (Acts 7:46-47 NTE)

Solomon built God a house: *oikos* in Greek, directly corresponding with *bayith* in Hebrew. However, the vow of David never mentions either of these two words. *Oikos* and *bayith* were not placed in his heart because a house with restrictions was not God's desire for future generations. That's why the Lord's desire, even to this day, is to rebuild the Tabernacle of David which Solomon took down! The Zionist Freemasons, on the other hand, are obsessed with rebuilding the Temple of Solomon on the Temple Mount. Their overwhelming desire is to rebuild a house for their false-Messiah. He is the antichrist, who will set himself up inside this Temple and make the bogus-claim that 'he is *god'* (2 Thess. 2:4). Let's stick to the correct pursuit by rebuilding what God desires us to rebuild and leave the rest alone. (Col. 3:1-3)

In Acts 7:46, Stephen was not speaking of David's desire to build the Temple; he is expressly referencing *the Psalm 132 vow*, which was a desire he had well before the desire for the Temple entered his heart. The passion which resulted in the oath came when he was a young boy in Bethlehem, long before the Ark had ever come into Jerusalem. In his purity of devotion, he simply wanted to provide a place where God could inhabit and people could dwell: a mishkân/skēnōma/tabernacle.

It was only after David had built his cedar palace that thoughts of a temple originated in his mind. All of a sudden, he felt sorry for God; he had a majestic palace, and God only a humble little tent. These thoughts are first recorded at the beginnings of 2 Samuel 7 and 1 Chronicles 17. By this time, David would have been in his forties. We know that this new heart-desire of David's was never fulfilled, but on David's part, it was simply an error of failing to discern divine timing. A temple was not in God's plan for David's life, even though preparations for it were (1 Chr. 28:1-3). This apparent failure did not render his previous vow incomplete. God made it clear to us that what David mentioned in the original vow was the mishkân or skēnōma, thus it was already fulfilled through the Tent of David. God told David that residing there pleased Him greatly;

> ^{5}I have never lived in a house, from the day I brought the Israelites out of Egypt until this very day. My home has always been a tent, moving from one place to another in a Tabernacle. ^{6}Yet no matter where I have gone with the Israelites, I have never once complained to Israel's leaders, the shepherds of my people. I have never asked them, "Why haven't you built me a beautiful cedar house?" (1 Chr.17:5-6 NLT)

Showing David His pleasure with the current arrangement further confirmed that the vow had been brought to fulfilment. God had even bigger plans than a temple project for David going forward. He was actually going to build David another house; a dynasty of kings culminating in the Messiah, who would reign from David's throne forever (2 Sam 7:11-14 NLT). That's how pleased God was with David's tabernacle. If David had built God a temple, then Jesus' throne would have been connected to the temple and not the tabernacle. Because of this, God would be unable to rebuild the tabernacle of David in the last days, as it would not directly correspond with David's throne. (Is. 16:5)

Now back to Acts 7:46-47: Contrary to my earlier belief, Stephen is not illustrating Solomon's success at the expense of David's failure. He is stating what both of them achieved in their lifetime.

1) David completed his vow in Psalm 132:5 by setting up the TOD; and

2) Solomon also completed his mandate to build the Temple.

Moreover, Stephen is illustrating a distinction in the heart motivation David possessed compared with Solomon. David desired a 'dwelling place of God-relationship'; a place where he could delight in the glory of Yahweh. But Solomon's prime motivation was simply to 'build God a house'. He was just like any modern-day builder; not overly concerned about who is going to live there. Such builders do not live in the house after they finish the build or come back to visit the residents; their obligation is simply to complete the contract.

Solomon's mandate, although confirmed by the Lord, never became more than second-hand revelation handed down from his earthly father. At the time, Solomon did have a degree of love towards God and he was committed to serving His will. But for him, the project was not primarily about intimacy with God, neither was it fuelled by desperation to draw close. *It* was simply an architectural design God had commanded him to build. This made it more about the grandeur of the outside presentation, rather than the One who would dwell on the inside.

Solomon was so used to growing up in God's thick manifest glory it was always familiar to him. He never truly grasped the significance of the access he had been granted inside David's tent, because he had never been without it. This would have negative ramifications later on in his life: In the midst of worldly success, he would gradually drift away from the Lord. David, on the other hand, would never allow earthly achievement to supersede his dedication to humility and worship. He knew full-well that the daily commitment to his vow was the cornerstone of kingly success.

Chapter 25

WHERE WOULD MY RESTING PLACE BE?

[7]We will go into his tabernacles: we will worship at his footstool. [8]Arise, O Lord, to Your resting place, You and the ark of Your strength. [9]Let your priests be clothed with righteousness, and let your saints shout for joy. (Ps. 132:7-9 KJV, NASB, ESV)

Immediately after David speaks concerning the two tabernacles of entry (Tabernacle of David and the Heavenly Sanctuary), he says; "Arise Lord, and come to your *resting place, You and the Ark.*"

First of all, we must establish when and where this occurred. The context is defined for us in verse 6; *'we found it in the fields of the Forest'*. 'The Lord rising up' is symbolic of David's entourage lifting up the Ark to move it out of Abinadab's house in Kiriath-jearim. After a three month lay-off at Obed Edom's house, the Ark finally made it to the Lord's 'resting place', the tent David pitched on Mount Zion. This is verified in the final two verses of Psalm 132;

> *For the Lord has <u>chosen Zion</u>; he has desired it for his dwelling place: [14]"This is my **resting place forever**; here I will dwell, for I have desired it."* (Ps. 132:13-14 ESV)

It is abundantly clear; God has chosen ZION as His resting place. We must keep this at the forefront of our minds to correctly interpret *what's coming next...*

Building a proper understanding of God's true resting place must be achieved *before* fast-forwarding to the inauguration day of Solomon's Temple, *constructed on Mount Moriah*. As a part of proceedings, Solomon had to speak a prayer of dedication. This is found in 1 Chronicles 6:12-42. In view of such a momentous occasion, Solomon made a custom-built bronze platform and placed it at the centre of the temple courtyard. Then he knelt to pray.

In Solomon's introduction, he mentions his father three times. Each time he implores God to fulfil the promises he made to David. It already seems like Solomon's mindset was focused on David's past loyalty rather than forging his own unique partnership with God. While it was important to honour David's legacy, Solomon also needed to take ownership of the vision moving forward.

Instead, he was relying too heavily on the generational blessings passed down by his father. Psalm 132:10-12 tells us that the generational blessings promised to David and his descendants would only be experienced by the future kings who kept faithful to the 'covenant terms' given to David. It is never enough to rely on the faithfulness of our ancestors as a guarantee that God must bless us regardless of our actions;

> *[10]For the sake of your servant David, do not reject your anointed one. [11]The Lord swore an oath to David, a promise he will not abandon: "I will set one of your offspring on your throne. [12]__If your sons keep my covenant and my decrees that I will teach them__, their sons will **__also__** sit on your throne forever."* (Ps. 132:10-12 CSB)

In verses 10 and 11, we see that the promised Messiah coming through David's lineage was indeed guaranteed by oath regardless of the behaviour of David's future generations. This is known as 'the sure mercies given to David' (Isa 55:3, Acts 13:34). For the sake of David's faithfulness, 'Christ the Anointed One' was assured to come through one of David's sons and He would never be rejected by God. All the sufferings and hardships David endured in God's name would certainly not be in vain, even if the majority of his descendants rebelled.

After David passed, each subsequent king was required to 'keep *the terms* of the Davidic Covenant' to be made worthy of an eternal seat alongside Christ. If they kept the Lord's decrees, they would *also* sit on David's throne forever. Sadly, the majority ended up being evil kings rather than righteous. Those who were disobedient never got to experience 'the sure mercies of their father David.'

The sure mercies of David are: 'the steadfast, reliable covenant mercies promised to David'. They have been handed to Jesus, the Son of David, and are assured to all who enter into the Davidic Covenant by receiving Him as Lord. In light of Christ's sacrifice, there has been made available an abundance of God's mercy to be lavished upon humanity, enabling Jesus to receive His full inheritance (Ps. 2:8). All we have to do to receive this 'sure mercy' is come to Him with a broken and contrite heart, trusting completely in His Spirit of grace to cleanse us from any previous sins and then lead us from there into all righteousness.

Solomon's Good Intentions

I must highlight two passages of Solomon's dedication speech. Immediately after the introduction he prays;

> *"But will God actually dwell with mankind on the earth? Behold, heaven and the highest heaven cannot contain You; how much less this house which I have built!"* (1 Chr. 6:18 AMP)

And now Solomon's conclusion;

> *And now arise, O LORD God, and go to your <u>resting place</u>, you and the ark of your might. Let your priests, O LORD God, be clothed with salvation, and let your saints rejoice in your goodness.* (1 Chr. 6:41 ESV)

If you have been paying attention, you would recognise Solomon's conclusion. It is a direct quotation from David's vow found in Psalm 132:8-9, which was our scripture reference at the beginning of this chapter. Solomon seems convinced that shifting the Ark out of the Tabernacle of David and into his Temple is the fulfilment of these verses. But didn't we just establish that the actual fulfilment of this occurred when the Ark was placed in Zion? Verses 13 and 14 of Psalm 132 clearly show us that.

> *For the Lord has <u>chosen Zion</u>; he has desired it for his dwelling place:*
> [14] *"This **(ZION) is my <u>resting place forever</u>**; here I will dwell, for I have desired it."* (Ps. 132:13-14 ESV)

There is also a second issue with Solomon's conclusion. It concerns the priests;

> [8] *"Arise, O Lord, to Your resting place, You and the ark of Your strength.*
> [9] <u>*Let your priests be clothed with righteousness, and let your saints shout for joy.*</u>*"* (Ps. 132:8-9 NASB, ESV)

Above is the quote from Solomon, as recorded in Psalm 132. What David said in verse 9 is very interesting. When David spoke about the resting place of God upon Mount Zion, he said that *'the priests will be clothed with righteousness, and the saints will shout for joy.'*

What David is actually emphasising is that *all* the saints are shouting for joy *because on Mount Zion, all* the saints are permitted to *be* priests! Through the TOD, the priests and the saints become one and the same group. This means there is to be no 'class distinction' (of clergy and laity) within the body of

Christ. We are all royalty: a kingdom of priests. That's a cause for celebration! All of us are also 'clothed with righteousness' because the righteousness of Christ has been imputed to us at the new birth. That is the blessing of the New Covenant in Jesus' blood. Every single believer becomes a saint, and as a saint, they immediately become a priest through the ordination of Melchizedek. We know for certain David was referring to the priests at His tabernacle, because later in Psalm 132 it says;

> *¹³For the Lord has __chosen Zion__; he has desired it for his dwelling place: ¹⁴"This is my resting place forever; here I will dwell, for I have desired it. ¹⁵I will abundantly bless her provisions; I will satisfy her poor with bread. ¹⁶__Her (ZION's) priests I will clothe with salvation, and her (ZION's) saints will shout for joy.__"* (Ps. 132:13-16 ESV)

The 'her' mentioned twice in verse 16 is the *Zion from verse 13: 'Zion's priests* will be clothed with salvation, and the *saints of Zion* will shout for joy'. That is us!

Verse 16 of Psalm 132 proves to us that David's vow explicitly refers to Zion because (after the mention of Zion in verse 13) he re-iterates the <u>final verse of his vow (V9)</u>. (David's vow starts at verse 3 and ends at verse 9). Let's check out both v9 and 16 below;

> *⁹Let your priests be clothed with <u>righteousness</u>, and let your saints shout for joy."* (Ps. 132:9 ESV)

> *¹⁶Her (ZION's) priests I will clothe with <u>salvation</u>, and her (ZION's) saints will shout for joy."* (Ps. 132:16 ESV)

The only other change between verse 9 and verse 16, is that the word 'righteousness' is exchanged with 'salvation'. As New Testament believers, to be clothed with salvation *is* to be clothed with righteousness. There is no difference.

Quoting David's Vow out of Context

When Solomon quoted Ps. 132:8-9 at the inauguration of his temple, it was utilised *out of context* because he was actually taking the priesthood *away from the saints*. Anyone not directly descended from Aaron had now been effectively 'laid off'. Though this is not recorded in the scriptures, I would surmise that there were many people in Israel who were grieving when they saw the Ark being carried away from the Tabernacle of David. Their time of close proximity to the Ark and sweet fellowship with God had now been cut off. This was surely cause for sorrow rather than joy!

"Arise, O Lord, to Your resting place, You and the ark of Your strength."

(Ps. 132:8 NASB – David's vow)

"Arise, O Lord God, to Your resting place, You and the ark of Your strength."

(2 Chr. 6:41 NKJV – Solomon's dedication)

The Temple of Solomon was located on Mount Moriah. However, we know Psalm 132:13 shows the resting place of God *is Mount Zion!* There is clearly something aloof about Solomon placing this portion of David's vow at the conclusion of the temple's 'dedication-prayer'. It was by no means complete heresy on Solomon's part, but when being considered within its original context (spoken by David) we have proven that Solomon quoted it outside of its proper framework. Even so, the verse still had a certain amount of relevance; the Ark was going to rest in the Temple permanently from that time on. In an overall sense, it was probably a suitable enough scripture considering what the people were witnessing. Let's put the relevant portions of Psalm 132 consecutively;

*[8]Arise, O Lord, to Your **resting place**, You and the ark of Your strength.*
(Ps. 132:8 NASB)

*[13]For the Lord has <u>chosen Zion</u>; he has desired it for his dwelling place: [14]This is my **resting place forever**; here I will dwell, for I have desired it.*
(Ps. 132:13-14 ESV)

The Hebrew word for 'resting place' in both verse 8 and 14 is *mĕnuwchah.* In the Septuagint they split v8 and v14 into two different Greek words: *anapausis and katapausis.* We will study these Greek words later, but for now, our focus is *mĕnuwchah.*

God's true 'Resting Place' confirmed by Stephen

There is an obscure mention of *mĕnuwchah (resting place)* in a prophecy from Isaiah which may be deemed of little relevance except for the fact that it is propelled into the limelight of the New Testament by our friend Stephen in

Acts 7. Not only is this prophecy in Isaiah 66:1-2 quoted by Stephen, the place where he quoted it was immediately following the section of his message we covered in the last chapter;

(The TOM) remained in the land until the time of David, [46]who enjoyed God's favour and asked that he might provide a dwelling place for the God of Jacob. [47]But it was Solomon who built a house for him. [48]"However, the Most High does not live in houses made by human hands. As the prophet says: [49]**"Heaven is my throne, and the earth is my footstool. What kind of house will you build for me? says the Lord. Or where will my resting place be?** [50]**Has not my hand made all these things?"** (Acts 7:45b-50)

The text highlighted in bold comes from Isaiah 66:1-2a. The resting place in Hebrew is *mâqôwm měnuwchah*. Through Isaiah, God affirms what Solomon said at the beginning of his dedicatory prayer (2 Chr. 6:18), yet at the same time stands in direct opposition to the quoting of David's vow in his concluding remarks. (2 Chr. 6:41)

In Acts 7, Stephen quotes a passage of Scripture where God is essentially rebuking the Jewish people for calling the temple on Mount Moriah (oikos/bayith) His resting place! Stephen strategically includes this directly after mentioning about Solomon building 'a house' for God. The people living in Isaiah's time may have got this false idea from Solomon's dedication in 2 Chronicles 6:41. Yet at the same time, Solomon was wise enough to know that any sort of earthly dwelling could not contain the God of Heaven, even the most expensive and elaborate in human history!

For your recollection, here's what Solomon prayed just after completing his intro;

"But will God actually dwell with mankind on the earth? Behold, heaven and the highest heaven cannot contain You; how much less this house which I have built!" (1 Chr.6:18 AMP)

There is perfect agreement between this and what Stephen and Isaiah spoke;

[48]*However, the Most High does not live in houses made by human hands. As the prophet says:* [49]**"Heaven is my throne, and the earth is my footstool. What kind of house will you build for me? says the Lord. Or**

where will my resting place be? [50]Has not my hand made all these things?" (Acts 7:48-50)

In verse 48, Stephen refers to God as the 'Most High'. If He is Most High, then He is higher than the highest of all the heavens. Like Solomon said, God cannot be contained within a house we can build.

Then Stephen follows with the quote from Isaiah 66. Let's break down what God is saying here;

1) *Heaven is My throne, and the earth is My footstool. What kind of house will you build for me? Says the Lord. Has not my hand made all these things?*

"I AM all encompassing: enveloping the entire cosmos. Therefore, what kind of house could you build for Me that would be big enough to contain all that I AM? Have not My hands created all these things to begin with?"

2) *Or where will my resting place be?*

"If heaven is My throne, and the earth My footstool, where would My true resting place be?"

Think about where a king rests: Does a king take a rest on his footstool? Certainly not! That rules earth out. A King rests *by sitting down on His throne!*

God's resting place (mâqôwm měnuwchah: Isa 66:1) must therefore be located in heaven; even more specifically, at the place where *His throne has been set in place.* When the Psalmist said *'the Lord has chosen Zion; he has desired it for his dwelling place' (v13),* he used the word for 'dwelling place' we touched on last chapter: The word *môwshâb.* If you recall, this word involves more than just dwelling somewhere, but also 'taking a seat of authority'. So Psalm 132:13-14a could easily say; **'The Lord has chosen Zion, He has desired it as *His seat of authority.* "*This throne* is My resting place (měnuwchah). Here I will dwell.'"**

Tabernacle on Zion: Home address of Jesus Christ

God has set up His throne on Spiritual Zion in the heavenly Jerusalem (Heb. 12:22). According to Psalm 132:5 and 7, the dwelling place containing this throne is the mishkân or skēnōma: the *Tabernacle* on Zion. God is omnipresent (everywhere), but the place where He rests is where an open manifestation of His glory dwells. *We* must get to this place!

> [13] *"The Lord has chosen Zion; he has desired it for his <u>dwelling place</u> (môwshâb: seat of authority)* [14] *"This is my <u>resting place</u> (mĕnuwchah) forever; <u>here I will **dwell (yâshab)**</u>, for I have desired it."* (Ps. 132:13-14 ESV)

This reference to 'dwell' in verse 14 (the Hebrew word 'yâshab') should be the only time where the English word 'dwell' or 'dwelling' appears in Psalm 132. God *yâshab's on his môwshâb*. Translation: He abides/dwells on His throne of authority (in Zion).

Yâshab means 'make my home', 'take up residency' or 'the place where you hang out'. God's home is where the Magnificence of His Glory dwells, resonating out from His resting place: His throne; the Ark. God's dwelling place is inside a tabernacle that has an open entrance, granting free and unhindered access to all!

This **Yâshab** [Psalm 132:14b] (God's dwelling/home) comprises;

The four M's from Psalm 132

    1. <u>Mishkân:</u> (tabernacling/intimacy/fellowship) [Psalm 132:5b.7]

    2. <u>Môwshâb:</u> (seat of authority – throne) [Psalm 132:13]

    3. <u>Mĕnuwchah:</u> (place of rest) [Psalm 132:8, 14a]

    4. <u>Mâqôwm:</u> (take our stand / occupy ground) [Psalm 132:5a]

Now consider God the Son. The Ark is a picture of Him. Like the Ark, which was lifted up and transported by David's men onto Zion, Jesus rose from the dead and entered His resting place when He ascended to heaven and was *seated* at the right hand of the Father. Jesus Christ sits enthroned between the Cherubim according to Psalm 99:1. His throne is the Mercy Seat inside the heavenly Holy of Holies, God's *yâshab* and true tabernacle. The Father said to Him, *"Son, sit down and rest at My right hand, and watch as your enemies become your footstool"* (Ps. 110:1). Jesus has sat down in His seat of authority, and from this position of rest He waits for His enemies to be utterly subdued;

Now Christ has gone to heaven. He is seated in the place of honour next to God, <u>and all the angels and authorities and powers accept his authority</u>. (1 Pet. 3:22 NLT)

Jesus wants all of us to experience this same resting place through abiding in Him. Being 'restful' does not imply that Jesus does nothing; everything He does is orchestrated from 'a state of rest'. The authority of this resting place comes by faith, for only those who truly trust God's word can enter His rest. (Heb. 4:3)

Likewise, as we sit down with Him in heavenly places, we also find rest for *our own* souls (Matt 11:29, Eph. 2:6). From this place of authority, we can command the devil to become our footstool, then put our feet up and relax. That's what a footrest or a 'pouf' is designed to do. When you pull the lever on your sofa, it reclines you into a more relaxing position. When Satan and his princes become our footrest, we can experience spiritual relaxation and rest. This 'disarming of the devil' can only be achieved from within the manifest Majestic glory of God seated with Christ in the throne-room.

We must dive into the refreshing water of the river that makes glad the City of God. We must follow the rapids of God's Spirit up to the holy place where the Most High dwells (Ps 46:4). Most critically, as individuals we must cooperate with Him to find our custom made pathway leading up to Mount Zion. There is no specific formula: God has a unique pattern for each of us to discover.

Last chapter, we learned that the two tabernacles of entry will be merged into one during the millennial reign of Christ. The tabernacle in heaven, whilst still standing, is left vacant because Jesus is not there anymore; He will be physically situated on earth. Now let's examine what occurs at the end of the Millennium.

In Revelation 21:1, we discover that at the end of His 1000 year reign, Christ and His glorified saints will have worked together to create a completely new heaven and a new earth. The heaven and earth (as they were once known) will have disappeared from sight! At this time, the New Jerusalem will come down from the third heaven and touch down as the Capital city of earth forever (Rev. 21:1-2). As John saw it descending, he heard a loud shout coming from the throne;

Behold, the <u>tabernacle of God</u> is among men, and He will <u>dwell among them</u>, and they shall be His people, and God Himself will be among them. (Rev. 21:3 NASB)

The true heavenly tabernacle, after being vacant for 1000 years, will descend as part of the New Jerusalem. It will be a permanent fixture on earth, superseding the Tabernacle of David from that time onwards. The dwelling place of 'God the Father', 'God the Son' and 'God the Holy Spirit' will be with us on earth eternally. To 'dwell among them' is the same Greek word used of Jesus in John 1:14 when He came to earth the first time and *tabernacled* among us.

Now look at Revelation 21:22-23;

[22] I saw <u>no temple</u> in the city, for the <u>Lord God Almighty and the Lamb are its temple</u>. [23] And the city has no need of sun or moon, for the glory of God illuminates the city, and the Lamb is its light. (NLT)

For all eternity, there will be a **Tabernacle of God,** but there will be **no Temple!** God Himself is the Temple, because as Stephen pointed out to us; *'The Lord does not live in temples made by human hands'*. God is so expansive that He simply has to *be the Temple*. A building with rooms that restrict cannot contain our God. On top of all that, the Majestic Glory that used to be experienced only within close proximity to the tabernacle becomes the replacement for moonlight and sunlight. It will be felt world-wide without hindrance. The Tabernacle of God spreads His Glory over all the earth as yeast spreads through the whole batch of dough.

◊◊◊◊◊

"(The TOM) remained in the land until the time of David, [46] who enjoyed God's favour and asked that he might provide a <u>dwelling place</u> for the God of Jacob. [47] But it was Solomon who built a <u>house</u> for him. [48] "However, the Most High does not live in houses made by human hands. As the prophet says: [49] "'Heaven is my throne, and the earth is my footstool. What kind of house will you build for me? says the Lord. Or where will my resting place be? [50] Has not my hand made all these things?'" (Acts 7:45b-50)

By relating the two unique structures David and Solomon established to the prophecy in Isaiah 66:1-2a, Stephen skilfully shows us that God's desire was

236

the dwelling place (skēnōma) set up by David rather than the house (oikos) built by Solomon! The Temple would never be a suitable resting place; His resting place is forever the dwelling place of 'life in the Spirit' patterned after the Tabernacle of David. The level of supernatural revelation given to an operator of the church's 'food program' is extraordinary. In fact, it is said that Stephen "was a man full of faith and the Holy Spirit" and that "no one could stand up against the wisdom by which he spoke". (Acts 6:5, 10)

The finished work of Christ on the cross enables Jesus to take a permanent seat of authority (môwshâb) in the heavenly realms. Now He dominates the devil from this place of rest. However, there are certain occasions when Jesus still rises to His feet. Jesus stands up to honour courageous acts of heroism performed on account of His name.

When Stephen began his message in Acts 7, they said his face was shining like the face of an angel. After Stephen finished speaking, the Jews were so furious they gnashed their teeth at him. But Stephen said, *"I see heaven open and the Son of Man STANDING at the right hand of God"* (Acts 7:56). Jesus was standing to honour Stephen's stand for Him. When we stand up for Him; He stands up for us. The Jews, on the other hand, were blocking their ears. They seized Stephen and led him out to be stoned to death. As the rocks were flung his way, he was knocked to his knees and prayed; *"Lord, do not hold this sin against them",* and shortly after this, he graduated to heaven (Acts 7:60). Stephen was fulfilling the Hebrew word *mâqôwm;* He was standing at his post and occupying to the very death.

~ Chapter 26 ~

YOUR PERSONAL ZION

We are beginning to understand with greater clarity the most basic prophetic application of the word 'Zion' in the Bible. Though simple, it is utterly profound: a most vital concept to grasp. Zion represents 'life in the Spirit' and the Tabernacle on Zion is where 'life in the Spirit' transports us. Regarding Zion, Hebrews 12:18 says;

18You have not come to a mountain that can be touched

When you encounter the blessings and promises of Zion in the Word of God you can substitute 'Zion' for 'those who walk in the Spirit'. By so doing, the many references to Zion found in the Old Testament suddenly come alive to you as a Christian. Through abiding in the Holy Spirit, we receive all the benefits of Zion. Let's take Psalm 87:2, as one simple example;

The LORD loves the gates of Zion more than all the other dwelling places of Jacob. (NASB)

Translation: "Of all His people, the Lord loves those who walk in the Spirit the most."

We want to find our way up to the Heavenly Tabernacle upon Zion to meet with Jesus at the throne of grace. This is the mercy seat inside the heavenly Holy of Holies. Remember what David vowed: He would not enter his house, lie down in his bed, or give sleep to his eyelids until he found a resting place for God in his life.

David swore he would find *his Mount Zion*, the place where God dwelt *for him*; a special location where the Lord could always be found *by him*. Only then could he find rest for his soul, because he would be able to enter the true rest that can only be experienced *in God* alone. David went through all types of afflictions to see this become a reality, but he wouldn't let these trials deter him. He wasn't just establishing a resting place for himself, but was also helping others locate this same place in their lives. This is part of our calling, also.

We need to find our own personal Zion: the place specific to us where we can connect with God aside from the interruptions of this busy world. The pathway looks different for each one of us because God has created us all uniquely. He enjoys the variety of relational dynamics that come from all the individual expressions of the 'secret place'. (Matt 6:6)

Sometimes when we hear the term 'prayer closet' or 'secret place' we think of a claustrophobic chamber of confinement. A small room may be the way up to Zion for some of you, but the point Jesus was trying to make in Matthew 6:6 was that we need to find a place of seclusion where worldly distractions are completely blocked out.

This could be out walking in the forest or along the beach. Others prefer to be sitting down on a specific couch or lying in a bed. It may be out on the porch, or it could literally be a special prayer room you have set aside within your house. The principal thing is to find what works for you.

The way I connect with God is definitely through prayer walking and also bike riding. I prefer to be moving, so I find trails where I can be at peace. For others, it may be prayer-driving in the secret place of your car. Perhaps it is alone-time with God while surfing, fishing, playing golf, swimming or jogging. Fellowship with others is a must, but it is no substitute for the secret place. The primary aim is to clear our mind so that we can tune in to the frequency of heaven. Only you know the intricate way God designed you to have an intimate connection with Him. But we must be diligent enough to search out these pathways into the glory of the Lord if we want to effectively 'break through' into supernatural living.

In chapter one, I shared how *'the Father seeks those who worship in Spirit and in truth.'* The Father is seeking for the true worshiper, but in order to be a true worshiper, we must ensure we provide Him a resting place. It's no good for God to find us only to be told, like Mary and Joseph, that there's no room for Him in the inn. We need to be like the Shunammite woman in the days of Elisha who built an additional room on top of her house for the prophet to stay whenever he pleased (2 Kings 4:10). This room was literally 'a little chamber' which is the exact meaning of the Greek word Jesus used for 'secret place' in Matthew 6:6. Embracing the 'Tabernacle of David lifestyle' is to build the Lord a permanent lodging in our life. This encompasses scheduling, strategy, as well as repetition, but the most important element of all is 'time'.

Let me ask you again: *Have you set aside time to locate Mount Zion? Have you set foot upon that secret place of intimacy where you are certain to find God?*

Do you know how to withdraw out of the chaos and meet with Him in a personal, heart transforming manner? We must cultivate the holy altar within our prayer closet, where we open up a heavenly portal into Zion.

Relationship with Jesus Christ is personal, not corporate. We all have an individual responsibility to maintain our intimacy one-on-one, away from the congregation. This is where it is won or lost: Time alone with God! When the Lord sees what is done *in secret,* He begins to reward us *openly,* that is, in the public eye.

Let me be brutally honest; if you only experience God in church meetings, it is not enough to sustain you. While experiencing God in church gatherings is helpful, you cannot survive off that alone. It is part of the church's mandate to create times of corporate worship so that the body can be edified and encouraged, but it also their responsibility to train and equip the saints on how to meet with the Lord personally. If this is done correctly, the glory flowing out of multiple 'secret-places' will combine, unleashing the power of God exponentially.

God in Busyness / God in Seclusion

While reading this chapter, this thought may have crossed your mind; *"But God is always with me wherever I go, no matter how busy my life is."*

Granted: Our God can be found in the hustle and bustle of the technologically advanced planet that we now live on. He is with us in the midst of the busyness of everyday life, giving us the grace to complete immediate tasks at hand. Yet He is also the God who must be sought in the lonely, *faraway* places. This does not change just because we are constantly surrounded, and at times, consumed within a hyper-active environment. Jeremiah 23:23 says that God is not only a God who is close at hand. He is *far away* at the same time. Jesus understood this, for He often withdrew from the crowds into lonely places so He could connect with His heavenly Father and receive His direction while abiding in His loving embrace. (Luke 5:16)

In the 'faraway places' we actually connect with Him on a deep enough level to get a 'clear word' from the Lord for our life. Here God's promises are conceived and then birthed, and from this place of seclusion the Lord will anoint us with the unction of His Holy Spirit. This is where the things we do and the words we say carry a supernatural enabling of divine impact that attracts favour. But in order to connect in this way, we must disconnect from all the fanfare and continual bombardment of the internet crazed world that ruthlessly attempts to hem us in and ultimately distract us from our primary purpose. As this becomes more difficult to achieve in an ever-increasing social-media driven climate, God will reward in greater measure those who are disciplined enough to invest the time in the Tabernacle of David; their personal Mount Zion, a uniquely developed secret place of worship, intimacy, prayer, and private devotions.

Resting beside Still Waters

In this day and age, it is even more crucial to withdraw and find rest. You cannot continue to live in non-stop stimulation without crashing and burning. This is why I promised in the last chapter that we would complete the word studies on 'the resting place' of the Lord from Psalm 132. When we go to this resting place, *we* 'join in' with His rest as well.

> *[8]Arise, O Lord, to Your **resting place**, You and the ark of Your strength.* (Ps. 132:8 NASB)

> *[13]For the Lord has chosen Zion; he has desired it for his dwelling place: [14]This is my **resting place forever**; I will make my home here because I have desired it.* (Ps. 132:13-14 ESV, CSB)

For your recollection: The Hebrew word for 'resting place' in verse 8 and 14 is the same word; *měnuwchah.*

We previously examined how God used *měnuwchah* when He spoke through Isaiah; *"where will My resting place be?"* (Isa. 66:1) *Měnuwchah* simply means: *'resting place, rest, quietness.'*

We are familiar with this word from the famous Psalm 23. In verse 3, the Bible says the Shepherd leads us beside 'still' or 'quiet' waters. This means that when we are led by the Holy Spirit, we enter a sense of calmness and tranquillity in both mind and soul. The other relevant mention of this word is in Psalm 95:11, where God swore that the Israelites in the wilderness would never enter His 'rest'.

If you recall, in the Septuagint they split the two mentions of 'resting place' from v8 and v14 into two different words: *anapausis and katapausis.* We will now extract all the richness from these two Greek words.

The similarity between the two is that they both end in *pausis*. If you are cluey, you would see the English word 'pause' in here. The 'pausing' of God in our lives is not physically coming to a standstill (like a game of 'freeze'). It is a pause where our *mind* is stilled. Our thoughts have to be quietened and our emotions must be calmed. Only then can we accurately hear what God is saying.

Let's begin with *anapausis*. It means: *'intermission, cessation of any motion, business or labour.'* In other words, 'time-out!' We need to stop what we're doing and hear from the Coach. Only once we have learnt the game-plan for the next phase of play can we return to the match. Life is hectic, and on many occasions, we cannot differentiate between what is really important and what is menial and insignificant. God helps us in these strategic 'time-outs' to get our priorities straight, keeping us progressing towards His plan for our life. The key to this intermission is the cessation of 'business' or 'labour'. This is vitally important.

This leads into the second definition of *anapausis*: 'recreation'. When we rest in the Lord, it should always bring re-creation. Much like our spiritual conversion, God's rest releases rejuvenation, resulting in a revitalised fervour for life. But I also believe this can refer to recreation as we know it today, because recreation is not business or labour. That's why time with the Lord can also include playing that game of golf, getting out in the surf, hitting the ski-slopes, hiking, gardening, or kicking the football. All of these, when done properly, can be of great value to our overall well-being. Only we must ensure we include God in the recreation. It is fun to play a game or go on a vacation, but involving God in these things is the key to true re-creation. Have you ever come home from a vacation and felt like you needed a vacation from your vacation? This occurs when we fill our holiday with constant activity and hyper-stimulation but fail to truly rest.

When I do recreational things, I like to involve God and make it peaceful, talking to Him about what I'm doing. Celebrate a good golf swing, a magnificent kick, or a spectacular catch with God. I especially like to complement God about how awesome His creation is. We cannot get out of balance as servants of the Lord and only 'work, work, work'. Being a workaholic is not God's best for us. There is a restful, recreational regeneration that is a necessary part of our proper functioning in His kingdom on earth.

Now we will look at *katapausis*. This is *'a putting to rest, a calming of the winds: Peace, be still.'* Metaphorically, it is *'the heavenly blessedness where God dwells, which He has promised to make persevering believers in Christ partakers'*. If we persist in the disciplines of the 'Tabernacle of David lifestyle', we will enter this state of heavenly blessedness.

This is the same word used by Stephen in Acts 7:49 when he quoted Isaiah; 'where will my <u>resting</u> place be?' But more importantly, the *katapausis* is the place of God's rest regularly mentioned throughout Hebrews 3 and 4.

Earlier I spoke about Psalm 95:11, where God swore on oath that He would not allow the Israelites to enter His rest *(měnuwchah in Hebrew)*. In this case, the Lord was referring to Canaan, the Promised Land. They did not believe Joshua and Caleb's positive report concerning their ability to take the land, so they never entered it. Those who do not believe cannot enter God's rest, but we who believe can! For there is another day called 'today', where later on, God spoke through *David,* saying,

> *"<u>Today</u>, if you hear His voice, do not harden your hearts as they did in the rebellion, during the time of testing in the wilderness where your ancestors tested and tried me, though for forty years they saw what I did... So I declared on oath in my anger, 'They shall never enter my rest.'"* (Heb. 3:7-9, 11)

David describes a 'second chance offer' given by God to enter this rest. Even though those in David's tabernacle experienced a foretaste, this state of heavenly blessedness would ultimately be accessed through the New Covenant in Jesus' blood. Therefore, whenever we trust the Lord enough to be led by the Spirit, we shall cease from our own works of human striving and enter into the Sabbath-rest set-aside for the people of God (Heb. 4:9-10). Here we get re-charged for our grace-empowered existence.

The three stranded cord of Heavenly Blessedness

There are three primary benefits we receive each and every time we enter the rest of God. Without these graces, we will constantly struggle through life. God's rest comprises three gifts given by the Spirit of God: peace of mind, reassurance, and comfort.

1) **Peace of Mind:** *A state of mental and emotional calmness. In this state, the mind is quiet and you experience a sense of happiness and freedom.*

First, we experience a calming of the soul. This is what Jesus said would happen when those who are weary and heavy burdened come to Him for rest (Matt 11:28-30). Suddenly, a sense of joy and liberty overwhelms us as we sense the presence of God all around.

2) **Reassurance:** *The action of removing someone's doubts or fears. It relieves or removes unnecessary anxiety.*

This happiness and freedom also comes because God has removed doubts and fears, replacing them with trust in His goodness and sovereign plan. All anxiety we face is unnecessary because Paul said *"Be anxious about nothing, instead, pray about everything, and the peace of God will guard your heart and mind in Christ Jesus."* (Phil. 4:6-7)

3) **Comfort:** *The easing or alleviation of a person's feelings of grief and distress.*

The Holy Spirit is our Comforter. He comforts us in all our afflictions so that we can comfort others with the same comfort we have received from God (2 Cor. 1:3-5). When we have to endure hardship in all kinds of painful trials (Acts 14:22), the loving embrace of the Father will cause grief and distress to fall away like the chains fell off Peter in his prison cell in Acts 12:7. These trials have come so that the testing of our faith, which is far more precious than gold refined by fire, will be proved genuine (1 Pet. 1:7). Jesus told us in John 16:33;

"I have told you these things, so that in Me you may have [perfect] peace and confidence. In the world you have tribulation and trials and <u>distress</u> and frustration; but be of good cheer [take courage; be confident, certain, undaunted]! For I have overcome the world. [<u>I have deprived it of power to harm you and have conquered it for you.</u>]" (AMPC)

~ Chapter 27 ~

MAKING US FEEL RIGHT AT HOME

Beautiful in elevation, the joy of the whole earth is Mount Zion on the sides of the north: The city of the great King. (Ps 48:2 NKJV)

Going up Mount Zion and into the tent where Jesus dwells is a strange phenomenon. From the spiritual point of view, we are heading up into the heavenly places, whereas from the physical point of view, it is as though God's glory has descended from heaven to dwell with us. Whichever way we look at it, there is an open invitation for all humanity to come and spend quality time with the King of kings and Lord of lords, and to do so with such intimate connection that each of us feels as though we are His favourite. Such is the depth of His love for all of us.

Remember the word **yâshab** from Psalm 132:14? It represented the Lord's 'hang-out'. According to this verse, Jesus Christ has taken up residency in Zion. God wants us to familiarise ourselves with His home. This does not imply that we should become 'familiar' with His home (take it for granted). Rather, I am saying that we should go there so often that it becomes a lifestyle. It's just like the family home. You become part of the fabric: Not only are you always welcome, you belong.

Mishkân (from Psalm 132:5, 7a) shows us that the type of dwelling *is a tent* patterned after the Tabernacle of David from the Old Testament. This doesn't insinuate that the heavenly tabernacle literally has to be a tent. *Mishkân* means that he abides in/remains constantly/totally inhabits. He is always home; He never leaves. That's why the Bible says that Jesus will never leave or forsake us (Heb. 13:5). Yet despite this, we can choose to leave His presence if we don't abide in the Spirit.

Mishkân also denotes tabernacling, which is intimate fellowship. As branches, we are called to 'abide in the Vine' and produce much fruit. Abiding is an un-severed connection, and this Hebrew word encompasses that. Most importantly, we have never-ending access to God's help in time of need as we come boldly to the throne of grace: the only piece of furniture in Jesus' house beside His footstool.

Môwshâb (from Psalm 132:13b) is another word for dwelling or habitation, but more specifically it highlights the sitting down *on a seat* within that dwelling. It is the seat of authority (the throne or mercy seat) where we sit down with Jesus in heavenly places after bowing low at His footstool. If Jesus was not already sitting there, we wouldn't even have the right to go anywhere near it, let alone sit on it. In Psalm 2:6 God declares; *"I have set My King on My holy hill of Zion."* (NKJV)

In Psalm 1:1 we are told that we should not *'sit in the seat of the scornful'*. 'Sit in the seat' here is 'yâshab môwshâb'. We are not to 'hang out' on the same seat with the scornful, but we are to go into Jesus' house and dwell with Christ on the same seat where He sits. In Ephesians 2:6, the Greek word *sygkathizō means 'to sit down together'.* It means to *'sit with someone on the same seat'*. All the powers of hell are under our feet when we take up this position in the Spirit.

Môwshâb is also used on two occasions in 1 Samuel 20: The royal family of King Saul were about to celebrate a new moon festival, and David, who had a seat at the king's table, was going to be absent. In verse 18 Jonathon uses *môwshâb* to refer to David's seat, and then in verse 25, *'yâshab môwshâb'* is used referring to King Saul who *'sat in his seat'*. This shows us that God has given us a seat at His royal table. He desires to lavish us with all the bountiful blessings of His banqueting table. He also wants to set this table up for us in the presence of our enemies (Ps. 23:5). But pay careful attention: This table is not a snacking table where you race in, grab a quick bite to eat, and then rush out. The substance of God's house is only granted to those who *sit and dine*, who tabernacle with the Lord for substantial amounts of time.

After David became king, he granted Mephibosheth, Jonathon's son, a permanent seat at the king's table. David's wealth and estate was made available *to* Mephibosheth, and he was given a seat equal to one of the king's own sons. (2 Sam 9)

Měnuwchah (from Psalm 132:8, 14a) has already been covered extensively in the previous chapter. It is the receiving of God's rest in the form of 'peace of mind, reassurance and comfort'.

Mâqôwm (from Psalm 132:5a) is the ability to stand at our post and occupy the territory God has given us. It is the anointing to carry out the call of God on our lives. As long as we stay intricately connected to the Lord's home, we will find the empowerment to occupy ground and invest our talents until we sleep in death or Jesus comes back.

When David pitched the tent on Mount Zion, it established a *mâqôwm* (place) where he could stand firm and defeat the attacking enemy. The tent was on the top of the greatest stronghold or fortress in the land. There was no way the enemy was going to break in and interrupt the flow of God's glory in the hearts and minds of the Zionists. Zion was a safe-haven for them, and from this 'place' they were able to stand strong against the enemy while they expanded the kingdom by taking territory. During the 33 years of the Tabernacle of David, his kingdom was enlarged so greatly that he died not merely a king, but the emperor of the known world!

The corresponding Greek word for *mâqôwm* found in the Septuagint *is topos*. It means *'a portion of space marked off'*. In the New Covenant, this implies that when we ascend into Zion, it forms a safe-haven guarding our heart and a protective shield around us, barring the devil access. The Lord is our shield and buckler (Ps. 91:4). We will be immovable and unshakable as we stand strong in the power of His might;

> *Those who trust in the Lord <u>are like Mount Zion, which cannot be moved</u>, but abides forever.* (Ps. 125:1 NKJV)

In summary, when we dwell in Zion by 'abiding in the Spirit' we have unlimited, never-ending access to God's help. We will rest with the peace of mind, reassurance, and comfort of the Holy Spirit. We will partake of the abundance of spiritual blessings upon Jesus' table, seated in authority with him in heavenly places (Eph. 1:3, 2:6), and we will be fortified, enabling us to take our stand and occupy our post.

These four elements of God's home are ours if we desire to *'make the Lord our refuge, the Most High our dwelling place'* (Ps. 91:9). Becoming a permanent resident in God's hometown of Zion is contingent upon our willingness to cultivate the simplicity of pure devotion to Christ Paul talks about in 2 Corinthians 11:2-4. So ascend up to the top of God's mountain. I guarantee; He'll make you feel right at home!

Loyalty to the Oath leads to Covenant

David, the son of Jesse, speaks—David, the man who was raised up so high, David, the man anointed by the God of Jacob, <u>David, the sweet psalmist of Israel</u>. [2] "The Spirit of the Lord speaks through me; his words are upon my tongue.

[3]The God of Israel spoke. The Rock of Israel said to me: 'The one <u>who rules righteously, who rules in the fear of God</u>, [4]is like the light of morning at sunrise, like a morning without clouds, like the gleaming of the sun on new grass after rain.'

[5] "Is it not my family God has chosen? <u>Yes, he has made an everlasting covenant with me</u>. His agreement is arranged and guaranteed in every detail. He will ensure my safety and success." (2 Sam 23:1-5 NLT)

The prerequisite to the Covenant agreement God made with David (1 Chronicles 17:1-14 and Psalm 89:3-4, 19-37) was his diligence to make good on the oath he swore to God as a young boy. The establishment of David's tent on Zion led to major <u>covenantal blessings</u> (both for his own life and for every subsequent generation), all of which were obtained through connection with the Promised Son. Beholding the glory of God in his worship tent ensured David ruled righteously in the fear of God, and this kept the covenant operating effectively.

The Lord bless you out of Zion (Ps. 128:5 NKJV)

The end of Psalm 132 (v15-18) contains an assortment of blessings that flow from Zion. These blessings are incorporated *within the Davidic Covenant*. All of the benefits are established upon the foundation called 'the sure mercies of David' (Isa. 55:3, Acts 13:34). Through the death, burial and resurrection of Jesus Christ, the Father made entry into this covenant available to all who would receive Him. All who confess with their mouth that Jesus is Lord and believe in their heart that God raised Him from the dead are guaranteed access to this mercy; God's continual, ongoing ability to forgive. Repentance is the substance that keeps this mercy flowing in our direction.

[15]"I will abundantly bless her provision; I will satisfy her poor with bread. [16]I will also clothe her priests with salvation, and her saints

shall shout aloud for joy. [17]There I will make the horn of David grow; I will prepare a lamp for My Anointed. [18]His enemies I will clothe with shame, but upon Himself His crown shall flourish." (Ps. 132:15-18 NKJV)

There are many more promises which make-up God's covenant with David other than these listed at the end of Psalm 132 (the subject of a later volume). Our goal here is to complete our study of this epic psalm. What we read above is the culmination of what will occur for those who have completed the vow of David: locating their Zion by establishing a resting place for God. Get ready for these benefits to show up in your life as you implement the Tabernacle of David lifestyle.

[15]*I will abundantly bless her provision; I will satisfy her poor with bread.*

The phrase 'I will abundantly' is actually the identical term in Hebrew used by God when He told Abraham; *"By Myself I have sworn, says the LORD, because you have done this thing, and have not withheld your son, your only son—That in blessing I will bless thee, and in multiplying I will multiply thy seed"* (Gen 22:16-17 KJV). The term is 'barak-barak' and it is a strong affirmation meaning; God will *certainly* do it. It is effectively a 100% guarantee.

When God told Abraham ten chapters earlier that he would bless him so abundantly that all nations of the earth would be blessed through him, this promise was still contingent upon Abraham's subsequent obedience and trust in the fear of the Lord. It was only after he sacrificed his son Isaac on the altar that the scripture was fulfilled saying; *'Abraham believed God, and it was credited to him as righteousness',* even though God first pronounced this over Abraham in Genesis 15:6 (Refer Jam. 2:21-23). Now that Abraham (many years later in Genesis 22) had fulfilled the righteousness spoken over him, God would CERTAINLY bless him. Prior to this, God was not obliged to fulfil any of His promised blessings. It's time for us as Christians to fulfil the righteousness of Christ by *putting on* the breastplate and implementing it (Eph. 6:14). Empty claims of: 'I am the righteousness of Christ' with no evidence seen through our character and actions is hypocrisy. We cannot enter the abundant blessing of God's provision without *'living out'* righteousness in the fear of God. David said;

*"The Lord has dealt with me according to **<u>my righteousness</u>**; according to the <u>cleanness of **my** hands</u> he has rewarded me."* (2 Sam 22:21)

The Psalmist states in Psalm 132:15 that if we faithfully fulfil the vow of David, the abundant provision of God's covenant blessings are made certain. If we do not fulfil the vow, God has every right to withhold them. The word for provision here is written in a cognate form for the word in Psalm 78:25 translated 'meat'. In this Psalm, the meat was given 'to the full'. Sounds like John 10:10, doesn't it? In Scripture, the word 'meat' often refers to a 'whole nourishing meal'. It denotes overflowing, abundant provision, while bread usually speaks of merely 'satisfying our needs'. By satisfying Zion's poor with bread, God fulfils Psalm 23:1, *'I shall not be in want'*, but then He goes far over and above that. He gives us life in abundance, to the full, till it overflows. (John 10:10 AMP)

The first and primary blessing flowing from Zion is spiritual provision in the form of wisdom, revelation and divine strategies. Those who have given up selfish pursuits in order to ascend Zion have reason to be content without anything this world has to offer (lusts of the eyes, lust of the flesh and the pride of life) because God has prepared better things for them (Heb. 6:9, 11:16). After putting off the deceitful lusts of the old man, God will abundantly bless and nourish the new man, satisfying the poor in spirit with the bread of life and the God-fearer with solid meat.

Our provision in verse 15 also includes 'natural resources'. David gave up everything to follow God's will. He was left with nothing in a cave. But in the end, God honoured David's steadfast loyalty by showering him with blessings of material riches beyond what anyone had ever seen before. Because his old self had been put to death, he was able to handle such abundance without being corrupted.

I always like to refer to finances as 'resource' rather than 'wealth'. Resource is 'supply drawn upon' but wealth is 'money stored up'. Therefore, God wants us to draw upon the supply He has poured into our lap and put it to work for kingdom purposes. This does not mean we have to give it all to a church organisation. We may be called to invest our money into launching a marketplace ministry. But one thing's for certain: We must be willing to invest our mina and see it increase. Jesus showed us it's a sin to keep it in a handkerchief or hide it in a hole in the ground. (Luke 19:11-27)

16I will also clothe her priests with salvation, and her saints shall shout aloud for joy.

We have covered this verse already, so I won't repeat myself unnecessarily. Needless to say, God does offer his priests salvation, which means we will be delivered from all attacks of the enemy. We can shout aloud for joy as we see the mighty hand of Yahweh taking down strongholds and every evil thing that exalts itself against the knowledge, purposes, and plans of God. This salvation refers to 'deliverance, rescue unto safety, uninterrupted welfare, prosperity and *overwhelming victory.*' Despite all our afflictions we are more than conquerors through Christ who loved us. (Rom. 8:37)

What, then, is our priestly assignment? It comprises two elements. First is our ministry before God's throne in intercessory prayer, worship and private devotions. These are signified by the harps (worship) and bowls (intercession) mentioned in Revelation 5:8. Second is the role of 'middle man', where we stand in the gap between God and human beings. As ambassadors of reconciliation, we are commissioned to show lost people the way towards God. The Apostle Paul said; *"Christ Jesus gave me the <u>priestly duty of proclaiming the gospel of God</u>, so that the Gentiles might become an offering acceptable to God, sanctified by the Holy Spirit."* (Rom. 15:16)

17There I will make the <u>horn of David grow</u>; I will prepare a lamp for My Anointed.

Until Christ the King arose out of the house and line of David, God would bring down every plan designed to utterly destroy it. Once Jesus accomplished His earthly mission, He would sit upon the throne of his Father forever as the ultimate 'Son of David'. All the promises given to David and his descendants now centre on Him.

When the Psalmist wrote that the horn of David would 'sprout forth', he was speaking about the might and power of David's kingdom and its ongoing legacy. In an overall sense, it would continue to grow and increase in strength through His anointed 'kings'. When stating that the Lord had prepared a lamp for His anointed, the Psalmist is showing us that the light of David's kingdom will never fade out. The Heavenly Father would preserve David's rule through His chosen King. For He states emphatically; *"I have determined that my chosen king's dynasty will continue."* Who is this King? He is the preeminent King descending from David: the Lord Jesus Christ. How then does His kingdom continue to increase in strength and influence? By shining His light through His anointed kings! After all, Jesus is the 'King of kings'.

When Zechariah, the father of John the Baptist, regained the power of speech upon the naming of his messianic forerunner, he prophesied about the One whom John would prepare the way for;

> *"He has raised up a **horn of salvation** <u>for us in the house of his servant</u> <u>David</u>... **because of the <u>tender mercy</u> of our God**, by which the <u>rising sun</u> <u>will come to us from heaven to shine on those living in darkness</u> and in the shadow of death, to guide our feet into the path of peace."* (Luke 1:68, 78-79)

Jesus is the horn of David, and He is a light that pierces darkness. Zechariah says that the horn of Jesus' kingdom increases through granting people salvation. This is the overriding goal and ultimate motive behind any kingdom advancement by His people on earth. Zechariah also refers to the tender mercy of God, alluding to the 'sure mercies given to David'; the foundation by which the horn of salvation is offered to all mankind. (Rom. 11:30-32)

◊◊◊◊◊

David was a king and a priest. When we are born of water and the Spirit, we enter a kingdom that is based on both the *throne and tabernacle* of David; a kingdom of priests (Rev. 1:6). In verse 17-18 of Psalm 132, the focus shifts primarily to the kingly dimension of our covenantal calling in God, but our role as a king is so vitally linked to our role as a priest that the two can never be separated. The domain we acquire as kings is only given to us to build a platform conducive for priestly evangelism. Even so, the exaltation of our horn and the bright shining of the lamps of God's anointed people will be made manifest through kingdom pursuit. By becoming marketplace missionaries, we can shine the light of the gospel to God's lost sheep. When Jesus said: *"you are the light of the world. A city on a hill cannot be hidden; neither do you buy a lamp and hide it under a basket",* He was talking about bringing hope to a dark and dying world (Matt 5:14-15).

By demonstrating the gospel of the kingdom, we 'legislate righteousness' as we orchestrate the ethics of the kingdom of God throughout our sphere of influence. As our kingdom territory expands, love abounds within that territory, bringing the lamp of hope instead of the darkness of despair found in a world system filled with pride, corruption and deception. Because of this hope, those within our sphere will want to become citizens of the kingdom by inviting the King into their hearts.

As we put forth an authentic witness of the Son of God; *"the people living in darkness will see a great light; on those living in the land of the shadow of death a light will dawn"* (Matt 4:16). Rays of ever-increasing sunshine will radiate upon those living in the land of the shadow of death (Luke 1:78-19). Those who respond to the warmth of His love and call upon His name are removed from the despair of darkness into His marvellous light, bringing an immediate transition into hope and destiny. (Jer. 29:11, Col. 1:13)

God has promised to make the horn of David grow. The powerful expansion of the kingdom of God and its King, Jesus Christ, will forever be exalted throughout the earth (Isa. 9:6-7). It's time for us to partner with Jesus through the promises laid out in the Davidic Covenant. By utilising the anointing of the Holy Spirit combined with divine strategies of heaven and the righteous morals of kingdom culture, we will see our 'horn' (our strength, influence, and kingdom territory) rapidly expand. If we continue in humility by serving people through our kingdom calling, our lamps will shine ever brighter and fruit will be borne for eternal life.

> *"The way of the righteous is like the first gleam of dawn, which <u>shines ever brighter</u> until the full light of day."* (Prov. 4:18 NLT)

~ Chapter 28 ~

A FLOURISHING CROWN OF REVIVAL

[18]His enemies I will clothe with shame, but upon Himself His crown shall flourish. (Ps. 132:18 NKJV)

In order for our crown to flourish, we must have victory over our enemies, and so here, in verse 18, we find a counter-promise for those who decide to be adversaries of the Lord Jesus. In Psalm 132:16, those who accept and choose to live for Him are "clothed with salvation", and in stark contrast, those who reject Him in Psalm 132:18 are given "garments of shame" to wear. These clothes signify 'the unexpected disappointment from the failure of all their vain hopes and wicked designs.' Though those who oppose Him may temporarily get ahead through their conniving and scheming, it doesn't last for long. In the end, they will be brought low, while the humble will be lifted into a place of exaltation. (Luke 14:11)

Those who walk in the righteous ways of King David can be certain that their crown will flourish. As they go about the work of the kingdom assigned to them, their kingdom pursuits will prosperously expand and produce much fruit for eternal life. No weapon formed against them shall prosper, and the Lord will silence every tongue that rises in judgment. (Isa. 54:17)

The kings of Judah (the lineage of David) inherited the royal covenant made between Yahweh and David. The common denominator of a move of God in their tenure as king was the re-establishment of the 24/7 devotional worship set up by David in his Tabernacle at Zion.

When Solomon finished building the temple, the Tabernacle of David ceased to exist, but the worship order established by David was maintained. As long as the people's hearts and minds were set upon worshiping Yahweh, the kingdom of Judah continued to flourish, but in times of apostasy, it would decline as their enemies prevailed. Whether our enemies prevail or are clothed with shame predominantly depends on the yielding of our will and the corresponding level of intimacy we have with the Lord.

> *"And in mercy shall <u>the throne be established</u>; and He shall sit upon it in truth <u>in the tabernacle of David</u>, judging and seeking judgment and hastening righteousness."* (Isa. 16:5 KJV)

Commentators have debated about what Isaiah meant when he mentioned the tabernacle of David in this prophecy. It is the Hebrew word 'ōhel, which is the same word used when David pitched his tent on Zion. Yet many scholars have concluded that because a throne is mentioned here, the 'ōhel of David references David's throne in his cedar palace, not the worship tent. Their approach centres on this: By the time Isaiah spoke these words, the house of David had fallen and declined to such a low state that all that was left was a dilapidated kingdom *the size* of a tent or booth. In Amos 9:11, when Amos said; *"In that day I will raise up the fallen booth of David";* he used the word 'sukkah', which is the same word used for the feast of *tabernacles*. Considering these tents were 'little houses' or 'booths', they also interpret the rebuilding of David's Tabernacle in Amos to be David's royal throne and palace, now a 'little house' compared to its former glory.

But as is often the case, all this contention is unnecessary. Just as it is impossible to separate our role as kings and priests, the throne of David and the worship tent of David are so vitally connected you cannot isolate one from the other. Combined within Zion was a political and ecclesiastical unity within the nation's governmental headquarters. Therefore, believers in Jesus are welcomed into New Covenant Zion inside the heavenly Jerusalem. We have access into the *Royal House and Worship Tent* of David, representing both kingly and priestly ministry. Both Scriptural interpretations are valid and cohesive.

It was through the worship, praise, prayer, adoration, and the proclaiming of God's word in David's tabernacle that his throne was established and prospered. David's dedicated lifestyle of fellowship with the Lord was the backbone behind the increase of his kingdom authority and the expansion of his rule and territory. David even prophesied in Psalm 110:4 that he was functioning as a priest after the order of Melchizedek, in the same likeness as the coming Messiah. The throne of Jesus Christ is located between the Cherubim in the Holy of Holies (Ps. 99:1). That is where the *true* throne was established for David, inside the *'ōhel* pitched on Zion where he worshiped at the footstool of the Ark, heeding Yahweh's voice of command. If the worship tent had been removed from its place, David's throne inside his palace would have been totally devoid of power, and its authority would have dwindled fast. Of course, David was human. There were times when he veered off track or made a mistake, but each time he was quick to repent and continue the call (2

Sam 11-12, 1 Chr. 21). Because David kept the 'simplicity of devotion to Jesus Christ' as his lifelong pursuit, his crown continued to flourish till the day he died.

We are called to rebuild the fallen tabernacle of David, because we, along with the rest of humanity, have been given the precious opportunity to 'seek the Lord' (Acts 15:17). People didn't 'seek the Lord' at the throne in David's palace. They sought the Lord *in the worship tent*. It is obvious what Isaiah and Amos are trying to communicate. By raising up again the worship of the Lord through 'life in the Spirit on Zion', we fulfil the vow of David and as a result, the crown upon our heads will flourish. This is the predetermining factor for any lasting success in all our kingdom-endeavours. Only by abiding in the Vine can we produce fruit *that will remain.* (John 15:7-8, 16)

Let's further validate this by examining the post-David generations. Once the royal covenant with David had been duly established, we discover a re-emerging theme throughout Scripture concerning the way in which the kingdom of God either flourishes or diminishes.

King Solomon

First, there was the reign of Solomon, who began well but finished poorly. David had pre-arranged all the worship teams for transition into temple worship, giving Solomon the schedule of how this new structure was to function. This was called *'the Davidic order of worship'*, or *'worship according to the commandment of David'.* (1 Chr. Ch16 & 25)

It was a glorious start to Solomon's reign as he faithfully implemented what his father David had ordered (2 Chr. 5:11-14). Solomon quickly became the richest man who ever lived and was also touted as the wisest man alive. Unfortunately, there was a breach in his intimacy with the Lord, and for Solomon it was a slow but steady progression away from God towards foreign wives and then foreign gods (1 Kings 11:1-13). In the end, what had begun with the dominance of David's empire had deteriorated into a kingdom filled with strife and division. Upon Solomon's death, it was split in two: Israel in the north and Judah in the south. The northern kingdom of Israel would never have a righteous king and they were taken away as captives by the Assyrians in 722BC, becoming what is now known today as 'the ten lost tribes.' In the southern kingdom of Judah, there was a mix of good and evil kings until they were eventually taken as exiles to Babylon in 597BC. Their captivity lasted seventy years.

King Asa

King Asa was the third king of Judah after Solomon. He did what was right in the eyes of the Lord by removing all the detestable idols from the land. Then he repaired the altar of the Lord in front of the temple:

> *[11]On that day they sacrificed to the LORD 700 cattle and 7,000 sheep and goats from the plunder they had taken in the battle. [12]Then they entered into a covenant **to seek the LORD**, the God of their ancestors, with all their heart and soul. [13]They agreed that anyone who refused to seek the LORD, the God of Israel, would be put to death—whether young or old, man or woman. [14]They shouted out **their oath of loyalty** to the LORD with trumpets blaring and rams' horns sounding. [15]All in Judah were happy about this covenant, for they had entered into it with all their heart. They earnestly sought after God, and they found him. And the LORD gave them rest from their enemies on every side.* (2 Chr. 15:11-15 NLT)

Here, the people made an oath similar to the vow made by David, and they dived headlong into it. The covenant agreement was to "seek the Lord", which is exactly what the rebuilding of David's tabernacle requires according to Acts 15:17. The result was complete and utter victory over their enemies *on every side.* (Prov. 16:7)

King Jehoshaphat

The next king was Asa's son Jehoshaphat. The LORD was with Jehoshaphat because he followed the example of his father's early years and did not worship the images of Baal. He sought the God of his father David and obeyed his commands instead of following the evil practices of the kingdom of Israel. Thus the LORD established Jehoshaphat's control over the kingdom of Judah. All the people of Judah brought gifts to Jehoshaphat, so he became very wealthy and highly esteemed. He was deeply committed to the ways of the Lord.

After Jehoshaphat sent Levites to teach the Word of God across all the towns of Judah, the fear of the Lord fell upon the surrounding nations so that *none of them* wanted to declare war against him (Prov. 16:7). Talk about freedom from your enemies! But after several years had passed, the enemy finally decided to have a crack at defeating Jehoshaphat in battle. Although living faithfully for God will keep the devil off your back the majority of the time, this does not insinuate you will never have to fight him in battle. Jesus was the epitome of faithfulness to God, yet after being tempted and prevailing, the Bible says that the devil left him *until the next opportunity came* (Luke 4:13). Jesus had a season of respite, but the devil was always planning to come at Him again.

The only way the enemy could muster up the courage to go up against Jehoshaphat was to combine three nations in an alliance against him. Israel had treated these nations kindly in the days of the wilderness wanderings when they passed around them and did not destroy them (Deut. 2:9, 19). Now this was how they repay the Israelites for their kindness! Unfortunately, there are times when people we have sacrificed for, invested in, and given our heart to suddenly turn on us and become our enemy. This is hard to bear, but we must be not caught unawares by such an occurrence.

When Jehoshaphat heard the news, his first inclination was to beg for the Lord's guidance. He ordered everyone in Judah to fast while the entire nation sought the Lord: men, women, and children alike. After the king asked God for His help on behalf of the people, the Spirit of the Lord came upon a man named Jahaziel, son of Zechariah.

> *[15]He said, "Listen, all you people of Judah and Jerusalem! Listen, King Jehoshaphat! This is what the LORD says: Do not be afraid! Don't be discouraged by this mighty army, for the battle is not yours, but God's. [16]Tomorrow, march out against them. You will find them coming up through the ascent of Ziz at the end of the valley that opens into the wilderness of Jeruel. [17]But you will not even need to fight. Take your positions; then stand still and watch the LORD's victory."* (2 Chr. 20:15-17 NLT)

The next day when they reached the battlefield, King Jehoshaphat said;

> *"Listen to me, all you people of Judah and Jerusalem! Believe in the Lord your God, and you will be able to stand firm. Believe in his prophets, and you will succeed." [21]After consulting the people, <u>the king appointed singers</u> to walk ahead of the army, singing to the Lord and praising him for his holy splendour. <u>This is what they sang</u>: "Give thanks to the Lord; his faithful love endures forever!" [22]At the very moment they began to sing and give praise, the Lord caused the armies*

of Ammon, Moab, and Mount Seir to start fighting among themselves.
[23]The armies of Moab and Ammon turned against their allies from
Mount Seir and killed every one of them. After they had destroyed the
army of Seir, they began attacking each other. [24]So when the army of
Judah arrived at the lookout point in the wilderness, all they saw were
dead bodies lying on the ground as far as they could see. Not a single
one of the enemy had escaped. (2 Chr. 20:20-24 NLT)

The king put the worship leaders ordained by David up front and saw a
miraculous, mighty and comprehensive victory. They didn't even have to lift a
finger!

King Hezekiah

Now we move down several generations to King Hezekiah. He was the earthly
king that Isaiah was referring to when he declared Isaiah 16:5, being a partial
type and representation of the coming Messiah. When he became king, he
purified the temple and reopened its doors. The previous generations had
abandoned the Lord's dwelling place, shutting up the doors of the temple so
that the priests stopped burning incense, baking the Bread of the Presence or
even presenting burnt offerings.

Once all was in readiness, they rededicated the temple just prior to the feast of
Passover. The Levites had recovered all the items discarded by King Ahaz and
they were now in front of the altar; purified and ready for use. Once they had
sacrificed bulls, rams and goats for the atonement of the people's sins, the real
action started;

[25]Hezekiah set the Levites in the house of the Lord with cymbals, with
*psalteries, and with harps, <u>according to the **commandment of David**</u>,*
and of Gad the king's seer, and Nathan the prophet: for so was the
commandment of the Lord by his prophets.

*[26]And the Levites stood <u>with the **instruments of David**</u>, and the priests*
with the trumpets. [27]And Hezekiah commanded to offer the burnt offering
upon the altar. And when the burnt offering began, the song of the Lord
*began also with the trumpets, and <u>with the instruments **ordained by***
***David** king of Israel.</u>*

[28]And all the congregation worshipped, and the singers sang, and the
trumpeters sounded: and all this continued until the burnt offering was

*finished. ²⁹And when they had made an end of offering, the king and all that were present with him bowed themselves, and worshipped. ³⁰Moreover Hezekiah the king and the princes commanded the Levites to sing praise unto the Lord with the **words of David**, and of Asaph the seer. And they sang praises with gladness, and they bowed their heads and worshipped.* (2 Chr. 29:25-30 KJV)

This was a worship service that had not been seen in Jerusalem since the time of David's Tabernacle! Hezekiah restored the worship according to the *commandment* of David. They used the instruments *ordained* by David, and sung praise songs *written* by David!

³⁴But there were too few priests to prepare all the burnt offerings. So their relatives the Levites helped them until the work was finished and more priests had been purified, for the Levites had been more conscientious about purifying themselves than the priests had been. (2 Chr. 29:34 NLT)

The revival that ensued following this extravagant display of worship was monumental. They did not have enough priests to prepare all the burnt offerings brought to them by the people! Likewise, when the glory of God hits the church through the restoration of Davidic style worship, there won't be enough church leaders to look after the influx of new converts. What a great problem to have! In the case of Hezekiah's dilemma, the Levites quickly came to the aid of the priests to help get the task completed.

The Levites had been *'more conscientious about purifying themselves'* than the priests. When *'the harvester overtakes the reaper and the treader of grapes him who sows seed'* we will be surprised how many believers God has prepared in 'hiddenness' who are ready and willing to step up and fill the void and help bare the heavy load of discipleship during the massive End-time Harvest which will come 'one thing fast on the heels of another'. What will shock us most is that these new leaders who emerge seemingly out of the woodwork will be even more capable and anointed than many of those who have been in the limelight for years, even decades!

King Josiah

Josiah was the last righteous king. The previous king, Ammon, had been a wicked king following on from the sins of Manasseh before him. Josiah had the

260

temple cleansed again around the time of Passover, just as Hezekiah had done a few years previous.

> *³Josiah said to the Levites who taught all Israel and who were holy to the LORD, "Put the holy ark in the house which Solomon the son of David king of Israel built; it will be a burden on your shoulders no longer. Now serve the LORD your God and His people Israel. ⁴Prepare yourselves by your fathers' households in your divisions, <u>according to the **writing of David** king of Israel</u> and according to the writing of his son Solomon."* (2 Chr. 35:3-4 NASB)

The previous kings had been so wicked that the Levites had actually taken matters into their own hands and confiscated the Ark out of the Holy of Holies in order to keep it protected from the detestable profanity happening there. Now Josiah eased the burden from their shoulders by letting them know it was now safe to return the Ark into its rightful place. The Passover service was prepared, the priests stood in their places, and the Levites assembled in their respective courses (2 Chr. 35:10). Then we are told;

> *"the singers the sons of Asaph were in their place, <u>according to the commandment **of David**</u>, and Asaph, and Heman, and Jeduthun the king's seer."* (2 Chr. 35:15 KJV)

Were there any positive results from such action and reform?

> *¹⁸<u>Never since the time of the prophet Samuel had there been such a Passover. None of the kings of Israel had ever kept a Passover as Josiah did</u>, involving all the priests and Levites, all the people of Jerusalem, and people from all over Judah and Israel. ¹⁹This Passover was celebrated in the eighteenth year of Josiah's reign.* (2 Chr. 35:18-19 NLT)

Thus, every awakening in Judah under godly kings was not a return to a material tent, but to the *spirit* of the Tabernacle of David—the glorious *order of worship* established under David's mighty reign.

The Returning Exiles

For our next example, we must look post the Babylonian exile. When King Cyrus of Persia saw his own name mentioned in bible prophecy, he issued a proclamation releasing the Jewish people to return to Jerusalem and rebuild the temple which King Nebuchadnezzar of Babylon had destroyed.

A remnant of the house of Judah responded to the call. Among them were Ezra, the scribe-priest and Zerubbabel who would take on the role as governor. In all, there were 42,360 people who initially returned to Judah, and most critically, among them were 200 singers! (Ezra 2:64) The Bible says;

> So the priests, the Levites, <u>the singers</u>, the gatekeepers, the Temple servants, and some of the common people settled in villages near Jerusalem. The rest of the people returned to their own towns throughout Israel. (Ezra 2:70 NLT)

The foundation of the temple was finished on the Feast of Trumpets; the same festival that the Temple of Solomon had been dedicated on centuries earlier.

> *[10]When the builders completed the foundation of the Lord's Temple, the priests put on their robes and took their places to blow their trumpets. <u>And the Levites, descendants of Asaph, clashed their cymbals to praise the Lord, just **as King David** had prescribed. [11]With praise and thanks, they sang this song to the Lord:</u> "He is so good! His faithful love for Israel endures forever!" Then all the people gave a great shout, praising the Lord because the foundation of the Lord's Temple had been laid.* (Ezra 3:10-11 NLT)

What began as a glorious reviving of David's fallen kingdom abruptly grinded to a halt shortly after this. Construction on the temple ceased when opposition arose from the enemies of Judah and Benjamin. These agitators wanted to 'help' them build the temple, but it was obvious to Zerubbabel that their request was sinister. They wanted to desecrate the purity of God's house by mixing in elements of idolatry. When Zerubbabel denied them this request, the local residents tried to discourage and frighten the people of Judah to keep them from their work. They bribed agents to work against them and to frustrate their plans. So the work on the temple came to a standstill until the second year of the reign of King Darius. (Ezra 4:1-5, 24)

◊◊◊◊◊

A long while after the first exiles had returned, a man named Nehemiah, who was the cup-bearer of Artaxerxes, King of Persia, had a burden placed upon him by the Lord. Although by this time the temple had now been fully restored and parts of the city were being rebuilt, the people were in grave danger because the walls that protected the city still lay in ruins.

Artaxerxes granted Nehemiah's request to rebuild the walls of Jerusalem and gave him access to the materials he would need (Neh. 1-2). There was plenty of opposition for Nehemiah as he and his men rebuilt the walls and installed the gates. So much so, that at times half of the people had to be stationed as guards with spears, shield, bows and coats of mail. Even the men who were building had to do so with one hand supporting the load and the other hand holding a weapon. (Neh. 4:16-18)

Eventually, the monumental task was completed, shaming their enemies. Attending the dedication of Jerusalem's walls was a number of Levites descending from those who had returned with Zerubbabel over a century earlier.

> *These were the family leaders of the Levites: Hashabiah, Sherebiah, Jeshua, Binnui Kadmiel, and other associates, who stood opposite them during the ceremonies of praise and thanksgiving, one section responding to the other, as commanded **by David**, the man of God.* (Neh. 12:24 NLT)

The Levites had been sought from all the places near Jerusalem to come and keep the dedication with gladness. They took part in *'the joyous occasion with their songs of thanksgiving and with the music of cymbals, harps, and lyres.'* [28]*The singers were brought together from the region around Jerusalem and from the villages of the Netophathites."* (Neh. 12:27-28 NLT)

The Levites had been appointed once again to the ministry given to them by David:

> [45]*They performed the service of their God and the service of purification, as commanded **by David** and his son Solomon, and so did the singers and the gatekeepers. [46]The custom of having choir directors to lead the choirs in hymns of praise and thanksgiving to God began long ago in the days **of David** and Asaph. [47]So now, in the days of Zerubbabel and of Nehemiah, all Israel brought a daily supply of food for the singers, the gatekeepers, and the Levites.'* (Neh. 12:45-47 NLT)

In these glorious times, there was even a daily supply of food provided for the singers. Everywhere you looked, there was abundance! This was a far cry from when the prophet Haggai turned up and there was nothing but the foundation of the temple and no walls. Back then, they had meagre harvests and money was falling through their pockets because they were building their own houses rather than the Lord's (Hag. 1). Now there was a full rededication to the things of God. The temple was in full operation; the walls were secure, and the Davidic worship movement was back in motion. Even the Word of God had been re-established, leading to mass repentance as Ezra taught the entire assembly. (Neh. 8-9)

The Body of Christ

Now we have covered all the major times of renewal in the dynasty of David, but it would be remiss of me to fail in giving mention to the greatest of all worship revivals in history thus far. We are talking about Acts 15:16-17. When James announced that what was occurring in the early church was a fulfilment of Amos 9:11-12, it became apparent that this new worship movement called 'the Way' had been founded and built upon the Tabernacle of David and the Davidic order of worship, rather than the superficial regulations and carnal ordinances contained within the LOM. The early church took the world by storm, so that it was said that wherever they went they turned the world upside-down! (Acts 17:6 NKJV) That was the opinion of their enemies, of course. From God's perspective, they were turning the world 'right side up'.

There is a clarion call to the body of Christ to haul in the End-time Harvest, ushering in the second coming of Jesus Christ. We know how it will be achieved: Worship unto glory. It is that simple. We are to follow the sacrificial example of the early disciples, whilst using the modern wineskins available to us. The church, as a movement, will get back to its early roots, meeting from house to house and in larger gatherings as the Spirit leads. The institutional church and all its organisations will come crumbling down as God merges everyone back into one body, His body. There will be no class distinctions between clergy and laity. Church leaders will help mature the saints then equip *them* for the work of *their* ministry. The body of Christ will once again have its primary influence in the marketplace outside the four walls of the church building. Just as the 120 ran *out* of the upper room into the centre of town when the tongues of fire came and sat upon them, so will the 'last-days church'. The Holy Spirit will propel us into the lush green pasture outside the sheep-pen. Every believer will be trained on how to hear the Chief Shepherd's voice and follow Him *for themselves*.

We are not going back to the book of Acts. We are going *beyond* the book of Acts! It's time for our crowns to flourish.

SECTION VI:

ZION BOUND

~ Chapter 29 ~

A TRAGIC FALSE START

In the final two sections, we will examine the process whereby David fulfilled the precious oath he made to the Lord as a young boy back in Bethlehem Ephrathah (Ps. 132:6). It wasn't as smooth and faultless as David would have hoped, but he made it in the end, and that's what counts.

King David is now 37 years old. After overcoming many afflictions, he is finally crowned king over all of Israel. Shortly thereafter, he successfully secured control over Jerusalem by defeating the Jebusites (1 Sam 5:1-7). The city where David had taken Goliath's head years earlier was now under Israeli control for the very first time. It was the geographic location God had promised David as a boy, and it had now been delivered over into his hands. Thus, the fortress of Zion was aptly renamed the 'City of David' (1 Sam 5:7). The time had now come to establish "a permanent dwelling place for the Lord, a tabernacle for the Mighty One of Jacob". (Ps. 132:5)

Psalm 84:5-7 describes the results David knew would occur at this holy site, and why there was such an intense longing for this setup to become a reality;

> [5]*"How blessed is the man whose strength is in You; in whose heart **are the highways to Zion**! [6]When they walk through the Valley of Weeping, it will become a place of refreshing springs. The autumn rains will clothe it with blessings. [7]They go from strength to strength; Every one of them appears before God in Zion."* (NASB, NLT)

David had a vision that extended far beyond himself. Wrapped up in the fulfilment of his own personal vow were personal encounters for multitudes of God-seekers. Whenever hard times hit, David would imagine this glorious reality. He knew God was going to liberate many from spiritual bondage into magnificent freedom. For the sake of these people, David would never give up.

As 'spiritual David's', this is our calling as well. We are ushering in the glory of God not only for ourselves (although that is a great by-product), but also for those around us. We are living out this lifestyle so that others may come into an experiential knowledge of the Lord through His manifested glory.

King David was getting super dooper, ultra-excited. The procession of the Ark from Abinadab's house in Kiriath-jearim along the highway to Mount Zion was fast approaching. The plans were finalised, the day was set, and the tent had been pitched. Now all David needed was for everything to run smoothly. It was going to be the greatest time of festivity ever celebrated in Israel. There were no less than 30,000 troops involved, and they were just the officials so the overall participation rate was predicted to be high. (2 Sam 6:1)

> *David consulted with all his officials, including the generals and captains of his army. [2] Then he addressed the entire assembly of Israel as follows: "If you approve and if it is the will of the Lord our God, let us send messages to all the Israelites throughout the land, including the priests and Levites in their towns and pasturelands. Let us invite them to come and join us. [3] It is time to bring back the Ark of our God, for we neglected it during the reign of Saul." [4] The whole assembly agreed to this, for the people could see it was the right thing to do.* (1 Chr. 13:1-5 NLT)

Even though David's plan was the general consensus amongst the assembly, I'm sure there were some priests who, being overly fond of the Tabernacle of Moses, had their reservations. These plans didn't seem to fit the protocols laid out in Moses' Law.

> *"What's this crazy king doing? Is he going to get us all killed? No one except the High Priest is permitted to enter the Holy of Holies, and even then, it's only on one day of the year!"*

> *"Why isn't he putting the Ark back where it belongs in the Tabernacle on Mount Gibeon? We finally had a chance to place the Ark back in its proper place, and now David does this!"*

Though David seems cocky and over-confident, he is actually exuding God-confidence. There was no presumption on his part, for he knew God was allowing this. In Acts 13:36, the Apostle Paul states that David "served his own generation *by the will of God*". David understood this tent was a restoration of God's original design for His children. It would go down in history as a foreshadowing of the upcoming dispensation of grace.

> [5] *"So David summoned all Israel, from the Shihor Brook of Egypt in the south all the way to the town of Lebo-hamath in the north, to join in bringing the Ark of God from Kiriath-jearim. [6] Then David and all Israel went to Baalah of Judah (also called Kiriath-jearim) to bring back the*

Ark of God, which bears the name of the LORD *who is enthroned between the cherubim."* (2 Chr. 13:5-7 NLT)

Here we see a confirmation of Psalm 99:1; the Word of God once again declares that Jesus' throne is the atonement cover between the cherubim. The general public would soon be able to approach the very footstool of God; the privilege of petition at the base of His throne! No wonder everyone was filled with such anticipation and perhaps even trepidation!

[3] *"They placed the Ark of God on a **new cart** and brought it from Abinadab's house, which was on a hill. <u>Uzzah and Ahio, Abinadab's sons, were guiding the cart</u> [4]that carried the Ark of God. <u>Ahio walked in front of the Ark</u>. [5]David and all the people of Israel were celebrating before the* LORD, *singing songs and playing all kinds of musical instruments—lyres, harps, tambourines, castanets, and cymbals."* (2 Sam 6:3-5 NLT)

Here we find out that David had a new cart custom-designed for the occasion. He was mimicking what the Philistines had done when the mother cows towed the Ark back into the land of Israel. The old one (crafted by the Philistines) had been burnt to make a fire for the sacrificial offering of these mother cows to the Lord. Therefore, David decided to make a brand spanking new version of this cart.

So far, things were running smoothly. Two of Abinadab's sons were in charge of guiding the cart as it was towed along by the yoke of oxen. These two, Ahio and Uzzah, were not literal sons in the way we would speak of today; they were most likely great grandsons. By this time, Abinadab was no longer alive. Perhaps these two boys were grandchildren of Eleazar, who was the actual son of Abinadab placed in charge of caring for the Ark when it first arrived at their family home in the outskirts of Kiriath-jearim. (1 Sam 7:1)

Ahio and Uzzah successfully guided the Ark down the hill, navigating the most treacherous terrain with no problems whatsoever. They were now approaching the smooth, flat area of the threshing floor of Nacon. The most dangerous part of this journey was behind them; now they could relax a little, or could they?

◊◊◊◊◊

King David and all his newly appointed worship team were having a great time singing songs and playing all types of musical instruments as they followed the

Ark along. Onlookers who gathered at the edges of the parade must have felt slightly awkward and a little bewildered by such an extravagant display of adulation and emotion. Those who were taught about the Ark were not used to seeing that kind of 'irreverent' behaviour in the presence of the Almighty. The Mosaic priests also watched on with caution. Something about this tent pitched on Zion didn't sit right with them. It was definitely not congruent with the ritualistic duties of their religious occupation.

> *⁶But when they arrived at the threshing floor of Nacon, the oxen stumbled, and Uzzah reached out his hand and steadied the Ark of God. ⁷Then the Lord's anger was aroused against Uzzah, and God struck him dead because of this. So Uzzah died right there beside the Ark of God. ⁸David was angry because the Lord's anger had burst out against Uzzah. He named that place Perez-uzzah (which means "to burst out against Uzzah"), as it is still called today.* (2 Sam 6:6-9 NLT)

At the most unexpected moment, the oxen stumbled. On the smoothest, flattest part of the journey, tragedy struck. That's why Paul tells us; *"Be careful when you think you stand, lest you fall"* (1 Cor. 10:12). It is in these seemingly innocuous times that the devil can catch us off guard and cause us to stumble. Earlier I spoke about how Satan left Jesus until *the next opportune time.* Satan is an opportunist. Most of the time, it is when we are 'at ease in Zion' that he pounces and knocks us off our perch.

Uzzah was dead, and in the eyes of the people, David was to blame. The priests shouted at David; *"See; we knew this was a bad idea! Don't you know the proper way to transport the Ark?"*

King David was crushed; he became furious at God. How could the Lord do this to Uzzah, and to him? After all David had done for Him and all the rejection he had endured to get to this moment, and this is how God repays him?

Numbers 4:4-6 shows us that *according to the Law of Moses,* the sons of Aaron (the priests), had to prepare the Ark for travel by inserting wooden carrying poles. The Levite clan of Kohath would then bear the weight of the Ark on their shoulders and transport it to the next destination. *David did not follow these laws.*

David chose to use a man-made, heathenistic method for transporting the holiness of God. He copied the ways of the Philistines, which was not according to God's due order. Fair enough, this was wrong: David made a mistake, but I personally do not believe that he was deliberately naïve concerning the Word of God. In my opinion, David only misinterpreted the type and shadow that was being played out in the procession up to Zion, and only regarding this did he fail in seeking God properly. After all, David was thoroughly educated in the strict Jewish tradition, so we can be almost certain that David knew the Torah inside and out.

In his over-exuberance, David presumed they had already fully entered the New Covenant foreshadowing, so he 'went for it' with a sheer lack of prudence and caution. He should have checked everything over with God, but if we re-examine 1 Chronicles 13:1, it says that David *"consulted with **all his officials"*** instead of the Lord.

◊◊◊◊◊

Here's a different perspective on David's choices: He set up the Ark on a *new* cart. This was symbolic of the New Covenant—the new and living way through the curtain. The yoke of oxen pulling the cart signified the divine service of Jesus Christ: He made Himself of no reputation, taking the form of a *bondservant*, coming in the likeness of men. Being found in appearance as a man, He humbled Himself and became obedient to death, even death on the cross (Phil. 2:7-8). The Lord Jesus did all the work on Calvary's cross so that we don't need to bear the works of our flesh, the works of the law and the weight of sin *on our shoulders*. Instead, we can walk alongside the Ark in complete liberty, praising the Lord with psalms, hymns and spiritual songs, and worshiping by making melody in our hearts (Eph. 5:19). The yoke upon the oxen's shoulders represents Jesus' yoke, which is easy and His burden light (Matt 11:30). David typified what was *soon* to come; that's why he thought it was unnecessary to consult the LOM on the correct protocol for transporting the Ark. Unfortunately for David, excessive amounts of exuberance may have caused him to jump the gun a little…

Uzzah's brother Ahio got in the correct position by stationing himself *in front of the Ark* (2 Sam 6:4). This left Uzzah behind the Ark, or perhaps next to it: If the Ark was going to fall off, Ahio was not going to see it. I could just imagine Ahio barging in; *"I-I-I'll take the front, Uzzah, cheers mate"*: Smart thinking.

Ahio means 'brotherly' signifying the brotherly love or fraternity that occurs between the brethren: all believers in Christ. At the conclusion of many epistles, we read, *"greet one another with a holy kiss."* Kiss here is the Greek word *philema*. It means 'a sign of fraternal affection'. It is another reference to brotherly love: the 'holy love amongst' and the 'sense of belonging within' the Christian family. Jesus is the ultimate display of brotherly love. No greater love is there than what our firstborn brother displayed: He laid down His life for His friends, and we are His friends if we do what He commands us (John 15:13-14).

Church life should not merely be defined merely by *ekklēsia*; 'an assembly', but by the intimate fellowship and deep communion derived from the Greek word, *koinōnia*. This is where we not only meet together, but share our very lives and when required, even our possessions; a true community or 'common-unity' comprising joint participation and contribution. As Paul said; when the churches assembled, he and his companions were delighted to share not only the gospel of God but their own lives as well. This is how true family is formed within Christ's body. (1 Thess. 2:8)

David means 'beloved'. His life is also a pattern of a Christian who has been truly accepted in the beloved. Amazingly, there is only one church in the book of Revelation who are given 'the key of David: the beloved'. It is Philadelphia, and what does Philadelphia mean in Greek? You guessed it: 'brotherly love'. We are called to this, so much so, that Jesus said it would be the sole witness to the outside world that the Father sent Him to earth (John 17:23). That's why Peter told us that we should 'add to godliness, brotherly kindness ('philadelphia'), and to brotherly kindness, *agape* love. For if we do these things in increasing measure, we will never fall away and shall receive a rich welcome into the eternal kingdom of our Lord and Saviour, Jesus Christ. (2 Pet. 1:7-8, 10-11)

Uzzah means 'strength'. He signifies the 'human strength and effort' by which men try to earn their way to God through the works of the flesh resulting in 'works of law'; a religious display of outward activity that denies the power that could truly make them godly (2 Tim 3:5). All of these 'righteousnesses' are filthy rags before God (Isa. 64:6 KJV). They cannot save us or earn any favour with God.

In light of these revelations, let's re-examine what happened.

³They placed the Ark of God on a <u>new cart</u> and brought it from Abinadab's house, which was on a hill. <u>Uzzah and Ahio, Abinadab's sons, were guiding the cart</u> ⁴that carried the Ark of God. <u>Ahio walked in front of the Ark...</u> ⁶But when they arrived at the threshing floor of Nacon, the oxen stumbled, and Uzzah reached out his hand and steadied the Ark of God. ⁷Then the Lord's anger was aroused against Uzzah, and God struck him dead because of this. So Uzzah died right there beside the Ark of God. (1 Sam 6:3-4, 6-7 NLT)

Ahio (brotherly kindness) was walking in front of the Ark amongst the yoke of oxen. Uzzah (human effort) was at the back fixated on the shaking and swaying of the Ark. Ahio was at rest, yoked together with Christ. Uzzah was heavily burdened with apprehension, trying to appease God whilst living life in his own ability.

In His lifetime, Jesus escaped through the crowd on many occasions, avoiding multiple assassination attempts by the Jews. In similar fashion, the Ark made its way successfully through the hilly descent. Jesus miraculously survived these plots all the way up to Palm Sunday, just like David's procession reached the smooth threshing floor of Nacon without incident. In both these cases, the danger seemed behind them. Jesus' disciples, in particular, thought that the worst of the persecution was over. Look at how the whole world was going after Him! (John 12:19) Surely He was primed and ready to take back the kingdom for Israel, they presumed.

But look what unexpectedly occurred. Only five days after the whole world celebrated Jesus, He was swiftly condemned by the very same people and crucified on a Roman cross. Jesus 'stumbled', but He rose again on the third day! In the same way, the oxen stumbled on the flat surface. The oxen stumbled, but they rose again without falling over and recovered their footing. The Ark was never going to hit the ground, just as Christ was never going to stay in the grave. There was a brief moment of doubt during the shaking, but no complete dislodging. Uzzah was so irrationally paranoid and uptight that his emotional reactions took over. The man representing human effort and works of law presumptuously tried to save the Ark through his own feeble strength, just as Peter attempted to prevent Christ from going to the cross. (Matt 16:21-22)

The threshing floor is the place where God takes hold of His winnowing fork and separates the wheat from the chaff after the oxen have treaded over the grain. Ahio hung onto the yoke and did not fall. Uzzah was not yoked to Christ and so in the stumbling he reached out the arm of the flesh and suffered death.

Ahio and Uzzah are a picture of those who enter the New Covenant versus those who stay in the LOM. Those who trust in Christ's sacrificial death to atone for their sins will never stumble so as to fall. For Jesus has risen! *He* did not stumble beyond recovery. But those who trust in their own good works and religious piety stumble at the cross and are offended by it (Gal 5:11). Anyone who still advocated circumcision after the resurrection was cut off from Christ, signing themselves up instead for slavery to carnal ordinances, thereby separating them from God's grace (Gal. 5:3-4). They remained in a religious form of godliness, but denied the power of God, which would impart true righteousness, holiness, and redemption. (1 Cor. 1:30)

That's why David was so upset with God. The arm of the flesh had ruined his parade! *"Lord, didn't you reveal to me that there was a new and living way? Isn't it free access into the glory without fear of negative repercussions? You told me contact with the Ark is now judgment free! What is going on?"* The only blockage to experiencing New Covenant glory is submission to our flesh. A continual life of carnal religious worldliness will still incur judgment in the Holy of Holies.

Doubt-filled thoughts begin to flood David's mind: He suddenly begins to question everything he has heard from God up until this point;

> *"Have I totally missed God? Is this whole thing a sham? Has God been baiting me up all these years to snare me in this trap? Maybe the priests were right all along. Perhaps I have been going mad!"*

Imagine the spiritual warfare and the intense waves of dread flowing through David's emotions during this time. The devil was having a field day inside David's mind. So deep the despair, it's as if David's entire relationship with God is under question. Think about it: David now doubts his life's mission! This promise had been the burning passion inside of his heart since his youth. Now the whole dream seems to be in tatters. The day that began as the happiest day of his life had turned into a nightmare: What a disaster!

> [9]*David was now afraid of the Lord, and he asked, "How can I ever bring the Ark of the Lord back into my care?"* [10]*So David decided not to move the Ark of the Lord into the City of David. Instead, he took it to the*

house of Obed-edom of Gath. [11]*The Ark of the Lord remained there in Obed-edom's house for three months, and the Lord blessed Obed-edom and his entire household.* (1 Sam 6:9-11 NLT)

David's fury quickly turned into fear. Initially, he was *angry* at God, now he became *afraid* of God. This was not the righteous fear of God: David was *scared of God.* A true fear of the Lord will draw you closer to God. In this holy posture, you don't want to displease Him or do anything to bring distance between yourself and Him. But when you are afraid of God, you sprint in the opposite direction, far away from God's presence. David's mind was running wild; *"Who is this God I've been following all these years? I don't even know who Yahweh is anymore. Has my relationship with Him been nothing but a fraud?"*

Have you ever felt like this? I had a season about ten years into my Christian journey where everything went into crisis and the previous decade of commitment to God seemed totally in vain. In fact, at the times of deepest darkness, I felt like it would have been better if I'd never become Christian to begin with! My whole Christian existence was shaken to the core. Had I actually been hearing God, or had it been the devil all along? Like David, at first I ran away from God, but then slowly but surely I began the process of seeking His face once more. I just couldn't bear living life without Him.

I'm pleased to say that God brought me through that dark time and shone His light on the truth. God *had indeed* been with me in the first ten years. It just hadn't turned out the way my human reasoning thought that it should. In hindsight, that crisis was the best thing that could have ever happened to me. I came out the other side knowing the faithfulness of my Lord in a whole new dimension, and I still live in that assurance to this day. King David was going to come through this also: He was not going to run away from God forever. It may have taken a little time, but God was going to separate the truth from lies and make clear to His beloved David the steps going forward.

In the meantime, King David had the Ark taken to Obed-Edom's house. After Uzzah dropped dead, David was too frightened and disillusioned to have the Ark brought into the city. What if they incurred deaths on an even higher scale? That would be utterly disastrous! There were too many unanswered questions floating around in his head. So the Ark had a pit-stop on the way to Zion until David was ready to face up once again to his God-ordained assignment.

~ Chapter 30 ~

SERVANT OF THE GENTILES

Just who exactly was this man called Obed-Edom the Gittite? Where did he live and why did God choose him?

Given that; 'the Bible explains the Bible', let's search inside the Word of God for answers. In the majority of cases, God has already provided us with the information we require, so we need not jump to outside sources to find the answers already contained within His holy Word.

In order to apply this technique, we must let the Scriptures speak for themselves. There may be times where we examine all the relevant verses and are still not able to establish our findings with 100% surety, but if we base our conclusions on the overwhelming evidence, we will rarely go wrong.

For starters, where does Obed-Edom live? The word 'Gittite' is the key here. A Gittite was a native of the Philistine city of Gath. There is another similarly named city just north of Philistia called 'Gath-rimmon', which, according to Joshua 21:24-26, was a Levite town given to the Kohathites (a Levite clan) by Joshua. But when you look up all the references to 'Gittite' in the Bible, there is not a single connection to Gath-rimmon. Every single time, the Word of God links the Gittites to the town simply referred to as 'Gath' (Josh 13:3, 2 Sam 15:18-22). In 2 Samuel 21:19 and 1 Chronicles 20:5, we even find Goliath of Gath, the giant killed by David, referred to as a Gittite. It is therefore clear that Obed-Edom was indeed a resident of Gath.

"So then, Obed-Edom must be a Gentile", I hear some of you say. Hold on a minute; don't come to such a hasty conclusion! Just because someone lives in a Gentile city doesn't mean they are automatically a Gentile. Remember that around a decade earlier, David had killed Goliath and scattered the Philistines, and then just recently he had defeated the whole Philistine army again (2 Sam 5:17-25). Could it be that many Jewish people took advantage of the vacuum created by these victories and had taken up residency in Gath? The region of Philistia was a part of the land promised to Abraham in Genesis 15, so there certainly would have been attempts by the Jewish people to migrate into that land.

*"Thus the ark of the LORD remained in the house of Obed-edom the Gittite three months, and the LORD **blessed** Obed-edom and all his household."* (2 Sam 6:11 NASB)

The clue we must take from this verse is that 'The Lord *blessed* Obed-Edom'. This is important for when we look at the descendants of Korah in a genealogy given by David to Solomon. This was a list of Levitical roles given to the clan of Merari. They ended up being the gatekeepers around the temple complex.

"These are the divisions of the gatekeepers: ⁴The sons of Obed-edom, also gatekeepers, were Shemaiah (the oldest), Jehozabad (the second), Joah (the third), Sacar (the fourth), Nethanel (the fifth), ⁵Ammiel (the sixth), Issachar (the seventh), and Peullethai (the eighth). God had richly blessed Obed-edom." (1 Chr. 26:1, 4-5 NLT)

Can you see what the Word of God says at the end of Obed-Edom's family list? It re-iterates that God had *indeed, certainly or surely*, blessed him. That's what the word for 'richly' means here. It is a confirmation of what has been given to us in 2 Samuel 6:11 regarding the three-month period when the Ark was in his house. It reveals that the blessing continued on *beyond* that time. In fact, it is the only mention of the word 'blessed' in this whole chapter of genealogies. God strategically inserts the minutest of extra detail into 1 Chronicles 26:5, confirming to us He is speaking of the same Obed-Edom who courageously housed the Ark. According to verse 15, the south gate went to Obed-Edom, and his sons were also in charge of the storehouse. *His* family was the only lineage of gatekeepers *who were richly blessed*.

Now we know that Obed-Edom was in fact a Levite from the Korahites of the *clan of Merari*, one of Levi's three sons. He was not from Gath-rimmon. That town was given to the *clan of Kohath*. The fact that he was a Levite makes sense, because it is unlikely that David would have broken another Levitical law after what had just happened to Uzzah by having the Ark shipped away to a Gentile. The time was close at hand for the Gentiles to be given access to the Ark, but at this point in time, God was still requiring the Mosaic Law to be upheld.

Another confirmation that Obed-Edom was a Levite can be gleaned from the extensive roles he was given at the Tabernacle of David once the Ark left his house. He was employed there *full time*, and only someone from within the

Levitical tribe of Israel would have the time to work these long hours in service to the Lord.

The other factor to consider here is that David emulated past history: the Ark had been taken back to Gath, the same Philistine city it had been whisked away to over a century earlier. When the Philistines had the Ark in their possession, they broke out in tumours and there was a mice plague. At the time of King David's rule, the Philistines were still worshiping their false God Dagon, so it would be reasonable to assume that these same results would have occurred if Obed-Edom had not been a sanctified worshiper of Yahweh.

Through the Ark's re-appearance in Gath, God revealed that there would come a time when His presence would dwell securely and safely in all nations of the earth. God's glory would be permitted to manifest outside of Israel through the Body of Christ globally. When David killed Goliath, representing the demonic stronghold of Gath, he took his head and placed it in Jerusalem. Soon David was going to come and fetch the Ark from Gath, and take it on the very same trip to Jerusalem as evidence of God's complete and utter victory over the strong men of Satan. (Matt 12:26-29)

◊◊◊◊◊

What is the definition of the name Obed-Edom? Obed is 'servant', and Edom refers to the Edomite's, who were descendants of Jacob's twin brother Esau (Gen. 32:3, 36:1). Of extreme relevance to us is the contents of the verse we are becoming quite familiar with, Amos 9:11-12;

> *"In that day I will raise up the fallen booth of David, And wall up its breaches; I will also raise up its ruins and rebuild it as in the days of old; [12] That they may possess the <u>remnant of Edom</u> and <u>all the nations</u> who are called by My name," declares the Lord who does this.* (NASB)

Do you see the mention of 'remnant of Edom' here? Edom is a term representing the 'residue of the nations' who would believe in the Jewish Messiah. This is confirmed by James the Apostle, when he quoted the Greek Septuagint translation of this verse to the Jerusalem council;

> *"After these things I will return, And I will rebuild the tabernacle of David which has fallen, And I will rebuild its ruins, And I will restore it, [17] So that the <u>**rest of mankind**</u> may seek the Lord, And <u>all the Gentiles</u>*

who are called by My name," Says the Lord, who makes these things known from long ago. (Acts 15:16-17 NASB)

The *remnant of Edom* is a term God uses to refer to *the rest of humanity.* The people called by God from all nations are not Jewish people scattered among the nations; they are fully-fledged Gentiles! This shows us that Edom can refer, in a broader sense, to Gentiles, heathens, pagans; all those estranged from God. Thus, Obed-Edom's name means 'servant of the Gentiles'. Through this servant of the Gentiles, a remnant of the heathen would be called out and set apart to bear the name of the Lord! (Amos 9:12, Acts 15:17) The remnant or residue is 'the remainder'. At the end of the age, the field of the whole world is reaped. The 'harvester angels' first task is to separate the tares from the wheat and place them into bundles to be burned. After this, the wheat *that is left over* is brought into the barn. (Matt 13:24-30, 36-43)

Being a Levite doesn't insinuate Obed-Edom's name loses its prophetic meaning. His name is translated 'servant of the Gentiles' because the Ark came to his house, a prophetic picture of the Lord Jesus coming to planet earth. To do what? 'Serve the Gentiles'. Just as Israel was destined to possess what was left of their archrival Edom, Jesus, through His atonement, has possessed a remnant from the Gentiles for Himself and brought them into His sheepfold. (John 10:16)

The Lord Jesus didn't come down from heaven only to serve his natural descendants, the Jews, but to die as a sacrifice *for all humanity.* This central truth of the good news was a message the Jewish people couldn't get their heads around. They thought their Jewish Messiah was going to come as a military commando like David and free Israel from the tyrannical control of Rome. Instead, He came as a humble servant to all nations. (Luke 24:47, Acts 1:6-8)

Have the same mindset as Christ Jesus: [6]who, being in very nature God, did not consider equality with God something to be used to his own advantage; [7]rather, he made himself nothing by taking the <u>very nature of a servant</u>, being made in human likeness. [8]And being found in appearance as a man, he humbled himself by becoming obedient to death—even death on a cross! (Phil 2:5b-9)

Jesus made it abundantly clear *that "the Son of Man did not come to be served, but to serve, and to give His life as a ransom for many"* (Mark 10:45)

Throughout his earthly ministry, we see Jesus serving and blessing Gentiles. He gave true living water to the Samaritan woman at the well and even asked her for a drink of water from her 'unclean' pitcher. He healed a Canaanite woman's daughter of an impure spirit, and ministered multiple times to the inhabitants of Tyre, Sidon and those from across the other side of the Jordan. (John 4, Mark 3:8, 7:24-28, Luke 6:17)

Obed-Edom's name was a foreshadowing of a later time when the Lord God would visit the Gentiles in the form of a human Servant. Through His servanthood, they would ultimately gain access into the Holy of Holies! Jesus was coming to earth to serve *them* all the way to His death. After rising again, He gave them free access through the veil via His blood atonement.

The typology of this was about to come to fruition when the Ark was finally brought into Jerusalem by King David. The rest of humanity, along with God's firstborn Son (Israel), would all be welcome inside David's tent (1 Chr. 16:28-30). In the tabernacle of David, both Jew and Gentile could seek Yahweh. The only stipulation was that they approach in holy fear. That's why God took a detour and stayed with Obed-Edom. It was a newsflash! The Gentiles were going to be grafted in!

~ Chapter 31 ~
BEARING PROPER WEIGHT

> [9]*__David was now afraid of the Lord__, and he asked, "How can I ever bring the Ark of the Lord back into my care?"* [10]*So David decided not to move the Ark of the Lord into the City of David. Instead, he took it to the house of Obed-edom of Gath.* [11]*The Ark of the Lord remained there in Obed-edom's house for three months...* (1 Sam 6:9-11 NLT)

Obed-Edom graciously accepted the Ark into his own home after such a tremendously traumatic false-start in the establishing of David's Tabernacle. Meanwhile, David is back in Zion, trying not to think about the tragic events that have occurred. He is desperately attempting to block his mind from replaying what had just transpired. *"Just try and pretend like it never happened"*, he tries to convince himself.

But here's the deal: David is not praying. David is not worshiping. He is not seeking God! In his mind, he has become afraid of God and fled from His presence. How can David keep his thoughts off past hurts and failures without the healing hand of the Holy Spirit? It is nearly impossible!

The only answer is 'escapism'. Fortunately for David, the construction of his cedar palace had been scheduled to begin around the same time as the tent on Zion was pitched. The structure that would facilitate his function as king, and the structure to outwork his function as priest, were being established at the same time. Immediately after the Ark was placed at Obed-Edom's house, King Hiriam of Tyre sent messengers to David, along with the cedar timber, and the stonemasons and carpenters began to build the palace (1 Chr. 14:1). "Phew, perfect timing," he thought. "Something to keep my mind occupied."

David could now 'busy himself' by getting all caught up in the architecture of his new living quarters. Living in a state of 'busyness' would keep his thoughts away from the things he really needed to deal with in his heart. This enabled David to escape from the pain, guilt and offense, but this was only a bandaid solution. His 'issues' were still lurking under the surface. Until he dealt with the wounds deep on the inside, he could never live in freedom.

The only positive thing David could dwell on was the fact that by some miracle, he was still king. The people had not revolted and kicked him out of the kingdom! Not only that, but David came to realise during this time that even despite the setback, the Lord had *'confirmed him as king over Israel and had greatly blessed his kingdom for the sake of his people Israel'* (1 Chr. 14:2). The general population could see this clearly and still held him in high regard. God's hand of favour and blessing had always been on David, and it hadn't lifted even after the mishap with the Ark. This gave David a minimal amount of comfort amidst the spiritual warfare going on in the battlefield of his mind.

Astounding News

About two months after the incident, messengers came to David with a staggering report: *"Do you know that the house of Obed-Edom has been supremely blessed since the moment the Ark came into his possession? Everything he owns has multiplied and everything he puts his hands to has prospered!"* (1 Sam 6:12a)

In a state of perplexity, King David responds: *"Hey! That's what God told me would happen when we brought the Ark into my tent on Zion! Only it would have been for all the inhabitants of the surrounding lands, not just one man! Maybe I was not so far off the beaten track after all?"*

David's heart comes alive with the news! The longing to get reacquainted with God suddenly overwhelms his being: *"I just can't live another minute hiding from the Lord. I need to get away from all this hustle and bustle and seek Him for answers to heal my soul. Only the Lord my God can permanently remove this hurt and pain."*

David finds a solitary place where he can be alone, withdrawing to terrain much like the sheep paddocks where he used to connect with God as a young boy. He desperately desires to get back to his first love. Out comes the harp. *"Gee"* he thinks, *"I haven't played this for a while: Probably going to sound a little bit rusty."*

David begins to play. At first, he misses a few chords and stumbles upon the wrong note, but all of a sudden, the Spirit takes over. Now he is in the flow, he is ministering under the anointing. Next thing he knows, demons of torment flee from his mind just as they used to do for King Saul when David played for him years earlier. Almost instantly, David can see clearly: God begins downloading why things turned out the way they did and also gives him the corrective plans to move forward and get back on assignment.

David asks the Lord; *"Lord God, I thought there was a new and living way through the curtain? I truly believe you told me that people would be able to approach, and even touch, the Ark without fear of negative consequences. Why did you kill Uzzah?"*

The Lord replied; *"My beloved Son David, the moving of the Ark into your tent is 'transitionary'. It denotes the time period when the Messiah of Israel will walk this earth. During that time, there will be a transition from law into grace, but the full reality of My wrath being removed cannot occur till My Son rises from the dead and sits down at My right hand. That is symbolic of the time when you place the Ark inside the tent. From that time on, people can approach my footstool without fear of judgment. And don't worry about Uzzah, he is safe and being comforted in paradise with Abraham."*

Galatians 4:4 tells us that *"when the fullness of time had come, God sent forth his Son, born of woman, <u>born under the law, ⁵to redeem those who were under the law</u>, so that we might receive adoption as sons."* (ESV)

Jesus came to redeem those 'under the law', but in order to do this He had to be born 'under the law'. He needed to fully comply with everything the Law of Moses commanded men to do in order to remain in right standing with the Father. Jesus did the humanly impossible. Not as an earthly priest, but as an ordinary Jewish man, He fully obeyed His Father. By the power of the Holy Spirit and the enabling virtue of His divine blood, He shrugged off every temptation from His human flesh and fulfilled the Mosaic Law to perfection. Jesus never sinned, not even once. He did this so that we can be free from the 'letter of the law' which kills, and transfer across into the 'spirit of the law' which brings life. (2 Cor. 3:6)

◊◊◊◊◊

The 33-year period when Jesus walked the earth was a strange time. Although Jesus was announcing the New Covenant gospel of the kingdom, He was *at the same time* perfectly fulfilling the 'letter of the law' from the first covenant. People were getting water baptised, but the Holy Spirit was not yet living in their hearts. Jesus and John preached a baptism for the forgiveness of sins, but the people were also bringing their animal sacrifices to the temple for the same reason. Jesus was touching unclean people and making them clean, but then He also said *"go show yourself to the priest and offer the sacrifices that <u>Moses</u>*

commanded for your cleansing" (Mark 1:44). Everything was a blend. They had placed one foot into the new, while the other was still in the old.

In bringing up the Ark to Jerusalem, David had to clarify with the Lord what was acceptable and unacceptable down to the very last detail, so that first, the type and shadow of Jesus' earthly life was accurately fulfilled and second, no one else would be brought into harm's way.

During this time of rededication, things became crystal clear to David. He now had full assurance that the procession would go smoothly second time around. There was now no room for presumption because David had fully sought the Lord for 'His way'.

Let's Try Again!

When the time came for the next attempt, the first thing David said was;

> *"No one except the Levites may carry the Ark of God. The LORD has chosen them to carry the Ark of the LORD and to serve him forever".*
> *³Then David summoned all Israel to Jerusalem to bring the Ark of the LORD to the place he had prepared for it.* (1 Chr. 15:2-3 NLT)

From here, the descendants of Aaron (the priests) and all the Levites were called together;

> *¹¹Then David summoned the priests, Zadok and Abiathar, and these Levite leaders: Uriel, Asaiah, Joel, Shemaiah, Eliel, and Amminadab. ¹²He said to them, "You are the leaders of the Levite families. You must purify yourselves and all your fellow Levites, so you can bring the Ark of the Lord, the God of Israel, to the place I have prepared for it. ¹³Because you Levites did not carry the Ark the first time, the anger of the Lord our God burst out against us. We failed to ask God how to move it properly." ¹⁴So the priests and the Levites purified themselves in order to bring the Ark of the Lord, the God of Israel, to Jerusalem. ¹⁵Then the Levites carried the Ark of God on their shoulders with its carrying poles, just as the Lord had instructed Moses.* (1 Chr. 15:11-15 NLT)

Jesus was born onto this earth 'under law'. Therefore, the Ark (representing Jesus) had to be carried according to the instructions taught by *Moses*. The Levites had to carry it upon their shoulders with the prescribed carrying poles in place. That was the foot that was still in the old, but there was also the other in the new. Let's look at the next verse;

[16] "David also ordered the Levite leaders to appoint a choir of Levites who were singers and musicians to sing joyful songs to the accompaniment of harps, lyres, and cymbals." (1 Chr. 15:16 NLT)

Amongst the old system, the new was emerging: the inauguration of worship in the form of music, dance and song! David had asked the Lord; *"Can we still celebrate with the new order of worship you've shown me, or does that have to wait too?"*

The Father replied; *"Yes David, you can sing, dance and play with all your heart, for when Messiah comes to earth, people will worship Him as the Lord God and He will accept their worship. He is the great 'I AM', just as I AM."*

As a Jewish man from the tribe of Judah, Jesus was living under the law, but as God, He simultaneously accepted the worship reserved only for Yahweh. Therefore, David was permitted to keep the worship element to his parade. People didn't wait until Jesus rose from the dead to worship Him as God. In the same way, David didn't have to wait till the Ark was placed in his tent. All David had to do to ensure safe passage for the Ark and everyone surrounding it was to change the oxen and cart back to the old Mosaic custom of shouldering the load on carrying poles.

In this instance, the carrying poles give us two specific revelations;

First, the shoulder is symbolic of 'government, support, and strength in responsibility'. In Deuteronomy 18:3, the shoulder of the meat was a special portion given to the priests. In 1 Samuel 9:24, Samuel ordered that the shoulder of the meat be given to King Saul right before he was anointed as Israel's first king. The priests carrying the Ark on their shoulders revealed that Jesus Christ would have the government of God's kingdom on his shoulders as He functions in His role as both King and Priest. Isaiah 9:6-7 NKJV says;

*"For unto us a Child is born, Unto us a Son is given; And the government will be upon His shoulder…Of the increase of His government and peace there will be no end, **upon the throne of David and over His kingdom."***

A second revelation of the carrying poles has to do with us. As was previously pointed out through King David's first attempt with the ox and cart; in the New Covenant, we are not required to carry the WEIGHT OF OUR SIN. The cross emboldens us to walk alongside the Ark in full freedom, or better still, go up front like Ahio and yoke ourselves with Christ. However, *there is* a price to pay if we want to carry THE WEIGHT OF HIS GLORY. We are not required to bear the weight of past sin, but we are invited to swap it for a new weight of glory. Jesus does have a yoke and a burden for us to carry, but the load of sin is too heavy to bear. The weight of His glory, however, is easy and the burden of it is light.

It is a privilege and an honour to carry the weight of His glory. That is why the remnant go through such intense trials and testing to ensure they are fit to carry this weight. This was emphasised in David's instruction to the priests and Levites. He told them to follow the correct process with respect to the LOM, but above all this, he told them to 'consecrate' themselves;

> *"You are the heads of the fathers' houses of the Levites. <u>Consecrate yourselves</u>, you and your brothers, so that you may bring up the ark of the LORD, the God of Israel, to the place that I have prepared for it. [13]Because you did not carry it the first time, the LORD our God broke out against us, because we did not seek him according to the rule."* (1 Chr. 15:12-13 ESV)

Bearing the weight of His glory *demands consecration*: that is 'purification and sanctification resulting in holiness'. Once we have come to the cross and placed our past sins under His blood, we do not have to bear that weight any longer. But we are expected to bear weight in God's kingdom; the right kind of weight. It is the weightiness of the *kâbôwd Yĕhovah:* the Glory of the Lord. In order to achieve this, we must cooperate with the Holy Spirit, Who will guide us into all truth *and righteousness*. Only disciples are qualified to carry His glory, converts cannot. Jesus said that anyone who does not carry the weight of their cross and follow Him cannot be His disciple (Luke 14:27). The weight of His glory is directly proportionate to the weight of our sacrificing of self. These two 'weights' are directly correlated.

The essence of consecration is **'setting yourself apart in dedication for spiritual service'.** *Spiritual* service is the antithesis to the *superficial* service laid down as the bedrock of Mosaic Law (Heb. 9:9-10). To correctly divide the word of truth, we must clearly differentiate between the two…

~ Chapter 32 ~

I DESIRE MERCY, NOT SACRIFICE

As previously discussed, the time-period where Jesus roamed the earth was a transitory season. It had a 50-50 blend of both the old and new covenants. One of the primary and most revolutionary concepts Jesus was instilling as He taught the Jewish people was first mentioned by God through the prophet Hosea;

> *"For I desire mercy, not sacrifice, and acknowledgment of God rather than burnt offerings."* (Hos. 6:6)

As Jesus neared death, a teacher of the law (scribe) came up and asked Him about which commandment in the law was the greatest. Jesus answered by emphasising the centrality and primary focus of the first and greatest commandment; 'love the Lord your God with all our heart, soul, mind and strength' and then He mentioned that the second was just like it; 'to love our fellow human beings as we do ourselves'. These were *by far* the most important commandments, leading to the true fulfilment of all the others. (Rom. 13:10, Gal. 5:14)

It was almost as if this scribe knew Jesus' answer in advance, because immediately after Jesus finished, the man excitingly replied;

> *32 "Well said, teacher! You are right in saying that God is one and there is no other but him. 33 To love him with all your heart, with all your understanding and with all your strength, and to love your neighbour as yourself is more important than all burnt offerings and sacrifices."*
>
> *34 When Jesus saw he had answered wisely, he said to him, "You are not far from the kingdom of God."* (Mark 12:32-34a)

The kingdom of God is 'the true heavenly reality of the earthly Davidic kingdom'. This man was *not far off* entering it. For him, the transition away from 'sacrifice' and into 'mercy' was almost complete. We have to admire the tender-heartedness of this scribe. To have such a grasp on this type of spiritual truth was very unusual for a teacher of the law. Their upbringing and indoctrination as a strict 'instructor of the Pharisees' would make them most resistant to this type of revolutionary change.

In responding to the man in this way, Jesus clarified that this transition in thinking was one of the primary pathways into the kingdom. It is a key element in breaking us out of the 'old', enabling us to fully explore the 'new'. No one would accept the invitation into the kingdom of God (through accepting Christ) if they did not first grasp this shift in paradigm. A short time later, Jesus rebuked the teachers of the law when He gave this summation of the stereotypical scribe;

> *13 "Woe to you, teachers of the law and Pharisees, you hypocrites! You <u>shut the door of the kingdom</u> of heaven in people's faces. <u>You yourselves do not enter, nor will you let those enter who are trying to</u>.*

> *15 "Woe to you, teachers of the law and Pharisees, you hypocrites! You travel over land and sea to win a single convert, and when you have succeeded, you make them <u>twice as much a son of hell</u> as you are."*
> (Matt 24:13, 15)

Ouch! Jesus didn't sugar-coat His rebukes. Fortunately, the scribe who inquired of Jesus (concerning the greatest commandments) didn't fit this stereotype. He refused to go along with what was popular or what could get him ahead in life. Instead, he was a seeker of the truth.

One day, Jesus and His disciples went through the grainfields on the Sabbath. Because the disciples were hungry, they began to pick some heads of grain and eat them. When the Pharisees saw this, they said to him, "*Look! Your disciples are doing what is unlawful on the Sabbath.*" (Matt 12:1-2)

Jesus hit back at the Pharisees with a masterful response;

> *"Haven't you read what <u>David did</u> when he and his companions were hungry? 4He entered the house of God, and he and his companions ate the consecrated bread—which was not lawful for them to do, but only for the priests. 5Or haven't you read in the Law that the priests on Sabbath duty in the temple desecrate the Sabbath and yet are innocent? 6I tell you that something greater than the temple is here. 7<u>If you had known what these words mean, 'I desire mercy, not sacrifice,' you would not have condemned the innocent</u>."* (Matt 12:3-7)

Jesus knew it was greatly beneficial to give an example of King David when debating with those who idolise Moses' Law. According to the rigid interpretation of the rules found in Leviticus 24:9, King David and His companions were guilty of breaking the commandment stating that only the priests could partake of the old loaves of showbread from within the Holy

Place. God overlooked this law on two accounts. 1) He allowed men who were not priests to use the Bread of the Presence, satisfying their intense hunger, and 2) He also did not require them to eat it in the prescribed location either, for David was alone at the time and was meeting up with his companions to eat later (1 Sam 21:3). God did not count any of the actions by David or his travelling party as transgression because He considered the current crisis of greater importance than the 'rules' He laid down at Mount Sinai, placing more weight upon the desperate situation they were in. It was a case where 'common sense prevailed'. (Prov. 2:7, 8:14 NLT)

Jesus then throws in the command from Numbers 28:9, where priests are enabled to sacrifice two lambs on the Sabbath, breaking the Sabbath law in doing so. The Sabbath was made to benefit man, not man to be a slave of the Sabbath. (Matt 12:5)

On the surface, the focal point of contention appears to be 'Sabbath day regulations', but Jesus is hitting on something deeper here. He is actually delving into the condition of their hearts. There was an ungodly motivation behind the guise of these strictly enforced Sabbath rules taught by the Pharisees, and Jesus identifies it, bringing it to the surface. The issue the Pharisees *really* have is that they elevate sacrifice above mercy. In their pride, self-righteousness was taking precedent over the urgent needs of others. Let me explain…

Legalism 'Super-charged'

In the Law of Moses, there were 613 laws to keep. Hebrews 9 shows us that the service conducted by the priests and the laws kept by the people were *regulations of outward service (dikaiōma latreia- Heb. 9:1)* that were performed only *in the flesh (sarx - Heb. 9:10)*. These carnal ordinances were imposed upon them only until the 'time of reformation' which came through Jesus (KJV). As we learnt back in chapter 3, they were merely outward, external, or worldly, meaning there was no 'heart connection' or 'spiritual element' attached to them.

This in itself was hard enough to bear, but wait till you hear what the Pharisees believed and what they taught. *They* took religious duty to a whole new level! The teachers of the law added 'the traditions handed down by the fathers' on top of these 613 laws. This became known as the 'oral law', while designating the original LOM the 'written law'. Whenever an elder in the party of the

Pharisees came up with a new rule, they would add it to the oral law, and this continued on down the generations. By the time of Christ, there were so many extra laws of 'man-made tradition' being kept, that it was impossible to bear up under the weight.

Another deeply rooted problem was the fact that the traditions handed down by the fathers were handed down orally and never written down. If you have a book of laws fully documented that you can reference any time, and then another set that had to be recalled by memory, which do you think would be widely emphasised and taught more often?

Keeping the LOM as the only 'official Scriptures' also gave the illusion that they believed the LOM to be the actual Word of God, with the oral tradition as lesser or secondary to it. But in actual fact, we find in Matthew 15:1-7 and Mark 7:5-13 that when these traditions contradicted Moses, the scribes would conveniently elevate their own traditions of the elders above the inspired Word of God! Jesus rebuked the Pharisees and scribes for this when they were using one of these traditions to berate Jesus' disciples for not washing their hands before they ate. This was not a requirement in the LOM, yet they were accusing the disciples of being ceremonially unclean.

With these thousands of integrated rules, all that the Pharisees (and in particular the scribes) would do day-in, day-out was attack people for not keeping this rule, disobeying that rule, not keeping themselves ceremonially clean, or not performing this 'religious duty' or that 'pious ritual'.

Their entire life calling was all about 'religious police duty'. In their teaching, there was no emphasis on matters of the heart; it was all based on outward actions of rigid and insanely strict obedience. According to them, they were the superior ones that 'knew all the rules' and performed them to a tee: the 'epitome of holiness'. Everyone else could never be righteous enough. Thus, they exalted themselves as holy figures to be reverenced and honoured by the rest of the ordinary scum. But Jesus saw straight through their facade;

> "You are the ones who _justify yourselves in the eyes of men, but God knows your hearts_. What is highly valued among men is detestable in God's sight." (Luke 16:15)

Because of these additional laws, the followers of Judaism who had a heart to follow the Torah could never attain to the same mark of perfection as their teachers. This erroneous indoctrination led to class distinctions and double standards, all rooted in pride, self-centredness, and personal exaltation. This is the complete opposite of true discipleship. The end-goal of discipleship is for the student to emulate the character of their teacher, and to become like their Master. This was impossible under this ultra-legalistic framework. Truth be told, in the inner recesses of their hearts and behind closed doors, most of these Pharisees were actually the worst sinners of the lot! Jesus even told them to their faces that "their hearts were far away from God" and that "they worshipped the Lord in vain." (Matt 15:8)

Saturday's at the synagogue were nothing more than a time of finger-pointing, accusation and law enforcement: *"Clean this kettle and wash this pitcher: If you miss anything, God will judge you! By the way, here's a new tradition we added during the week. Quickly commit it to memory, then we'll recite all the traditions out loud. Also, before you go, don't forget to tithe the herbs from your garden by giving them to us right here on your way out."*

This was the 'holier than thou' club. Everyone who came under the oppression of their ministries left feeling condemned, inferior and under the heavy hand of an angry God armed with a whacking stick. No matter what their followers did out of the goodness of their hearts, it would never be enough to please God. This was fundamentalism gone mad! Eventually, Jesus was so fed up with them that in Matthew 23:33, he imitated his cousin John and called them a 'brood of vipers'. What Jesus said at the beginning of His righteous tirade sums this all up;

> [2] *"The teachers of the law and the Pharisees sit in Moses' seat.* [3] *So you must be careful to do everything they tell you. But do not do what they do, for they do not practice what they preach.* [4] *They tie up heavy, cumbersome loads and put them on other people's shoulders, but they themselves are not willing to lift a finger to move them."* (Matt 23:2-4)

Not only did the Pharisees tie heavy loads of their own man-made legalistic rules and place them onto men's shoulders, not one of them would even *lift a single finger* to help them carry these unnecessary burdens. Are you beginning to see the severe lack of mercy accompanied by an abundance of flesh-driven sacrifice?

Defining True Legalism

What the Pharisees were teaching was the epitome of legalism. In basic terms, legalism is when we place greater importance on following the commands of

God than having a relationship with Him. But legalism is more than that; it is when someone teaches rules or laws that are *outside of the terms of the Covenant*. It is not at all legalistic to teach obedience to terms contained *within* the covenant. For example, if the New Testament says, *'among you there must not be even a hint of sexual immorality'*, then, as a part of the Law of Christ found in the New Covenant, you are not legalistic if you teach this to Christians or aim to implement this righteous standard into your own Christian walk. But always remember; if God's laws become your sole focus, then your balance is out and you will still find yourself stuck in legalism. Jesus said that the aim of obeying His commandments is so that we can abide in His love (John 15:9-10). This is the motivation behind law-keeping; that we may remain in intimacy with Him.

What we must understand, though, is that as ministers of Christ, it is not enough to merely 'teach' holy commands. Our role is to equip and to assist people in walking them out. We must empower and teach disciples *how* to overcome by the wisdom and power of the Spirit. Mentioning the standard is only half of the job. Loving people into implementation of that obedience through gentle exhortation and kind teaching is what is most important.

We must separate true legalism from 'misinterpreted legalism', or else we fall into error. Free, sloppy, or hyper-grace teaching is the extreme case of misinterpretation concerning the true nature of legalism. Adherents of this false doctrine are the 'Christian liberals' who call out any form of self-examination or focus on personal holiness as legalism. They don't understand the terms of the New Covenant, the difference between accidental and deliberate sin, or the differentiation between Moses' Law and Christ's law, which operate from two totally separate approaches toward obedience. (Works of Law vs Spirit-led)

So what does legalistic teaching look like for us today?

1) An overwhelming emphasis on the laws of God that lacks a focus of communion with Him.

2) Being commanded to return to regulations in the Law of Moses which Christ has done away with by fulfilling the type and shadow (including forcing people to participate in feast days and compulsory offerings—Col. 2:16, Gal 4:10)

3) Advocating obedience to God through human striving of our flesh rather than 'Spirit-led obedience' through the enabling grace of God.

4) Adding strict man-made traditions that are not in the New Testament for Christian living. Here are some examples; *"you are required to say this phrase at this specific time", "you have to bow at this spot", "you must perform this or that action". "In order to earn God's acceptance, you must serve on this team or complete this duty"*, or absurd holiness standards like, *"it's a sin to dance at a wedding: flashing lights, drums and electric guitars are of the devil; women are sinning if they wear make-up or pants and if you play golf on Sunday, you're desecrating the Lord's Day"* etc.

When the Pharisees accused the disciples of harvesting grain of the Sabbath back in Matthew 12, they were misapplying the meaning of the Sabbath because of these extra 'traditions of men', but they were also showing the motive behind everything they did as religious extremists. It was a system of control and a method to prop themselves up in the sight of the common people.

Jesus says; *"Hey you so-called teachers who supposedly represent Me: Go away and learn what this means; 'I desire mercy, not sacrifice.' You lack mercy, but you abound in sacrifice. It should be the other way around."*

What Hosea 6:6 refers to, and what Jesus was saying to the Pharisees, is this;

"I desire *acts of* mercy *to be shown to others* rather than *a performance of meaningless self-*sacrifice."

The true 'sacrifices of God' are *merciful acts for the benefit of another*. These are the spiritual sacrifices mentioned in 1 Peter 2:5 that please God and are an integral part of the New Covenant. It is when we decide to lay down our selfish desires and give assistance and care to others. Religious rituals and duties are a meaningless form of self-sacrifice that are of no advantage to those around us. That's how you can tell if something is 'mercy driven' or 'sacrifice driven', whether it's worthwhile or pointless.

What God wants to see is loving-kindness on display. This is how we fulfil the second of the two greatest commandments mentioned by Jesus to that faithful scribe. It amazes me how this teacher of the law in Mark 12 could be so in tune with God's heart when all his colleagues were peddling such vain religion to the multitudes.

The first and greatest commandment to love God with everything we have is fulfilled through the spiritual sacrifices of praise, worship and prayer inside the TOD within our secret place. This is the 'simplicity of pure devotion to Christ' we discussed in chapter 2.

By fulfilling the first commandment, we are empowered to go out into the world and fulfil the second, which is to love those we come into contact with as we love ourselves. This is the 'mercy' Jesus desires to find present in all of our lives. The entire New Covenant requirement of sacrifice is summed up in this simple operation of loving God through worship and then dispensing the love of God to others through the empowering influence of His marvellous grace. It is the difference between the *living* sacrifices found in Romans 12:1 and the *dead* sacrifices modelled by the Pharisees.

God wants to fill you up to pour you out; then fill you up again to be poured out once more. Believe it or not, remaining in the secret place (away from others) all the time can end up in selfishness. Though this time with God is vitally necessary and the cornerstone of everything contained within this book, on its own, it isn't enough. Eventually, God is going to send you out of the prayer closet so that you can be emptied by selflessly serving others just like Jesus did when He came to earth (Phil. 2:7). Jesus withdrew to faraway places and spent extensive periods of time with His Father, but He never stayed there permanently. He always came back and displayed God's mercy by serving hurting people once more (Luke 5:16, Acts 10:38). Without this outworking, the kingdom cannot expand.

What exactly is showing mercy to others?

'Showing mercy' is encapsulated by love and servitude. And the definition God gave me is;

'Helping others in an area where they cannot help themselves' (i.e. are helpless)

Our ultimate example of this is Jesus, the King of kings, who took the place of 'slave of all' and died on a Roman cross. He gave up His life to extend God's mercy through forgiveness of sin to the entire human race. This was an area where 'we could not help ourselves'; there was nothing *we* could do to get our sins forgiven. So Jesus stepped in and served us in this area by taking the lowest place. This is true kingship in the kingdom of God. God's promotion (in church or marketplace ministry) comes when we take least position and value others more highly than ourselves. (See Phil. 2:3-10)

Look at all the mercy we receive from God. Isaiah 16:5 says "in *mercy* shall a throne be established and Jesus will sit on it in truth in the Tabernacle of David." The whole foundation of Jesus' throne is based on the mercy He extends to mankind. Then, in Hebrews 4:16, the Bible tells us that we receive *mercy* as we come boldly to the throne of grace, the very same throne mentioned in Isaiah 16. Without Jesus' blood on the mercy seat, we could never enter boldly into His presence to be forgiven, let alone find the enabling grace to move forward and show mercy to others. As has been mentioned multiple times, according to Psalm 99:1, the 'mercy' seat *is* Jesus' throne. No wonder the throne is established on *mercy*; that's its actual name!

Given that God has shown us such mercy shouldn't we then, as imitators of Him, be called to extend mercy also? This is why Romans 12:1 begins with the phrase: 'in view of God's mercy' when speaking of us presenting our bodies as living sacrifices holy and pleasing to God; because He has shown us mercy, we should respond likewise.

Now obviously we can't go around atoning for and then forgiving people's sins, but we can find ways to help others in areas where they are helpless. Our first response does not always have to be preaching the gospel of salvation by telling them about Jesus. Religion has taught us this, and we need to get that out of our heads! The truth is, even though this is our ultimate goal, most of the time this will occur much later on. Yes, leading people to Christ is our main objective, but it is the end-game, not always the first move. We need to learn how to switch our minds away from the priestly frequency and adjust it over to the kingly frequency. Showing mercy can be displayed in any area of a person's life where we are able to assist and bless them, alleviate a burden, or make life easier. I am talking about helping them by solving a physical problem or dilemma. The appreciation that grows from 'good works' completed with no strings attached builds a platform of influence which God can use at the right time for the ultimate purpose: our priestly function.

~ Chapter 33 ~

SPIRITUAL SACRIFICES PLEASING TO GOD

"Therefore, I urge you, brothers, __in view of God's mercy__, to offer your bodies as a living sacrifice, holy and pleasing to God—this is your spiritual act of worship." (Rom. 12:1)

Jesus' throne is established on God's mercy toward us as sinners. *In view of that mercy*, we should respond by laying down our lives as *living* sacrifices, consecrated and pleasing to Him. Whoever claims to live in Him must live as Jesus did (1 John 2:6). The entirety of Jesus' earthly life was consumed with God-given purpose, and that purpose came from a fully surrendered life of extended mercies to the people around Him. If we can get our eyes off ourselves and onto what God has commanded us, we will enter into the life-giving flow of infinite glory He has prepared for us. We will enter the abundant life He promised us in John 10:10.

"Therefore, I urge you, brothers, in view of God's mercy, to offer your bodies as a __living sacrifice__, holy and pleasing to God—this is your spiritual act of worship." (Rom. 12:1)

In the sacrificial system, the sacrificed animals *died*. They were no longer living and therefore were of no help to anyone. The priests who sacrificed the animals were also dead in their own transgressions and sins, which the animals could never actually take away (Heb. 10:4, 11). The priesthood had their focus on dead animals and religious duty instead of bringing life to their fellow citizens and caring for them.

As priests in the royal priesthood, like our High Priest Jesus Christ, we are both the priest *and the sacrifice*. Our lives therefore become sacrifices that are *living* in the natural, but our flesh is dead on God's altar. On this altar, we get lit up with the fire of God, and our focus is renewed on showing mercy through love and servitude to those around us. These are spiritual sacrifices that are instilled with God-purpose and bring forth *zōē* life. This supernatural 'life' exudes out of believers who are animated by the life-source of the Spirit of God. Being possessed with vitality, we abide in the absolute fullness of life that can only be found through obedience to Jesus Christ: For it is more blessed to give than to receive. (Acts 20:35)

*"Therefore, I urge you, brothers, in view of God's mercy, to offer your bodies as a living sacrifice, holy and pleasing to God—this is your **spiritual act of worship**."* (Rom. 12:1)

When we offer our bodies as living sacrifices for the sake of helping others, it is seen by God as a *spiritual act of worship*. There is the spiritual type of worship that is directed to God via soaking and waiting upon the Lord, but then there is another form of spiritual worship which is seen through our actions of loving kindness toward our neighbour.

The Greek for 'spiritual act of worship' is *'logikos latreia'*. This is the spiritual version of *latreia* that has zōē life attached to it. Because it is spiritual and not carnal, the *latreia* can be defined as worship, not mere service.

Back in chapter 4, we examined how Hebrews 9:1 paints the grim picture of the *latreia* in the Tabernacle of Moses. It was *dikaiōma;* merely 'regulation driven'. The spiritual component was missing. The Old Testament priests were given religious ordinances of superficial service to perform ritualistically. We have been given the spiritual element which gets our minds off meaningless sacrifice and onto the purity of extending God's mercy. This results in actions that can be included as part of true worship unto God!

The word logikos can mean 'logical or what is reasonable', but also 'pertaining to the soul', which I believe is what Paul and Peter are referring to when they use this word. When you examine the only other verse where this word appears in our Bible, it is in this context;

[2]*"like newborn babies, long for the pure milk of the word, so that by it you may grow in respect to salvation"* (1 Pet. 2:2 NASB)

Here, Peter is referring to the undiluted, pure milk of God's word. What form of milk is this? Is it natural milk we derive from a mother or from cows? No, it is *spiritual*. This is brought out in the NIV translation;

"Like newborn babies, crave pure spiritual milk, so that by it you may grow up in your salvation"

◊◊◊◊◊

In the Bible, *logikos* is always referring to spiritual things; things that pertain to our soul or 'inner-man'. Therefore, the *logikos latreia* is correctly categorised as *'spiritual* worship'. As we already know, the second word; *latreia*, denotes 'service rendered for hire' or 'action', and this mention in Romans 12:1 also correlates with *spiritual worship* because these selfless actions spring forth from becoming a living sacrifice, not a dead one! Therefore, 'your spiritual *actions* of worship' would also be an acceptable translation for *logikos latreia* at the end of the verse. In this context, it encompasses, **'*spiritual* service that affects the soul and transforms the mind *of another*.'**

These actions of true worship are mentioned by Peter only three verses after his reference to spiritual milk;

> *"You also, like living stones, are being built into a spiritual house to be a holy priesthood, offering <u>spiritual sacrifices</u> acceptable to God through Jesus Christ"* (1 Pet 2:5)

The first facet of spiritual sacrifice as a priest of God is praise, thanksgiving and adoration *towards God*, as well as our intercessory prayer life and private devotions in His Word.

The second facet of spiritual sacrifice is when we offer our bodies as living sacrifices *for the sake of others*. 'Living sacrifices' then are believers who **'lay down their lives to show mercy to others.'**

These spiritual acts of worship are living and active, full of loving purpose. They fulfil God's desire for 'mercy over sacrifice'. These selfless actions are the spiritual version of the natural, external service of the priests in the TOM. They are sacrifices that produce a heart transaction, unlike those of the old Mosaic order, who performed meaningless, 'self-absorbing' duties.

These two facets of spiritual sacrifice comprise the two distinct forms of our divine worship which work in tandem to see God's name glorified in the earth;

1) <u>The Davidic order of Worship</u>

2 Cor. 11:3: simplicity of pure devotion to Christ (soaking, prayer and time in His Word)

Heb. 13:15: sacrifices of praise and thanksgiving *toward God* (Praise and worship)

2) <u>Spiritual Service of Worship</u>

Matt 12:8: showing mercy *to others*, rather than *meaningless self*-sacrifice

Rom. 12:1: offering our bodies as living sacrifices, holy and pleasing to God

Freedom from Dead Religion

There are only five times where *latreia* is used in the Word of God. We have our most honourable mention here in Romans 12:1. Jesus only used this word one time, in John 16:2, which I will come back to later. The other three occurrences (Heb. 9:1, 9:6 & Rom. 9:4) are all references to the divine service of the priests at the TOM.

It wasn't just the animal sacrifices that amounted to empty service. All the assigned tasks within the Holy Place also came under the same category; the lighting of the lampstand, the baking of the consecrated bread, and the burning of incense. In all these roles, the hearts of the priests were not connected to any of it. It was just a 'mental apprehension of' and robotic obedience toward a natural command.

The priest stood in the Holy place bored out of his brains;

> *"mmm, that section of bread has puffed up nicely; I think I'll bags that one for my lunch on the weekend".*

> *"Ah yes, that's right, keep enough oil in the menorah to keep the lamps burning"*, the priest mused as he flicked through his notifications; *"oh no, quick, I got distracted, run and get the oil, QUICK! The light of God is going out!"*

> *"That incense stuff we have to burn makes it difficult for me to breathe: how about you?"*

> *"Yeah, sort of, but I guess it's a health hazard that comes along with the job. Maybe we can seek some kind of compensation once this is all over?"*

Their concepts of why they were doing these things were all worldly. They had no idea of the spiritual significance hidden within the type and pattern they were performing day in and day out. It kept them busy, that's about all. It was like running on a treadmill or sitting in a rocking chair: a lot of activity was going on, but no spiritual progress was being made!

◊◊◊◊◊

Funnily enough, I have stories from my Catholic upbringing related to all three: Within Catholic tradition, they have a special red light called the 'sanctuary lamp'. According to the traditional custom, near the altar, a special lamp, fuelled by oil or wax, should be kept alight to indicate the presence of Christ. In modern times, it is just an electric light globe in a red glass casing. It was the light that signified 'God was in the church building'.

One day, as a seven-year-old, I got slightly over confident. My Dad was the person in charge of the choir and locking up after Saturday night mass. We would stay back and be last to leave, and could roam around in all the special places, like up around the altar and in the sacristy. As we were about to leave, I said to my Dad;

"Don't worry, I'll turn the lights off. I know what I'm doing: I've watched you plenty of times".

My Dad said;

"Ok, you know the ones to turn off and the one to leave on?"

"Yeah, of course I do", I replied.

I went to the switches, and turned off all the white ones, and somehow, to this day I still don't know how, I also accidentally flicked off the *red switch of the sanctuary lamp!* The next day, the priest walked in for the Sunday morning service, and to his horror, Jesus had left the building! He rang my dad and exclaimed; *"who turned the red light off?!"* Oh dear, the news got relayed to me.

The next time I went near the church, my teeth were chattering and my knees were knocking together. I snuck into the doors and tiptoed over to the place where you kneel for prayer.

"Hi G-g-g-god, s-s-sorry for kicking you out of your church, in the name of the Father, the Son, and the Holy Spirit. Amen."

"Quick, get outta here", I thought. I scrambled for the exit.

"Oh no! I forgot to genuflect...!"

I hurried back in; knelt down on one knee, and back up. Now, I was once again off toward the light of freedom. *"Ah! Don't miss the holy water, splash, splash, 'Father-Sn-Holy Sp'rit-men', and phew, what a relief."* Finally, I was outside. I was saved!

Haven't we been told by Stephen in Acts 7 that: *"The Most High does not live in temples made by human hands"?* But being immersed in religion, I didn't know any better.

◊◊◊◊◊

After I had recovered from that traumatic experience, I became an altar server at age 9 to keep occupied through the boringness of mass. Very quickly, I became the 'pro' altar server who knew the ins and the outs of everything. Before long, I was the oldest and most capped altar server in the parish. I helped teach the newbies everything, including how to tie the fancy knots in the red cord that held up our white robes.

We did all sorts of jobs like carry in a golden crucifix on a pole, with Jesus still dead on there, of course. We rang the bells at the specified times, went to the hole in the wall and gathered the cruets of water and wine, then took them up to the priest at the altar.

Every single mass at the church I attended, the priest only ever gave the congregation the body of Christ. None of us ever partook of the symbol of the blood, which was port wine. The priest completed all the fancy rhetoric and blessed both the bread and the wine, but no one would ever get any wine!

I started to think to myself; *"why don't I get to have a taste of the blood of Jesus. This isn't fair!"* But as time went on, I started to realise why. The priest would go back up to the altar after he had given out communion and skull the whole chalice-full of wine. Clearly, he needed a boost to get him through the mass as well!

Eventually, my curiosity got the better of me. While alone in the sacristy, I nudged my younger brother, Darren, who was also an altar server. I said; *"you know the bottle of port wine in the cupboard over there, why don't we have some? We'll never get to have it any other way."* That was my justification. I snuck over and quickly took a swig. Finally, I had my first taste of the blood of Jesus, and it hadn't even been blessed by the priest! No, let's be real here; it actually wasn't the blood of Jesus, just my first taste of alcohol! But for all of you who are concerned for me; don't worry. I never took a liking to alcohol and I still dislike the taste, even to this day.

◊◊◊◊◊

The third experience has to do with the incense. If you were an experienced altar server, you could serve at funerals. This gave you extra jobs, in particular, burning incense. We had a golden thurible on a chain, and we burnt a round piece of charcoal over a flame, then placed it in the thurible. Once the hot charcoal was inside, we would sprinkle the incense mixture on top and the smoke would come out of the holes in the thurible. We kept it burning by swaying it from side to side to keep the oxygen flowing. Right near the end of the funeral, we brought it out to the priest, who circled the coffin, placing the smoke all around.

I was going to the Catholic primary school attached to the church at the time, so every now and again there was a knock on our classroom door. The priest would come in and ask me, *"Hey, Justin, I've got a funeral at 12:30. Want to serve it?"*

I always said yes without hesitation because I wanted to get out of class and even better, I usually got paid 5 bucks!

It saddens me now when I think about the attitude I took into those funerals when other people were mourning loss and suffering intense grief. All that concerned me was what I was going to do with my extra $5. That is what dead, dry, boring religion does to you, especially if you are exposed to it as a young kid. It desensitises your capacity to love and suffocates the ability to discern the needs of the people around you.

All of these Catholic duties were very similar to the three items the priest would attend to inside the Holy Place of Moses' Tabernacle. Can you believe that after Jesus freed us from all that religious bondage, the deceitfulness of human flesh drives people straight back into it?

The amazing thing about the tabernacle of David is you quickly discover that these Mosaic priestly roles became completely redundant. There was no Holy Place in the TOD, only the '*Most* Holy Place'. Even an altar of burnt offering was not required on Zion, except for the first day, as you will find out in the next chapter. Everyone was now permitted to minister as priests, and the sacrifices they offered were now living and meaningful. The *dikaiōma latreia* (regulations of divine service) that were part and parcel of the Mosaic priesthood, found no place in David's liturgy.

Why only Priests and Levites?

At the TOD, there was no difference between priests and Levites. Absolutely no class distinction remained. In Moses' tabernacle, the descendants of Aaron (the priests), could minister in the Holy Place and also sacrifice animals on the brazen altar. The Levites were not allowed to do any of this. They were selected only as 'tabernacle assistants' who served the priests in various roles (Num. 3-4). But now at the TOD, the two groups had been merged together. The priests no longer had anything to do, so David incorporated them in with the Levites.

So if the priests were redundant and everyone was now equal with regard to approaching the Lord, why then did David appoint *only Priests and Levites* to be a part of the worship band and all other roles within his tabernacle? (Refer 1 Chr. 15-16) What about the rest?

The reason no one from any other tribe was selected for tabernacle service was not because God wouldn't allow it. Rather, the decision was made solely on *time constraints*. The others did not have enough time in their schedules to serve full time in this capacity. The tribe of Levi, (which included the priests) were set aside by the Lord for full-time church ministry. They were not given any farming land in Israel because their income was supplied by the tithes of everyone else in marketplace ministry. (Num. 18:20-24)

The non-Levites actually needed to enter David's tabernacle to soak and get re-filled so they could gain strength and continue pursuing the will of God through their own entrepreneurial initiatives. Marketplace ministers were the backbone behind the growth of David's kingdom territory, so it was vital that they receive from the Lord whilst ascending Mount Zion.

Regarding proximity of access to God, there was no longer any distinction between Levites and any other Israelite. The rationale behind David's selection criteria was purely logistical. The priests had to come to the realisation that they were now equal to everyone else, and not a class above. Yet despite this, they had still been given an even better opportunity than they ever had before: access through the veil right up to the Ark itself! God had not brought the priests down to a lower level. He had brought everyone up to *His* level.

A Touching Moment

Despite all the pointless religion, there was one shining memory I treasure from my days as a Catholic.

The Catholic religion has a practice known as 'reconciliation' or 'confession'. This is where you go into a secret room one-on-one with a priest and confess your sins to him. The priest acts as the arbitrator between you and God, pronouncing your sins forgiven, but only after he prescribes a certain amount of penance for those sins. So, for example, he might say; *"those sins are worth, 2 Hail Mary's, 3 Our Father's and 1 Glory be, then do two extra chores next week and also be nice to your parents"*.

Hopefully by now you would recognise that I deem the Catholic practice of confession and the priest's role in it totally unscriptural. The priest is usurping the role of Jesus by once again going back to the days of the TOM. Penance also is an unbiblical perversion of repentance.

Anyhow, we had to wait until Grade 3 to complete our first reconciliation. After this, we were permitted to do it whenever the priest offered it. On one such occasion, my entire family was taken by surprise. I was around 13 years old. My Dad, myself, Darren and April were going to church for reconciliation. My youngest sibling, Grant, was too little at the time I believe, and my mum was not catholic so she didn't take part. The priest came over and said;

> *"Tonight, we're going to do reconciliation differently. You are going to do it together as a family."*

Whoa, this was weird. Instead of going out to a secret room one at a time, the priest had a little table set up just in front of the altar with some candles. We all had to stand around the table in a circle holding hands.

Then the priest said; *"share with each other what you've done wrong"*. (See Jam. 5:16)

So we all confessed ours sins *in the presence of each other*. When it came to my turn, the priest said;

> *"So Justin, what have been your sins since your last reconciliation?"*

I probably said something arbitrary like; *"Ah, well, a couple of times I lied to my parents... the other day I was mean to Darren and... I sometimes call April bad names."*

We progressed around the unbroken circle, and what happened next was the part I still remember vividly. To my shock, the priest said;

> *'Tonight, you don't need to perform any penance. All you have to do is look each other in the eyes one by one and tell them "I love you"'.*

So I softly responded; *"I love you Dad, I love you Darren, I love you April."*

It was weird and also extremely powerful because, although I have very caring and devoted parents, the one thing we always struggled with as a family was showing affection. I don't recall ever hearing the words "I love you" in my whole life up until that point. We never said it to each other.

That night the priest got us to show each other mercy, forgiveness and unfailing love. This was the true role of a teacher and a priest in the New Covenant! What's even more stunning is that the love we showed *replaced the penance.* For that one day, the priest did away with the meaningless self-sacrifice and replaced it with merciful love. I don't know if that type of action lines up with the official doctrines of the Catholic Church but hey, let's give credit where credit is due; he did it anyway. The priest facilitated a moment of tender mercy where we unknowingly followed Hosea 6:6 and it did something *inside* our hearts, bonding us closer together as a family.

Are you offering service to God?

Let's find the context in which Jesus used *latreia* that solitary time. At the last supper on the night of his betrayal, Jesus was teaching His disciples about things that would occur after He returned to heaven;

> *"All this I have told you so that you will not fall away. [2]They will put you out of the synagogue; in fact, the time is coming when anyone who kills you will think they are <u>offering a service</u> to God. [3]They will do such things because they have not known the Father or me."* (John 16:1-3)

The underlined section above is *latreia.* Jesus was talking about the deceptive zeal of religious zealots. These insurrectionists originated from the Pharisees, but on most occasions, were conveniently deployed on behalf of the Sadducees.

In their blindness to the truth, they sincerely believed that killing Christians was offering *latreia*; that murdering them was a sacrificial service pleasing to God.

Who was the first major terrorist from the party of the Pharisees that went around killing Christians and throwing others into prison? It was the Apostle Paul. And who did he obtain letters of permission from? The chief priests, who were Sadducees (Acts 5:17, 9:1-2, 22:5). I have no doubt Jesus was thinking about Paul when He gave this warning in the upper room.

Yet who was it that ended up writing Romans 12:1, saying we should offer our bodies as living sacrifices in actions of *spiritual latreia?* The very same man! The transforming power of the cross of Jesus Christ took Paul from a John 16:2 murderer of Christians in service to God and converted him into a Romans 12:1 spiritual servant who dispensed mercy daily by continually offering *his own body as a living sacrifice*: What a transformation!

Like Paul, we must enter into the true mercy God desires to outwork through us and discard 'meaningless self-sacrificial duties'. By soaking in the 'simplicity of pure devotion to Christ', we will fill ourselves up to overflowing with the love of God, equipping ourselves to be poised and on the alert: ready to show mercy; to **'help others in areas where they cannot help themselves'.**

~ Chapter 34 ~

SACRIFICES 'ONCE AND FOR ALL'

King David is over the moon; his relationship with Yahweh has been fully restored! Not only that, but the Lord has also given more precise instructions on how to transport the Ark into Jerusalem with success. Fortunately for all in attendance, these new guidelines would not take away from any of the celebrations David was planning. This was still going to be the greatest time of jubilation that the people of Israel had ever participated in. The new wineskin of passionate expression was about to be unleashed, never to be taken away.

> *[12]Then King David was told, "The LORD has blessed Obed-edom's household and everything he has because of the Ark of God." So David went there and brought the Ark of God from the house of Obed-edom to the City of David with a great celebration. [13]After the men who were carrying the Ark of the LORD had gone six steps, David sacrificed a bull and a fattened calf.* (2 Sam 6:12-13 NLT)

As the procession began, David halted the parade after only six steps to sacrifice a bull and a fattened calf. A few people muttered under their breath;

> *"Is David usurping the roles of the priests? Who does he think he is?"*

David took only six steps before stopping, because it signifies the number of man. King David was saying to God;

> *"We are only human. We can make mistakes. So just in case anyone makes a mistake along this path, I sacrifice these animals as a blood sacrifice to cover any accidental faults that may transpire."*

This line of thinking relates directly to the 'bull'. Leviticus 4:13-14 shows us a bull sacrifice was required as a sin offering if the community of Israel sinned unintentionally. David is covering all of his steps here. Although he is now following God's guidelines to the letter, he wants to ensure that if someone accidentally steps out of line, they are covered and not subject to the same fate as Uzzah.

Second, the six steps signify the six places where the Ark had been kept since it was stolen from the Israelites by the Philistines. It had been in Ashdod, Gath, Ekron, Beth-shemesh, Kiriath-jearim, and Obed-Edom's house. There was going to be a sense of finality to the seventh place the Ark would enter. The tabernacle of David was a type and shadow of God's eternal resting place, as we discovered in our study of Psalm 132. This relates directly to the second animal David sacrificed; the fattened calf. Never being used in the LOM, this is the first time this animal, a 'fatling', is mentioned in the Bible. It is equivalent to the fattened calf from the parable of the lost son spoken by the Lord Himself. Just like the prodigal moved away from his father into all types of mayhem and dysfunction before returning, so the Ark had been taken away into foreign lands and was now returning to the Father's dwelling place.

Then the Bible says;

> *Because God was helping the Levites who carried the ark of the covenant of the Lord [to do it carefully and safely], they sacrificed seven bulls and seven rams.* (1 Chr. 15:26 AMP)

After a safe start, David realised the Lord was empowering the Levites. He quickly perceived that no one was going to step out of line this time. Because God was guiding their every step, David ordered that the procession come to a halt for a second time. This time, however, he sacrificed seven bulls and seven rams.

The number seven speaks of perfection, completeness, or fullness. It is symbolic of Christ's perfect, sinless, once-for-all sacrifice. (Heb. 10:1-14)

Oxen are castrated bulls. Castration makes them easier to train and control as draft animals. We previously examined that oxen are representative of divine service, but they also represent 'strength for service'. The *divine* service was Jesus' finished work on the cross, and *strength for service* is the anointing for priestly duty because, in Exodus 29, we see that the bull was sacrificed in the consecration ceremony for the priests. (v1, 3, 12-14)

The rams are symbolic of substitution and consecration. In Exodus 29, the ram is sacrificed along with the bull in the priestly dedication ceremony (v1-3, 15-28). What King David was actually doing here was consecrating himself, and *all those in Israel,* as priests unto the Lord. Under the 'new and living way' everyone was now a priest, gaining access through the veil.

Linking directly with the 'divine service' of the bull is the 'substitution' of the ram. In Genesis 22, we find God testing Abrahams's faith. He told Abraham to sacrifice his only son, Isaac, as a burnt offering. Just as Abraham was going to plunge the knife into Isaac's heart, the angel of the Lord stopped him. Then Abraham looked up and saw a ram caught in the thicket (Gen. 22:13). This specific animal was the substitutionary burnt offering for Isaac. This was the very occasion which Jesus referred to when He said to the Jewish leaders; "Abraham saw My day and was glad" (John 8:56). Through His finished work of divine service, Jesus became our substitute. On the cross, He took our place and paid the wages of our sin, which was death.

A ram was also required in Leviticus 5:14-6:7 as a guilt offering for breaking one of the Lord's commands or defiling the Lord's sacred property. Jesus died so we can be freed from the guilt associated with previous violations of God's righteous decrees. We are liberated from our past so that we can live fully for Him without being held back. (2 Cor. 5:15)

In 1 Chronicles 15:27, the Word of God reveals that David designed a uniform for the Levites who were carrying the Ark, as well as the musicians and singers who followed alongside. Interestingly enough, David also dressed himself in one of these special robes. Though this was a beautiful robe, it looked nowhere near as stylish as his fancy royal robes. The priests would have wondered why David wanted to identify with the Levites when he could have distinguished himself as king.

Worshiping with Reckless Abandon

As the procession drew closer to the city, David couldn't contain himself any longer. He threw off his special uniform and, to the dismay of the Levites, he revealed nothing but a linen ephod underneath. This was the plain, bland, ordinary garment of a priest. For a king who would normally wear extravagant royal attire, it could easily be misinterpreted as underwear. David danced before the Lord with all his might in front of the entire crowd, wearing nothing but this ephod (1 Sam 6:14). Now the Mosaic priests were certain that David had gone loopy; here was a king trying to take on their role as a Levitical priest! The tent setup was one thing, but presuming the dualistic role of king-priest and dancing around like a hooligan? In their eyes, this was definitely against prescribed protocol.

When we analyse David's sprightliness, we must consider the dark place he had experienced in the previous three months. He had been stuck in the mud and the mire: a pit of despair. It was in light of this victory that David totally abandoned himself to God without a thought of what on-lookers might think. He had been lifted out of the miry clay and now his feet were placed on solid ground. The lord had given David a new song to sing, a hymn of praise to his God (Ps. 40:1-3). We must be careful not to judge those who praise so exuberantly that they seem 'over the top', or even seemingly trying to gain attention. At times this may indeed be the case, but we do not know the dark places God has delivered certain people from. Many are praising God with everything they have because that's the only genuine reaction that can exemplify the depth of gratitude inside their heart for all God has done.

There was a murmuring amongst the religious; *"David's surely going to get himself killed this time"*.

But David replied; *"No, it's fine. I've sought God, and he has allowed it. I'm operating as a priest after the order of Melchizedek, you'll 'get it' soon."*

These joyous actions of David launched the new pattern of worship by demonstrating the liberty of this fresh and life-enhancing way. By dancing with all his might, he showed us that no amount of active expression is too much for God. This opens the way for everyone to be totally unrestrained in their worship.

The sceptics fired back at David: *"This guy just wants to complicate matters: why can't he just stick to the book and keep it simple!"*

But David said; *"You want simple? Wait till you see how gloriously simple this new way is compared to the old. Believe me, you don't want the Ark going back to Gibeon, that's the administration of death which condemns you! You require mercy from God, not empty sacrifices; your sins 'taken away', not merely covered. Come to my tent and receive complete forgiveness."*

Slowly but surely, the people decided to follow David's lead. He was modelling the freedom we currently enjoy in Christ Jesus. There was now a dancefloor full of unrestrained, praise-filled worshipers. The Spirit that had come upon David had spread into the crowd so that even sceptical priests were caught off-guard. Mosaic priests were meant to act 'solemn'. They were meant to act 'restrained'. They were meant to act 'proper'. Suddenly, without warning, the Spirit of God came upon one of them and the holy joy in the atmosphere broke him out of his religiosity. His foot began tapping to the rhythm, his hands suddenly swayed to the beat. Before his mind could catch up with what his body was doing, he broke out into a jig! *"Whoops, s-s-sorry God, don't judge me,"* he said, trembling.

When David stripped off into the most basic priestly gown, he was breaking the stereotype of class distinction amongst God's people. There was to be no celebrity Christians in David's procession; no separation between clergy and laity, between the five-fold ministers on the stage and those called out into the marketplace. This is because, under the New Covenant in David's tabernacle, we are all priests. We are all 'ordinary', meaning; we are all on the same level as each other. There are no first-class and second-class citizens. In the Body of Christ, no one should be exalted over another. Only Jesus is worthy to be glorified. We are all bland compared to Him. We are cloaked in humility as we imitate David by wearing our simple priestly gown.

God will give some a church platform. But remember this, a platform is given for influence; it is not a stage for performing. Church leaders are not celebrities; they are equippers. It is all about training those in the pews to get out of the pews and become shining stars to the world around them!

Paul said, 'as children of God without fault', we are to 'shine like stars in the night sky' among the crooked and corrupt generation which surrounds us (Phil. 2:15-16). In light of this, we cannot deny the fact that God desires for us to glow in our various roles and giftings, but we do this by reflecting the glory of Jesus, not our own glory. This is what David was modelling for us. The glory on his countenance came from his adoration of the Ark (Jesus), not from fancy attire, self-exaltation or attention seeking.

There is no doubt that we are called to 'let our light shine before men' (Matt 5:16), but when we are among one another, we are all body parts vitally connected to Christ; the only Exalted Head. God wants to distinguish us among unbelievers, but whether we excel in church leadership roles or as marketplace missionaries doesn't matter. As long as we all shine brightly to glorify Jesus out in the world and maintain equality among one another when we fellowship, the *entire* work of the ministry will be completed and a truly unified family will be cultivated to the glory of God.

Safe passage into a new home

So all Israel brought up the Ark of the LORD's Covenant with shouts of joy, the blowing of rams' horns and trumpets, the crashing of cymbals, and loud playing on harps and lyres. They brought the Ark of God and placed it inside the special tent David had prepared for it. (1 Chr. 15:28, 16:1a NLT)

Everything went off without a hitch. The Ark finally made it into the tent pitched by David! He couldn't wipe the smile off his face, and the commoners among Israel were having a jolly good time. The priests and the Levites who were part of David's team were loving life! A few of the remaining Mosaic priests also began to let their hair down, but only slightly. On the whole, they were still rather guarded and reserved. For them, the tabernacle of David would have to prove itself over time before they fully embraced the new wine God was pouring out.

They brought the Ark of the LORD and set it in its place inside the special tent David had prepared for it. And David sacrificed burnt offerings and peace offerings to the LORD. (2 Sam 6:17 NLT)

Now the priests of Gibeon were utterly astounded: After the Ark was firmly set in place, David came back out to those in attendance and sacrificed burnt offerings and peace offerings.

"Here David goes again doing his 'priestly thing'. Relations of Judah are not allowed to do all this. Besides, he's not even using the correct altar!"

They were certain God's wrath which had been simmering against David would soon reach boiling point. *"We know David is God's beloved, but how much more of this wilful disobedience can Yahweh take"*, they whispered to each other.

In the LOM, the burnt offerings are found in Leviticus chapter 1 and the peace offerings are found in Leviticus chapter 3. They are administered by priests on behalf of the people. *Both of these were voluntary*, an animal presented as a freewill offering to the Lord. They therefore represent Christ's voluntary offering of Himself. Jesus came to earth as a bondservant to do His Father's will. He abided in the Father's love as He completed what the Father commanded Him. (John 15:10)

> *"No one can take my life from me. I sacrifice it voluntarily. For I have the authority to lay it down when I want to and also to take it up again. For this is what my Father has commanded."* (John 10:18 NLT)

Jesus received the command from His Father to lay down His life for the sin of all mankind and then resurrect it up again. The Son obeyed His Father's voice and complied out of *His own free will.* According to Jesus, this obedience was the proof that He truly loved Him and that the Father loved Him back. (John 10:17, 14:31)

~ Chapter 35 ~

SACRIFICES BROUGHT TO AN END

*And as soon as David had **made an end** of sacrificing burnt offerings and peace offerings, he blessed the people in the name of the Lord of hosts.* (1 Sam 6:18 KJV)

The Holy Bible states that after completing the burnt and peace offerings, David 'made an end' to the sacrifices. This actually means that he made an end of them *for good.* These sacrifices were for one-day only. Each of the various dedicatory sacrifices David performed on this inauguration day pointed to Calvary's cross. Here, the ultimate dedicatory sacrifice took place 2000 years ago. The cross is the altar to which all other altars pointed, fulfilling the true substance behind the typology and thus abolished animal sacrifices *for good.*

Jesus Christ, the greater Son of David, offered His own body and blood as the spotless, sinless, dedicatory sacrifice to God. His blood was shed for the inauguration of His tabernacle, opening up the way through the veil into the heavenly realms where all may worship Him freely, without restraint.

There is no account of animal sacrifices ever taking place again at the Tabernacle of David on Mount Zion. After these initial sacrifices, the only ones that remained from that time on were sacrifices of praise, joy, and thanksgiving offered by the priesthood of Yahweh, which included everyone!

The New Testament fulfilment of this typology is evident: When Jesus Christ offered Himself on the hill called Golgotha, His perfect, once-for-all sacrifice fulfilled and thus abolished the former, inferior sacrificial system. All such sacrifices have now become an abomination in His sight; an insult to our Redeemer's death on the cross.

Now that the Father has given the body and blood of His unique, one-of-a-kind Son, there will never be another time when God will require an animal sacrifice. Any attempts to do so would be a reversal of the New Covenant to re-establish the Old. If that is indeed the case, we should not incorporate *any other part* of the Mosaic Covenant into the freedom by which Christ has set us free. Paul commands us in Galatians 5:1 to remain totally liberated. The only set of laws we are subject to in the New Covenant is the 'law of God', which is also known as 'Christ's law' (1 Cor. 9:20-21). We obey this system of law by living in the Spirit, not through works of our flesh.

> *And as soon as David had made an end of sacrificing burnt offerings and peace offerings, he blessed the people in the name of the Lord of hosts.* (1 Sam 6:18 KJV)

Once David had brought the sacrifices of his Tabernacle to a permanent conclusion, he 'blessed the people in the name of the Lord'. This is none other than the priestly blessing given to Aaron and his sons to speak over the people of Israel! (Deut. 21:5) After hearing this, the Mosaic Priests became livid;

> *"Does this king want to make us totally redundant? Is there anything from the priesthood David is not going to usurp today?"*

This 'Aaronic blessing' is found in Numbers 6:24-26;

> *[24]"The Lord bless you and keep you; [25]the Lord make his face shine on you and be gracious to you; [26]the Lord turn his face toward you and give you peace."*

In response to this pronounced blessing, God says in verse 27;

> *"in this way they will put my name on the Israelites, and I will bless them."* (EHV)

Take this in carefully; v26 and 27 state that when the Lord turns His face toward you, *He puts His name on you.* What does it mean to have God's name written on you? When you declare the name of Jesus, it actually works. The power of His name will back up your confession and produce results. Therefore, with Jesus' signature of authority on the end of your prayers, Satan always has to bow and obey any official document sealed with Christ's divine autograph. It is a similar concept to having God's name written on our foreheads, which is borrowed terminology from the Book of Revelation. (7:3, 9:4, 14:1)

> *[11]I am coming soon. Hold on to what you have, so that no one will take your crown. [12]The one who is victorious I will make a pillar in the temple of my God. Never again will they leave it. I will write on them the name of my God and the name of the city of my God, the new Jerusalem, which is coming down out of heaven from my God; and I will also write on them my new name.* (Rev. 3:11-12)

*³No longer will there be any curse. The throne of God and of the Lamb will be in the city, and his servants will serve him. ⁴They will see his face, **and his name will be on their foreheads**.* (Rev. 22:3-4)

◊◊◊◊◊

In light of this, let's look at what Peter wrote when he quoted King David from Psalm 34;

¹⁰For, "Whoever would love life and see good days must keep their tongue from evil and their lips from deceitful speech. ¹¹They must turn from evil and do good; they must seek peace and pursue it. ¹²For the eyes of the Lord are on the righteous and his ears are attentive to their prayer, but the face of the Lord is against those who do evil." (1 Pet 3:10-12)

By quoting King David, Peter shows us that the face of the Lord *turns away* from those who *do* evil. This reverses the Aaronic blessing, which essentially means the authority of His name comes *off* you. But for those who live righteously, His eyes are always upon you, the priestly blessing stays on you, and His ears are always listening to your prayers.

Satan is fearful of those who have the signature of Jesus; the seal of God, upon their forehead. They are the ones the Lord has inscribed His name upon. We don't want to allow Satan the opportunity to say; *"Jesus I know, and I know about Paul, but who are you?"* (Acts 19:15)

In Psalm 34:16, there is an additional line which Peter left out. It says; "the face of the lord is against those who do evil, *to blot out their name* from the earth." If you do not have the name of Christ written on your forehead, *your name* will be blotted out from the earth. This means that when you pray, Satan won't recognise you as one bearing Christ's authority, even if you conclude your prayers with a religiously formulated "in Jesus name" at the end.

King David spoke the priestly blessing over all those who were going to enter his Tabernacle. In the same way, Jesus has spoken this same Aaronic blessing over every born-again believer. All we have to do is keep the Lord's face shining on us by turning away from evil and continuing to do good. We must seek peace and pursue it! Then we will abide in the power of the Most High's signature, the Name that is above all other names. Jesus has done His part. Now we must do ours to see His divine autograph splattered across the earth.

Bring out the Party Food!

And he dealt among all the people, <u>even among the whole multitude</u> of Israel, as well to the <u>women as men</u>, to every one a cake of bread, and a good piece of flesh, and a flagon of wine. (2 Sam 6:19 KJV)

After pronouncing the priestly blessing, David dished out a meal for everyone in attendance. It wouldn't be much of a celebration without party food. David was performing all of this with an open veil behind him and the Ark of God's glory fully visible to those who approached the table.

The Hebrew word for 'even among the whole multitude' shows us that David did not leave anyone out. It was offered to the entire crowd present with no discrimination. No identification checks were necessary. Whoever wanted to partake of this meal was able to come forward. And it wasn't just for the men, but also for the women and their children. This covenant meal even included foreigners residing in the land. Just after David died, Solomon counted 153,600 foreigners in the land of Israel (2 Chr. 2:17). You could be sure that many of them were present on this monumental day. The Septuagint goes a step further, telling us it was *"all the host of Israel from Dan in the north to Beersheba in the south"*. This term is used nine times in the Hebrew Bible, referring to the full extent of the entire land of Israel. Any human being who lived within those boundaries and came to celebrate the Ark was allowed to be fully involved, regardless of gender, age, background or ethnicity.

David had three items on the menu. He gave to each person a small ring-shaped loaf of bread, a choice piece of meat, and the third was 'a grape-cake, a cluster of grapes, or perhaps wine'. The New Life Version says it this way in 1 Chronicles 16:3;

> *"He gave to every man and woman in Israel a loaf of bread, a share of meat, and a loaf of dried grapes."*

The cake of bread was the round dough baked for sacrificial meals (Lev. 8:26). Being hollow in the centre, it was shaped like a large doughnut. The 'share of meat' was a portion of choice flesh. In other words, David portioned out the meat from the animals he had just sacrificed, and gave it to all! John Wycliffe translated it 'a piece of roasted ox flesh'. The 'choice' piece of meat was the priestly portion of the animal. There was no sorting of the animal meat into ordinary cuts and priestly cuts. It was an all in spit-roast. Sounds a little bit like; *'Eat whatever is sold at the meat market without raising questions of conscience'*, doesn't it? (1 Cor. 10:25)

According to the LOM, women were not permitted in the priesthood, children were under the priestly age-limit, and foreigners came from the wrong ethnic group. Yet they were all permitted to partake of the priestly portion of sacrificial meat from the altar of God! This is why it says in Hebrews; *'We have an altar from which those who minister at the tabernacle (of Moses) have no right to eat.'* (Heb. 13:10) Everybody was now being treated equal.

◊◊◊◊◊

The grape-cake is the Hebrew word *'ăshîyshâh,* and this is its first mention in Scripture. Many translators believe it to be a jug of wine, others a cake of raisins. A cluster of either grapes or raisins seems to fit most logically when catering for such a huge crowd. They had already been given a cake in the form of bread, and each receiving a large jug of wine would have cost a fortune and been a logistical nightmare. So it comes down to a cluster of grapes or raisins. This word is used two other times subsequent to this story. It appears once in Hosea, and once in Song of Solomon.

> *Then the LORD said to me, "Go again; show love to a woman who is loved by another man and is an adulteress, just as the LORD loves the Israelites though they turn to other gods and love <u>raisin cakes</u>."* (Hos. 3:1 CSB)

In Hosea 3:1, *'ăshîyshâh* is eaten in pagan feasts of idol worship with a context of turning toward other gods. Cakes of raisins are used in various pagan religions, but within the kingdom of God there is no such connection. The consistent theme throughout Scripture for the kingdom of God is grapes in a vineyard. A raisin is a dried grape, dried out so that there is no grape juice left inside. Isn't it interesting that grape juice is an element of communion representing Christ's shed-blood?

When translating the word *'ăshîyshâh* in Hosea 3:1, the word 'raisin' is appropriate because pagans deny the blood of Jesus. But Jesus didn't feed raisin cakes to His disciples, so we dare not remove a reference to the blood of Jesus from Scripture. Therefore, it is reasonable to assume that David handed out a cluster of red grapes to each person, foreshadowing Christ's shed blood. David dishing out this meal is prophetic of Jesus offering wine to His disciples along with bread when He taught his brand-new royal priesthood what it truly meant to eat of His flesh and drink of His blood. (John 2:1-11, 6:53-54, 1 Cor. 11:23-25)

The bread and the grapes signify the communion elements brought out by Melchizedek for Abraham and by Jesus for the Twelve at His last supper (Gen. 14:18, Matt 26:20-28). It is the bread of everlasting life and the New Covenant of forgiveness in Christ's blood. Jesus is High Priest of this order in the likeness of Melchizedek, and we are His royal priests.

There is no mention of the Lord giving out meat at that Passover meal. Jesus' life *was* the lamb to be sacrificed. When King David dished out choice portions, the meat represented the ingesting the supernatural 'zōē-life' of Jesus Himself through the cross: His voluntary peace and burnt offering (John 5:26, 6:33). We enter into this zōē-life by becoming partakers with Him in His death in order that we may also become partakers in His resurrection; an existence where death no longer has any grip or mastery (Rom. 6:3-9, Phil. 3:10-11).

Resurrection life can only be attained after 'dying to self'. In Christ, neither circumcision nor uncircumcision means anything; what matters is a new creation (Gal. 6:15). The old version of us has passed away and the brand new version has been rolled out onto the showroom floor! (2 Cor. 5:17) As new creations, therefore, we are called to keep ourselves shiny and attractive by escaping the cravings of the world caused by lustful desire and partake of the divine nature as we abide in the Holy Spirit. In this way, we inherit all the very great and precious promises God has freely given us. (2 Pet. 1:3-4)

With every action David performed on this day, he completely shattered the old paradigm. As he formed the food lines, the religious conservatives, already beside themselves, were now plain horrified; *"Now it all makes sense. David doesn't just want to get himself killed; he wants all of us dead! The judgment of God is going to smite the entire nation in one fell swoop! Looks like terrorist activity to me: He must be stopped!"*

Another distant onlooker replied; *"What are you going to do? He's the king! Listen, God is no respecter of persons. If we don't eat any of the food, the Lord will protect us and we'll be preserved. Let's just keep our distance from all these unlawful shenanigans!"*

So the people ate their fill; men, women, children and God-fearing foreigners, and at the end of it all, there was nothing but the sound of satisfied tummies.

The only way this could have been possible without incurring God's wrath was if the Lord esteemed everyone who ate as a priest. Under the new priestly order of Melchizedek, this was indeed the case! There was no sign of judgment and no sign of death anywhere to be seen. Never had the people felt such freedom and liberty in the presence of God. They were fully accepted in 'the beloved', for that is the meaning of David in Hebrew. (Eph. 1:6 NKJV)

Open Access for all Nations

After David had finished the official proceedings, he had the worship team recite a special song of thanksgiving to the Lord, recorded in 1 Chronicles 16:8-36. Within the lyrics of this song we can find many of the emphases of Davidic worship.

Of particular interest to us are verses 28-30a;

> *O **nations of the world**, recognize the Lord, recognize that the Lord is glorious and strong. ²⁹Give to the Lord the glory he deserves! Bring your offering and come into his presence. Worship the Lord in all his holy splendor. ³⁰Let all the earth tremble before him.* (NLT)

David's Tent really was open to people of *all* nations. There was no dividing wall between Jew and Gentile during this momentous season of outpouring. After the song came to its conclusion, everyone present shouted "amen!" and praised the Lord. It was now time for Asaph and his fellow Levites to begin the first shift in the 24/7 praise and worship. (1 Chr. 16:4-6, 37)

What were the 'common occurrences' witnessed inside David's tent? What kind of culture was birthed from this revolutionary form of worship unto God? If we are adhering to the mandate of rebuilding David's fallen tabernacle, we should see the appearance of *at least some* of these 'expressions of worship' when we gather as the Body of Christ. On the next page is a list of expressions which were the ingredients that formed this new culture…

1) God's presence: Unlimited Access for *all nations*: (1 Chr. 16:28-30, 37-38, Heb. 6:19-20)

2) Reverential Fear/Trembling: (1 Chr. 16:30, Ps. 96:9 AMPC)

3) Seeking (waiting upon) the Lord/Prayer: (1 Chr. 16:11, 2 Chr. 7:14, Ps. 27:14, 37:7, 40:1, Isa. 40:31 KJV) (including intercession and spiritual warfare)

4) Recording the Word of the Lord/writing down prophecy: (1 Chr. 16:4 KJV, 28:19)

5) Singing Songs: (1 Chr. 15:16-18, Ps. 96:1-3, Col. 3:16)

6) Playing Musical Instruments: (1 Chr. 15:19-22, 23:5b, 25:1-7, Ps. 33:3)

7) Song-writing/composing: (1 Chr. 16:7 NLT, Ps. 98:1, 1 Ki. 4:30-32, Rev. 5:9)

8) Praise: (1 Chr. 16:4, 36. Eph. 5:19 AMPC)

9) Thanksgiving: (1 Chr. 16:4, 8, 41, Phil, 4:6)

10) Rejoicing/Joy: (1 Chr. 16:10, 25-31, Ps. 27:5, Luke 2:10-11)

11) Clapping Hands: (Ps. 47:1, 98:8, Isa. 55:12)

12) Shouting/Exclamation: (1 Chr. 15:28, Ps. 47:5, Is. 12:6, Rev. 19:1)

13) Dancing: (1 Chr. 15:29, 2 Sam 6:14, Ps. 149:3, 150:4)

14) Lifting Up Holy Hands: (Ps. 28:2, 63:4, 134:2, 141:5, Neh. 8:6, 1 Tim. 2:8)

15) Bowing Low/kneeling/prostrating: (2 Sam 12:20, 1 Chr. 16:29, 29:20, 2 Chr. 20:18)

16) Empowerment for Spiritual Service/Calling/Living Sacrifice: (1 Chr. 16:24, Rom 12:1, Phil. 4:18, 1 Pet 2:5, Heb. 13:15)

17) Saying 'Amen' (Power of Agreement): (1 Chr. 16:36, Matt 18:19-20)

Keep this checklist handy as a tool to assist you in your quest to repair the ruins of David's fallen shelter through your own life and also within your local fellowship. (Always remember, this list is merely a guide: everyone has their own way of worshiping. We are not expected to manifest all 17 of these within our unique style. All that is required is to be led personally by the Holy Spirit)

Obed-Edom follows the Glory

Now let's briefly reconsider Obed-Edom: faithful caretaker of the Ark. David did not leave him out on this grand occasion. David actually gave Obed-Edom the honour of guarding the Ark as they brought it into Jerusalem, along with a man called Jehiah (1 Chr. 15:24). This would have been a daunting proposition after what had happened to Uzzah three months earlier. Nevertheless, Obed-Edom had the courage and faith to comply.

He followed the Ark from his house into Zion *and then stayed involved on a permanent basis.* Three months in God's glory wasn't enough. It had to be lifelong from here on! Obed-Edom would not let the favour of God lift off his family. After the Tabernacle began its function, he enrolled as one of the seventy chosen doorkeepers who would stand at the entrance. He would *'rather be a doorkeeper in the house of his God, then dwell in tents of wickedness'* (Ps. 84:10 NKJV). As long as his legs would permit him to stand, he would usher people into God's glory (1 Chr. 16:38).

On top of this, when Obed-Edom was 'off-duty', he also had stints in the worship team as a muso (1 Chr. 15:21). His specialty was playing the lyre. Once he had experienced the glory in his own home, he couldn't get enough of serving the Lord! His legacy lived on through his eight sons, who followed in their Father's footsteps and also became doorkeepers. (1 Chr. 26:4-8)

~ Chapter 36 ~
WHOSE HOUSE DO YOU LIVE IN?

The processional march transporting the Ark into Jerusalem was accompanied by the blowing of trumpets, the clashing of cymbals, and loud playing on harps and lyres. According to Psalm 68:25, the maidens danced in and out between the singers and musicians as they marched along. It was certainly not a quiet, subdued service, but one of utter gladness, excitement, and great enthusiasm.

In the midst of all this, David was dancing with all his might before *the Lord*, not before *the people.* He wasn't acting like a celebrity, nor attempting to steal any of the limelight. Quite the opposite: By wearing only a basic linen ephod, he was *blending in* with the common people. This ensured the Ark remained the central attraction! The only reason many people had their eye on him was because they were religious critics who thought that a king should not be acting this way.

As David danced along his merry way, there was one person who was the most distant of all onlookers. This woman held the privileged elevated position within the king's palace. She could stand up high on the top floor and look out her window from a vantage point no one else had access to. Unfortunately, this entitled position actually caused her to miss out on all the fun!

This was Michal, David's first, and the most cherished of all his wives. David and Michal were teenage lovers. She was David's first love, and by stealing his heart at a young age, she had always been most precious to him. She was the daughter of King Saul, and David wanted to marry her so much that he went and bought her from Saul with the price of 100 Philistine foreskins: Talk about dedication!

Michal even saved David's life in 1 Samuel 19, when her father's troops were gathering outside the house to murder him. She told him to flee out a back window while she pretended he was sick in bed. From this time on, they lost contact with each other. After Saul found out what Michal had done, he did not allow her to reunite with David. If that wasn't evil enough, Saul then forced her to marry a new husband named Palti. (1 Sam 25:44)

In the meantime, David married many other wives, but none could compare or would ever replace his first love, Michal. There was a special bond between David and Michal that none of his other wives had. David loved her so much that one of the first things he did when he became king of Judah after Saul's death was to ask to be reunited with her;

¹²Then Abner sent messengers to David, saying, "Doesn't the entire land belong to you? Make a solemn pact with me, and I will help turn over all of Israel to you." ¹³"All right," David replied, "but I will not negotiate with you unless you bring back my wife Michal, Saul's daughter, when you come." ¹⁴David then sent this message to Ishbosheth, Saul's son: "Give me back my wife Michal, for I bought her with the lives of 100 Philistines." ¹⁵So Ishbosheth took Michal away from her husband, Palti son of Laish. (2 Sam 3:12-15 NLT)

Instantly, Michal had become a queen! Not only that, but during the time when the Ark had stayed at Obed-Edom's house, she had moved into the brand-spanking new cedar palace. It was located so close to the site David reserved for his tent, she only had to look out the window to see what was happening.

But there was something wrong inside Michal's heart, something that must have sprung from her childhood upbringing. She was raised in *the household of Saul*, who neglected the Ark of God and despised the Lord's presence. This had come down generationally to Michal, yet it did not manifest until the Tabernacle of David was launched.

¹⁶But as the Ark of the LORD entered the City of David, Michal, the daughter of Saul, looked down from her window. When she saw King David leaping and dancing before the LORD, she was filled with contempt for him. (2 Sam 6:16 NLT)

David wasn't simply dancing before the Lord. He was leaping high into the air! *Now* the issue lodged deep within Michal's heart came to the surface. *"What is David doing?! Why isn't he wearing his kingly robes? He looks like he's prancing around in his underwear!"*

The problem had already begun well before she saw David out the window. That morning, she had already decided not to attend the parade. Think of the position she could have enjoyed in this procession. If she had wanted to, she could have been David's number one dance partner and had a whale of a time! She was already manifesting resentment toward David even as he left to collect the Ark. There was clearly some kind of barrier between Michal and the Ark of God's presence.

We know this because when she peered out the window, all she could focus on was David. She did not even look toward the Ark, not even for a moment. Her only concern was her reputation as queen. *"Gee, my husband is making me look bad. This is totally ridiculous! The dignity of the royal family is being demeaned. I'm ashamed to be married to that moron!"* That may sound like strong language, but that is exactly what she says later on.

There was an underlying bitterness and deep resentment that had arisen between Michal and the Lord. Her father and brother had died on the same day on the battlefield, and while estranged from David, he had married many other wives.

Michal was focused on the flesh rather than the glory of God. This caused her to despise David because she couldn't relate to the hilarity of his passionate reaction. Had she been down in the Lord's midst, she probably would have been set free and rejoiced much the same. The offence she was carrying caused her to view the most glorious and epic event in Israel's history in a completely negative light. Michal found herself 'on the wrong side of the window'.

Returning Home to Bless the Family

David returned to bless his household. But Michal the daughter of Saul came out to meet David... (2 Sam 6:20a ESV)

The first thing David did after completing this intense day of ministry was to head straight home and *bless his household.* He was not going to let 'the ministry' become more important than his priestly duty to his own family. No matter how much God raises our level of influence, we can never use it as an excuse to neglect our role as King-Prophet-Priest over our family.

But Michal the daughter of Saul came out to meet David and said, "How the king of Israel honoured himself today, uncovering himself today before the eyes of his servants' female servants, as one of the vulgar fellows shamelessly uncovers himself!" (2 Sam 6:20b ESV)

David had been on a high. This was probably the best day of his life. Now he comes back, and out of the goodness of his heart begins to bless his household. Then Michal storms into the room! Unfortunately, this day was not going to end as David had hoped.

Michal says sarcastically; *"Well David, you really distinguished yourself as king today, didn't you? You looked like a man in his underwear, and you did it in complete view of all the maidservants. How highly do you reckon they think of you now after you pranced around like the village idiot?"*

It seems evident that Michal is jealous of the young servant-girls who had the opportunity to dance with David throughout the procession. When she looked down and saw them locking arms and skipping joyously as they swung through the worship band, she got terribly annoyed because of regret. She knew she should have been down there dancing with David, too.

The first thing Michal accuses David of is 'indecent exposure', the word *galah* in Hebrew. But she is not referring to the indecent exposure of Noah in his tent when he was stark naked (Gen. 9:21). She is referring to David taking off his royal robe and stripping down to a plain white linen ephod. As stated previously, a linen ephod *seemed like* underwear when compared to the pageantry of the king's royal garb.

There are two aspects to this. The first is that Michal despised the fact that David blended himself in as one of the common people in Israel. The basic priestly garment looked bland and ordinary because God never wanted the priesthood to exalt themselves over anyone else. This was the perfect attire for David to show his adoration and praise to God. David was being used by God to demonstrate the humility of true worship, which is a priestly function. He had to lay the correct foundation from the get-go. No one can boast in the presence of God. (2 Cor. 10:17-18, Gal. 6:14)

The second is that Michal could not reconcile David adding the role of a priest to his kingship. When her father Saul attempted to do this, the kingdom was taken from him! The linen ephod symbolises righteousness in Scripture, but Michal couldn't discern the purity of David's actions in all of this. She saw indecency when God saw righteousness. This is still the claim of the modern Pharisaical Christian, even up to this very day. They view passion filled worship as 'indecent and out of order'. But as long as the Lord sees righteousness, it doesn't matter what the judgmental think or say. We are seeking God's pleasure, not the praise of man.

What I also found hilarious is that this word for uncovering yourself 'galah' is a variety of bird; a pink and grey cockatoo found in Australia. Funnily enough, 'a *Flaming Galah*' is Australian slang for someone who is 'a bit of a doofus, plays the fool, or acts stupid'. And this leads straight into the next point.

*"How the king of Israel honoured himself today, <u>uncovering</u> himself today before the eyes of his servants' female servants, as one of the **vulgar** fellows shamelessly <u>uncovers himself!</u>"* (2 Sam 6:20b ESV)

Not only did Michal accuse David of indecent exposure, she also greatly despised his exuberant expressions of worship before God. If you look back over verse 20, the word 'galah' for uncovering oneself is used twice, but in-between them Michal calls David 'vulgar'. This is translated into the English text as 'vulgar' because of the context of the supposed 'indecent exposure'. But the Hebrew word *rêq* used here does not mean vulgar. It should be translated 'foolish, stupid or empty-head'. Michal was not accusing David of vulgarity, but *moronic* behaviour. This is where it gets even deeper. If we go across into the New Testament and look at Jesus' Sermon on the Mount, we find an intriguing link. In Matt 5:22b Jesus says;

[22] *"But I tell you that <u>anyone who is angry with a brother will be subject to judgment</u>. Again, anyone who says to a brother, '**Raca,**' is answerable to the Sanhedrin. But anyone who says, '**You fool!**' will be <u>in danger of the fire of hell.</u>"* (NIV)

Raca in Greek is very similar to *rêq* in Hebrew. It means you are *'senseless and good-for-nothing, an empty-headed person with no brains!'* Calling someone this name was answerable to the Jewish Court, but the word for "You fool" is *moros* which is where we get the English word 'moron'. This is also implied in the Hebrew word *rêq*.

In calling David *"rêq"*, Michal was calling David 'raca' and 'you fool' combined. By making such a serious accusation concerning David's character, she actually put herself in danger of the fires of hell, according to Jesus! Anyone who hates a fellow believer is in the darkness and walks around in the darkness. They do not know where they are going, because the darkness has blinded them (1 John 2:11). Therefore judge nothing before the appointed time; wait until the Lord comes. He will bring to light what is hidden in darkness and will expose the motives of people's hearts. At that time, each one of us will receive our praise from God (1 Cor. 4:5). This is serious business! We must be super-vigilant to keep our lives 'Michal-free'.

Freedom of Expression

From the very start, David modelled the new worship order God was establishing. He showed us that there is no limit to the outward expressions we can display toward God, as long as the gestures are not obscene or attention seeking. Michal, on the other hand, was trying to *hinder* this full expression of worship.

If a person is not trying to steal the limelight through ridiculously over the top antics, we can be certain God will accept their worship as pure and undefiled. What the critics say carries no weight. By the same token, through intimacy we must develop our own unique expression that is a true indication of who we are. David gave us a license for full expression, but that looks different for each individual. We don't have to go all out in exuberance if that is not natural to us. We must discover the way we are wired to connect with God and be unhindered in that unique expression as the Spirit leads. Most critically, we must ensure we don't fall into the trap of judging someone else's style of worshiping.

Now let's look at David's response to Michal;

> ²¹*So David said to Michal, "It was before the LORD, <u>who chose me above your father and above all his house</u>, to appoint me ruler over the people of the LORD, over Israel; therefore I will celebrate before the LORD. ²²I will be more lightly esteemed than this and will be humble in my own eyes, but with the maids of whom you have spoken, with them I will be distinguished."* (2 Sam 6:21-22 NASB)

David says; *"I'll tell you what's truly happening. I know where these accusations are coming from. The Lord chose me above your father and **above all his house**! I didn't choose this; God did. I didn't touch the Lord's anointed or plan to do him any harm. The hand of God's grace has raised me into this marvellous position of favour. Do you think I'll neglect to show Him my gratitude?"*

David is not gloating here. He is trying to show Michal why she is so troubled. She thinks it's because David danced before a wooden box, but the real problem is much deeper than that. She has a heart-issue that has sparked such an unreasonable reaction. Then David adds;

"All I did was take my royal robes off, played some instruments and had a dance. There's nothing immoral about that. I was celebrating the Lord and don't need to boast in my royal robes to honour Yahweh. When we're in the presence of Almighty God, none of us can compare to Him. We are all equal. Do you think I'm undignified because I didn't insist on flaunting title, pomp

and ceremony? Were you insulted because I seemingly lowered our royal status before the people of Israel? Like everybody else, I am poor and needy; a broken man in need of God's grace. Israel will still respect me as their king when they see me acknowledging that I am a weak man before God."

> *"Yet I will demean myself even more than this, and will be humbled (abased) in my own sight [and yours, as I please], but by the maids whom you mentioned, by them I shall be held in honor."* (1 Sam 6:22 AMP)

In effect, David goes on to say; *"If this type of behaviour causes me to be lightly esteemed, so be it. And if you thought I was worshiping the Lord with everything I've got today, you haven't seen anything yet! I am willing to humiliate myself even more than I did today, so you better get used to it. But one thing's for sure; those handmaidens who you say despise me, <u>they do indeed think I'm distinguished</u>."*

In this final rebuttal, David actually deflects Michal's sarcasm back on her. The same Hebrew word that was used by Michal, meaning 'distinguished' or 'honoured' *(kâbad)* is also used here by David. She said; *"How the king of Israel 'distinguished' himself today" (v20),* and David replied; *"you know what? You may say that sarcastically, but it's genuinely the truth." (v22)*

Two Distinct Houses

The house of Saul (represented by Michal) despised the worship of King David, but the servant girls who were dancing with David adored him because of his humility. What's more, they would continue to do so as David remained relatable; he would never lord it over the people by flaunting his authority as king.

In the same way, the Son of David - Jesus Christ, would come down to earth and take the humble position of a bondservant. He did not consider equality with God or His position as Creator of the universe something to flaunt, but made Himself *of no reputation*. (Phil. 2:6-7)

When they looked at Jesus, the modern day house of Saul (the Pharisees, Sadducees and religious leaders of Israel) despised their Messiah just like Michal did David. They were looking for a mighty, conquering 'show-off' of a Messiah. But the handmaidens, representative of the believing remnant of Israel and the gentile church, highly esteem the Lord and adore Him. Not many of us are of noble birth or royal lineage, yet God has invited us into His household and granted us an inheritance as kings and priests through the humble example of our loyal King, Jesus.

The religious onlookers of David's day (representing *the spirit* of the house of Saul), would readily accept a king who would deliver the kingdom into their hands; a king that brought them power and control over their enemies. They admired David when he did that. But could they accept a king who lowered himself through humility, served others as a priest, and led them into the unashamed, unscripted, off-the-chart worship where love is elevated as the highest law? It seemed not! And just like the Jewish leaders in the time of Jesus, *their* house was left to them desolate. (Matt 23:37-38)

> *Therefore Michal the daughter of Saul had no children to the day of her death.* (2 Sam 6:23 NKJV)

Michal was barren for the rest of her life, which may have been because David was no longer intimate with her. Jesus wants us to be intimate with Him. Therefore, we must worship Him in the same spirit as King David. By operating in the spirit of her father, Michal was standing in direct opposition to the Lord. One thing was clear; there would never be fruitfulness coming out of the womb of the house of Saul. There is nothing but desolation for members of Saul's house, but God is faithfully rebuilding David's.

The same will happen today to anyone who 'sticks their nose up' at Tabernacle of David style worship, or those who attend a church that does not facilitate an environment for its expression. They will see limited growth and scarce amounts of blessing. Even more critically, a lack of exposure to the manifest glory will hinder their ability to experience the fullness of 'life in the Spirit'.

There will always be 'Michals' amidst the true worshipers of Yahweh. Religious onlookers will stand far off in the distance, judging with a critical, haughty spirit when the Spirit of God is moving and the glory of God manifesting. Just like the Judaizers, they are there *'to spy on us and take away the freedom we have in Christ Jesus'* (Gal. 2:4). We should not be surprised or taken aback when such ridicule occurs, nor should we allow it to hold us back; for all those who desire to live godly in Christ Jesus will suffer persecution (1 Tim 3:12). Let's be found residing in the house of the family line of David, and not in the house of the family line of Saul.

Chapter 37

WORSHIP LIVES ON

King David was not permitted to build the temple because he was a man of war with too much blood on his hands (1 Chr. 22:8). However, God did grant David the privileges of designing the architectural plans, collecting the required materials, and the establishing of laws, ordinances, and worship involved in its daily operations.

David delivered these plans over to his son Solomon before he died. Solomon had a full blueprint for the construction of the temple and its ongoing function. Many of these details are given to us in 1 Chronicles 22-29 and 2 Chronicles 2-4. King Solomon built the temple according to the pattern that was given to him by his father.

The Tabernacle of David had been in operation for 33 years under David, from the age of 37 till when he died at 70. Amazingly, this is exactly the same number of years the Son of God came and also functioned as King-Priest on the earth.

The last verse of 1 Kings 6 tells us it took Solomon 7 years to build the temple and the first verse of the same chapter reveals he began construction in the 4th year of his reign. This means that after the 33 years under David, there was an 11-year period where the Tabernacle of David continued to function under Solomon until he took it down (1 Kin. 8:4). This 11-year period was a time of rich intimacy with the Lord and outward success for Solomon.

At the beginning of his tenure, Solomon felt completely out of his depth, being young and inexperienced. King Solomon was thankful for God's hand of favour upon his life, but he also needed to inquire of Him desperately. He decided the best place to go in order to gain God's approval and hear Him speak would be the bronze altar; the official place of sacrifice found at the TOM on Mount Gibeon.

Solomon decided he would offer an enormous 1000 burnt offerings to God as a freewill gesture to show his appreciation for the favour on his life. Given that there was no bronze altar at the TOD in Jerusalem, Solomon called the entire assembly of Israel's leaders and invited them to go up with him to Gibeon and celebrate this wonderful occasion. (2 Chr. 1:2-6)

God was pleased with Solomon's generosity and responded almost immediately. That very night, while Solomon was still in Gibeon (2 Chr. 1:13), He appeared to Solomon in a dream and said; *"Ask for whatever you want me to give you."* (1 Kin. 3:5)

The primary reason Solomon came to inquire of the Lord is indicated in the portion of his prayer below;

> *"Now, LORD my God, you have made your servant king in place of my father David. But I am only a little child and do not know how to carry out my duties. ^{8}Your servant is here among the people you have chosen, a great people, too numerous to count or number. ^{9}So give your servant a discerning heart to govern your people and to distinguish between right and wrong."* (1 Kin. 3:7-9)

God was very pleased that Solomon had not asked for the death of his enemies, long life or wealth. He had asked for *wisdom; a discerning heart to govern the people and the ability to distinguish right from wrong.* God granted his request then threw in riches and honour as added extras (1 Kings 3:10-13). **IF** *he would continue to follow God* by obeying His commands and decrees as David, his father, did, then he would also be granted a long life. (1 Kings 3:14)

King Solomon was so enamoured by this mighty visitation that when he awoke, he did not go back to the altar of burnt offering at the TOM. Instead, he raced back to Jerusalem and stood worshiping before the Ark of the Lord's Covenant *inside the tabernacle of David*. After this, he went out and stood at the entrance and sacrificed peace and burnt offerings just like his father David at the inauguration of Zion's tent. David had done this in front of the whole multitude of Israel, but as far as we can tell, Solomon was on his lonesome. Then, with his next move, Solomon again imitated what his father had done: He took all the sacrificial meat and put on a feast for all his court. (1 Kin. 3:15, 2 Sam 6:17)

Although he had captured God's attention at the bronze altar of sacrifice in Gibeon, Solomon knew the location to truly thank the Lord was the place of intimacy and fellowship in the tent of his father, David. It had been declared at Solomon's coronation that the authority of his rule and reign would be firmly established from this very hill, just like his father's was. God had now fully installed Solomon upon Mount Zion: His holy mountain! (Ps. 2:6)

The key verse in Solomon's visitation was always going to be 1 Kings 3:14; *"if you follow me and obey my decrees and my commands as your father, David, did, I will give you a long life."* That was the big 'IF' in the equation. Riches and fame were guaranteed to Solomon from the beginning. Longevity, however, was conditional upon ongoing obedience.

After Solomon had completed both the temple and his palace, the Lord appeared to him a second time, just as He had done at the beginning of his reign in Gibeon (1 Kin. 9:1-9). Aware that there was danger on the horizon, God came to reiterate the promises *and the terms (the IF's)* of the Davidic covenant. No longer having access to David's tabernacle, Solomon now had plenty of opportunity to become complacent in his new mansion. Making this even more tempting was the fact that David's comprehensive victories had given Solomon rest from his enemies on every side. To protect himself from falling into 'the comfort zone', Solomon would have to be extra vigilant to seek God's face morning and night.

Unfortunately, in the end he didn't heed the word of the Lord twice given (1 Kin. 3:14, 9:4-9) and ended up violating the terms of the covenant by marrying foreign wives and serving other gods. The nation of Israel suffered greatly for centuries because of this. Even so, there had been a glorious 11-year period where Solomon and the people in Israel could continue to enter David's tabernacle. So in total, David's tent stood for approximately 44 years. After this, the typology of the New Covenant ceased until the genuine article and actual substance came in the man, Jesus Christ.

David, the type of king-priest in the order of Melchizedek, had died. The one who had been experiencing the powers of the coming age was now removed from the scene. Thus, after 11 more years, the foreshadowing of New Covenant realities came to a close, *though not entirely...*

Focal Point of the Temple Dedication

By studying 1 Chronicles 25, we find that David's 24 divisions of worship (that had been operating in the TOD) were incorporated into the daily operations of Solomon's Temple as an integral component. Let's relive the dedication of Solomon's Temple a third time, as there is one facet I have purposely neglected to mention until now. But don't get the impression that it's not important; I've actually saved the best till last...

It was time to put the finishing touches into place. Solomon's final act was to go and fetch the Ark from Zion, remove it from the TOD, and then bring it into its newly upgraded 'double-sized' Holy of Holies.

> *[4] When all the elders of Israel arrived, the Levites picked up the Ark. [5] The priests and Levites brought up the Ark along with the special tent and all the sacred items that had been in it.* (2 Chr. 5:4-5 NLT)

Solomon had read about the *kâbôwd Yĕhovah* that had filled the Tabernacle of Moses when the Ark had first been placed inside, and he was fully expecting a similar occurrence in the temple. The air was thick with anticipation. The Levites carried the Ark up to where the bronze altar was, just outside the entrance, and Solomon told them to rest it there temporarily.

King Solomon had a plan: He remembered the time when God visited him in a dream after sacrificing 1000 burnt offerings. He thought to himself, *"I'm going to go all out this time. This will impress God way more than last time!"*

> *[6] There, before the Ark, King Solomon and the entire community of Israel sacrificed so many sheep, goats, and cattle that no one could keep count!* (2 Chr. 5:6 NLT)

Solomon went on a slaying frenzy. He kept telling the priests; *"Sacrifice another one, and another one, and another one..."* There was no way of keeping count. The priests were utterly exhausted when Solomon finally brought the sacrifices to a halt. He looked toward the temple and... nothing, absolutely nothing! *"Oh ok, well ummm, that didn't seem to achieve anything... oh well, yeah I know, it's going to happen when the Ark is placed in the Holy of Holies. That's what happened back in Moses' day. Besides, it hasn't been in there for over a century. God's surely going to be rapt to see it back in its rightful place."*

So Solomon ordered the priests to bring the Ark into the Oracle:

> *[7] Then the priests carried the Ark of the LORD's Covenant into the inner sanctuary of the Temple—the Most Holy Place—and placed it beneath the wings of the cherubim. [8] The cherubim spread their wings over the Ark,*

forming a canopy over the Ark and its carrying poles… ¹¹Then the priests left the Holy Place. All the priests who were present had purified themselves, whether or not they were on duty that day. (1 Kin. 3:7-8, 11 NLT)

The Ark went in. The priests came out, and still… nothing! *"Well, that's embarrassing. What an anticlimax. Mmmm, what should I do now… quick Solomon, think of something… I know! I'll crank up the worship band. Hopefully that'll cause everyone to forget about this awkward moment and buy me some time while I work out what I'm going to do next."* *"Asaph, you're up!"*

¹²And the Levites who were musicians—Asaph, Heman, Jeduthun, and all their sons and brothers—were dressed in fine linen robes and stood at the east side of the altar playing cymbals, lyres, and harps. They were joined by 120 priests who were playing trumpets. ¹³The trumpeters and singers performed together in unison to praise and give thanks to the Lord. Accompanied by trumpets, cymbals, and other instruments, they raised their voices and praised the Lord with these words: "He is good! His faithful love endures forever!" **_At that moment a thick cloud filled the Temple of the Lord_**. *¹⁴The priests could not continue their service because of the cloud, for the <u>glorious presence of the Lord</u>* (kâbôwd Yĕhovah) *filled the Temple of God.* (2 Chr. 5:12-14 NLT)

Solomon couldn't contain himself: *"The kâbôwd Yĕhovah! Kâbôwd Yĕhovah! The Lord has responded to WORSHIP, HURRAY! Worship lives on!"*

The Tabernacle of David had been removed from its place, but worship never would be! By waiting until the enacting of worship to pour out His glory cloud, God is sending us this message;

"Since the time David established Zion's tabernacle, I have no longer been about meaningless self-sacrifice or restricting the sound of My praise. From that time forward and forevermore; **I am all about worship.** *Once unleashed through My servant David, there will be no turning back; for My people shall never be silenced. Into perpetuity, I will always hear the echo of worship reverberating throughout the earth!"*

Solomon quickly realised that from now on, the glory of the Lord would *only* be manifested via worship, not by any religious rituals or superficial works of the flesh. God's greatest pleasure is to see His children worshiping and adoring Him from the closest proximity (His loving embrace/lap: John 1:18). Through intimacy, it thrills God to lavish His love and blessings upon those who set aside time to draw near to Him. (Jam. 4:8, Heb. 11:6)

As we learned in chapter 28, this true form of worship beautifully combines 'the simplicity of pure devotion' with 'the laying down of a life through spiritual sacrifices of selfless service (actions of mercy toward others)' (2 Cor. 11:3 + Rom. 12:1). Both must be present if we are to fully worship the Lord in Spirit and truth. This authentic combination is pure worship that always catches God's attention. (John 4:24)

SECTION VII:

END-TIME HARVEST

~ Chapter 38 ~
THE HARVEST: AN 'EVER-EXPANDING' REMNANT

The prophet Amos was from the small, inconsequential town of Tekoa in the Judean hills, 10 miles south of Jerusalem. He was not a prophet by occupation, nor had he been trained in the 'school of the prophets'. Unlike Jeremiah or Ezekiel, he was not the son of a priest, nor was he the son of a prophet like Isaiah. In order to make a living, he was a sheep-breeder and also one who tended sycamore-fig trees. The sycamore-fig, being smaller than ordinary figs and of inferior quality, was regarded as 'the poor man's fig'. Despite his ordinary background, his skill with words and the strikingly broad range of general knowledge (with regard to history) preclude him from being classified as merely an ignorant peasant.

Despite not being a professional prophet, or a native of Israel's kingdom, he was called to travel north and deliver God's message (Amos 7:14-15). Hosea was a contemporary prophet of Amos who was also sent to warn Israel around this time.

After splitting with Judah at the conclusion of Solomon's reign, the ten northern tribes of Israel had fallen into great apostasy. Parting ways with the capital city of Jerusalem, they desired to set up their own temple. But they went one better: they created two of them; one at Bethel and the other in Samaria. But instead of setting up their temples according to the pattern laid out by King David, they rehashed the idolatrous golden calf system from way back in the wilderness wanderings. (1 Kin. 12:26-31)

At the time Amos arrived, the inhabitants of Israel thought they were pleasing God because they *seemed* to have His blessing (Amos 5:14). Israel had gained control of the international trade routes that intersected their land, and the economy was booming. They were positioned directly at the crossing of the main road from Europe to Arabia, and the main road from Egypt to Asia. When God promised Abraham this land for his chosen descendants, it truly was the choicest piece of real estate available. The Israelites were making the most of this, forming a merchant class to maximise commerce in the trade industry via importing and exporting. Quickly becoming an affluent society, one of the most sought after careers was in real estate. Most of the people were so rich that they owned two houses: a winter house and a summer house. Not only that, but these dwellings were 'houses of ivory'; mansions decorated with ivory inlay (Amos 3:15). They could also afford to plant 'pleasant vineyards' in their backyards (Amos 5:11). And so God sent a poor, shabby prophet in shepherd's clothing to a lavishly decadent society overflowing with luxury. (1 Cor. 1:26-31)

This was a time of relative peace and prosperity, but not because of the people's righteous behaviour. It was actually due to a mighty move of God's Spirit caused by the preaching of the prophet Jonah in the Assyrian capital of Nineveh. A decade or two earlier, Jonah had displayed with convincing utterance and a visible sign (being spat out of a whale after three days—Luke 11:30) that God was going to wipe Nineveh off the map in response to all the evil they were committing. When the city repented, God relented and this revival unto righteousness in Assyria had postponed the immanency of their threat toward Israel. The fear of Assyria had been removed for a time, and a generation had grown up in Israel who did not know war. They had been raised with vast amounts of material wealth without even a trace of neighbourly instability; they were 'living the good life.' In chapter 7, Amos refers to them twice in intercessory prayer as 'Jacob' rather than Israel, because that was the perfect analogy to show how far Israel had fallen. They had gone back to being Jacob, the schemer and supplanter who used deceit and trickery to get ahead in life. (Amos 7:1-6)

When Amos first came along, he began prophesying to Israel about the judgment that would fall upon all the surrounding nations (Amos 1:3-2:5). The people of Israel thought, *"We like this guy! This Judean is a true prophet of the Lord!"* But Amos was baiting them before unloading truth-bombs. There was far more that displeased God happening in Israel than anywhere else! They had installed temple prostitutes at their golden calf setup (Amos 2:7b) and when conducting international trade, they *'made the ephah small, and the shekel large, falsifying the scales by deceit'* (Amos 8:5b). These are only two examples among many other detestable practices.

Though at this time Assyria had withdrawn their bloodthirsty conquest, the threat of takeover was still to come if Israel did not repent within this grace period. As the Israelites neared the precipice of destruction, God spoke of the Assyrians this way, when He stated through Isaiah;

Woe to Assyria, the rod of My anger [against Israel], The staff in whose hand is My indignation and fury [against Israel's disobedience]! ⁶I send Assyria against a godless nation and commission it against the people of

My wrath; to take the spoil and to seize the plunder and to trample them down like mud in the streets. (Isa. 10:5-6 AMP)

The Lord had still preserved Assyria as 'the rod of His anger', even though they had previously repented at the preaching of Jonah. They would surely come against Samaria and Bethel soon enough if there was no sign of change on the part of the sinful kingdom, Israel.

◊◊◊◊◊

Even before the fury of Assyria had been unleashed, the land had been rocked by an enormous earthquake. This occurred only two years after Amos began to prophesy (Amos 1:1). It was such a major event that it was even mentioned by Zechariah 250 years later! (Zech. 14:5)

In fact, judgment already began the moment Amos arrived. According to Amos 4:6-11, God sent famine, followed by drought, then crop failure, then plague, then war, and lastly, the natural disaster. It seems from the reference to Sodom and Gomorrah in verse 11 that the earthquake may have also contained a volcanic eruption. God was using these judgments to awaken the people to their sin. However, when referring to all these things, Amos repeats the phrase; *'"Yet you have not returned to Me", says the Lord'*.

Throughout chapter 5 Amos asks the house of Israel (also known as the house of Joseph), to respond:

"Seek the Lord and live, Lest He break out like fire in the house of Joseph, And devour it". (Amos 5:6 NKJV)

In light of the judgments that had already occurred, the Israelites should repent before worse disasters hit their doorsteps. If Israel refused to respond correctly to the prophet's warning, they would inevitably experience 'the day of the Lord'; a coming day when God will 'settle the score' for all their wilful sins, fulfilling Amos' words of complete and utter destruction (Amos 5:12-20). But after refusing to heed his call to repentance, Amos tells them this;

Woe to you who are at ease in Zion, And trust in Mount Samaria... Woe to you who put far off the day of doom; (the day of the Lord) Who cause the seat of violence to come near; ⁴Who lie on beds of ivory, Stretch out on your couches, Eat lambs from the flock And calves from the midst of the stall;

⁵Who sing idly to the sound of stringed instruments, And invent for yourselves musical instruments like David; ⁶Who drink wine from bowls, And anoint yourselves with the best ointments, <u>But are not grieved for the affliction of Joseph</u>. ⁷Therefore they shall now go captive as the first of the captives, And those who recline at banquets shall be removed.

⁸The Lord God has sworn by Himself, The Lord God of hosts says: "I abhor the pride of Jacob, And hate his palaces; Therefore I will deliver up the city And all that is in it." (Amos 6:1a, 3-8 NKJV)

The Israelites were like; *"Ah, who cares about a few minor hiccups such as famine and drought, or even the odd natural disaster. We're rich! We can eat, drink and be merry. There's plenty stored away for many years to come."* (Luke 12:13-21, 1 Cor. 15:32)

That response spelled the end for Israel: Ignoring Amos' admonitions sealed their impending doom. They were a basket of summer fruit, overripe and fermenting, no good except to be tossed aside (Amos 8:1-2). About 30 or 40 years after Amos prophesied in the land, the Assyrians came and destroyed their capital city of Samaria, conquering Israel.

The lead up to the resurrection of David's fallen Tent

Amos speaks about this coming day of judgement in greater detail throughout the final chapter of his book, culminating in a restoration of Davidic worship and revival. We will begin with verse 8;

"Behold, the eyes of the Lord God are upon <u>the sinful kingdom</u>, and I will destroy it from the surface of the ground, except that I <u>will not utterly destroy</u> the house of Jacob," declares the Lord. (Amos 9:8 ESV)

'The sinful kingdom' here refers to the northern kingdom of Israel, even though the southern kingdom of Judah wasn't much better. The Lord viewed Israel as entirely apostate. Having utterly revolted from the spiritual ideals of worship and the plumb line of Jehovah's righteous standards, they had now passed the grace period of repentance as a collective people. The Hebrew used here by Amos could just as easily be translated 'the sinning kingdom' or 'the kingdom of sin'. It speaks of a kingdom *addicted to sin; a place where sin prevails and reigns supreme with no moderation or restraint.* Through Hosea and Amos, God had given them ample warning, but to no avail. Total obliteration was now inevitable. The Assyrians were going to come and level Samaria and the entire land of Israel to the ground.

Yet amid this entire calamity, God also says; *"I will not utterly destroy the house of Jacob."* Despite the fact that they were desperately wicked as an overall nation, God would supernaturally preserve a 'surviving remnant' from the people of Israel. That's why immediately after declaring Assyria as God's judgment rod toward Israel, Isaiah also prophesied;

> *[20]And it shall come to pass in that day that the remnant of Israel shall no more join themselves with, and the saved of Jacob shall no more trust in, them that injured them; but they shall trust in the Holy God of Israel, in truth. [21]And the remnant of Jacob shall trust on the mighty God. [22]**And though the people of Israel be as the sand of the sea, a remnant of them shall be saved. [23]He will finish the work, and cut it short in righteousness: because the Lord will make a short work in all the world.*** (Isa. 10:22-23 LXX)

Isaiah states that even though Israel be like the sand on the seashore, *only a remnant would be saved.* This remnant would no longer partner with the evil rulers who were only causing them pain, but would place their trust in the Holy God of Israel.

In the New Testament, the portion of this scripture highlighted in bold is echoed by Paul in Romans 9:27-28, which when linked with Romans 11:23-26, refers to an End-time ingathering of the Jews immediately before God cuts this age short in righteousness by *"carrying out His sentence on earth with speed and finality"*. This then I believe, is the time period when the ultimate fulfilment of this 'Jewish remnant' occurs, where an ever-increasing number of Jews (those who call themselves Jews/identify as Jewish) will have their eyes opened and be grafted back into God's kingdom along with a multitude of Gentiles.

> *[23]And if they do not persist in unbelief, they will be grafted in, for God is able to graft them in again. [24]After all, if you were cut out of an olive tree that is wild by nature, and contrary to nature were grafted into a cultivated olive tree, how much more readily will these, the natural branches, be grafted into their own olive tree!*

> *[25]I do not want you to be ignorant of this mystery, brothers, so that you may not be conceited: Israel has experienced a hardening in part until*

*the full number of the Gentiles has come in, ²⁶**and so all Israel will be saved**. As it is written: "The deliverer will come from Zion; he will turn godlessness away from Jacob.* (Rom. 11:23-26)

Romans 11:26 foretells a conversion of the Jews so universal that they are separated into an 'elect remnant' while the "rest who were hardened" disappear from God's radar altogether. This infers, then, that all the believing remnant (from Romans 9:27) shall be saved, because according to Romans 9:6-8, not all Israel are truly Israel, only the children of the Promise. The 'true Israelites' Paul is referring to are all the Messianic Jews, the ones who have repented and no longer bow their knee to Baal (the antichrist one-world system). It is the Gentile believers' job to make the people of Israel envious through the Tabernacle of David lifestyle; the simplicity of pure devotion to Christ. This will ensure that the full quota of natural branches are grafted back into their own olive tree. This believing remnant from Israel, numerous in itself, will be wholly converted!

◊◊◊◊◊

The sinful kingdom from the days of Amos would become known as 'the ten lost tribes' from the Assyrian invasion onward. Yet despite this, even at that time, God would keep track of *a loyal remnant*, ensuring they would return to the land when the Judean exiles were sent back to rebuild Jerusalem after their Babylonian captivity. The Lord would ensure that the descendants of these faithful Israelites were in Israel when Christ came, thus preserving the Israelite remnant through faith in Him.

⁹For behold, I will command, and shake the house of Israel among all the nations as one shakes with a sieve, but no pebble (kernel of grain) shall fall to the earth. ¹⁰All the sinners of my people shall die by the sword, who say, "Disaster shall not overtake or meet us." (Amos 9:9-10 ESV)

An Assyrian takeover would be the tool in God's hand for the sifting *of His own people*. In this case, God would refer to the sieve used in the sifting of wheat. This is the last of *three* processes in the separation of wheat from chaff (the thin, dry, scaly protective casing that forms a dry husk around the grain). This means God was going to do *a thorough sorting* of His people into those of the faithful remnant and those who were mere lip-servants. Those who declared outward allegiance to Yahweh but lived a life contrary to that declaration would fall to the earth like chaff falls through the sieve. This reminds me of what Jesus said to the Pharisees; *"these people honour Me with their lips, but their hearts are far from Me."* (Matt 15:8)

The surviving remnant, still loyal to the Lord, would be a pebble remaining in the sieve. This refers to the kernel of grain, which is approximately the size of a small stone. It was grain to be consumed for food, or seed to plant for next season. They too would have to endure being run-over by the Assyrians and scattered among all the nations, yet God kept His heavenly tracking devices locked in on who they were.

◊◊◊◊◊

The separation of wheat from chaff is often used in Scripture for the sifting of God's own people. At the very beginning of the New Testament, we see John the Baptist describing his baptism of repentance using this same analogy. Only John did not mention the 'sieve'. Instead, he mentioned the 'winnowing fork'

> *"His winnowing fork is in his hand, and he will clear his threshing floor, gathering his wheat into the barn and burning up the chaff with unquenchable fire."* (Matt 3:12)

This was the *second* process in the harvesting of wheat. When the Messiah of Israel arrived on the scene, it was time to separate the wheat from the chaff among those in the household of God! The same thing happened to Israel when Amos' predictions of destruction were fulfilled.

By separating wheat from chaff, God sorts His own people corporately in order to remove those who are not genuine disciples, thus leaving the remainder behind as a pure, consecrated remnant. This sifting is achieved primarily through tribulation and persecution (Mark 4:17). True disciples are completely determined to follow Jesus no matter the cost and are fully committed to becoming like their Master. Only these will endure such trials without falling away. God's desire is not for us to suffer, but He will sift His people for a season so that only a pure bride without spot or blemish remains (Lam. 3:33). Once this process is complete, He will remove the trials and fast-track the remnant into the Majestic Glory and the supernatural increase of His pure-white harvest.

> *And the God of all grace, who <u>called you to his eternal glory</u> in Christ, after you have **<u>suffered a little while</u>**, will himself restore you and make you strong, firm and steadfast.* (1 Pet. 5:10)

◊◊◊◊◊

Jeremiah 51:33 says—*'Daughter Babylon is like a threshing floor at the time it is trampled'*

In this scripture, we again see the threshing of God's chosen people. Here the Lord is referring to Judah. As grain on a threshing-floor, they have been sorely bruised and trodden under foot by the Babylonians. This speaks of the *first* process, when the grain is placed on the threshing floor and run over by a threshing sledge, also known as a 'tribulum' where we derive the English word 'tribulation'. But I love God's exhortation in Isaiah 41:15;

> *"Do not be afraid, you <u>worm Jacob, little Israel</u> (remnant), do not fear, for I myself will help you," declares the Lord, your Redeemer, the Holy One of Israel. "See, I will make you into a <u>threshing sledge, new and sharp, with many teeth</u>. You will thresh the mountains and crush them, and <u>reduce the hills to chaff</u>."*

Those who prevail as wheat through all three processes (threshing sledge, winnowing fork and sieve) become the purified remnant; the faithful leftovers of God's people. They will overcome and shame the wicked; those who have destined themselves for destruction having chosen to remain obstinate toward God. After becoming pure wheat, the remnant are transformed into the threshing sledge or 'tribulum' used to thresh God's enemies, reducing them to chaff. The sharp teeth are the shards of sharpened rock attached to the underside of the tribulum.

Being opposed to God's people, these antagonists make themselves enemies of God Himself, Who blows them away like chaff in the wind (Ps. 1:4-5, 83:13, Isa. 17:13, 29:5-6). To achieve this, God starts this process by using His remnant as the threshing sledge. He then tosses them into the air with His winnowing fork (Jer. 15:7). This reveals a dual purpose for the remnant in the harvest: Not only are they cultivating the grain for eternal life, they are threshing the enemies of the Lord with sharp teeth. The angel of the Lord drives them away as chaff in the wind (Ps 35:5). There is no malicious intent in the hearts of the remnant, but as they abide in the glory, speak the truth in love and war in the Spirit over their region, they dispossess the enemy along with those who stubbornly identify as his children.

With their opposition removed, the wheat (God's remnant) can then go about the work of the kingdom unhindered, bringing in many souls ordained for eternal life. These new converts will be effectively 'discipled'. Through this genuine discipleship, the remnant expands. There is no cap on how big a remnant can become. Some towns, regions or states could have over 50% of the population as the chosen elect. We have been programmed to think of the remnant as the teeny-weeny minority who are always oppressed by the masses. But this does not have to be the case. During the harvest, we are going to see small remnants expand into large percentages of the total population, so don't limit the Body of Christ to an outnumbered minority. Let's believe for as big a yield as possible! More importantly, let's ensure that no matter the size, we create an environment where every believer is growing into maturity. Our commission is always to make disciples of all nations, not converts. Remember, God will not permit lukewarm-ness in the coming End-time Harvest. (Rev. 3:16)

Individually brought forth as Wheat

Separation of the wheat from chaff not only refers to the sifting of His corporate body at large, but these processes also occur within an *individual believer's life*. God implements this personal sifting to rid us of the chaff of 'disloyalty, human reasoning, and trust in other things'. He blows aside the allegiances we carry inside that are not of the Lord. Like Peter, we must go through a personal sifting to qualify for our place in the harvest.

> [31] *"Simon, Simon, <u>Satan has asked to **sift all of you** as wheat</u>. [32] But I have prayed for you, Simon, that your faith may not fail. And when you have turned back, strengthen your brothers."* (Luke 22:31-32)

Simon Peter had to undertake the sifting by the sieve, just as the Israelites did in Amos 9:9. Through Peter's threescore denial, a thorough work of all three processes was performed by the Lord inside Peter's heart. Each denial represented a particular process in the sifting of wheat.

1) ***Tribulum:*** *A sled constructed with shards of rock or iron driven into the sled's heavy wooden underside. Oxen or other livestock dragged the threshing sledge repeatedly across sheaves of wheat to detach chaff from the grain.*

The threshing sledge separated Peter's self-centeredness from the wholesome kernels of submission. The chaff of 'self-preservation' was exposed through this crushing.

2) ***Winnowing Fork:*** *After the tribulum, labourers in the Middle East winnowed (separated) the chaff from the wheat by tossing the broken, crushed stalks repeatedly in the air with large wooden pitch forks. An evening breeze blew this chaff away, leaving the wheat kernels along with stems and specks of sediment on the threshing floor.*

Remorse, self-pity and confusion lay upon the threshing floor of Peter's soul—along with the little remaining courage. What would he do this second time? Should he declare his allegiance and submit himself to the same suffering Christ was experiencing? Not at this point in his life: More of the chaff remaining in Peter's heart became separated as the grain was tossed into the air.

3) ***Sieve:*** *Women now gathered this winnowed mixture for the final sifting. A woman sat on the ground with a woven sieve that allowed the debris to drop through tiny holes. Then, with care, she picked out every visible speck of sediment left among the kernels before pouring the grain into containers for storing. It was painstaking, tedious work separating the larger pieces of debris (like tiny rocks and dirt) from the wheat grain by hand.*

After the third accusation came Peter's way, he panicked and spoke damnation upon himself; *"A curse on me if I'm lying—I don't know the man!"* (Mark 14:71 NLT) The confusion caused by his human reasoning unveiled his true heart-condition; a reality which was too much to bear in the moment. Immediately after this third denial, the rooster crowed the second time, and the Lord looked across and locked eyes with Peter (Mark 14:72, Luke 22:61). In this moment, Peter's heart shattered into what felt like a million pieces. From this, he thought he would never recover. But on the contrary, Peter was going to find out that Jesus Christ can bind up even the most shattered of broken hearts. Once Peter turned back, he became one of the boldest of all preachers and a chief apostle of the Jerusalem church. Whenever he felt like cowering in fear, he would recall his denials, visualise the disappointment on Jesus' face, and determine that such a failure would never happen again. He had become pure wheat; separated, sifted, and qualified to share in the coming harvest...

~ Chapter 39 ~

ONE THING HOT ON THE HEELS OF ANOTHER

[11] "In that day will I raise up the tabernacle of David, the fallen hut or booth, and close up its breaches; and I will raise up its ruins, and I will build it as in the days of old, [12]That they may possess the remnant of Edom and of all the nations that are called by My name, says the Lord Who does this." (Amos 9:11-12 AMPC)

THEN...

Look, the days are coming — this is the Lord's declaration; (CSB)

"Things are going to happen so fast your head will swim, <u>one thing fast on the heels of the other</u>. You won't be able to keep up. Everything will be happening at once—and everywhere you look, blessings! Blessings like wine pouring off the mountains and hills." (Amos 9:13 MSG)

When the Tabernacle of David is rebuilt, the Body of Christ will be correctly positioned to haul in the final harvest of souls immediately before the culmination of the age. We are given information concerning the make-up and conditions of this worldwide move of God's Spirit in Amos 9:13. The fact that this overflowing abundance of harvest immediately follows the call to resurrect Davidic worship in the Majestic Glory shows that this rebuilding *is the prerequisite* to the release of the global outpouring.

For the Lord will carry out his sentence on earth with <u>speed and finality</u>. (Rom 9:28)

This scripture (which Paul quoted from Isaiah 10:23 LXX) explains how God will operate right near the end of the age. He will therefore execute the End-time Harvest in this very fashion.

1. SPEED (Gk: syntemnō)

Things are going to happen so fast your head will swim, one thing fast on the heels of the other.

God is going to move swiftly. It will be a quick work with *no delay!* When Paul refers to 'quick' *(syntemnō)*, he is not saying that it 'lasts only a short time'. The harvest is quick in the sense that God is moving immense speed performing so many miracles across the world at the same time. It will not be *over* quickly, but throughout its entire duration, God is going to be *moving* so quickly it'll feel like our brains are going to explode.

You won't be able to keep up. Everything will be happening at once!

We will find ourselves saying things like; *"Whoa, whoa, whoa, slow down God, my head can't keep up!"* It's safe to say, God is going to blow our minds! The Greek word for 'quick' meaning: 'to dispatch briefly, execute or finish quickly', shows us that God is not wasting any time. He is moving at breakneck speed to complete the job in the briefest time possible. That's why this word can also be translated 'a short word,' also referring to 'expedited prophecy'. (Expedite means to speed up the process)

This infers that God will not delay this process one iota. Yet when we consider the monumental extent of the Lord's plan, we quickly realise that from our limited human perspective, it will indeed take a decent amount of time. We are talking about a bare minimum of a tithe of the earth's population coming into the kingdom of God. Even at Godspeed, that is going to take a while. We must also grasp that any 'time-period' is regarded as quick by God because He inhabits eternity. What is *quick* to God seems *a long time* to us who dwell in the slow-motion-ness of this fallen world. For with the Lord a day is like a thousand years, and a thousand years like a day. (2 Pet. 3:8)

2. *FINALITY (Gk: synteleō)*

The secondary factor is the 'finality' aspect. This means that God is not so hasty that He misses things or does a half-baked job. The Lord will both quickly *and thoroughly* complete His glorious ingathering with exceptional precision. When we rush (as human beings), the result is a less precise effort ending up in a shoddy job. But this is not the case with God. The Lord only brings His work to an abrupt end because He has finished it to utter perfection. Jesus is the Author and *the Finisher*, but He's also the author *and Perfector*. The reason there is such a sudden halt to the 'execution of His Word' is because once God begins to move He quickly accelerates to top speed and remains there full throttle all the way to the finish line. All of a sudden, as he crosses, He's done! Then enter 'the Day of the Lord'. (Refer Rom. 9:28 NASB)

◊◊◊◊◊

Everywhere you look, blessings! Blessings like wine pouring off the mountains and hills.

What exactly are the 'blessings' we will see poured out during this celebration season? While I appreciate Eugene Peterson's Message paraphrase of verse 13 because it so vividly captures God's mode of operation, to understand these blessings we will need to examine the intricate details by going back to a more direct translation of the original Hebrew;

> *"Behold, the days are coming," says the Lord, "When the plowman shall overtake the reaper, And the treader of grapes him who sows seed; The mountains shall drip with sweet wine, And all the hills shall flow with it"* (Amos 9:13 NKJV)

There are four hyperboles here;

That the ploughman shall overtake the reaper: He who breaks up the ground, and prepares it for the seed, shall be ready to tread on the heels of the reaper; who shall have a harvest so large, that before he can gather it all in, it shall be time to plough the ground again.

The treader of grapes him that sows seed: This is a similar concept to the statement above: so great shall their vintage be, that before the treaders of grapes have finished their work, the seedsman shall be sowing his seed against the next season. In both cases, seed-time and harvest are merged together; they essentially become one and the same!

The mountains shall drop sweet wine: Vineyards shall be so fruitful, and shall produce such an abundance of grapes, that wine shall appear to be as plentiful as if it were running down the sides of the mountains.

And all the hills shall flow: The implication is; they have such a plentiful supply of rich feeding for the cattle that they should, by consequence, give a large quantity of milk. This expression is found in the parallel prophecy of Joel 3:18;

> *"And it will come to pass in that day, That <u>the mountains shall drip with new wine, The hills shall flow **with milk**</u>, And all the brooks of Judah shall be flooded with water; A fountain shall flow from the house of the Lord And water the Valley of Acacias"* (NKJV)

The blessings in this harvest season will be so great that Amos compares them to land producing so quickly and so abundantly that it is difficult to finish one cycle before the next cycle begins. Are we spiritually prepared for the intensity of the workload that is going to be upon us when this breaks forth? We need to seriously ask ourselves that question, and prayerfully consider it in our hearts.

The Ploughman shall overtake the Reaper

When God speaks of the wheat harvest, He is referring to the harvesting of souls for eternal life spoken of by Jesus in John 4:34-36;

> *[34]Jesus said to them, "My food is to do the will of him who sent me and to accomplish his work. [35]Do you not say, 'There are yet four months, then comes the harvest'? Look, I tell you, lift up your eyes, and see that the fields are white for harvest. [36]__Already the one who reaps is receiving wages and gathering fruit for eternal life__, so that sower and reaper may rejoice together."* (ESV)

When Jesus spoke these words in the early part of December, there would usually be four months until the wheat harvest in April. But Jesus told His disciples to *"look up"*, because the fields He was referring to (fruit for eternal life) were "*already* white for harvest". Here Jesus is alluding to an acceleration of the usual harvest time, when the sowing and reaping become closer and closer together as the end of the age approaches. If we think we have to wait, Jesus says we're wrong: *one thing hot on the heels of another.* The harvest is plentiful, and it is already ripe.

The ploughman overtaking the reaper also relates to the parable of the wheat and the tares when an enemy sowed tares amongst the wheat. In the early stages, when the grain is immature, there is no way to tell the difference between a tare and a kernel of wheat. If you attempted to pull out the tares at this point, you would uproot much of the wheat with them. So the wisest strategy is to wait until the harvest is fully mature. At that time, the wheat bows down in humble submission while the tares remain upright in a posture of arrogant defiance.

The field of this current gospel age comes into its full maturity during the End-time Harvest. Ever increasingly, there will emerge a clear distinction between those who are true sons of God and those who are not. The lukewarm will be spewed out of God's mouth because there will no longer be the option of fence-sitting with one foot in the world and one foot in the kingdom. People will either be red-hot or ice-cold, with nothing in-between. (Rev. 3:16)

Treader of Grapes him who Sows Seed

When God speaks about 'treading grapes', He is referencing the crushing of the believer in the winepress to bring forth sanctification. This comprises all the fruits of righteousness that develop through relationship with Christ Jesus, referred to by Paul in Philippians 1;

> [10]*so that you may be able to discern what is best and may be pure and blameless for the day of Christ,* [11]*filled with the fruit of righteousness that comes through Jesus Christ* (Phil 1:10-11 NIV)

> *"May you always be filled with the fruit of your salvation—the righteous character produced in your life by Jesus Christ—for this will bring much glory and praise to God."* (Phil 1:11 NLT)

We must, through many tribulations, enter the kingdom of God (Acts 14:22). We have authority to enter the harvest fields of the kingdom through the gateway of tribulation. Many of us have been going through this process over the past decade or so in order that we may be set apart for our position in this last great move of the Holy Spirit. Once we have passed the stern test of 'willing obedience through suffering' we are handed the key that unlocks the gates of the kingdom, and the land allocated to us in the harvest field is ours for the reaping.

> [1]*Therefore, since Christ suffered in his body, arm yourselves also with the same attitude, because he who suffers in his body is done with sin.* [2]*As a result, he does not live the rest of his earthly life for evil human desires, but rather for the will of God...* [19]*So then, those who suffer according to God's will should submit themselves to their faithful Creator and continue to do good.* (1 Pet. 4:1-2, 19)

In John 15, Jesus told us that He is the grapevine and we are the branches. If we remain in Him, we will produce much fruit, showing ourselves to be His disciples. It is clear from Scripture that this 'fruit of the vine' represents holy living, because when we abide in the Spirit, we cannot fulfil the lusts of our flesh. (Gal. 5:16)

Jesus spoke another 'grape parable': one about evil tenant-farmers or 'vinedressers';

[33] 'Listen to another parable: there was a landowner who planted a vineyard. He put a wall round it, dug a winepress in it and built a watchtower. Then he rented the vineyard to some farmers and moved to another place. [34]When the harvest time approached, he sent his servants to the tenants to collect his fruit. [35]The tenants seized his servants; they beat one, killed another, and stoned a third. [36]Then he sent other servants to them, more than the first time, and the tenants treated them in the same way. [37]Last of all, he sent his son to them. "They will respect my son," he said.

[38]But when the tenants saw the son, they said to each other, "This is the heir. Come, let's kill him and take his inheritance." [39]So they took him and threw him out of the vineyard and killed him. [40]Therefore, when the owner of the vineyard comes, what will he do to those tenants?'

[41]"He will bring those wretches to a wretched end," they replied, "and he will rent the vineyard to other tenants, who will give him his share of the crop at harvest time."

[42]Jesus said to them, 'Have you never read in the Scriptures: "The stone the builders rejected has become the capstone; the Lord has done this, and it is marvellous in our eyes"? [43]Therefore I tell you that the kingdom of God will be taken away from you and given to a people who will produce its fruit.' (Matt 21:33-43)

The master expected the vinedressers to correctly harvest the grapes and then give him his fair share. Instead, they wanted nothing to do with their Landlord, or His Son, for that matter. They preferred to usurp His lordship in a feeble attempt to seize the Son's inheritance. This represented the Jewish leadership at the time of Christ, who although having an outward veneer of piousness, were not living righteous lives before God. They were like whitewashed tombs which looked beautiful on the outside but inside were full of dead men's bones. On top of this, they were also leading the people astray because they were denouncing the Son He had sent. The kingdom of God would be taken away from them and given to a new, born-again people who would *produce its proper fruit.* That's why the grape symbolises 'the righteous character produced in you by Jesus Christ' shown to us above in Philippians 1:11 NLT.

Along with the coming harvest, there will arrive a higher standard of holiness, purity and sanctification, such as we have not seen since the days of the early apostles. The Spirit of Elijah will return so that people will once again be taught 'repentance *for* the forgiveness of their sins' (Luke 24:47, Matt 3:1-2) rather than forgiveness of sins for free with repentance as an optional extra. There will be such an intense spirit of conviction accompanying God's labourers wherever they go, similar to Charles Finney (a prominent leader of the 2nd Great Awakening). Like Finney, mass conviction will emanate out from the manifested Glory carried by these labourers, causing deep repentance among the people.

Mountains dropping Sweet Wine

Such is the excess of grapes that the mountains appear to be dripping with wine. The abundance of plump grapes is the fatness of blessing and spiritual maturity amongst the elect. Fruits of righteousness abound and overflow. People actually talk and act like Jesus! The church has become a bride prepared for her husband without spot or blemish. (Eph. 5:27)

We can gain further insight concerning the sweet wine dropping from the mountain (mentioned in Amos 9:13 and Joel 3:18) by examining the time when Jesus turned water into wine.

> *[7]Jesus said to the servants, "Fill the jars with water"; so they filled them to the brim. [8]Then he told them, "Now draw some out and take it to the master of the banquet." They did so, [9]and the master of the banquet tasted the water that had been turned into wine. He did not realise where it had come from, though the servants who had drawn the water knew. Then he called the bridegroom aside [10]and said, "Everyone brings out the choice wine first and then the cheaper wine after the guests have had too much to drink; but you have saved the best till now."* (John 2:7-10)

To understand what is coming, a comparison can be made between water and wine. Water is bland, wine is decadent. Water is colourless, wine is rich in colour. Water is inexpensive, wine is luxurious. Water is common, wine is precious.

The sweet wine flowing from the mountains is showing the rich qualities of God's abundance, which has been made available for faithful labourers to utilise in the coming harvest. God has not left His servants without necessary provision.

What I am talking about is this: There will no longer be only the water of the natural. We shall abide in the wine of the supernatural. We no longer have to abide in the ordinary, but shall enter the realm of the extraordinary! We don't have to remain in tasteless, bland religion; but can enter the richness and intoxication of Spirit-filled pungency. Forget past feelings of weakness and powerlessness; strength and potency in the atmosphere of His Glory shall be your acquired portion. We are moving out of the commonalities of this world into a new heavenly existence.

But the most critical shift of all will be an abrupt ending of the *watered*-down gospel and the seeker friendly model of church. Springing forth with a new robust clarity shall be the undiluted truth of the Word, the wine of deeply fermented revelation. *Jesus really has saved His best wine till last!* This will be the death knell of cheap Christianity and the re-igniting of 'counting the cost' Christianity.

Financial Provision

One last revelation regarding wine that we cannot overlook is that water is inexpensive, while wine is expensive. At the wedding, they essentially ran out of finances. They we unable to afford enough wine for all the guests that were invited. Jesus gave them financial assistance by turning water into wine and He didn't even take a dime from their wallets.

I believe that true believers in the harvest will be amply financed as they go about the work of the kingdom, yet the acquisition of *personal wealth* will be of lowest priority to them. At times, God will *supernaturally* provide like He did at the wedding, but most of the provision will be skilfully dug through trade, commerce, and 'doing business' in the marketplace (Luke 19:13 CSB). God has creative ideas, witty inventions and new meaningful services that will fund His children in the very last days.

On top of all of this, we have been given the promise found in Isaiah 60, that as we shine with His glory, people of great wealth and prominence will be sent by the Lord and lay their treasures at our feet;

> *Nations will come to your light, and kings to the brightness of your dawn... you will look and be radiant, your heart will throb and swell with joy; the <u>wealth on the seas will be brought to you</u>, to you the <u>riches of the nations will come</u>. [6]Herds of camels will cover your land, young camels of Midian and Ephah. And all from Sheba will come, <u>bearing gold and incense and proclaiming the praise of the Lord</u>. [7]All Kedar's flocks will be gathered to you, the rams of Nebaioth will serve you; they will be accepted as offerings on my altar, and <u>I will adorn my glorious temple</u>.* (Isa. 60:3, 5-7)

Hill's flowing with Milk

The flowing milk is a restoration back to the fertility of the Promised Land, which was described as a land flowing with milk and honey (Deut. 27:3). In the Final Great Awakening, the body of Christ is once again moving out of the barren wilderness into the land where plentiful harvests abound!

This milk also refers to the vital need for pure spiritual milk, that it may satisfy the craving of the multitude of newly born again believers, enabling them to grow up strong in their salvation;

> *[2]Like newborn babies, crave pure spiritual milk, so that by it you may grow up in your salvation, [3]now that you have tasted that the Lord is good.* (1 Pet. 2:2-3).

God is currently preparing and setting into place anointed 'teacher-harvesters' who are skilled in distributing the milk of the Word to new Christian converts, fast-tracking their progress beyond the elementary teachings about Christ towards 'solid food'.

Anyone who lives on milk, being still an infant, is not yet acquainted with the teaching about righteousness. What else does an abundance of fattened cows produce? A huge amount of red meat! At the appropriate time, the Lord's faithful servants will distribute the meat of the Word to those who are ready for it. Solid meat is for mature disciples; those who by constant use have had their senses trained to distinguish good from evil. (Heb. 5:13-14)

~ Chapter 40 ~

THE RESTORATION OF ALL THINGS

[15]For I am the Lord your God, <u>who stirs up the sea so that its waves roar</u> — the Lord Almighty is his name. [16]I have put my words in your mouth and covered you with the shadow of my hand—I who set the heavens in place, who laid the foundations of the earth, <u>and who say to Zion, "You are my people"</u>. (Isa. 51:15-16)

The final great move of the Spirit is coming like a tsunami wave enveloping all four corners of the earth. We need to prepare ourselves by climbing to the spiritual high ground of Mount Zion! This will not be a localised event. Just like a tsunami impacts the entirety of the land it invades, so will this Third Great Awakening. The nations it hits will be inundated with widespread outpouring. This will require every believer to be involved and activated within all spheres of influence. This will be the greatest of great awakenings, a mega outpouring of dynamic power; 'Holy Spirit supercharged!'

Revivals tend to be localised to a specific region and usually last only a few years. They bring a decent number of souls into eternal life, but do not typically reform society. *Awakenings,* however, last for over a decade and end up transforming the culture of entire nations. With them comes more than a spiritual reviving, but also societal reformation. Our witness and positive influence revolutionises not only individual lives, but the policies of public and private institutions. Every believer is out and about, spreading the aroma of heaven, performing signs and wonders while they implement kingdom principles and divine strategies into their local community and spheres of influence. In the midst of all this, the greatest ingathering of souls will be ushered into a relationship with Jesus Christ.

Spirit of Elijah

In fulfilment of Malachi 4:5-6, we are entering the days of 'the Spirit of Elijah' where, like John the Baptist, we will prepare the way for the Lord's *second* coming by turning *'the hearts of the fathers to their children and the hearts of the children to their fathers'*. This speaks of the healing of relationships between generations. For many decades, the previous generations have been so caught up believing that Jesus was coming back in their generation that they often neglected to pass on the baton to the next. They were preoccupied with the tribulation instead of this season spoken of in Malachi 4. This is one of many reasons I believe the second coming of Christ is still multiple generations away, because according to Malachi, the very last of the last days *has a generational focus.* This indicates that the end time awakening *will span generations.* The previous generation's ceiling must become the next generation's foundation to build upon. This will require the fathers and sons to be unified so they can effectively pass on the baton of fire, allowing the next crop of youngsters to continue running with the flames of revival. In order for Malachi 4 to come to fruition, it will most likely require a period of at least 50 years, maybe even more.

But what else does the 'Spirit of Elijah' bring forth? In Luke 1:17, we see the angel Gabriel announcing John the Baptist's role to his father Zechariah: "turning the hearts of the Fathers back to their children" (to pass on the baton) and *"the disobedient back to the attitude of the righteous".* Here we also see God's End-time labourer's carrying a spirit of conviction bringing mass repentance to those currently living in disobedience. They will turn to the Lord and receive a new 'righteous' attitude.

Yet even more fascinating is the Septuagint version of Malachi 4:6. It says that the Spirit of Elijah "shall turn again the heart of the father to the son, and *the heart of a man to his neighbour."* This 'pioneering spirit' is not only given for the mending of relationships between generations but also between *every man and his neighbour!* The forerunner anointing comes to prepare the way for Jesus' return by restoring *every type* of relationship that occurs between the believers God places along our path. This will enable comprehensive unity to be found within His body, and because of this, people on a worldwide scale will recognise that the Father sent Jesus. (John 17:23)

Calves loosed from the Bonds

By examining Malachi 4:2, we see another key component to the move of God as the end draws near. The Hebrew text in the second half of verse two is difficult to translate into English, hence translations vary. But to get the correct meaning, we must refer once again to the trusty Septuagint;

"But to you that fear my name shall the Sun of righteousness arise, and healing [shall be] in his wings: and ye shall go forth, <u>and bound as young calves let loose from bonds</u>." (Brenton LXX)

Malachi 4:2b is referring to calves being *set free* from confinement; it is not talking about young calves being well-fed *in* the stall. The NIV and NLT are therefore, good English translations of this verse;

But for you who revere my name, the sun of righteousness will rise with healing in its wings. And you will go out and leap like calves <u>released</u> from the stall. (NIV)

But for you who fear my name, the Sun of Righteousness will rise with healing in his wings. And you will go free, leaping with joy like calves <u>let out to pasture</u>. (NLT)

The key word here is 'released'. This End-time Harvest will be characterised by every believer being released and sent out into *their* area of expertise. Every one of us has our own part to play. It will no longer be the 'super-evangelists' and 'mega-revivalists' doing the bulk of the heavy lifting from a solitary platform, as in times gone by. This will truly be an awakening at the grassroots level.

And you will go forth and <u>frolic</u> like calves from the stall. (Mal. 4:2b NASB)

A calf frolics or 'skips about' when it is let out of the stall because it is free to roam. They jump playfully as they anticipate exploring their harvest field. We also see this in Jeremiah 50:11, where the same Hebrew word for frolic *(pûš)* is used; *'You <u>skip around</u> like a heifer in the grass'* (AMP). Here we see once again the link between leaping for joy and being led out into the sustenance and freedom of green pastures. The focus of Malachi 4:2b is on the excitement of being let out to explore territory and consume fresh, lush grass.

Jesus used the same imagery when He spoke in John 10 about His sheep;

*The man who enters by the gate is the shepherd of his sheep. <u>The watchman opens the gate for him</u>, and the sheep listen to his voice. <u>He calls his own sheep by name and leads them **out**</u>. When he has brought **out** all his own, he goes on ahead of them, and his sheep follow him because they know his voice.* (John 10:2-4)

Jesus says that His sheep belong *to Him*; they hear His voice and they follow *Him*, but *where* exactly do they follow Him? The answer is *outside* of the sheep pen (the four walls of the church), and the watchman; that's the pastor, actually *opens* the gate, allowing Jesus to take them out. *What a revolutionary concept!* The heart of the father is to multiply the kingdom and that doesn't happen by hoarding and holding people to a church mission but by championing the sheep by genuinely getting behind their unique assignments.

Why would Jesus put such an emphasis on the going out? Here is the answer;

> *I am the gate; whoever enters through me will be saved. He will come in and __go out and find pasture__. [10]The thief comes only to steal and kill and destroy; I have come that they may have life, and have it to the full. I am the Good Shepherd.* (John 10:9-11a)

We see here that there is indeed a time to come in, but most critically, also a time to go out. The sheep must come in to find protection, shelter, rest and rejuvenation, but it is only when they follow the Good Shepherd out that they *find pasture.*

'Pasture' here refers to nourishment and sustenance. It is something you depend on for survival. This means that if you don't go *out,* you will not survive; you become internalised and self-destruct in the sheep pen, having no greater vision. On the other hand, the sheep that are eating the pasture will grow and be able to produce offspring, causing a multiplication effect in the Body of Christ.

Feeding on the pasture is the 'life in abundance, to the full, till it overflows' that Jesus spoke about in John 10:10. The End-time Harvest will be multitudes of everyday believers being led out by Jesus into this supernatural life of frolicking joy and extra-ordinary impact.

Drawing this Age to a Close

"The harvest is the end of the age" (Matt 13:39). This involves the harvesting of wheat from amongst tares. Wheat and tares are totally separate entities which look almost identical until harvest. They are not united on the one stalk (as is the case with wheat and chaff). That's why the parable of the wheat and the tares represents *the entire human race*, the global population comprising 'sons of God's kingdom' and 'sons of the evil one'.

As previously indicated, the separating of wheat and chaff *from the one stalk* primarily speaks of a sifting within the community of God's people, or within the life of an individual believer (Amos 9:9, Luke 22:31). This sifting among God's people is occurring as God prepares His true remnant as labourers for this final upcoming harvest. The 'end of the age' however, is the time for the wheat to be separated into sheaves (that are stored) *and the tares* into bundles (to be burned). (Matt 13:30)

> *"He who sows the good seed is the Son of Man.* [38]*The field is the world, the good seeds are the sons of the kingdom, but the tares are the sons of the wicked one.* [39]*The enemy who sowed them is the devil, the harvest is the end of the age, and the reapers are the angels.* [40]*Therefore as the tares are gathered and burned in the fire, so it will be at the end of this age.* [41]*The Son of Man will send out His angels, and they will gather out of His kingdom all things that offend, and those who practice lawlessness,* [42]*and will cast them into the furnace of fire. There will be wailing and gnashing of teeth.* [43]*Then the righteous will shine forth as the sun in the kingdom of their Father. He who has ears to hear, let him hear!* (Matt 13:37-43 NKJV)

In comparing the last great ingathering of souls to a wheat harvest, Jesus is showing us that there must be a maturing of the crop before He returns to gather the wheat into His barn (Matt 13:30). This is another reason why I believe the harvest will last for an extensive period. The wheat must become mature enough to confront the spirit of antichrist, which reaches its climax as the end draws ever closer.

As the head, Jesus works *through His body* as we sow the seed of the gospel to plant the wheat. We are also wheat in the crop, planted by others who have ministered to us and/or prayed for us. At the time of the crops full maturity, Jesus coordinates the 'gathering into the barn' when He dispatches the angels to separate the wheat from the tares. We are the *earthly labourers* who *sow and tend* the field during the outpouring; the angels are the *heavenly harvesters* who, *by sorting* the crop bring this age to a close (Luke 10:2, Matt 13:39).

I believe this culmination of the harvest season (spoken of by Jesus in the parable of the wheat and the tares) is the event we see in Revelation 14:14-16;

the final siren of this age as we know it and the conclusion of the End-time Harvest:

> [14]*"I looked, and there before me was a white cloud, and seated on the cloud was one like a son of man with a crown of gold on his head and a sharp sickle in his hand.* [15]*Then another angel came out of the temple and called in a loud voice to him who was sitting on the cloud, "Take your sickle and reap, because the time to reap has come, <u>for the harvest of the earth is ripe</u>."* [16]*So he who was seated on the cloud swung his sickle over the earth, <u>and the earth was harvested</u>.*

The time is fast approaching for 'the restoration of all things' (Acts 3:21). The end is near, glory is on the horizon. A plentiful harvest awaits yet Jesus warns us that the labourers are few! The Lord has sent out His clarion call, urging us to get the ball rolling by making ourselves ready. The Body of Christ both individually and corporately must resurrect David's fallen tent to become carriers of the Majestic Glory, and by doing so they will be equipped to release and steward the worldwide awakening.

God will then begin the process of wrapping this age up as the darkness descends and the lawless one is overthrown by His second coming. Once we've helped usher in the harvest, Jesus and His angels will take care of the rest.

Thanks for reading!

Please add a review on Amazon and let me know what you thought...

Amazon reviews are extremely helpful for authors, thank you for taking the time to support me and my work. It is greatly appreciated!

If you enjoyed the book, please share your amazon review on social media to encourage others to read the message too!

◇◇◇◇◇

COMING SOON!

Volume II in the End-Time Harvest series: **"Trinity of the Stone!"**

DON'T FORGET TO SIGN UP FOR THE MAILING LIST

TO RECEIVE YOUR FREE PDF BONUS CHAPTERS, BLOG ALERTS FROM THE AUTHOR & INFO ON NEW RELEASES, subscribe at:

www.justinfarrugia.org

◇◇◇◇◇

CONNECT with Justin aka "GIFT OF THE GAB"

Gab: www.gab.com/JLF538
Gettr: www.gettr.com/user/JLF538
Telegram: http://t.me/JLF538
YouTube: www.youtube.com/giftgab
Facebook: www.facebook.com/JLF538

Made in United States
Orlando, FL
26 June 2022

19166429R00200